CW01183696

Also available

Interpreting the Orient: Travellers in Egypt and the Near East
2001 • 284pp • 235 x 155 mm • Cased £35.00 • ISBN 0 86372 258 X

The British Arabists in the 20th Century
2001 • 252pp • 235 x 155 mm • Cased £35.00 • ISBN 0 86372 288 1

Egypt: Caught in Time
1997 • 160pp • 260 x 210 mm • 17 colour & 155 duotone pictures • Cased £19.95 • ISBN 1 873938 95 0

Narrative of the Residence of Fatalla Sayeghir among the Wandering Arabs of the Great Desert
1996 • 216pp • 210 x 120 mm • Cased £19.95 • ISBN 1 85964 0885

Sexual Encounters in the Middle East
1999 • 332pp • 235 x 155 mm • Cased £35.00 • ISBN 0 86372 253 9

Travels of Ali Bey in Morocco, Tripoli, Cyprus, Egypt, Arabia, Syria and Turkey
Vol. I • 1993 • 384pp • 235 x 168 mm • 44 engravings, 2 maps • Cased £30.00 • ISBN 1 873938 39 X
Vol. II • 1993 • 388pp • 235 x 168 mm • Cased £30.00 • ISBN 1 873938 40 3

Available from your local bookshop; alternatively, contact our Sales Department on +44 (0)118 959 7847 or e-mail on **orders@garnet-ithaca.demon.co.uk** to order copies of these books.

UNFOLDING THE *Orient*

Travellers in Egypt and the Near East

EDITED BY
PAUL AND JANET STARKEY

ITHACA PRESS

UNFOLDING THE ORIENT
Travellers in Egypt and the Near East

Ithaca Press is an imprint of Garnet Publishing Limited

Published by
Garnet Publishing Limited
8 Southern Court
South Street
Reading
RG1 4QS
UK

Copyright © Paul and Janet Starkey 2001

All rights reserved.
No part of this book may be reproduced in any form or by any electronic or mechanical means, including information storage and retrieval systems, without permission in writing from the publisher, except by a reviewer who may quote brief passages in a review.

First Edition

ISBN 0 86372 257 1

British Library Cataloguing-in-Publication Data
A catalogue record for this book is available from the British Library

Jacket design by David Rose
Typeset by Samantha Barden

Printed in Lebanon

Contents

Introduction   1
Paul and Janet Starkey

1 A Textual Landscape: The Mapping of a Holy Land in the Fourth-Century *Itinerarium* of the Bordeaux Pilgrim   7
Glenn Bowman

2 The Grand Tour in the Ottoman Empire, 1699–1826   41
Philip Mansel

3 Dressing Native   65
John Rodenbeck

4 English Pleasure Travel in the Near East, 1580–1645   101
John Ghazvinian

5 Egypt in 1615–1616 as seen through the Eyes of the Armenian Simeon of Poland   111
Angèle Kapoïan

6 Adam Olearius's Travels to Persia, 1633–1639   119
Elio Brancaforte

7 The British in Oman since 1645   131
Sir Terence Clark

8 Ruins and Landscapes from Sardis to Stowe: The Work of Giovanni Battista Borra   143
Jane Ayer Scott

9 Ottoman Women through the Eyes of Mary Wortley Montagu   157
Mary Ann Fay

10 James Silk Buckingham (1786–1855): An Anecdotal Traveller   169
Peta Rée

11	Lord Belmore proceeds up the Nile in 1817–1818 *Deborah Manley*	179
12	From Cairo to Petra: Léon de Laborde and L.M.A. Linant de Bellefonds, 1828 *Pascale Linant de Bellefonds*	193
13	James Burton and Slave Girls *Neil Cooke*	209
14	The Reverend Jolliffe's Advice to Travellers *Patricia Usick*	219
15	Italian Travellers in Egypt *Marta Petricioli and Barbara Codacci*	225
16	Nile Notes of a *Howadji*: American Travellers in Egypt, 1837–1903 *Martin R. Kalfatovic*	239
17	Romances and Realities of Travellers *Nadia El Kholy*	261
	Select Bibliography	277
	Index	311

Introduction

Paul and Janet Starkey

Egypt and the Near East have enchanted many people, both from within the region and from outside it. Travellers from the West, in particular, have journeyed to the region over the centuries for a variety of motives, both good and bad: they have travelled on pilgrimages; they have set out in pursuit of knowledge, of power, diplomacy and trade; they have travelled for pleasure and adventure, to plunder and to discover the exotic – or sometimes simply to discover themselves. Some have been influenced more than others by what they saw; others have brought back tangible evidence of their visits in the form of antiquities or other collectors' items; many have used their experiences and observations for their own literary or artistic ends.

The collection of papers in this book has its origin in the conference: 'Travellers to Egypt and the Near East' held at St Catherine's College, Oxford, in July 1997. The conference was a successor to that held in Durham in 1995, papers from which were published as *Travellers in Egypt* (London, 1998). Like its predecessor, the Oxford conference was a multidisciplinary affair, notable as much for the enthusiasm of the contributors as for the academic excellence of their contributions. Like its predecessor, much of the conference, for understandable reasons, also centred on the nineteenth century; however, a significant group of contributions took a wider perspective, extending the chronological and intellectual horizons of the participants and stimulating much lively discussion. This is the first of two volumes of fascinating material presented at the conference. The second volume is titled *Interpreting the Orient: Travellers in Egypt and the Near East* and includes papers on Carl Haag, Sir David Wilkie, Amelia Edwards and Gertrude Bell. For convenience, the papers in the collections are arranged in approximately chronological order, though with so many common themes running through them it has proved impossible to order them in a strict sequence according to a single criterion. In addition to the chronological sequence, the reader will detect a number of common themes – religion, gender, economics, colonialism, perceptions of literature and art and so forth – that haunt the essays and form webs of interconnection between them.

The first paper in this collection stands somewhat apart from most of the others, both chronologically and in spirit, but it serves as a useful reminder that travel to the Middle East is far from being a modern, or even a medieval phenomenon. In 'A Textual Landscape: The Mapping of a Holy Land in the Fourth-Century *Itinerarium* of the Bordeaux Pilgrim', Glenn Bowman compares two accounts of pilgimages to the Holy Land sites: the enthusiastic first person narrative of Egeria; and the later, more detached and impersonal *Itinerarium Burdigalense*, an account of a pilgrimage from Bordeaux to the Holy Land in AD 333. Bowman shows that although only half a century separates the two journeys, there had been massive changes in Christian perceptions of their world and the place of religion in it during that time, and he detects a shift from an interest in purely historical narratives to their topographical associations. As a practical guidebook for a trip to Palestine, the *Itinerarium* is unreliable: rather, the text is a gloss on biblical materials, to be used as a spiritual itinerary leading to the eternity of promised redemption.

The next two essays, 'The Grand Tour in the Ottoman Empire, 1699–1826' by Philip Mansel and 'Dressing Native' by John Rodenbeck, play a critical role in weaving many of the succeeding individual contributions into a consistent and comprehensible whole. In 'The Grand Tour', Philip Mansel describes the process by which the grand tour in the Ottoman Empire displaced the traditional grand tour centred on Italy that had provided two to three years' pleasurable travel with a semi-educational purpose for young gentlemen, particularly in the eighteenth century. From 1579, or even earlier, the Ottoman Empire had had close commercial and diplomatic links with Europe, and, as relationships grew closer in the eighteenth century, more travellers went there and were able to see the power of the Empire and its court. It became fashionable for them to adopt Turkish costume and architecture when they returned to the West, and young men were often painted in Ottoman dress to commemorate the success of their grand tour. During the early years of the nineteenth century, turmoil in Europe made travel to the Ottoman Empire even more popular: a visit to the ruins of Greece

Introduction

and the Middle East became part of the training of British architects, and writers such as Byron and Hobhouse drew inspiration from their experiences there.

John Rodenbeck's paper 'Dressing Native' elaborates the dress theme touched on by Philip Mansel, discussing in some detail the motives that prompted Western travellers to adopt local dress when travelling in the Middle East. Edward Said claimed in *Orientalism* that E.W. Lane wore Turkish clothing as a disguise, and dressing in native clothes has been seen by some commentators as evidence of espionage, schizophrenia or megalomania on the part of the travellers. Rodenbeck, however, convincingly argues that such accusations bear no relation to the well-documented realities of the Middle East between 1600 and 1850: local clothing was worn for a wide variety of motives, including comfort and safety, and official compulsion also played a part; espionage and aggression were almost certainly among the least important motives. Eighteenth-century Europe had been gripped by Turcomania, which set the fashion in costume, art and entertainment, and even Western military styles were adaptations of Turkish costume with Cossack influences. Lewis and many other Western artists wore Turkish clothes in Cairo in the 1840s and expected their Western subjects to do the same, though the fashion died out in the 1850s, when Ottoman and Egyptian government officials adopted Western dress.

The next group of essays takes us back to the pre-modern period. John Ghazvinian's essay, 'English Pleasure Travel in the Near East, 1580–1645', argues that 'curiosity travel' (a term that covers both the travellers and the texts they produced) deserves more attention than it has traditionally received in most histories of travel, which have often concentrated on those travelling for reasons of trade, military conquest, missionary zeal or diplomacy. The travellers he describes – many of whom were young, well-off, recent graduates – were passionately curious about foreign lands. Learning new languages and seeking places mentioned in classical sources, they seemed distinctly more fond of the empirical approach than the older, affirmation-based epistemological one of medieval times.

Angèle Kapoïan's contribution entitled 'Egypt in 1615–1616 as Seen through the Eyes of the Armenian Simeon of Poland', presents us with an unusual phenomenon, for although Simeon was born in Europe he was ethnically of Middle Eastern origin. Simeon, an Armenian deacon and scribe born in Poland, journeyed on a pilgrimage to the Near East, Ottoman Empire and Egypt. In 1635 he wrote *Travel Account*, which modestly describes the people, buildings and way of life he encountered in Alexandria and on his journey up the Nile, where he met Copts and fellow Armenians and admired the religious fervour of the Egyptian Muslims.

The purpose of Adam Olearius's journey to Persia, described by Elio Brancaforte in 'Adam Olearius's Travels to Persia, 1633–1639', was to persuade Persia to export its silk to Germany via the Volga and so end the Turkish monopoly of the trade. The entire mission was recorded by Olearius in a travel account crammed with information and published in 1656. Partly written in the third person and partly as a first person narrative, his work brought scientific criticism to bear on the author's observations, juxtaposing his descriptions of customs in the Near East with those of Europe.

Trade was responsible for the first contact being established between Britain and Oman, and as elsewhere in the period of British expansion, from the seventeenth century, the flag followed. In his essay 'The British in Oman since 1645', Sir Terence Clark describes how the East India Company led the way, following an initiative from the Omani side in 1645, when the Imam offered the company trading facilities in Sohar. It was not until Napoleon's threat to invade British India in 1798, however, that the British consolidated their position in Muscat, and their initial enthusiasm was short-lived, for in ten years four British Residents died in Muscat as a result of the debilitating climate. In the nineteenth and twentieth centuries, many travellers, especially from the Indian services, explored Oman and wrote of their adventures, including Sir Percy Cox (between 1899 and 1904), Bertram Thomas (between 1927 and 1930) and the last of the great travellers in Oman, Sir Wilfred Thesiger (in 1946 and 1947).

Jane Ayer Scott's essay, 'Ruins and Landscapes from Sardis to Stowe: The Work of Giovanni Battista Borra', reveals a somewhat different aspect of travel in the Near East. The architect Borra, an outstanding draughtsman familiar with classical monuments, accompanied the politician Robert Wood to the Near East in 1750, producing magnificent drawings of the great Hellenistic and Roman cities of Asia Minor – Palmyra, Baalbek, Smyrna and Sardis. Borra took great care to measure the ruins accurately, to record their topographical settings and to make clear drawings of their ornamentation, and the accuracy of his work at

Introduction

Sardis is still appreciated by excavation teams in the twentieth century. On his return to England in 1751, he contributed to the interior decoration of several great houses; his decorative schemes included Severan baroque, Doric and Ionic, as well as specific elements from Baalbek, Palmyra and Asia Minor.

A feminine view of the Near East at this period is provided by Mary Ann Fay's essay on 'Ottoman Women through the Eyes of Mary Wortley Montagu', which describes how Lady Mary lived in Istanbul from 1716 to 1718 as wife of the English ambassador, writing a series of letters about her experiences. Her letters wittily described Ottoman harems and baths, to which, unlike most male writers of the period, she had regular access. In contrast to received opinion, Lady Mary thought the veil a useful device; and her writings draw an unfavourable comparison between the position of women in eighteenth-century England – where the law accorded women neither property rights nor a separate legal personality – and the laws of Islam, under which a woman has a right to own property.

As already noted, it was after the French invasion of Egypt in 1798 that Western travel to the Near and Middle East began to become commonplace. Succeeding essays recount the adventures of a variety of travellers, whose motives for travel were as varied as their personalities. In 'James Silk Buckingham (1786–1855): An Anecdotal Traveller', Peta Rée recalls the life of the accomplished gossip and artful adventurer who arrived in Alexandria as a financially ruined seaman in 1813, and enjoyed a delightful social life as guest of the consul before travelling up the Nile. In 1815, using money assigned to him for transactions in India, Buckingham instead toured the Levant and was recognised as a swindler by W.J. Bankes. In 'Lord Belmore Proceeds up the Nile in 1817–1818', Deborah Manley relates the progress of Lord Belmore and his party on an elegant grand tour of Egypt; among the characters they met on their travels were Henry Salt, Belzoni, Comte de Forbin, Irby and Mangles. Pascale Linant de Bellefonds in her essay 'From Cairo to Petra: Léon de Laborde and L.M.A. Linant de Bellefonds', describes the visit of the two Frenchmen Laborde and Linant de Bellefonds to Petra in 1828, when, after entering Petra from the south via Sinai (rather than through the Sīq), they produced the first near-accurate layout of the site, drew high-quality illustrations of the monuments and became the first Europeans to visit the Deir; both David Roberts and J.L. Stephens made use of their illustrations in their own work.

Neil Cooke's paper, 'James Burton and Slave Girls', discusses the purchase of slaves by European travellers – a phenomenon that continued even after the Abolition of Slavery Act of 1833 had effectively brought slavery to an end in England. The nature of slavery in the Middle East was seen by English travellers as being essentially different from that of slavery in America (which persisted until 1865), and many travellers regarded the purchase of slaves as being a normal part of the lifestyle of an upper-class Turk. Some travellers brought their slaves back to England, and even, as Burton did, married a slave mistress.

A fascinating sidelight on travel to Egypt and the Near East in the early years of the nineteenth century is provided by Patricia Usick, who discusses 'The Reverend Jolliffe's Advice to Travellers', prepared by him to assist other travellers after a visit to Egypt and Syria in 1817 and published in 1820 as *Letters from Palestine*. Before the publication of a plethora of guidebooks in the mid-nineteenth century, there was little information available to someone on a grand tour, and travellers relied largely on networking, often enjoying hospitality from local consuls in Cairo and Alexandria.

The next two papers discuss travellers from Italy and America respectively. In 'Italian Travellers in Egypt', Marta Petricioli and Barbara Codacci show that Italy produced few accounts of the region comparable to those of French writers, such as Flaubert or Lamartine, and suggest that Italian travel writers did not reflect their country's knowledge of or interest or involvement in Egypt during the nineteenth century. By contrast, American travellers of the period, discussed in Martin R. Kalfatovic's 'Nile Notes of a *Howadji*', included not only prominent literary figures such as Mark Twain, but also a US president and his staff. As Nadia El Kholy shows in 'Romances and Realities of Travellers', however, the descriptions of the world that these and other travellers gave were often influenced by preconceived romantic and exotic ideas derived from the *Arabian Nights* and elsewhere, restructured for the benefit of a Western audience. In contrast to earlier travellers' accounts, which were primarily concerned with the need to inform, these used the Oriental world as a metaphor for dream, fantasy, imagination and unreality. Descriptions of Egyptian architecture were fettered by European artistic conventions, and Muhammad Ali was portrayed as a capriciously cruel Oriental despot living in luxury – like a figure from the *Arabian Nights*.

1

A Textual Landscape: The Mapping of a Holy Land in the Fourth-Century *Itinerarium* of the Bordeaux Pilgrim

Glenn Bowman[1]

In a recent article Robert Markus queries, with reference to the fourth century CE emergence of a Christian network of holy sites, 'why, how was it possible that any place should become holy?'[2] He proceeds to analyse how places come to be considered and treated as sacred in popular perceptions and practices as the reflection of a shift in Christian devotion 'from the eschatological meaning of the historical narratives to their topographical associations'.[3] This shift prepared the ground for the Constantinian church-building programme that affected not only Palestine but also the entire Roman Empire. It came about, according to Markus, because early fourth-century Christians felt it necessary to elaborate cult practices around tombs and relics of martyrs in order to assert continuity between their church – increasingly enjoying the support of the Roman state – and the church of early Christians, who discerned the signs of their divine election in the wounds of martyrdom that the same Roman state had inflicted on them. Markus writes that 'the veneration of martyrs . . . served to assure the Christians of a local church of its continuity with its own heroic, persecuted, past, and the universal Church of its continuity with the age of the martyrs'.[4] Martyrs and their relics came to be seen as resting 'in place', and the place of the cult became a site for sanctifying individuals and events of an increasingly distant past and contemporary Christians who wished to participate in that sanctity. 'Places became sacred as the past became localised in the present',[5] and the logic of the cult practices that brought fourth-century Christians into contact with their martyred forebears was easily extended from places explicitly connected with martyrdom to sites associated with other elements of Christian and pre-Christian history.

Scripture into site: text and monument in the fourth-century Holy Land

In the Holy Land, the sites sanctified were less commonly those associated with martyrdoms (notwithstanding the powerful exception of Golgotha) than those linked through biblical narratives with Jesus's prefiguration, his incarnation and the dissemination of his message through his disciples' activities. Constantine, as is well known, initiated a massive programme of churchbuilding in Jerusalem in AD 325, with the construction of a shrine complex composed of a basilica known as the Martyrium, a rotunda-shrine over Jesus's tomb, named the Anastasis, and a chapel at Calvary. This was quickly followed by the erection of three other memorial compounds: one near Hebron at Mamre, where Abraham was said to have been visited by God and two mysterious companions (Gen. 18:1–22); another at Bethlehem, where Jesus was reputed to have been born; and a third, the Éléona, on the Mount of Olives, from where, according to Acts 1:6–12, Jesus ascended into the heavens. These and other sites provided local and pilgrim Christians with settings in which they could engage – by means of liturgy and the imagination – with signal events drawn from a sanctified past.

We see, for instance, in the enthusiastic narrative of a late-fourth-century pilgrim who has come to be known as Egeria,[6] a compulsive siting of biblical references in the landscape:

> All along the valley [below Mount Sinai] they [local monastics serving as guides] showed us how each Israelite had a house, and they were round stone houses, as you can still see from the foundations. They showed us where holy Moses ordered the children of Israel to run 'from gate to gate' (Exod. 32:27) when he had come back from the Mount. They also showed us where holy Moses ordered them to burn the calf which Aaron had made for them; and the bed of the stream from which, as you read in Exodus, holy Moses made the children of Israel drink (Exod. 32:20). And they pointed out the place where a portion of Moses' spirit was given to the seventy men (Num. 11:25), and where the children of Israel had their craving for food (Num. 11:4). They showed us also the place called 'The Fire' (Num. 11:3), a part of the camp which was burning, where

the fire stopped when holy Moses prayed. And they showed us where the *manna* and the quails descended on the people (Num. 11:6, 31). So we were shown everything which the Books of Moses tell us took place in that valley beneath holy Sinai, the Mount of God.[7]

When Egeria returns from the Sinai to Jerusalem to participate in its extended Holy Week liturgy, she witnesses, on Palm Sunday, how the Christian liturgy – enacted in the Holy City in the same places the events it celebrates were alleged to have been carried out originally – re-presents and thus re-enacts the past:

> The bishop and all the people rise from their places, and start off on foot down from the summit of the Mount of Olives. All the people go before him with psalms and antiphons, all the time repeating 'Blessed is he that cometh in the name of the Lord'. . . . Everyone is carrying branches, either palm or olive, and they accompany the bishop in the very way the people did when once they went down with the Lord. . . . what I found most impressive about all this [the patterns of worship of the Jerusalem community] was that the psalms and antiphons they use are always appropriate, whether at night, in the early morning, at the day prayers at midday or three o'clock, or at Lucernare. Everything is suitable, appropriate and relevant to what is being done.[8]

In Egeria's praise of the verisimilitude of Holy Land sites and practices we see yet another instance of the evolving phenomenon of site sanctification, traced by Peter Walker through Eusebius of Caesarea's and Cyril of Jerusalem's discourses on the holy places.[9] Egeria *sees*, played out before her, the forms of scripture, whether these be read in the details of landscape or re-enacted in celebrants' movements across the field of the literal sites. Cyril, addressing catechumens *c.* AD 350, notes the sensory privilege enjoyed by those gathered on the literal site referred to in the biblical texts read to them by their instructor, 'one should never grow weary of hearing about our crowned Lord, especially on this holy Golgotha. For others merely hear, but we see and touch.'[10]

Emerging from these two texts one can discern the threat Gregory of Nyssa (AD 331–395) saw in the growing cult of holy sites: the danger that such sites would come to be seen as inherently sacred and that worship of the sites would come to supplant reverence for the divine to another . . . The book exhibits almost no theological interest. It moves indiscriminately from one place to another . . . [and] has no hierarchy of place.[19]

In the work of most commentators, the Bordeaux Pilgrim's narrative is overshadowed by the 'modern' first person narration of Egeria, which appears to offer a more immediately rewarding access to religion in the period. E.D. Hunt unfavourably compares its 'stark narrative' with that of Egeria, which 'furnishes a more penetrating glimpse into the devotion of the Christian traveller'.[20] Hunt's dismissal resonates with Mary Campbell's description of the *Itinerarium Burdigalense* and its source, the *Antonine Itinerary*, as 'barely more than lists of cities, *mansiones*, places of interest, and the approximate distances (given in *milia*) between them. These works are, in effect, verbal charts, designed for the convenience of subsequent travelers, not for the reader's spiritual exaltation.'[21] I will, however, argue in the following pages that the half century that separates the texts of Egeria and the Bordeaux Pilgrim effected massive transformations in Christians' senses of their world and the place of their religion in it, and that these changes deeply affect the narrative economies of the texts. I will contend that the *Itinerarium Burdigalense* is not a mere 'verbal chart' for the guidance of travellers, but is, instead, a carefully structured and deeply theological transposition onto topography of an eschatological history. The text, rather than seeking to direct pilgrims to the holy places of the Roman empire, works to lead catechumens to gateways that open on a kingdom not of this world.

Egeria's ecstatic response to the conjunction of place, text and pilgrim was symptomatic of the development of new attitudes towards holy sites in the decades following Constantine's conversion. Her narrative celebrates a world in the process of being transformed into a Christian domain, and the tone of her text is redolent of the same holy confidence that inspired Eusebius, in about AD 337–339, to suggest that the building of the Anastasis was the beginning of an inworldly fulfilment of Revelation's prophecy of a new heaven and new earth:

> On the very spot which witnessed the Saviour's sufferings, a new Jerusalem was constructed, over against the one so celebrated of old which, since the foul stain of guilt brought upon it by the murder of the Lord, had experienced the last extremity of desolation, the effect of divine judgement upon its impious people. It was opposite

this city that the emperor now began to rear a monument to the Saviour's victory over death, with rich and lavish magnificence. And it may be that this was that second and new Jerusalem spoken of in the predictions of the prophets.[22]

For Egeria, the newly Christianised empire is part of the project of world sanctification that she and her contemporaries saw prefigured in the texts of the Bible; the Christian world, and herself as a Christian in it, are enriched by that continuity and both self and site are rendered worthy. Egeria's narrative is densely charged by enthusiastic first person narration, 'we had been looking forward to all this so much that we had been eager to make the climb'.[23] It is marked by a confidence in the continuity of biblical past and sanctified present to the extent that Egeria is able to use her contemporary experiences to illuminate and elaborate biblical narrative:

> I kept asking to see the different places mentioned in the Bible, and they were all pointed out to me . . . Some of the places were to the right and others to the left of our route, some a long way off and others close by. So, as far as I can see, loving sisters, you must take it that the children of Israel zigzagged their way to the Red Sea, first right, then back left again, now forwards, and now back.[24]

Posteriority – the belatedness of visiting the holy places four centuries after Jesus's death – is not a condition of loss and distance, since the world has assimilated the biblical past and built upon it a contemporary structure of Christian community and authority. There was no rupture between the biblical past and the imperial present but only the signs of a community developing its structures and traditions building on that past and moving into its future. For Egeria, the Holy Land does not just contain monuments that refer to the founding moments of her faith but also shows evidence of that faith's development of local Christian communities and of the institutions it needs to grow and spread throughout Palestine and the rest of the known world:

> We were also shown the place where Lot's wife had her memorial, as you read in the Bible. But what we saw, reverend ladies, was not the actual pillar, but only the place where it had once been. The pillar itself, they say, has been submerged in the Dead Sea – at any rate we did not see it and I cannot pretend we did. In fact it was the

bishop there, the Bishop of Zoar, who told us that it was now a good many years since the pillar had been visible.[25]

It is not surprising that Egeria, having witnessed the monuments to the biblical past and seen the continuity between that past and her present in Jerusalem's fervent transformation into a ritual centre manifesting the word made flesh, announces her intention of following her pilgrimage through the holy places with a visit to places beyond the borders of the Holy Land, which have been caught up in and render evidence of the expansion of that incarnated and empowered revelation.[26]

Although the Constantinian basilicas were being erected as the *Itinerarium Burdigalense* was being composed, the tone of its discourse differs radically from that of Egeria. In it a detached impersonality prevails that tends to efface the subject positions of both narrator and reader:

> From here to Bethasora 14 miles, where the spring is in which Philip baptized the eunuch. From there it is nine miles to Terebinthus where Abraham lived and dug a well under the terebith tree and spoke and ate with the angels.[27]

In striking contrast to the passage from Egeria cited above in which the wanderings of the children of Israel are experienced in terms of a network of sites on a landscape that itself comes to serve as the grounds for biblical exegesis; the narrator and time of narration at times disappear in the Bordeaux Pilgrim's description of Bethel. In one case, the reader is introduced by the text into a terrain that does not abut on the contemporary site from where the narrative is launched, but is present only in the discourse of I Kings 13:1–32:

> From here it is a mile to the place where Jacob, on his way to Mesopotamia, fell asleep, and there is the almond tree, and here he saw a vision and the angel wrestled with him. Here was also King Jeroboam, to whom was sent a prophet so that he might be converted to the Most High God; and the prophet was commanded not to eat with the false prophet whom the king had about him, and because he was led astray by the false prophet and ate with him on his way back, a lion met the prophet on the way and killed him.[28]

In the Bordeaux Pilgrim's narrative the order of events is not organised with reference to the moment of observation but in terms either of a spatial contiguity that collapses temporality,[29] or, as I will demonstrate below, in terms of an eschatological periodicity that renders the narrator's role extraneous. The Bordeaux Pilgrim's text, rather than portraying the centre of an expanding new world order, seems to manifest to its audience a space contiguous to, but not continuous with, the secular world. The pilgrim who moves out of his or her native land and into that holy space seems simultaneously to 'lose' himself or herself, and to 'find' a way out of this life and into a world that takes its being from the events and prophecies of the Bible. The *Itinerarium* thus appears to map a passage between two distinct domains: the contemporary and fallen world of the Roman empire; and another world in which time is eschatological and leads towards the eternity of a promised redemption. The presence on that map of the four Constantinian basilicas would seem, however, to be a conundrum, inasmuch as they would seem to be very much of the time and order of empire. It will be necessary to move through the holy land represented in the *Itinerarium Burdigalense* to understand why, in a text that takes its bearings from a biblical past, the author should emphasise the fact that

> lately, by the order of the Emperor Constantine, was built a basilica, that is a house of the lord, with ponds of remarkable beauty beside it, from which water is taken up, and at the back a font, where children are baptized.[30]

Traversing the *Itinerarium*

The Bordeaux Pilgrim's text poses a critical reader with an immediate set of methodological questions. Is the text, for which we have no history of usage, to be read purely in terms of its internal logic? In so far as the text is, even with its descriptive addenda, in large part a listing of names, it seems clear that its author expects those seeking to understand the text to draw upon extra-textual information pertaining to the sites and events it names. Can we then use the contemporary Holy Land and its topographic peripheries as sources for the information that we need to make sense of the Bordeaux Pilgrim's text? Two things seem to militate against this mode of referencing. First, the *Itinerarium* appears to be an unreliable guidebook for a practical trip through Palestine. As Wilken points out, 'his route is puzzling; he sometimes turns back to visit places he could have seen when he was in the vicinity, and he makes few observations on the things he has seen'.[31] The text's erraticness and its striking omissions[32] suggest that it functions not so much as a guide to a literal place but as a discourse that uses places as a pretext for another exploration. Second, there is argument against using fourth-century Palestine as a hermeneutical device, because, in the text itself, real places seem to serve as doorways into a scriptural domain – as in the passage cited above, in which the reader is carried into I Kings 13 rather than directed along real fourth-century roads.

One is led to ask, then, whether the text is organised in terms of a logic existing outside of itself, not according to the order of sites along fourth-century pilgrim routes but to the biblical texts that early Christians would themselves have used as devices for interpreting events in their contemporary world. In this case, the literal Holy Land would be presented as a gloss on biblical materials, instead of, as it does in Egeria's text, serving as a primary text while the Bible serves to explicate. Interpretation would thus have to be based not primarily on the sites visited but, at least in the first instance, on the biblical references to which those sites offer access. In traversing the text of the pilgrim in the following pages, I will reverse the agenda Spitzer discerned in Egeria's gaze (see note 7 above) and will direct my eye from 'the *locus* (locality) in Palestine' to 'the Biblical *locus* (i.e. passage)' with which contemporary Christian knowledge would have associated it. In doing so, I hope not so much to show the land as it would have been perceived before place came to be seen as holy, as to provide an insight into what the Bordeaux Pilgrim was presenting if it was not a Holy Land.

The presentation of biblical material in the *Itinerarium Burdigalense* is framed, both at the beginning and the close of the narrative, with hundreds of brief entries of which the following, tracing the route between Antioch and Banias, are typical:

City of Antiochia	16 [miles]
From Tarsus in Cilicia to Antiochia	141 miles, 10 changes, 7 halts
To the palace of Daphne	5
Change at Hysdata	11
Halt at Platanus	8
Change at Bacchaiæ	7
Halt at Catelæ	16
City of Ladica	16
City of Gabala	14

> City of Balaneas 13
> The border of Cœle Syria and Phœnicia.[33]

The massive distances covered between Bordeaux and the borders of the Holy Land (by the text's own calculation the distance between Bordeaux and Sarepta is 3,190 miles) are, in large part, rendered as empty spaces by the text. The narrative marks borders (both natural and political), and makes occasional mention of curiosities dealing with water (the ebb and flow of the river Garonne at Bordeaux and 'a city in the sea two miles from the shore'),[34] but in large part restricts itself to the names of places at which the traveller rested or changed horses. Outside of the Holy Land, the text proffers little more than the homogenised mapping that characterises the military itineraries of the period. The only deviations from such models are a number of additions; on the way out:

> Viminatium, 'where Diocletian killed [Marcus Aurelius] Carinus';[35]
> Libyassa, where 'lies [the body of] King Annibalianus (Hannibal), who was once king of the Africans';[36]
> Andavilis, where is 'the villa of Pampatus, from which came the curule horses';[37]
> Tyana, where 'was born Apollonius the Magician';[38] and
> Tarsus, where 'the Apostle Paul was born';[39]

and on the return:

> Philippi, where the apostles 'Paul and Silas were imprisoned';[40]
> Euripides, where 'is buried the poet Euripides';[41] and
> Pellas, from 'whence came Alexander the Great of Macedonia'.[42]

It is when the text touches on territories that have parts to play in the biblical narratives[43] that the tenor of the *Itinerarium Burdigalense* changes radically. At Sarepta (biblical Zarephath), the narrative begins to sprout novel shoots of discourse, 'this is where Elijah went up to the widow and asked for food'.[44] A few lines later, another reference to the Bible emerges from the stem of the itinerary, 'this is where Mount Carmel is; there Elijah made sacrifice',[45] followed soon after by a third, 'there [Cessarea Palæstina] is the bath of Cornelius the Centurion, who gave many alms'.[46] A few lines later, the city of Isdradela (biblical Jezreel) is described as 'where Ahab reigned and Elijah prophesised; there is the field in which David killed Goliath'.[47] This is followed by a mention of Aser, which, inexplicably, according to Wilkinson,[48] the pilgrim claims was the site of Job's house. The text then presents Neopolis (Nablus) as 'the site of Mount Agazaren [Gerizim]':

> The Samaritans say that there Abraham offered sacrifice, and five hundred steps go up to the top of the mountain. From there, at the foot of the mountain, is that place called Sechar. There is the tomb in which Joseph is laid in the villa which his father Jacob gave him. From there, Dinah, Jacob's daughter, was abducted by the sons of the Amorites. A mile from here is the place called Sechar . . .[49]

From this point on, until the confines of the Holy Land are left behind, the form of the itinerary nearly disappears beneath a profusion of commentary that binds places to an apparently unstructured glossing of biblical associations and throws out the occasional contemporary observation. Despite this appearance of unstructured proliferation, which led the above-quoted commentators to characterise the *Itinerarium* as a 'verbal chart' that 'moves indiscriminately from one place to another . . . [and] has no hierarchy of place',[50] a theme emerges in the opening sections of the pilgrim's presentation of the Holy Land that sets the parameters of the rest of the text, determining what will be included and what excluded in the text's presentation of the territory.

The reader, emerging from a long crossing of the spiritual desert that surrounds the Holy Land, first encounters biblical *manna* at Sarepta, where the text's itinerary intersects with that of Elijah, who, directed by God, left his desert refuge by the brook Cherith and travelled to Sarepta to dwell in the house of the widow. The next digression, eight entries later, refers to the site on Mount Carmel at which Elijah offered sacrifice. Both incidents are part of a larger narrative (I Kings 16:29–18:46) that refers to the apostasy of Ahab and of the larger part of Israel and to Elijah's role in returning Israel from Baal worship to its dedication to Yahweh. Central to the story is a fierce drought that Elijah called down upon the land as a consequence of Ahab's following of the Baal. While the consequent famine wracked the land, Elijah hid from the wrath of Ahab by the brook Cherith, east of the Jordan, where he was fed by ravens until the brook itself dried up in the drought. He then went to Sarepta, where he not only fed the widow and her household with a jar of meal and a cruse of oil that miraculously refilled themselves as long

A Textual Landscape

as he stayed there, but also resurrected the son of the widow, who had fallen sick and died during his stay (I Kings 18:17–24).

Elijah's establishment of a small community sustained by divine power in the midst of a world dominated by famine and disease is followed, in the biblical narrative, by his challenge to the hegemony of the apostate king and the priesthood of Baal that propped up Ahab's power. Elijah's sacrifice on Mount Carmel is, of course, the bloody showdown between Elijah and the 450 prophets of Baal recounted in I Kings 18:20–40. Setting up the confrontation, Elijah challenges the king, the prophets and all Israel gathered on Carmel, 'How long will you go limping with two different opinions? If the Lord is God, follow him; but if Baal, then follow him' (I Kings 18:21). The failure of Baal's prophets to bring fire down upon their sacrificial offering is countered by Elijah's spectacular success in calling a voracious flame down upon his drenched bull. This is followed by the slaughter of the priesthood of the Baal and by the torrential end of the drought that Israel had suffered. Elijah not only 'repaired the altar of the Lord that had been thrown down' (I Kings 18:30) on Carmel, but also provided a convincing retort to those who could not decide which god – Yahweh or the deity of the rulers of the state – was the true god.

The richness in detail of these episodes is only alluded to in the text of the *Itinerarium Burdigalense* through the citation of Sarepta and Mount Carmel. The text uses sites as mnemonics to bring strategically significant moments in the history and prehistory of Christianity to the consciousness of a fourth-century audience already knowledgeable about biblical matters. To such an audience the stories of Elijah would be pertinent on several levels. Elijah's challenge to Israel and his spectacular proof of the power of the only true god would have presented a salient example to early-fourth-century neophytes who were poised to commit themselves to the worship of monotheistic Christianity and the abandonment of allegiance to the sanctioned divinities of the Roman state. Furthermore, Elijah's experiences at Sarepta would, for them, function typologically; the *Itinerarium*'s reference to Sarepta would – for early Christians to whom 'typology, the exposition of the foreshadowings of Christ in the history of Israel, was . . . a subject of elementary catechesis'[51] – have evoked Jesus's feeding of the multitude with loaves and fishes at the Mount of Beatitudes as well as his resurrection of Lazarus at Bethany (Elijah at Sarepta is the first of several Old Testament prefigurations of Jesus that crop up in the *Itinerarium Burdigalense*). Elijah's development[52] from an isolated bearer of truth hiding in the wilderness to becoming the mainspring of a small community, resident in the world but not subject to its life-destroying regime, and then becoming the victorious scourge of his enemies and bringer of life-giving rains to Israel – might itself stand as a prefiguration of the Christian community's own sense of past, present and future. This suggestion is supported by the fact that an historical motif recurs throughout the text, in which a dominant old order is mapped, then challenged by a divinely-endowed truth and finally shown to be overcome by that new power. An example – in typical topographical concentration – is shown a few lines later, 'City of Istradela [Jezreel]: there Ahab reigned and Elijah prophesized; there is the field where David killed Goliath.'[53]

The commentator on the Oxford annotated edition of the Revised Standard Version of the Bible notes, with reference to the opening of the Elijah sequence discussed above, that:

> The Canaanite (or Phoenician) god Baal (16.31–32) was held by his worshippers to be the one who controlled the rain. Elijah intended to show that his God, *the Lord the God of Israel*, was the one who really controlled the *rain*.[54]

Elijah's demonstration, graphically rendered in I Kings 18:41–46 when the rains pour torrentially over the burnt bull and the hecatomb of the slain Ba'alist prophets, meshes with a less spectacular, and similarly pedagogic yet more ambitious, exposition pertaining to water that runs through the whole of the *Itinerarium Burdigalense*. Soon after the pilgrim notes the location of Elijah's sacrifice there are two digressions directly associated with water:

> There is the bath of Cornelius the Centurion, who gave many alms. At the third milestone from there is Mount Syna, where there is a spring; if a woman washes herself in it, she will become pregnant.[55]

Then, a few lines later, the pilgrim speaks of Sechar:

> Sechar, from which the Samaritan woman went down to the same place where Jacob had dug a well, to fill her jug with water from it, and our Lord Jesus Christ spoke with her, and where there are plane

trees, which Jacob planted, and a bath, which gets its water from this well.[56]

If, as the constant mention of water-related sites throughout the text would suggest, water is a significant element in the pilgrim's presentation of the land, the reader should examine this early set of water associations for evidence of the narrator's motivation in including them.

The mention of the spring at Syna develops the theme of the life-giving powers of water earlier raised by the invocation of Elijah at Carmel, where he brought the rains and ended the killing drought. That the spring, even though extra-biblical and contemporary, does not simply maintain already existent life but miraculously engenders pregnancy, suggests that water in the Holy Land has a nature-defying power to replace barrenness with life. This link is demonstrated more forcibly later in the text, where the narrator locates the spring of Elisha outside Jericho:

> Before if a woman drank from that water she would not bear children. A vessel was brought to Elisha and he put salt in it and came and put it over the spring and said 'thus says the Lord: I have healed these waters'. Now if a woman drinks from it she will have children.[57]

With the mention of the bath of Cornelius the Centurion, the text again invokes life-giving water and, in so doing, effects not only a movement from the Old to the New Testament but also the first appearance of another recurrent motif of the *Itinerarium*: the overcoming of the old dispensation by the new. Cornelius, whose story is relayed in Acts 10, was one of the two first Gentile converts,[58] whose conversion follows the narrative of Peter being instructed in a vision to reject the dietary restrictions of Leviticus.[59] The divine instruction to overturn the Old Testament discriminations between the clean and the unclean is, in the rest of the chapter, extended to the laws separating Jews from Gentiles, and, as a result, Cornelius, a Gentile believer in the word of Christ, is baptised. Peter, at Cornelius's house, says:

> 'Truly I perceive that God shows no partiality, but in every nation any one who fears him and does what is right is acceptable to him . . .'
> While Peter was still saying this, the Holy Spirit fell on all who

heard the word. And the believers from among the circumcised who came with Peter were amazed, because the gift of the Holy Spirit had been poured out even on the Gentiles. For they heard them [Cornelius and his kinsmen and close friends] speaking with tongues and extolling God. Then Peter declared 'Can any one forbid water for baptizing these people who have received the Holy Spirit just as we have?' And he commanded them to be baptized in the name of Jesus Christ.[60]

The bath of Cornelius commemorates the fact that 'to the Gentiles also God has granted repentance unto life',[61] and so marks the historical moment at which the promise of divine election, previously restricted to the Jews, becomes universal. It is interesting that the site of this Gentile conversion, encountered as the pilgrim's text enters the Holy Land, is balanced, later in the text, as the narrative prepares to depart from the Holy Land, by the citing of other water – 'the spring . . . in which Philip baptised the eunuch'[62] – where the other originary Gentile baptism occurred. The text transposes onto the spatial boundaries of the Holy Land the temporal borders of the new and old dispensations. The limits of the Old Testament Promised Land are marked as simultaneously being the beginnings of the domain opened to redemption by the universal promise of the New Testament. This historical progression seems to be further marked geographically by the pilgrim's noting of Tarsus, where 'the Apostle Paul was born', and Philippi, where the apostles 'Paul and Silas were imprisoned' – beyond the boundaries of the biblical Holy Land at the front beyond which pagan holy men and mythographers, such as Apollonius of Tyana[63] and Euripides, still prevail.

The relation of the Old and New Testament dispensations is further developed in the excursus around the site of Sechim,[64] where the setting of Jacob's well allows the narrator not only to invoke the coming of the Israelites into their inheritance of the land[65] but also, through the tale of Jesus and the Samaritan woman, to suggest that that literal inheritance is superseded by the spiritual bequest brought by Jesus to Jews and non-Jews alike. In a gesture analogous to that made by Elijah at Sarepta, Jesus asks a woman for water at the well at Sychar:

> The Samaritan woman said to him, 'How is it that you, a Jew, ask a drink of me, a woman of Samaria?' For Jews have no dealings with Samaritans. Jesus answered her, 'If you knew the gift of God, and

who it is that is saying to you, "Give me a drink", you would have asked him, and he would have given you living water.' The woman said to him, 'Sir, you have nothing to draw with, and the well is deep; where do you get that living water? Are you greater than our father Jacob, who gave us the well, and drank from it himself, and his sons, and his cattle?' Jesus said to her, 'Everyone who drinks of this water will thirst again, but whoever drinks of the water that I shall give him will never thirst; the water that I shall give him will become in him a spring of water welling up to eternal life.'[66]

The woman, acknowledging Jesus as a prophet, queries whether God is to be worshipped on Mount Gerizim, as the Samaritans do, or in Jerusalem, as the Jews do. Jesus replies:

Woman, believe me, the hour is coming when neither on this mountain nor in Jerusalem will you worship the Father . . . the hour is coming, and now is, when the true worshippers will worship the Father in spirit and truth.[67]

This desanctification of place, seemingly an example of that early Christian tendency so well described by W.D. Davies in his *The Gospel and the Land*,[68] seems to sit oddly in a text that overtly bestows sacredness on a Christian holy land. It is, however, important to recognise that the Bordeaux Pilgrim uses topographical description precisely as a means of transcending the Judaic conception of a physical inheritance and stressing the spiritual, and thus universal, character of the Christian 'homeland'. This shift is evidenced in the juxtapositioning of Joseph's bones, which lie in a tomb 'in the parcel of the ground which his father gave him',[69] and Jesus's promise of 'a spring of water welling up to eternal life' that rests not on land but in the souls of all those who believe. From this point on in the text, the 'worldly kingdom' of the Old Testament is increasingly devalued while the despatialised domain of spiritual salvation is celebrated as the ultimate 'holy land'.

The pilgrim's presentation of Jerusalem interweaves the several themes discussed above to create a tapestry that is densely illustrated with evocations of the collapse of the worldly kingdom of the Jews and its supersession by the spiritual empire of their Christian inheritors. The description of the pools of Bethsaida, which marks the pilgrim's entry into Jerusalem, is drawn from the chapter in John that directly follows the story of Jesus's encounter with the Samaritan woman at the well below Gerizim. As in that story, the narrative of Jesus's Sabbath healing (without the use of water) of the paralytic[70] who had lain uncured next to the wonder-working pools for 38 years, serves simultaneously to abrogate Old Testament law and to demonstrate that the 'living water of Jesus's word is more powerful than the life-giving water of the land'. The remainder of John 5 distinguishes between the Jews, who sought to kill Jesus for breaking the sabbath and proclaiming himself equal with God,[71] and those who will, in believing the word of Jesus, pass 'from death to life'.[72]

The narrative moves from the pools to the Temple Mount itself, where it celebrates the wisdom and power of Solomon, the great kingdom builder of the Israelites, by noting the remains of his palace, his temple and the great underground pools and cisterns he had constructed. At the same time, however, the text, by merging elements of the second and third temptations of Jesus relayed in Matthew 4:5–10, shows Jesus rejecting the promise of earthly power to which Solomon had succumbed.[73] This is followed by the pilgrim's noting of 'a great cornerstone, of which it was said, "the stone which the builders rejected is become the head of the corner"'.[74] Matthew sets that psalmic phrase in a chapter in which Jesus demonstrates by means of a number of parables that the work of God is being taken from those originally assigned it and passed to a new people. In that chapter, mention of the cornerstone is followed by Jesus's statement, to the chief priests and the elders at the Temple, that 'the kingdom of God will be taken away from you and given to a nation producing the fruits of it'.[75] The *Itinerarium* then demonstrates that Solomon's Temple is ineradicably bloodstained 'in front of the altar . . . [by] the blood of Zacharias'.[76] The reference invokes Jesus's condemnation of the scribes and Pharisees for killing those God sends to inform them of his will:

> I send you prophets and wise men and scribes, some of whom you will kill and crucify, and some you will scourge in your synagogues and persecute from town to town, that upon you may come all the righteous blood shed on earth, from the blood of innocent Abel to the blood of Zechariah the son of Barachiah, whom you murdered between the sanctuary and the altar.[77]

This passage, which the Oxford annotators note refers to 'the sweep of time from the first to the last victim of murder mentioned in the Old

Testament',[78] is followed in the New Testament text by Jesus's retraction of the divine dispensation from Israel:

> O Jerusalem, Jerusalem, killing the prophets and stoning those who are sent to you. How often would I have gathered your children together as a hen gathers her brood under her wings, and you would not! Behold, your house is forsaken and desolate.[79]

The *Itinerarium* then demonstrates that desolation by mentioning the statues that the Temple's destroyers built over its ruins and noting the lamentations of the dispersed people over the loss of their kingdom and the ruin of their temple: 'there are two statues of Hadrian, and not far from the statues a pierced stone to which the Jews come every year to anoint and lament over with sighs, tearing their clothes and then going away again'.[80] The contrast that the pilgrim records is not only between the glory of the past and the desolation of the present – a contrast reiterated by the text's mention of Hezekiah, who, in II Kings 20:16–19, is told by Isaiah that the peace and security of his own days will be traded off against the absolute desolation of his house and his nation in the future – but also between the ruins of the Jewish Temple and the glory of the new Christian temple rising on a facing hill. This demonstration, overt but understated in the *Itinerarium Burdigalense*, is made more triumphantly and anti-semitically by St Jerome, later in the century, in *On Zephania*, I, 15–16:

> You can see with your own eyes on the day that Jerusalem was captured and destroyed by the Romans, a piteous crowd that comes together, woebegone women and old men weighed down with rags and years, all of them showing forth in their clothes and their bodies the wrath of God. That mob of wretches congregates, and while the manger of the Lord sparkles, the Church of His Resurrection glows, and the banner of His Cross shines forth from the Mount of Olives, those miserable people groan over the ruins of their Temple.[81]

From the Temple Mount the pilgrim's text moves first to Sion, and then across the city to Golgotha. Along this course it catalogues a number of monuments of the Old Dispensation, including Siloam – a pool of water that observes Judaic law by keeping the Sabbath – the remains of David's palace and the 'ploughed and sown'[82] sites of six of the seven

New Testament figure of Zacchaeus and Jesus's admonition to the chief priests and elders at the Temple in Matthew 21:31, 'the tax collectors and the harlots go into the kingdom of God before you'. Rahab, the harlot, was the only inhabitant of Canaanite Jericho saved from death, because she recognised that the spies who approached her were doing God's will and protected them from her own people. Analogously, Zacchaeus, who had lived a life of sin, was offered salvation by Jesus solely because he recognised Jesus and answered his call.

This emphasis on seeing and believing is further developed in the Book of John which describes Jesus, at the time of the Passover, re-enacting the Exodus incidents of the feeding of the multitudes[99] and the miraculous crossing of the waters.[100] Jesus, seeking to escape the crowds who, having participated in the miracle of loaves and fishes, had taken him for a worldly messiah and 'were about to come and take him by force to make him king',[101] walks across the sea of Galilee and husbands his disciples over. On the following day he tells those who, having heard of the feast, sought him out:

> You seek me, not because you saw signs, but because you ate your fill of the loaves. Do not labour for the food which perishes, but for the food which endures to eternal life . . . you have seen me and yet do not believe.[102]

Jesus continues, later in the same chapter, to develop the distinction between that which sustains life in this world and the spiritual food that gives life unto eternity:

> I am the bread of life. Your fathers ate the manna in the wilderness, and they died. This is the bread which comes down from heaven, that a man may eat of it and not die. I am the living bread which came down from heaven; if any one eats of this bread, he will live for ever.[103]

In overlapping the markers of the Israelites' crossing of the Jordan, so as to effect their triumphal entry into the land, with references alluding to Jesus's passage through the waters towards his fulfilment in Jerusalem, the *Itinerarium Burdigalense* posits the former as a sign or prefiguration of the latter. The Israelites who ate *manna* in the wilderness crossed over into the Promised Land and died, as the proliferation of their tombs in the following section demonstrates. Jesus passed over the waters of both the Galilee and death to be resurrected and to open a pathway for his disciples to follow into an eternal Promised Land. Those who carry out the divinely orchestrated acts while failing to discern their significance perish; those who see the signs through the forms that embody them inherit eternal life.

The movement from death to eternal life is mirrored in the text's movement from the site where Joshua initiated those Israelites born while the tribes wandered in the desert through the Dead Sea into the Mosaic Dispensation, to the site on the Jordan River where Jesus was baptised. The Israelites lived, built a nation and they and that nation died. The end point of that process – marked by the tombs in the desert and a water in which nothing can live and which turns those who enter into it 'upside down' – is countered by a movement developing out of it and transcending it that is demonstrated by Jesus's baptism in the Jordan:

> When Jesus was baptised, he went up immediately from the water, and behold, the heavens were opened and he saw the Spirit of God descending like a dove, and alighting on him; and lo, a voice from heaven, saying, 'This is my beloved Son, with whom I am well pleased'.[104]

This vertical passage between heaven and earth, which subsumes and sublimates the earlier lateral passage between desert and promised land, is followed by the mention of the site 'from whence Elijah was caught up into heaven'.[105] The mention of this site – outside the New Testament 'brackets' quoted above reminds us that Elijah, alone amongst all of the 'dead Jews' mentioned in the *Itinerarium*, was taken up alive into heaven, from where he later joins Moses to discuss with Jesus, immediately after the feeding of the five thousand, 'his departure, which he was to accomplish at Jerusalem'.[106] The site also invokes the mantle that Elijah used there to part the waters, and which Elisha, after his master's ascension, takes up and uses in the same manner to demonstrate that he has 'inherited a double share of [Elijah's] spirit'.[107] Both invocations – of Moses' and Elijah's participation in Jesus's death and resurrection and of the mantle that bequeaths its owner's power to its inheritor – imply a relay in which the work of redemption is passed on, after one labourer has completed his designated part, to another who 'takes up the mantle' of the divine mission. Elijah, who attempts to return Israel to the worship of the divinity who had chosen its people to manifest his will on earth, opens the text to the land on which that will was initially manifested. He effects his departure from the land and the book by passing that mission on to a new prophet, who carries that mission to a new Israel, no longer limited by the Dan and Beersheba, that gathers from all corners of the known world and takes up its inheritance in heaven.

Conclusion

In attempting to revive the text of the Bordeaux Pilgrim, I have undoubtedly read much into it that is not overtly there. That, however, the biblical materials associated with the site references made by the *Itinerarium* cohere to make up a systematic and complex discourse on the typological and historical relationships of the Old and New Testaments, implies that the text itself might originally have functioned in a setting in which such scriptural supplementation would have been part of the way its audience related to its reading.[108] The text's stress on the life-giving qualities of water would suggest that this setting was likely to have been one in which catechumens were being prepared for baptism into the Christian church.

Christianity, before it came to hegemonise religious expression in the Roman Empire, was shaped around its adherents' assertions that they had separated themselves from the profane world and joined with a new community ruled over by Christ rather than by the world's demonic powers. The literal movement of the Jews of the Babylonian exile out of the territory of their displacement and into the Promised Land was reiterated in place by early Christians through rituals that, re-enacting the death and resurrection of Jesus, effected for the participants a death to this world and a resurrection into a new society (that of the sect) located within a new reality (heaven). Since there was a delay in the translocation, insofar as the community of the saved was forced to reside in bodily form amidst the detritus of the fallen world until the Parousia (the second coming of Christ), Christians clearly mapped for themselves the radical divide that separated them from the unredeemed amongst whom they were forced to reside until as late as the sixth century of the Christian era.

Baptism appears to have developed out of the *tebilah*, the standard Jewish purification ritual, which served amongst Jewish congregations to cleanse individuals of impurity so that they could engage in the religious rituals and assert their solidarity with the larger community of Jews.[109] The rise of the Pharisees in the second century BC led to the redefinition of the *tebilah*, as a ritual that marked the borders between a community that perpetually observes the commands of the *Torah* and an 'outside' caught up in the defilement of political compromise and Hellenistic syncretisms.[110] Although ritual immersion here served to purify those who wished to maintain communion with an elect whose ritual purity was essential, purity was alway tenuous and ritual purification had continually to be enacted:

> Among the Pharisees there is implied . . . no permanent transition from the impure world into the pure community. The line between is constantly in flux; purity must be continually reestablished in response to voluntary or involuntary actions of the member of the sect, or to accidents that befall him. Thus the boundary between the sect and the world is wavering and porous, and the Pharisee does not, accordingly, represent his sect as the only 'real' Israel, nor does the immersion in the *mikveh* (immersion pool) become an initiation.[111]

In Christianity, on the other hand, baptism effected a permanent divide between distinct communities, and the rite itself was thus an irreversible initiation:

> The fact that [for early Christians] a water bath serves not just as a preparatory rite, as in most contemporary initiation, but as the central act of the whole ceremony vividly portrays life prior to the event – and outside the sect – as unclean. . . . [T]he whole ritual represents a dying and rising with Christ. It entails dying with respect to the structures and powers of the world (see Colossians 2:20), 'taking off' the 'old human' with his vices and his divisions and entanglements, and putting on a new life in Christ, the 'new human', distinguished by the unity of a new family of brothers and sisters, children of God. Clearly, then, baptism is a boundary establishing ritual.[112]

Christians occupied a different world to those among whom they lived, and, even though they were forced – as were the Jews of the Babylonian exile – to live in that other world in which their expectations and their identities were directed towards the community, they engaged in their rituals and through their meditations focused on the revelations and the Parousia.

This division is evident in the text of the Bordeaux Pilgrim, not only in the way the wasteland of illusion and deception stretching beyond the borders of the project of Christian missionisation is distinguished from the spiritual fertility of a terrain constituted out of the biblical word, but also in the way that, within that textual terrain, the life of the Christian 'new world' is separated from the dead 'old world' of the Jews. As a consequence of this St Ambrose, describing baptism in the late fourth century in his *De Sacramentos*, said:

> What was of greater importance than the crossing of the sea by the Jewish people? Yet the Jews who crossed over are all dead in the desert. But, on the contrary, he who passes through this fountain, that is to say, from earthly things to heavenly – which is indeed the *transitus*, that is to say, the Passover, the passing over from sin to life – he who passes through this fountain will not die, but rise again.[113]

The fact that the rituals of baptism and the text of the *Itinerarium* are both organised around reiteration of the radical divide between the worldly and the other-worldly leads me to posit that the former provides a context for the latter, and that, in this context, the alleged pilgrim's text was used as an *aide-mémoire* during the preparation of catechumens for baptism. The text refers, in the mnemonic form of a journey, to those portions of the Old and New Testaments that describe, literally or allegorically, the coming of the chosen of God into the promised land. In the text, however, the 'promised land' is only synonymous with the territory of biblical Israel for the Jews, and their final inheritance is clearly shown to be no more than a series of tombs in the desert. For the Christians, who are presented by the text as inheriting by relay the sobriquet 'chosen people', the promised land is elsewhere; the *Itinerarium*'s message, reiterated throughout, is that the kingdom of the Christians is a spiritual kingdom to which they owe allegiance even while living expatriate lives in this world. This argument is made explicitly by Jesus in his well-side discourse with the Samaritan woman, and is, I would contend, recognisable in the pilgrim's reduction of the central Constantinian basilica to little more than the setting for a baptismal font that is, in effect, a doorway to Paradise. That font – as is the case with the baptism sites of Cornelius, the Ethiopian eunuch that Jesus referred to in the text – draws together and fulfils the references to life-giving waters proliferating throughout the text.[114]

The series of interwoven references to the opposition of the worldly to the heavenly, and of the real Chosen People to predecessors who inherited a barren desert because they mistook the world for the heavens, appears, once its pattern is discerned, to provide the actual warp and weft of the *Itinerarium*. Discerning that structure and the principles informing it would not have been as difficult for catechumens during the month-and-a-half of rigorous, all-day catechetical instruction they went through during preparations for baptism[115] as it is for contemporary readers, who neither read the text under instruction nor live in a thought world similar to that of the early Christians. Baptism represented the same transit as that mapped by the *Itinerarium*, and the neophytes may well have been familiarised with the terrain of the spiritual voyage that they were about to make by a textual journey that carried them through a sequence of references rather than through a series of sites. It is not accidental that what would later become the Holy Land provided the frame for the terrain that they would travel; the land encompassed within its borders all of the loci around which the biblical narratives unwound themselves. As with a biblical onomasticon, however, the container was insignificant; it was the biblical texts, and their digressions and interconnections, that provided the grounds upon which the narrative found its footing, and through which its audience wandered as spiritual pilgrims.

Notes

1 I am grateful to John Elsner, of the Courtauld Institute, for incisive comments on the draft of this text. An earlier version of this paper, entitled 'Mapping History's Redemption: Eschatology and Topography in the *Itinerarium Burdigalense*' has been published in the proceedings of an eponymous conference held at the Tantur Ecumenical Centre for Theological Studies, Jerusalem, 3–28 June 1996. See I. Irvine (ed.), *Jerusalem: Its Sanctity and Centrality to Judaism, Christianity and Islam* (New York and Jerusalem, Continuum Press and Magnes Press, 1998), pp. 163–87.
2 Robert Markus, 'How on Earth Could Places Become Holy? Origins of the Christian Idea of Holy Places', *Journal of Early Christian Studies*, 2:3 (1994), 268.

3 *Ibid.*, 267.
4 *Ibid.*, 270.
5 *Ibid.*, 271; see also his *The End of Ancient Christianity* (Cambridge University Press, 1990), p. 92, as well as Jonathan Z. Smith, *To Take Place: Toward Theory in Ritual* (Chicago and London, University of Chicago Press, 1987) for a theological inquiry into ritual and place in early Christianity.
6 Egeria, 'Itinerarium', *Corpus Christianorum*, Series Latina 175 (Turnhout, 1965), pp. 27–90. I will use John Wilkinson's translation from Egeria's *Travels* (London, SPCK, 1971), hereafter cited as 'Wilkinson'.
7 Egeria 5.5–8 in Wilkinson, *op. cit.*, 107, pp. 91–147. Spitzer points out that 'the eye of the pilgrim wanders incessantly from the biblical locus (i.e. passage) to the locus (locality) in Palestine'. See Leo Spitzer, 'The Epic Style of the Pilgrim Aetheria', *Comparative Literature*, 1:3 (1949), 239.
8 Egeria 31.2–3 and 25.5 in Wilkinson, *op. cit.*, pp. 133 and 126.
9 Peter Walker, *Holy City, Holy Places? Christian Attitudes to Jerusalem and the Holy Land in the Fourth Century*, Oxford Early Christian Studies (Oxford, Clarendon Press, 1990).
10 Cyril of Jerusalem, 'Catecheses XIII.22' in Leo McCauley (ed.), *The Works of Saint Cyril of Jerusalem* (Washington, D.C., 1968), II, p. 19.
11 See William Moore and Henry Wilson (eds.), 'On Pilgrimage', *Selected Writings and Letters of Gregory, Bishop of Nyssa*, (Oxford, 1892), V, pp. 382–3.
12 Egeria 4.8 in Wilkinson, *op. cit.*, p. 96; my emphasis.
13 Egeria 19.7 in Wilkinson, *op. cit.*, p. 116.
14 Egeria 19.6–19 in Wilkinson, *op. cit.*, pp. 115–17.
15 Antoninus of Piacenza, 'Itinerarium' in P. Geyer and O. Cuntz (eds.), *Corpus Christianorum*, Series Latina 175, trans. John Wilkinson (Turnhout, 1965), pp. 79–89 (hereafter '*Corpus Christianorum*'). *Jerusalem Pilgrims before the Crusades* (Warminster, Aris and Phillips, 1977), pp. 79 and 81.
16 The term 'haptic' is drawn from Annabel Wharton's stimulating study of transformations of space and sensoria with the 'victory' of Christianity in *Refiguring the Post-Classical City: Dura Europos, Jerash, Jerusalem and Ravenna* (Cambridge University Press, 1995).
17 Gregory Dix's theories of the transformations effected in Christian liturgy by the corresponding move from private to public worship suggest, interestingly, that as monuments and ceremonials proliferated so the access of the lay public to scripture grew increasingly more attenuated. See his *The Shape of the Liturgy* (Westminster, Dacre Press, 1945), pp. 303–96.
18 I will provide my own translation drawn from the text in *Corpus Christianorum*, pp. 1–26 and will follow its editors (and Wilkinson) in citing P. Wesseling's pagination from his *Verera Romanorum Itinera* (Amsterdam, 1735). A complete English translation is available in Volume I of the Library of the Palestine Pilgrims' Text Society, *Itinerary from Bordeaux to Jerusalem: The Bordeaux Pilgrim AD 333*, trans. Aubrey Stewart (London, Palestine Exploration Fund, 1896), I, pp. 1–35. Wilkinson includes a substantial and well-annotated selection in his *Egeria's Travels*, pp. 153–63. The itinerary is dated by the pilgrim's reference by name to the consuls who were in power as he passed through Constantinople and by his references to the days of the months during which he passed through that city (Wesseling, *op. cit.*, p. 571).

19 Robert Wilken, *The Land Called Holy: Palestine in Christian History and Thought* (New Haven, Yale University Press, 1992), pp. 109 and 110.
20 E. D. Hunt, *Holy Land Pilgrimage in the Later Roman Empire AD 312–460* (Oxford, Clarendon Press, 1982), p. 86.
21 Mary Campbell, *The Witness and the Other World: Exotic European Travel Writing, 400–1600* (Ithaca, Cornell University Press, 1988), p. 27.
22 Eusebius, 'The Life of Constantine' in Ernest Cushing Richardson (ed.), *Eusebius: Church History, Life of Constantine the Great, Oration in Praise of Constantine* (Oxford, 1890).
23 Egeria 4.1, Wilkinson, *op. cit.*, p. 95.
24 Egeria 7.2–3, Wilkinson, *op. cit.*, p. 101.
25 Egeria 12.6–7, Wilkinson, *op. cit.*, p. 107. Wilkinson renders the text as though the pilgrim addresses the reader directly in the second person ('you'), while the Aubrey Stewart translation retains the coolness of the original Latin in its occasional use of the pronoun 'one'. See also John Elsner, 'Pausanius: A Greek Pilgrim in the Roman World', *Past and Present*, 135 (1992), 3–29.
26 Egeria 23.10, Wilkinson, *op. cit.*, p. 122.
27 Wesseling, *op. cit.*, 591.3–5.
28 Wesseling, *op. cit.*, 588.9–589.3, in Geyer and Cuntz, *op. cit.*, p. 95. An interesting analogy to the Bordeaux Pilgrim's use of the site of the village of Bethel as a means of entering the narrative space of the Bible is the way in which Greek Orthodox pilgrims ignore the specificities of events commemorated at holy places and use the places as 'doors' providing access to a generalised communion with the saints in the 'paradise' manifest to believers in the icon-dense interiors of all Orthodox churches. See Glenn Bowmann, 'Contemporary Christian Pilgrim to the Holy Land' in Anthony O'Mahony (ed.), *The Christian Heritage in the Holy Land* (London, Scorpion Cavendish, 1995), pp. 298–9.
29 'A mile from here is the place called Sechar, from which the Samaritan woman went down to the same place where Jacob had dug a well, to fill her jug with water from it, and our Lord Jesus Christ spoke with her, and where there are plane trees, which Jacob planted, and baths which get their water from this well'. (Wesseling, *op. cit.*, 588.2–6).
30 Wesseling, *op. cit.*, 594.2–4.
31 Wilken, *op. cit.*, p. 110.
32 The pilgrim, for instance, makes no mention of Nazareth or the Sea of Galilee, despite apparently passing within a day's journey of these salient sites in the life of Christ. See C. W. Wilson, 'Introduction' in Aubrey Stewart (trans.), *op. cit.*, pp. viii–ix.
33 Wesseling, *op. cit.*, 581.11–582.8.
34 *Ibid.*, 582.11.
35 *Ibid.*, 564.9.
36 *Ibid.*, 572.4–5.
37 *Ibid.*, 577.6.
38 *Ibid.*, 578.1.
39 *Ibid.*
40 *Ibid.*, 604.1.
41 *Ibid.*, 604.7.
42 *Ibid.*, 606.1.

43 Tarsus and Phillipi are, of course, biblical sites insofar as they are mentioned in Acts and Phillipians with reference to the events the pilgrim cites. As I will demonstrate below, they can, according to the logic of the text, be mapped as being within the 'Holy Land'.
44 Wesseling, *op. cit.*, 583.12; see also I Kings 17:10–16 and Luke 4:25–6.
45 Wesseling, *op. cit.*, 585.1; see I Kings 18:19–21.
46 Wesseling, *op. cit.*, 585.7–8; see Acts 10:19–48.
47 Wesseling, *op. cit.*, 586.4–6.
48 Wilkinson, *op. cit.*, p. 154, n. 5.
49 Wesseling, *op. cit.*, 587.3–588.3.
50 Wilken, *op. cit.*, p. 110.
51 Jean Danielou, *A History of Early Christian Doctrine before the Council of Nicea* (London, Darton, Longman & Todd, 1964), I, p. 406.
52 *Ibid.*
53 Wesseling, *op. cit.*, 586.4–6.
54 Herbert May and Bruce Metzger (eds.), *The New Oxford Annotated Bible, Revised Standard Version* (New York, Oxford University Press, 1973), p. 442 (note on I Kings 17:1).
55 Wesseling, *op. cit.*, 585.7–586.2.
56 *Ibid.*, 588.3–6.
57 Wesseling, *op. cit.*, 596.7–10. See II Kings 2:19–22, of which this is a close rendering. The fact that Elisha makes the water sweet and wholesome by salting it parallels Elijah's counter-inductive preparation of the sacrificial bull for immolation by pouring over it twelve jars of water (I Kings 18:33–5). In each case what is treated is not simply water, but water which, brought into association with divinity, operates supra-naturally.
58 The Oxford annotations refer to Cornelius as the first Gentile convert. See May and Metzger, pp. 1332–3, note on Acts 10:1–48), but Acts 8:26–39 describes Philip's baptism of the Ethiopian eunuch whom W. H. C. Frend calls 'the first non-Jewish convert recorded'. See his *The Rise of Christianity* (Philadelphia, Fortress Press, 1984), p. 89. That the *Itinerarium Burdigalense* treats both conversions indicates that it is concerned to mark the breaking out of the salvatory work from the confines of the Jewish people.
59 Acts 10:10–16.
60 Acts 10:44–48.
61 Acts 11:18.
62 Wesseling, *op. cit.*, 599.1–2; see Acts 8:26–40.
63 Apollonius of Tyana was an itinerant neo-Pythagorean teacher born early in the Christian era who was alleged to have had magical powers and to have travelled widely, even visiting India. Flavius Philostratus (*c.* CE 170) wrote a *Life of Apollonius of Tyana* in which the philosopher was attributed with a miraculous birth and the ability to work miracles. More significant, however, was the virulent anti-Christian polemic Sossius Hierocles presented as a biography in CE 302. In it, Hierocles contended that Apollonius was an excellent philosopher and exorcist and was in all ways far superior to Christ (see Frend, *op. cit.*, pp. 497–8). John Elsner has examined the role of Apollonius of Tyana in pagan hagiography in 'Hagiographic Geography: travel and allegory in the *Life of Apollonius of Tyana*', *Journal of Hellenic Studies*, 117 (1997).

64 Wesseling, *op. cit.*, 587.5–588.6.
65 Genesis 33:18–20 and Joshua 24:32. Interestingly, in the following section on Bethel, the pilgrim claims that Jacob wrestled with the angel at Bethel, whereas Genesis 32:24–30 sites this struggle at Peniel. Wilkinson in *Egeria's Travels* (p. 155, n. 6), sees this confusion arising from the fact that Peniel may have been commemorated at Bethel in the fourth century, but it is also salient that at both sites Jacob was recognised as 'Israel' (Genesis 32:28 and 35:10).
66 John 4:9–14.
67 John 4:21 and 23.
68 W.D. Davies, *The Gospel and the Land: Early Christianity and Jewish Territorial Doctrine* (Berkeley, University of California Press, 1974).
69 Wesseling, *op. cit.*, 588.1; see Joshua 24:32.
70 John 5:2–15.
71 John 5:16–18.
72 John 5:24.
73 The second temptation – in which the devil calls upon Jesus to throw himself from the pinnacle of the Temple so that the angels will prove his divinity by bearing him up – takes place where the *Itinerarium Burdigalense* sites the story, but the pilgrim appends to Christ's refusal a phrase – 'and him only shall you serve' (Matthew 4:10) – associates the pilgrim's rendering of Jesus's temptation with Satan's offer, from the peak of a very high mountain, to give Jesus dominion over all the kingdoms of the world.
74 Wesseling, *op. cit.*, 590.3–4: see Psalms 118:22–23 and Matthew 22:42.
75 Matthew 22:43.
76 Wesseling, *op. cit.*, 591.1–4.
77 Matthew 24:34–35; see also Luke 11:49–52.
78 May and Meeger, *op. cit.*, p. 1203. n. 35.
79 Matthew 23:37–38.
80 Wesseling, *op. cit.*, 591.4–6.
81 Quoted by F.E. Peters in *Jerusalem: The Holy City in the Eyes of Chroniclers, Visitors, Pilgrims and Prophets from the Days of Abraham to the Beginnings of Modern Times* (Princeton University Press, 1985), p. 144.
82 Isaiah 1:8.
83 Wesseling, *op. cit.*, 594.1–2.
84 *Ibid.*, 594.4. On the Constantinian baptistry, see Shimon Gibson and Joan Taylor, *Beneath the Church of the Holy Sepulchre Jerusalem: The Archaeology and Early History of Traditional Golgotha* (London, Palestine Exploration Fund, 1994), pp. 77–8.
85 Wesseling, *op. cit.*, 595.2–4.
86 *Ibid.*, 599.3–5; see Genesis 18:1–19.
87 Genesis 18:18–19.
88 Wesseling, *op. cit.*, 599.5–6.
89 *Ibid.*, 599.7–9.
90 *Ibid.*, 596.4–598.3.
91 *Ibid.*, 597.1; Joshua 2:1–21.
92 *Ibid.*, 597.2–3; Joshua 6.
93 *Ibid.*, 597.4–5; Joshua 4.
94 *Ibid.*, 597.5–6; Joshua 5:2–9.

95 *Ibid.*, 598.3; see II Kings 2.
96 *Ibid.*, 596.5–6; see Luke 19:1–10.
97 *Ibid.*, 598.1–2; see Matthew 3:13–17.
98 *Ibid.*, 597.7–10.
99 See John 6:5–13, and Exodus 16:2–19.
100 John 6:16–21.
101 John 6:15.
102 John 6:26–27 and 36.
103 John 6:49 and 51.
104 Matthew 3:16–17.
105 Wesseling, *op. cit.*, 598.3, and see II Kings 2: 4–15.
106 Luke 9:30–31.
107 II Kings 2:9.
108 E.C. Ratcliffe notes in 'The Old Syrian Baptismal Tradition and its Resettlement under the Influence of Jerusalem in the Fourth Century' in G. J. Cuming (ed.), *Studies in Church History: Papers Read at the Second Winter and Summer Meetings of the Ecclesiastical History Society*, 2nd edn (London, Thomas Nelson and Sons Ltd, 1965), p. 26, a reference to pre-baptismal anointing in the *Didascalia Apostolorum*, a mid-third-century manual of pastoral guidance, that 'the Didascaliast . . . expect[s] his readers to recall those passages of the Old Testament in which the spiritual effect of the anointing is described.' Although this does not explicitly confirm a general biblical literacy amongst early Christian catechumens, it does suggest that initiands in training for baptism would have had at hand a panoply of biblical materials pertinent to the process.
109 See Leviticus 14–15, and Numbers 19.
110 See Jacob Neusner, *A History of the Mishnaic Law of Purities* (Leiden, Brill, 1977) and *The Idea of Purity in Ancient Judaism* (Leiden, Brill, 1973).
111 Wayne Meeks, *The First Urban Christians: The Social World of the Apostle Paul* (New Haven, Yale University Press, 1983), p. 153.
112 *Ibid.*, p. 102. E.C. Whitaker argues convincingly that in Syrian Christianity until the end of the fourth century there was no confirmation and that the pre-baptismal anointing with oil noted in descriptions of baptism such as that of the *Didache* 'was an exorcism', serving only to formalise the completion of a process of separation from worldly powers that had already reached its end. See E.C. Whitaker, *The Baptismal Liturgy* (London, SPCK, 1981), p. xx. Post-baptismal confirmation accompanied by an anointing with oil was an innovation of the Western provinces of the Roman Empire and of centres of imperial innovation such as Jerusalem, and it would only later (and partially) be integrated into Syrian practices as 'an adventitious and optional addition' (*ibid.*, p. xxi). For the Syrian church 'the water is sufficient both for the anointing, and for the seal, and for the confession of him that is dead, or indeed is dying together with [Christ]' (the *Apostolic Constitutions*, c.375, quoted in *ibid.*, p. 32) and the new members of the community proceeded directly from baptism to taking the Eucharist.
113 St Ambrose, *De Sacramentos* I.12, quoted in Jean Danielou, *The Bible and the Liturgy* (Notre Dame, Indiana, University of Notre Dame Press, 1956), p. 92.
114 Tertullian, prior to his conversion to Montanism *c.* AD 195, carried out an extended examination of the sacred and profane uses of water in his *De Baptismo*

(Chapters 3–5). Here he rhetorically queries, 'What of the fact that waters were in some way the regulating powers by which the disposition of the world thenceforward was constituted by God? For the suspension of the celestial firmament in the midst He caused by "dividing the waters"; the suspension of "the dry land"? He accomplished by "separating the waters". After the world had been hereupon set in order through its elements, when inhabitants were given it, "the waters" were the first to receive the precept "to bring forth living creatures". Water was the first to produce that which had life, that it might be no wonder in baptism if waters know how to give life . . . It makes no difference whether a man be washed in a sea or a pool, a stream or a fount, a lake or a trough; nor is there any distinction between those whom John baptized in the Jordan and those whom Peter baptized in the Tiber, unless withal the eunuch whom Philip baptized in the midst of his journeys with chance water, derived (therefrom) more or less of salvation than others. All waters, therefore, in virtue of the pristine privilege of their origin, do, after invocation of God, attain the sacramental power of sanctification; for the Spirit immediately supervenes from the heavens, and rests over the waters, sanctifying them from Himself; and being thus sanctified, they imbibe at the same time the power of sanctifying' in Tertullian, *De Baptismo*, Chapter 4, quoted in Ernest Evans (ed.), *Tertullian's Homily on Baptism* (London, SPCK, 1964).

115 'Through Lent, candidates were disciplined with daily exorcisms and fasting. Concurrently they were catechized, that is, schooled in the behaviours and thoughts appropriate to Christians. The arduous mental and physical disciplining of the initiates was not usually an individual or private affair . . . Social patterns were disrupted – old habits were displaced by the new regimen, old acquaintances supplanted by new ones. Social intercourse was removed from the conventional sites of civic life – the bath, the forum, the theater – and recentered on the church', Annabel Wharton, *Refiguring the Post-Classical City: Dura Europos, Jerash, Jerusalem and Ravenna* (Cambridge University Press, 1995), p. 80. Wharton assumes that – at least by the fourth century – the period of pre-baptismal instruction was contemporaneous with Lent. However, in Hippolytus's *Apostolic Tradition* (c. CE 215), the author writes 'let a catechumen be instructed for three years'. See Hippolytus, *Apostolic Tradition* XVII.1, quoted in Whitaker, *op. cit.*, p. 3. Philip's instruction of the Ethiopian eunuch, which can be seen as a prototypical catechesis, appears nonetheless to have taken place in the course of a single afternoon's conversation (Acts 8:30–35).

2

The Grand Tour in the Ottoman Empire, 1699–1826

Philip Mansel

The Grand Tour is usually defined as a period of two to three years' travel for young men, with a semi-educational purpose, which is held to have reached its peak in the eighteenth century in Italy. It is often forgotten, however, that the Ottoman Empire was so accessible at the time that many travellers went on from Italy to Constantinople and further east. Grand Tourists were drawn to the Ottoman Empire for three reasons: power, pleasure and scholarship. The power and territorial extent of the Empire were the factors that made pleasure and scholarship possible. The Ottoman Empire was a great military and economic power, whose territory included modern Greece, Albania, Serbia, Bulgaria, Turkey, Syria, Iraq, Lebanon, Jordan and Egypt. The Grand Tour could extend to the Ottoman Empire because the political links between it and European states made travelling easy. Alliances with Christian powers had always been an aspect of Ottoman policy, since the first Ottoman troops had crossed into Europe in 1350. With the exception of Spain, the Knights of St John on Malta and the Papacy (which maintained the hostility of the crusader era towards the greatest Muslim power), most European states established embassies in Constantinople in the sixteenth century. The city became one of the diplomatic and commercial capitals of Europe.

After the early sixteenth century, France and the Ottoman Empire became allies, united as they were by a shared fear of the Hapsburgs who ruled in Spain, Naples and Austria. The 'union of the lily and the crescent', as one French noble called it, became one of the few fixed points in European politics. By the early seventeenth century, French 'Levant trade' (i.e. trade with the Ottoman Empire), consisting principally of cloth exports, was believed to comprise half of all French maritime commerce.

Trade also led to the establishment in 1579 of diplomatic relations between England and the Ottoman Empire. The first English ambassador, Harborne, was also a merchant who imported lead, tin and cloth to Constantinople and exported Malmsey wine and currants. Until the 1820s, the Levant Company, which he helped found, rather than the government, paid the ambassador's salary.[1] Later there was an important English merchant colony in Aleppo, two of whose merchants rediscovered the great Syro-Roman city of Palmyra in the Syrian desert in 1691. So the Ottoman Empire was both diplomatically and commercially part of Europe. It was in keeping with its interests and traditions to let merchants and travellers pass unhindered. Indeed, they were often provided, at their own expense, with official escorts by provincial governors.

Travellers had frequently written accounts of their journeys in the Ottoman Empire: John Sanderson, in 1584–1602; Henri de Beauvau, in 1604;[2] Thevenot, in 1655; Chardin, in 1665 and his fellow-jeweller and colleague, Grelot, in 1680. Philippe du Fresne-Canaye, in 1573, and M. Du Loir, in 1639, wrote accounts of their journeys from France to Constantinople in the company of a new French ambassador.[3]

More travellers began to arrive in the eighteenth century, as European relations with the Ottoman Empire grew closer, and more and more Grand Tourists arrived in Italy. In 1699, the Empire ceded most of Hungary to the Habsburgs, by the treaty of Karlowitz, and ceased to be an expansionist power. With the exception of wars in 1718–19, 1737–9, 1768–84 and 1787–92, the Ottoman Empire was mainly at peace thereafter. Most statesmen considered its preservation an European necessity, as a barrier against Russian expansion and influence. France assisted the Ottoman war effort against Russia and Austria in 1737–9 and as a result of the Ottoman Empire recovered Belgrade. Even Spain finally sent an embassy to Constantinople in 1784. In 1829, when Britain and France, not for the last time, were about to send fleets to protect the Ottoman Empire from the Russian army, the Duke of Wellington stated, 'The Ottoman Empire exists not for the benefit of the Turks but for the benefit of Christian Europe.'

Protected by the convergence of political, commercial and strategic interests of the Ottoman Empire and other European states, and by the order prevalent in most Ottoman provinces, travellers were able to visit Constantinople and the Ottoman Empire more easily than, for example,

Morocco, Russia or some districts south of Naples. Although many Italian artists worked in Constantinople (for example, L. Manzoni, G.M. Terreni and F. Tonioli), fewer Italians or even Venetians travelled through the Empire than in the sixteenth century.[4] For reasons that are unclear, Germans, Poles, Hungarians and Russians generally stayed away. Most travellers were British or French.

The power of the Empire, and the desire to observe the court and its splendour, were reasons for travel to Constantinople, as the latter was to visit other capital cities such as Vienna. Travellers might enjoy the privilege of accompanying an arriving or departing ambassador, even if not of the same nationality, on his ceremonial visit to the Ottoman Sultan in the imperial palace itself. For example, the imperial ambassador in 1699, Wolfgang IV Graf zu Oettingen-Wallerstein, was accompanied by eight princes and nobles, including Adolph August Duke of Holstein-Ploen, Graf von Kollonitz and Graf von Kueffstein.[5]

Even if there were no entertainments in the Ottoman palace that were open to westerners, the embassies in Constantinople, each of which had a staff of 50 or more, served as miniature courts and centres of news, protection and entertainment. According to William Hunter, author of *Travels through France, Turkey and Hungary to Vienna in 1792*, ambassadors visited each other in the evening in semi-royal state, escorted by guards, running footmen bearing *flambeaux* 'and a numerous train of attendants and servants . . . they are particularly scrupulous in observing the forms which have been established to distinguish their different degrees of rank and precedency, and according to the number of times a bell tolls it announces an ambassador, an envoy or a *chargé d'affaires*.'[6]

The future French Foreign Minister, Vergennes, served as French ambassador in Constantinople from 1756 to 1768, being greeted by the Sultan, at his audience on arrival, as representative of 'the oldest and the most faithful ally of the Ottoman Empire'. He boasted to his Foreign Minister, since hospitality was clearly an important part of his official duties:

> My style of life is superior to that of any ambassador . . . never has the Palace been better decorated than it is. My servants are clean and numerous; I have fifty people in my household. As for my table, it is served every day and *delicately* for fourteen heads and *every gentleman* is well received there.

Thirty years later, in 1788, an English traveller called Thomas Watkins, who arrived in Constantinople after a tour through France, Hungary and Italy, recorded that he was served twenty different wines after dinner with the British ambassador, Sir Robert Ainslie, 'the most rich and rare of Europe, the Greek islands, Jerusalem and the coast of Asia Minor'.

Watkins was pleased to visit the remains of ancient Greece at Athens and Troy, but became lyrical at the sight of Ottoman Constantinople, 'for I am persuaded that the whole earth has not in point of prospect any thing so grand, so various and so beautiful'.[7] Like all travellers, he was impressed by the Sultan's public procession to mosque on Friday:

> . . . the most magnificent and interesting [procession] I ever beheld. The rich and various costumes, the beauty and furniture of the Arabian horses, the comely appearance of the janizaries and bostangis or corps of royal gardeners (whose singularly formed caps of scarlet cloth are particularly remarkable), in a word the splendour, the novelty, the silence and solemnity of this spectacle cannot I think but make a most powerful impression upon every foreign spectator.[8]

As well as being the capital of a powerful empire, eighteenth-century Constantinople was becoming a city of pleasure – a role suggested by the words it gave the outside world: sofa, kiosk, coffee and kaftan. Dr Fonseca, a doctor of Portuguese Jewish origin who was frequently consulted on Ottoman policy by foreign ambassadors, wrote in 1724: 'Today all flourishes and lives for pleasure.'[9]

'The scales of the Levant' – the ports of Smyrna, Tripoli, Beirut, Saida and the great merchant city of Aleppo – had a reputation for being 'the worst school in the world for young men', beset by plagues and *un vin trop violent*.[10] Constantinople, however, had a healthier climate and a more open society. One of the supreme portraitists of the eighteenth century, Jean Étienne Liotard, recorded the daily life and pleasures of the city. He had been brought to Constantinople from Rome in 1737 by two young Englishmen on the Grand Tour, William Ponsonby, future Earl of Bessborough, and John Montagu, future Earl of Sandwich and First Lord of the Admiralty. Liotard's job, according to Montagu, was 'to draw the dresses of every country they should go into, to take prospects of all the remarkable places which had made a figure in history, and to preserve in their memories by the help of painting, those noble remains of antiquity which they went in quest of.' Montagu showed little of the condescension of some nineteenth-century travellers towards Muslims. Indeed he admired Muslims as models of conservatism,

> Their piety towards the creator, the exact observance of the laws of their religion, the obedience to the commands of the sovereign, the respect to their superiors, their charity towards all distressed persons, their sobriety, their moderation, their unexampled integrity in trade, and the gravity and solidity which they express in all their actions are virtues which are seldom wanting even to those of the meanest rank.[11]

Whereas his patrons continued on to Egypt, Liotard remained in Constantinople, drawing not places or remains but people – in addition to Montagu and Ponsonby themselves, in Ottoman dress, as was the custom, to commemorate the success of an Ottoman Grand Tour. Another drawing, *Helene Glavani and the English merchant, Mr Levett*, c.1740, now in the Louvre, shows the fascination of Ottoman costume and material objects for Western travellers. Liotard has represented his sitters wearing Ottoman dress and surrounded by symbols of Ottoman wealth and pleasures: a lute, a guitar, a jasmine-wood pipe and, on a writing box inlaid with tortoiseshell and mother-of-pearl, a perfume-sprinkler and an incense-burner. Other drawings show ladies playing backgammon, embroidering or drinking coffee. What makes these pictures so characteristic of the Ottoman Grand Tour is that they are not Orientalist romanticisations but realistic records.

In the eighteenth century, the Ottoman Empire influenced the West and vice versa. When he returned to the West, Liotard, who continued to wear Ottoman dress, was known as '*le Turc*'. The prints and drawings of Vanmour and Liotard helped inspire a fashion for Turkish dress in Western capitals, as can be seen in portraits by Longhi, Guardi, Vanloo and Angelica Kauffmann, and at such famous fêtes as the masquerade given by the King of Denmark in London in 1768 and the coming of age party of William Beckford, at Fonthill in 1781.[12] Similarly, because of the Constantinople embassies and the Ottoman Grand Tour, Ottoman architecture was more frequently a source of inspiration than the much closer Arab monuments of Granada. Ottoman-style 'mosques', tents and kiosks and 'Turkish rooms' were erected in the eighteenth century at, among other places, Schwetzingen Palace and the Marmorpalais at Potsdam, in Germany; Veltrusov and Tsarskoe Seloe in Russia; Haga in Sweden; and Lunéville and Armainvilliers in France. After the Café

Turc, opened on the Boulevard du Temple in 1780, decorated with views of Constantinople, a minaret and an Ottoman garden, it became one of the most fashionable cafés in Paris.[13]

Another pleasure-bent Grand Tourist, who later visited Egypt protected by an Ottoman *firman*, was Lord Charlement, a future leader of the Enlightenment in Ireland. Having visited the Hague, Turin, Rome, Naples, Athens and the Greek islands, he moved on to Constantinople in 1749, at the age of 21, accompanied, like most ambassadors and travellers to the Ottoman Empire, by an artist. This was Richard Dalton, who was to publish a book of prints of their journey, *Antiquities and Views in Greece and Egypt in 1751–2*, which was republished in an enlarged edition in 1791.[14]

Lord Charlemont admitted that, 'in Constantinople the first and most pressing object of my curiosity was to visit and examine the Porte, that source of Ottoman grandeur and dominion'. However, he was more interested in pleasure than in power. He reported:

> The mode of living at Constantinople is to a young man as pleasant as in any great city whatsoever. That quarter of the town which is called Pera and which itself forms a large city is entirely peopled with Franks [that is, Catholics or Protestants] and Greeks who live together in the most sociable manner and, with the public Ministers [ambassadors] form a society as pleasing as possible. The pleasures of the table are well understood and frequent and scarce an evening passes without balls, concerts or assemblies at all of which the intercourse between the sexes is as easy as can be wished.[15]

In contrast to the restraints imposed on Muslim women, Christian women could be hired by the month, through an arrangement known as '*mariage à cabine*', from a Turkish word for a form of temporary marriage called '*kabin*'. One eighteenth-century British ambassador was said to have spent 12 years in Constantinople 'upon a sofa with the women'.[16] According to Lord Charlemont, 'the women are exceedingly handsome and well-dressed and their manners are remarkably pleasing, a probable indication that they are no foes of love'. Since 'it is the duty of the traveller to leave nothing unseen', he visited brothels whose inmates were either Christian or Jews, 'many of whom are extremely beautiful and well-skilled in all the necessary arts and allurements of their calling'. At the end of the eighteenth century, the best brothel was beside the British embassy. Independent operators met clients in graveyards – where unaccompanied women could claim to be visiting the graves of their dead relations.[17]

Casanova himself visited Constantinople for three months in 1745, when on leave from a Venetian regiment in Corfu, in the entourage of the new Venetian representative, the Cavaliere Venier. He was 'surprised' in a kiosk, as he watched ladies bathing, by a Turk called Ismail.[18] A later traveller from Dublin, called Buck Whaley, who, after touring Europe in 1789, proceeded to Constantinople, Anatolia and Palestine, was horrified by another form of pleasure available in Constantinople – dancing boys – as was Byron's friend, J.C. Hobhouse, twenty years later. He referred to 'a spectacle so degrading to human nature . . . which no Englishman would patiently contemplate for a moment' – although he had just done so.[19]

Other sights visited by travellers to Constantinople included Aya Sofya and other mosques, thanks to 'golden rhetoric' – in other words, bribes. They enjoyed the Bosphorus (whose boatmen were considered by experienced travellers to be more skilled than gondoliers); the slave market; the bazaars; the baths; and whirling dervishes – although some were revolted by the smell of burnt flesh when dervishes held hot irons between their teeth to prove their piety.[20]

After power and pleasure, scholarship was the third reason for travel to the Ottoman Empire. Since it ruled over Greece, Asia Minor and Syria, the Ottoman Empire contained as many classical remains as Italy. Thanks to Ottoman order and diplomacy, the foreign scholar asking questions, or the artist drawing views, became familiar figures in the Levant. Beginning with Guillaume Postel in 1535,[21] many scholars had travelled to Constantinople or beyond, to collect medals, manuscripts (Oriental and classical) and antiquities for the king of France. Antoine Galland, thanks to whom the *Thousand and One Nights* was published in French in 1708, 70 years before the first French edition of Shakespeare, lived and worked in Constantinople at the French embassy in 1670–3. F. Spon came to collect manuscripts and antiquities for Louis XIV in 1674.[22] The Abbés Sevin and Fourmont were sent by the French government in 1728–9, in the hope of finding the lost books of Livy in the Topkapi Palace library.[23]

The British passion for classical antiquity reached its height in the eighteenth century. After a lengthy tour through France and Italy, in

1737–40, between the ages of 33 and 36, the scholar and theologian Richard Pococke visited Egypt, the Holy Land, Syria, Cyprus and Constantinople, where, like many visitors, he was painted in local costume by Liotard. Six years before the great Greek temples at Paestum, south of Naples, had been 'rediscovered', and possibly indulging in a private joke, he apologised for describing in his book, *A Description of the East and Some Other Countries*, 'the famous temple of Baalbek which has been so often mentioned by travellers'. He found the Ottoman authorities not only welcoming but polite – although suspicious of people who claimed to be travelling 'only for amusement'. Across barriers of language and religion, rank spoke to rank. Armed with a letter for the local pasha from the British consul at Tripoli, Pococke wrote:

> I delivered him my letter which he read with a pleasant countenance being a very good man, particularly civil to the Franks, having lately been a pasha in Bosnia. When I asked him leave to see the antiquities, he told me I might go where I pleased and called for a Janissary to attend me . . . both at my coming and going he saluted me with hosgeldi as much as to say I was welcome.[24]

In the absence of published Ottoman despatches, memoirs or letters, there is little first-hand evidence about Ottoman attitudes to travellers. According to Western accounts, however, most Ottoman authorities enjoyed entertaining foreign travellers and merchants.[25] When Lord Charlemont learnt how to hold a perfume-burner under his kaftan, 'the Reis Effendi laughed heartily and with great good humour told me that he was pleased to see me begin to accommodate myself to their customs, to which he hoped I should not long be a stranger'. According to Alexander Russell, author of *The Natural History of Aleppo and Parts Adjacent* (1756), who had travelled extensively in the Ottoman Empire and lived in Aleppo, 'the gentlemen of the British Factory at Aleppo' were treated by the pashas and, therefore, by the people, with 'civility and respect', 'so that we live among them in great security in the city and can travel abroad unmolested by Arabs and Curds where the natives dare not venture'.[26]

In the nineteenth century, partly in reaction to the rise of European imperialism, Damascus became a byword for religious fanaticism and a scene of massacres. In the eighteenth century, Pococke wrote:

> The Damascenes are much addicted to pleasure and love to pass their time in a lazy and indolent manner ... it is said that their women are the most beautiful in the world ... I spent my time very *agreeably* in Damascus passing my leisure hours in the coffee houses, and commonly taking my repasts in them ... I happened to see Constantinople at a time when the Turk was in good humour, and had no reason to be displeased with the Franks ... they had just made a very honourable peace for themselves with the Emperor [in 1739] and not a very disadvantageous one with the Muscovites whom they dreaded as a power superior to them; so that I went freely all over Constantinople and was so far from being affronted in the least that I rather met with civility in every place; entered publicly into such of the mosques as I desired to see and sometimes even on Fridays just before the service began and when the women were coming into the mosques to hear the harangers ... [needing to pay 'only a very small gratuity']. And indeed to speak justly of the Turks they are a very tractable people when they are well used and when they have no prospect of getting anything by ill treatment.[27]

After his return to London, in 1741, Pococke became a founder member of the Egyptian Society, which was devoted to discussion of history and antiquity over dinner and open to 'any gentleman who has been in Egypt' and to others. Early members included the Dukes of Richmond and Montagu; Frederic Louïs Norden;[28] Charles Perry; and, as *Sheik Pyramidum*, the Earl of Sandwich.[29] It appears to have been replaced in 1743 by the Divan Club, open to gentlemen who stated 'that they had the intention to go to Turkey', whose leading lights were also Sandwich (called 'El-Fakir Sandwich Pasha') and Pococke.[30]

Later British scholar-travellers included the architect James Stuart, who sailed in January 1751, after ten years' residence in Rome, from Venice to the Ottoman city of Athens, at the age of 32. He was sponsored by, among others, the British resident in Venice, Sir John Gray, the consul Joseph Smith and the Society of Dilettanti in London, founded in 1733 by 'some gentlemen who had travelled in Italy, desirous of encouraging at home a taste for those objects which had contributed so much for their entertainment abroad'. Members included Lords Bessborough and Charlemont, two veterans of Ottoman travel. Stuart went because, as he wrote in his celebrated work *The Antiquities of Athens*, which played a decisive role in the advancement of the knowledge of classical architecture 'Greece is the place where the most beautiful

Edifices were erected and where the purest and most elegant Examples of ancient Architecture are to be discovered.'[31] Stuart and Revett's observations in Athens provided direct inspiration for their work at, among other locations, West Wycombe, Shugborough and Spencer House. During the two years he stayed there, between 1751 and 1753, the Athenians enjoyed sufficient independence to drive out three Ottoman governors. Whereas travellers appreciated Ottoman pashas, they could detect few good qualities in the Greeks. Stuart was frightened by what he called 'the brutality and avarice of the natives'; Greeks were 'the worst of people' according to Thomas Watkins; 'utterly contemptible, bigoted, narrow minded, lying and treacherous', in the words of the architect C.R. Cockerell, in 1812.[32]

In Athens, Stuart met two other travellers on the Ottoman Grand Tour, Robert Wood and James Dawkins. The ease of travel in the Ottoman Empire is shown by the fact that, seven years before Robert Adam visited the more accessible Roman city of Split, on the Dalmatian coast, Wood and Dawkins, with John Bouverie, who died on the journey, had visited the great Roman sites at Baalbek and Palmyra (their visit was commemorated in Gavin Hamilton's painting *Wood and Dawkins entering Palmyra*, now in the National Gallery of Scotland). Like Pococke's and Norden's itineraries, Wood's and Dawkins's account confirms that the Ottoman Grand Tour was seen as a natural progression from the Italian one. They described themselves as 'Two gentlemen whose curiosity had carried them more than once to the continent particularly to Italy [who] thought that a voyage properly conducted to the most remarkable places of antiquity on the coast of the Mediterranean might produce amusement and improvement to themselves as well as some advantage to the publick.' Having met in Rome, they sailed for the coast of Caria and 'most of the inland parts of Asia Minor, Syria, Phoenicia, Palestine and Egypt'. They were accompanied by G.B. Borra, one of the king of Sardinia's architects at Turin, who had been recommended to Wood by Lord Charlemont, a friend of the king.

The resulting books, *The Ruins of Palmyra, Otherwise Tedmore in the Desert* (1753) and *The Ruins of Baalbec, Otherwise Heliopolis in Coelo-Syria* (1757), with many engravings of technical details such as capitals and architraves from drawings by Borra, also had a great impact on taste and architecture in Britain and France. 'Palmyra' Wood, as he became known, called Baalbek 'the remains of the boldest plan we ever saw attempted in architecture' and claimed that 'the desert was in great measure to Palmyra what the sea is to Great Britain, both their riches and defence'. Horace Walpole wrote, 'of all the works that distinguish the age none perhaps excell those beautiful editions of Baalbec and Palmyra'. Borra later worked as chief garden designer and architect at Stowe, one of the most famous parks and houses in England;[33] an entrance based on the Temple of the Sun at Palmyra was built at Osterley, in Middlesex, in 1770. Perhaps the most remarkable aspect of Wood's and Dawkin's work is that there is no mention of dangers from bandits. Evidently they were too trivial, or the travellers' Turkish guard too effective, for them to notice.

In 1764–6, sent and paid by the Society of Dilettanti, Richard Chandler travelled through Greece and Asia Minor with the artist, William Pars, 'in order to collect information and to make observations relative to the ancient state of these countries and to such monuments of antiquity as are still remaining'. Many of the marbles acquired during this journey are now in the British Museum. Chandler's travels were published as *Travels in Asia Minor or an Account of a Tour Made at the Expense of the Society of Dilettanti* (2 vols., Oxford, 1775), and, in massive limited editions with large folio plates, as *Ionian Antiquities*, (2 vols., 1769–97) and *The Unedited Antiquities of Attica*, edited by William Wilkins (1817).

The supreme example of the French Grand Tourist in the Ottoman Empire, one of the great art patrons of his age, was an erudite young courtier called the Comte de Choiseul-Gouffier. For Talleyrand, he was 'the man I have loved most', the only friend Talleyrand did not betray. In 1776–9, between the ages of 24 and 27, he travelled through Greece and the islands to Constantinople, with a train of scholars and artists almost comparable in quality to those who accompanied Bonaparte to Egypt, in 1798. His motives were, in his own words, to 'satisfaire la passion de ma jeunesse pour les contrées les plus célèbres de l'antiquité'. The works of Homer and Herodotus rarely left his hands. In 1782 he published the first volume of *Voyage pittoresque de la Grèce*, with 126 illustrations. In it he voiced the hope that 'ces climats peuvent encore produire des actes de patriotisme et de vertus susceptibles de surprendre les Nations les plus civilisées de l'Europe' and praised the plan of Catherine the Great to divide the Ottoman Empire with Austria and install her younger grandson, Constantine, as Emperor in Constantinople.[34]

However, what Choiseul-Gouffier had proposed as a traveller he opposed as a diplomat. After he returned to Constantinople as French ambassador, in 1784, he obeyed the traditional French policy of support for the Ottoman Empire, as Vergennes wrote, 'by all the means which will be in his [the king's] power'.[35] Choiseul-Gouffier brought a military and naval staff of 30 officers to help the Ottoman Empire modernise its armed forces. Two engineers, Kauffer and Le Chevalier, completed the first accurate map of the city in 1786. French engineers worked in a modern military engineering school and in the arsenal on the Golden Horn, and helped build a modern ship, launched in the Sultan's presence on May 30 1787. The first observatory since the Ottoman one of 1580, which had then destroyed by a fanatical mob, was established in the French embassy. The embassy printing press published *Eléments de la langue Turque ou table analytique de la langue Turque usuelle, avec leur développement, dédiée au roi*, by M. Viguier, Préfet Apostolique of the congregation de la Mission dans le Levant in 1790.[36]

Choiseul-Gouffier sent back many antiquities, which are now in the Louvre, that had been found for him by his antiquities dealer, Mr Fauvel. In the second volume of *Voyage Pittoresque*, however, classical ruins and Greek costumes are replaced by pictures of Ottoman officials and Constantinople street sellers, scenes of the departure of the Sacred Camel or the Captain Pasha and panoramas of the city itself. In 1784–1785, he despatched his artists, Jean-Baptiste Hilair and Louis-François Cassas, to paint views of Egypt and the Levant, many of which now hang in French, English and Irish private collections. Cassas was one of the few artists to paint in Turkey, Syria *and* Egypt, and produced what may be the first pictures of the pyramids and the Sphinx (now in a private collection in London) for an ambassador allied to the Ottoman Empire 12 years before Bonaparte's invasion of it.[37]

In addition to the ambassador's artists, many other Frenchmen travelled through the Levant in the 1780s. Whereas travellers had formerly come to the Ottoman capital to admire Ottoman power, now they toured the Ottoman Empire – whose vulnerability had been exposed by its defeat by Russia in the war of 1768–74 – to see which provinces might be ripe for conquest. After eight months spent in a Druze convent learning Arabic, the French philosopher, Volney, travelled through Egypt and Syria in order, as he wrote in the preface to *Voyage en Syrie et en Égypte pendant les années 1783, 1784 et 1785*, to judge its political and physical condition, 'prendre des notions exactes de son régime intérieur pour en déduire ses forces et ses ressources'.[38] Savary's *Lettres sur l'Égypte* (1785) was one of the books later used when preparing the *Expédition d'Égypte* of 1798. C.S. Sonnini toured the Greek islands reporting on their costume, commerce and daily life in preparation for the imminent end of what he called 'ce vaste et monstrueux empire'.[39]

As plans for the Empire's demise were being drawn up, it was visited by more travellers from more countries. In 1768, the Baron de Riedesel and, in 1784, the Orientalist Count Jean Potocki were the first German and the first Pole, respectively, to write accounts of their travels in the Ottoman Empire – on the whole favourable to the Turks and contemptuous of the Greeks.[40] In the summer of 1786, Lady Craven, who had swept down through Russia and the Crimea, stayed in Constantinople with Choiseul-Gouffier, whom she called 'a very fine scholar and a very polite and lively man'. She spent evenings looking through Cassas's drawings and enjoyed the splendour, hospitality and novelty of Constantinople before leaving for the Greek islands. In Constantinople she met, among other travellers, Richard Worsley, who had left Rome with the artist, Willey Reveley, for a tour of the Empire including Egypt, to collect gems and antiquities.[41] The son of the Dutch ambassador, M. de Dedem, also toured the islands, Greece, Egypt and Troy in 1791.[42]

Choiseul's rival, both as a diplomat and as an art patron, was the British ambassador, Sir Robert Ainslie. He formed one of the finest medal collections in Europe[43] and employed an artist called Luigi Mayer on a salary of fifty guineas a year plus travelling expenses. Mayer was an inhabitant of Rome and a pupil of Piranesi, who had previously worked for the king of Naples drawing 'all the views of the memorable ruins in Sicily'. In 1792, meeting him at the British ambassador's house and finding him 'an excellent draughtsman and a pleasant agreeable companion', a British traveller, Lord Guilford, took Mayer to Egypt and Syria.[44] In the next two years, Mayer and his wife, Clara, produced over three hundred drawings of the towns, inhabitants, ceremonies and ruins of the Ottoman Empire, in effect creating a pictorial encyclopedia of past and present of modern Greeks dancing at Tarabya as well as of Greek ruins at Ephesus. These drawings were later published as prints in London between 1801 and 1810.[45] In 1794, Luigi Mayer accompanied the ambassador back to London, where he died in 1803.

The wars of the French Revolution and Empire, rendering the Grand Tour in Europe more difficult, made the Grand Tour in the Ottoman Empire more popular. In Venice, after its occupation by Austria, according to Thomas Macgill, 'gaiety has given place to melancholy; and to the serenades of the lover, to the voice of pleasure and merriment have succeeded the groans of indigence and misery'.[46] In Constantinople, on the other hand, one early nineteenth-century visitor found that, 'In no place in the world, except Paris, are so many savants, artists, travellers and men of taste of every kind found together . . . the large receptions offer a charming mixture of the most diverse national qualities, blended with an exquisite taste and amiability.'[47] Travellers to Constantinople included J.B.S. Morritt of Rokeby in Yorkshire, who arrived overland from Vienna with two friends in 1794. He admired the classic sights: the Sultan's procession; the mosques where he experienced 'much less molestation than I have frequently found in *Roman Catholic* churches'; Topkapi Palace, which he compared to a small town; Athens, Salonica and the Greek islands; the ruins of Priene, Miletus and Pergamum in Anatolia; the beauty of the vegetation; and the warmth of Greek women. Staying near Troy with a Turkish gentleman, while looking for antiquities for his country house in England, he wrote to his family, 'You see how much we are at home among the Turks. I shall never believe in dangers again.'[48]

Constantinople Ancient and Modern with Excursions to the Shores and Islands of the Archipelago and to the Troad (1797) was specifically written for 'the English tourist' – possibly the first use of the term – by one of Morritt's travelling companions, James Dallaway, 'late chaplain and physician of the British Embassy to the Porte'. Devoted to power and scholarship, it described 'the political system in the seraglio and the office of vizier', and such major institutions as the Janissaries and the Greek and Armenian churches, as well as 'the present state of those ruins which were once the pride of classic antiquity'.[49]

Few individuals became so familiar with the Ottoman Empire as the great neo-classical artist and aesthetic theorist, Thomas Hope. In 1795–1797, in his own words, 'I resided nearly a twelve month in Constantinople; visited the arsenal and bagnio frequently; witnessed the festival of St George ; saw Rhodes, was in Egypt, in Syria and in every other place which I have attempted to describe minutely in *Anastasius*' – his great picaresque Ottoman novel published in 1819. Five volumes of his drawings now in Benaki Museum in Athens bear out his claim; his 1798 portrait by William Beechey in Ottoman dress, standing in front of a mosque, now hangs in the National Portrait Gallery.[50]

A visit to the ruins of Greece and the Middle East was becoming part of British architects' training. William Wilkins, future architect of the National Gallery and University College London, travelled there in 1800–2, with the artist, Agostino Aglie; Robert Smirke, architect of the British Museum that today houses so many antiquities acquired in the Ottoman Empire, visited in 1804–5. Charles Barry, future architect of the Houses of Parliament, made drawings and plans of the monuments of Anatolia, Egypt and Levant, now in the library of the RIBA, London, in 1817–20, charging another traveller, called David Baillie, a fee of £200 a year. Unlike many of their predecessors, they were more interested in the classical past than the Ottoman present. Ignoring the mosques of Constantinople, C.R. Cockerell, who travelled throughout Greece and Anatolia in 1810–14, wrote that, 'To architecture in the highest sense viz elegant construction in stone, the Turks have no pretension . . . the most charming things are the kiosks . . . such as you might imagine from reading the Arabian Nights . . . They are entirely of wood and even the most extensive are finished in about two months.'[51]

In 1806–7, Chateaubriand travelled throughout the Ottoman Empire, from Athens to Constantinople and Cairo. Contrary to what readers of Edward Said and other authors hostile to 'Orientalism' might expect, Europeans had, since 1650, been generally indifferent to the remains of the crusades and the sites and traditions of early Christianity. As he boasted, Chateaubriand was the first traveller to admire the latter, to prefer Jerusalem to Constantinople and to evoke the crusades, frequently quoting from a pilgrim's account of the twelfth century in his *Itineraire de Paris à Jérusalem et de Jérusalem à Paris, en allant par la Grèce et en revenant par l'Égypte, la Barbarie et l'Espagne* (3 vols., 1811).

Three years later, in 1809, Byron and Hobhouse arrived via Portugal, Spain and Malta – this was the favoured route during the Napoleonic wars. They stayed in the Ottoman Empire for more than a year. Byron employed one English servant, Fletcher; one Turk and two Albanians as guards and messengers; and an interpreter.[52] While Byron was fascinated by what he called in his poem, *Childe Harold*, 'the wild pomp of mountain majesty', and liked to gaze at stars and ruminate, Hobhouse, to Byron's annoyance, concentrated on topography and classical inscriptions. However, Hobhouse was also interested in the manners and customs of the modern Albanians, and in Ali Pasha, the Ottoman governor of northern Greece and Albania with ambitions to found an independent state. Indeed, between 1810 and 1822 Ali Pasha was an object of fascination for European travellers. Dr Henry Holland, in 1812, for example, recorded the details of the Pasha's face, 'the eye penetrating yet not expressive of ferocity; the nose handsome and well formed . . . the neck is short and thick, the figure corpulent and unwieldy'.[53] Byron later commented that he never judged from manners, for 'one of the mildest persons I ever saw was Ali Pasha'.[54] In reality Ali Pasha and his sons used torture as a means of government, and banditry as a source of revenue.

From 13 May to 14 July 1810, Byron and Hobhouse stayed beside the Embassies in Pera, first in a hotel, then in lodgings. They rode, swam the Hellespont, watched whirling dervishes, visited mosques and accompanied the British ambassador to the palace.[55] Hobhouse devoted nine chapters of his travel book to a description of the city. After visiting Constantinople they returned to Greece. By 1810, Athens had become as fashionable among the British as Rome had been twenty years earlier. Among the peers whom Byron met in Athens were Lords Sligo, Clare and Plymouth, and Mayer's patron, Lord Guilford (who lived in Greece from 1811 to 1824, converted to Orthodoxy and founded a university on Corfu). Other acquaintances were Henry Gally Knight, the writer on architecture; John Galt, the novelist;[56] Lusieri, the artist, who had accompanied Lord Elgin to Constantinople; Fauvel, the French consul and antiquities dealer; C.R. Cockerell, who enjoyed 'Elysinian days' in Athens; as well as French, Italian, German, Danish and American travellers.[57]

Another visitor whom Byron met in Athens in 1810 was Pitt's niece, Lady Hester Stanhope. What was unusual in her travels was neither her choice of destinations – Constantinople, Bursa, Palmyra, Aleppo, Damascus, Alexandria, Cairo – nor her close friendships with, and protection by, Ottoman officials, but her motivation. She was the first of the long line of Western travellers who went East not for power, pleasure or scholarship but to escape conventional society. Living in Lebanon in proud isolation, abandoned by her young lover, Michael Bruce, and pillaged by her servants, she became a *monstre sacré*, visited by travellers almost as eagerly as the nearby temples of Baalbek until her death in 1839.

The ten years after 1810 were the peak of the Grand Tour in the Ottoman Empire. A Foreign Office messenger called William Turner travelled throughout the Ottoman Empire in 1812–15, but proves the truth of Graham Gibbs's remark, 'travel narrows the mind'. Turner concluded, 'If indeed I have learnt any thing by my travels it is that England is the only country for an Englishman to live in.'[58] Between 1815 and 1819 a wealthy friend and mentor of Byron at Cambridge, William John Bankes, travelled, as he wrote *en grand seigneur* in the Ottoman Empire, from Albania to Cyrenaica. He stayed with Lady Hester Stanhope and desert shaykhs, copied Greek, Latin and Nabataean inscriptions and made the first accurate plans of some of the Roman cities of Syria and Jordan, such as Petra and Jerash ('the Pompeii of the East' had been rediscovered in 1806 by a Russian diplomat, U.-J. Seetzen, based in Constantinople). There are 1,500 plans and drawings (50 of Jerash, 22 of Bosra) in the Bankes collection ensure that there is a better record of many Syrian towns and monuments in the County Record Office in Dorchester than in Damascus. Since he travelled beyond Abu Simbel, Bankes became known as 'the Nubian explorer', although his indolence and mercurial temperament prevented him from publishing his findings. Finally, he transported a pink granite obelisk from the banks of the Nile to the lawns of Kingston Lacy, his country house in Dorset.

Just as few ambassadors had resisted having themselves painted with the Sultan or in Ottoman dress in Constantinople, so few travellers resisted having themselves painted in Eastern dress in front of Levantine ruins. George Cumming Bruce, for example, was painted in front of the ruins of Palmyra by Andrew Geddes, in 1817. Similar portraits exist by T.J. Phillips of Byron and Colonel Vivian in Albanian dress (in the National Portrait Gallery and Hadspen (Somerset) respectively), and of Thomas Legh, author of *Narrative of a Journey in Egypt and the Country beyond the Cataracts*, 1817, in Arabian dress at Lyme Park (Cheshire).

In 1816 the estranged Princess of Wales, Caroline of Brunswick, inspired by the tales of acquaintances like Lord Byron, and of her chamberlain, Sir William Gell, as well as by memories of her ancestors' exploits on the crusades, travelled through the Empire, visiting Tunis, Athens, Cairo, Jerusalem and Constantinople. In Tunis she received a guard of honour from the Bey and inspected his harems; to commemorate her visit to Jerusalem she founded the order of Saint Caroline of Jerusalem (motto: 'Honi Soit qui Mal y Pense'). Believing that 'the dear

Arabians and Turks are quite darlings', she returned to Italy with Turkish, Arabian and African servants, as well as textiles bought in Constantinople.[59] In 1817–19, the Comte de Forbin, Director of the Musées Royaux of France, was sent on a mission to the Levant in order to acquire antiquities to fill the gaps left in the Louvre by the enforced restitutions made to European powers after the battle of Waterloo.[60]

Travellers began to venture east from Syria into Mesopotamia and the Arabian desert. Between 1810 and 1817, the Swiss, John Lewis Burckhardt, travelled in Nubia, Syria and Arabia. He visited Mecca disguised as a pilgrim, rediscovered the Nabataean city of Petra in 1812 and the statues at Abu Simbel in 1813.[61] Other such travellers were Claudius James Rich, author of *Narrative of a Residence in Koordistan* (2 vols., 1836), and *Narrative of a Journey to the Sites of Babylon and Persepolis in 1811* (1839); John Macdonald Kinneir, who wrote *Journey through Asia Minor, Armenia and Koordistan in the Years 1813 and 1814* (1818); J.M. Tancoigne, responsible for *Lettres sur la Perse et la Turquie d'Asie* (2 vols., 1819); and James Silk Buckingham, the author of *Travels Among the Arab Tribes Including the East of Syria and Palestine* (1825), *Travels in Mesopotamia* (1827) and *Travels in Assyria* and *Medea and Persia* (1830).

By 1819, according to Edward Dodwell in *A Classical and Topographical Tour through Greece during the Years 1801, 1805 and 1806*, and published in that year:

> The classic regions of Greece have been recently explored by such a multiplicity of travellers that the Author of the present tour appeared to be precluded from the hope of making any considerable additions to that stock of information which they have already communicated to the public.[62]

Indeed, William Martin Leake, an officer who spent many years between 1799 and 1810 surveying portions of the Ottoman Empire and encouraging its governors to strengthen their defences against a possible French invasion, established the location of most ancient Greek sites, as he demonstrated in his books: *The Topography of Athens with some Remarks on the Antiquities* (1821), *Journal of a Tour in Asia Minor* (1824), *A Tour in the Morea* (1830), and *A Tour in Northern Greece* (1835).

Meanwhile, the prime facilitator of the Grand Tour in the Ottoman Empire, the order maintained there by the Ottoman authorities, was under challenge, both from within by rebellious Janissaries, pashas, Arabs[63] and Greeks, and from without by increasingly expansionist western powers. Already, Hobhouse had noted that the Greeks were longing to revolt, 'all their hopes are directed towards the restoration of the Byzantine kingdom in the person of any Christian, but more particularly a Christian of their own church'.[64] In 1821, as he predicted, a Greek revolt took place – although another traveller, John Fuller, believed that in Athens, at least, 'This was an anxious moment for the Greek inhabitants, the majority of whom were very well satisfied with their present condition, lived on very good terms with their Turkish neighbours and were very lukewarm in the cause for independence.'[65] Forgetting his earlier philottomanism, Byron soon provided funds, leadership and publicity for the Greeks. In 1826, the Janissaries themselves were suppressed by Sultan Mahmud II, whose 'milk white hand glittering with diamond rings', 'glossy jet black' eyebrows, eyes and beard, and air of ' indescribable majesty' Hobhouse had admired 16 years earlier.[66]

Never have so many travel books appeared on one area in such a short time as they did on the Ottoman Empire in the following ten years.[67] Travellers as varied as Disraeli (1830) – who, like Bonaparte in 1795, considered joining the Ottoman army and whose memories of the 16 months when he lived 'quite as a Turk' may have influenced his pro-Ottoman policy in the crisis of 1877–8[68] – Lamartine (1832–3), and Marshal Marmont (1834–5) arrived to observe the modernising revolutions that the Sultan, and his vassal, model and rival, Muhammad Ali Pasha of Egypt, were trying to impose from above. As the region became the focus of European diplomacy, and steamboats revolutionised the ease and speed of travel, a visit to the Ottoman Empire had finally become, in the words of a French visitor in 1826–8, Léon de Laborde, 'a banality'.

Indeed, for some the Grand Tour in the Ottoman Empire finally displaced the traditional Grand Tour centred on Italy. In *Doctor Thorne*, published in 1858, Anthony Trollope described Frank Gresham, after graduating from university, as

> doing the fashionable things, going up the Nile, crossing over to Mount Sinai, thence over the long desert to Jerusalem and home by Damascus, Beyrout and Constantinople, bringing back a long beard, a red cap and a chibook, just as our fathers used to go through Italy and Switzerland and our grandfathers to spend a season in Paris.[69]

NOTES

1. Pierre Masson, *Histoire du commerce français dans le Levant au XVIIIe siècle* (1911), p. 612; S.A. Skilliter, *William Harborne and the Trade with Turkey 1578–1582* (Oxford University Press for The British Academy, 1977), p. 50, cf. p. 115; Alfred C. Wood, *A History of the Levant Company* (London, Oxford University Press, 1935, repr. Frank Cass, 1964), p. 72.
2. Sir William Forster (ed.), *The Travels of John Sanderson in the Levant, 1584–1602* (London, Hakluyt Society, 1931); Henri de Beauvau, *Voyage du Levant* (Nancy, I. Garnich, 1619).
3. Philippe du Fresne-Canaye, *Voyage du Levant* (1573, repr. 1897); Jean de Thevenot, *Relation d'un voyage fait au Levant* (3 vols., Rouen and Paris, 1665–1684); Chevalier Chardin, *Voyage en Perse et autres lieux de l'orient* (Amsterdam, 1735); Guillaume-Joseph Grelot, *Relation nouvelle d'un voyage de Constantinople* (Paris, 1681).
4. When there were many works such as Ludovico de Varthema, *Itinerario . . . nello Egitto, nella Sorria, nella Arabia deserta e felice, nella Persia, nella India e nella Ethiopia* (Venice, 1525), describing a journey undertaken in 1502–7, and Marcantonio Pigafetta, *Itinerario di Gentil'huomo Vicentino* (London, 1585).
5. A. Ulrich Koch, 'Venezianische Maskerade', *Weltkunst*, Heft 4 (15 February 1996), 344–6.
6. William Hunter, *Travels through France, Turkey and Hungary to Vienna in 1792*, 3rd edn (2 vols., 1803), I, p. 323.
7. Thomas Watkins, *Tour through Swisserland . . . to Constantinople* (2 vols., London, J. Owen, 1794), vol. 2, pp. 139, 214, 218, 227; cf. Whaley praising 'an appearance of pomp and splendour that far surpasses that of any European court'. See B. Whaley, *Buck Whaley's Memoirs, Including his Journey to Jerusalem* (London, Alexander Moring, 1906), p. 116.
8. Cf. Lord Baltimore in *A Tour to the East in the Years 1763 and 1764, with Remarks on the City of Constantinople and the Turks* (London, W. Richardson and S. Clark, 1767), p. 53, who also called Constantinople 'that famous city which for its curiosity and situation exceeds every other in Europe.'
9. For the cult of pleasure among Dutch merchants in Constantinople, see C. Bosscha Erdbrink, *At the Threshold of Felicity: Ottoman-Dutch Relations during the Embassy of Cornelis Calkoen at the Sublime Porte 1726–1744* (Ankara, 1975), p. 138, Calkoen to States-General (22 March 1739).
10. Pierre Masson, *op. cit.*, p. 473, letter from French consul in Sidon (1 August 1695).
11. John Montagu, *A Voyage Performed by the Late Earl of Sandwich Round the Mediterranean in the Years 1713 and 1739* (1799), p. iii.
12. Anne de Herdt, *Dessins de Liotard* (1992), *passim*; Aileen Ribeiro, 'Turquerie: Turkish dress and English Fashion in the Eighteenth Century', *Connoisseur* (May 1979).
13. *Les Grands Boulevards* (Musée Carnavalet, 1985), pp. 159–61.
14. R. Dalton, *Antiquities and Views in Greece and Egypt in 1751–2* (London, T. King and H. Chapman, repr. 1791), pp. 163, 177, 181.
15. W.B. Stanford and E.J. Finopoulo, *The Travels of Lord Charlemont in Greece and Turkey in 1749* (London, Trigraph for A.G. Leventis Foundation, 1984), pp. 166–7, 204–5.

16 Wood, *A History of the Levant Company* (Oxford, 1935).
17 Alfred Wood, 'The British Embassy in Constantinople', *English Historical Review*, XL (1925), 551; Charlemont, pp. 3, 204–6; Elvis Habesci, *The Present State of the Ottoman Empire* (London, R. Baldwin, 1784), pp. 175, 393.
18 Casanova, *Histoire de ma vie* (Collection Bouquins, 1993), I, p. 279.
19 Whaley (*op. cit.*); J.C. Hobhouse, *A Journey Through Albania and other Provinces of Turkey in Europe and Asia, to Constantinople, during the Years 1809 and 1810* (London, J. Cawthorn, 1813), p. 885.
20 Whaley, *op. cit.*, p. 122; Watkins, *op. cit.*, pp. 220, 239, 243, 267, 275.
21 Author of *Des Histoires orientales et principalement des turkes ou turchiques* (1575).
22 *Vers l'orient*, catalogue of exhibition at the Bibliothèque Nationale (1983), pp. 33, 68.
23 Richard Stonemen (ed.), *Across the Hellespont: A Literary Guide to Turkey* (London, Hutchinson, 1987), p. 96.
24 Richard Pococke, *A Description of the East and Some Other Countries* (2 vols., London, J. & R. Knapton, 1743–5), vol. 2, pp. 108, 112.
25 Cf. Whaley, *op. cit.*, pp. 191, 226, 236; at Acre 'the governor received us with all that kind of politeness and pompous ceremony peculiar to Asiatic grandees'; C.R. Cockerell, *Travels in Southern Europe and the Levant 1810-1817* (London, New York, Longmans, Green and Co., 1803), p. 119, received in Athens with 'form and cordiality'; William Turner, *Journal of a Tour in the Levant* (3 vols., 1820), II, p. 60; 'the aga was very civil and begged that if I had need of anything here which he could do for me I would not fail to apply to him'.
26 Alexander Russell, *The Natural History of Aleppo and Parts Adjacent* (1756; repr. London, G. & J. Robinson, 1794), pp. 135–6.
27 Pococke, *op. cit.*, pp. 126, 133. The relative ease of access to Constantinople mosques is confirmed by many other accounts, e.g. Sir Francis Sacheverell Darwin, *Travels in Spain and the East 1808–1810* (Cambridge, The University Press, 1927), p. 49: July 1809, 'Mr Adair procured a firman to make the tour of all the principal mosques'; see also Hobhouse, *op. cit.*, p. 965.
28 A captain in the Danish navy, sent to Egypt by the king in 1737–1738, from Florence where he was a member of the Academy of Drawing. Author of *Voyage d'Egypte et de Nubie* (2 vols., Copenhagen, 1755), published by command of the king of Denmark.
29 BM Add. Mss. 52362. *Journal of the Egyptian Society 1741–1743*. Every year the Society celebrated the Feast of Isis with a dinner in London.
30 The last date in the minutes book is 25 May, 1746. I am grateful for this reference to Mr Giddings, of the National Maritime Museum archive, in Greenwich.
31 James Stuart, *The Antiquities of Athens* (4 vols., 1762–1816), vol. 1, p. x.
32 *Ibid.*, vol. 4, p. vii; Watkins, *op. cit.*, vol. 2, p. 317; Cockerell, *op. cit.*, p. 46.
33 Anita Damiani, *Enlightened Observers. British Travellers to the Near East 1715–1850* (Beirut, American University of Beirut, 1979), p. 109; some of Borra's drawings are in the Mellon Centre at Yale, others are at the Royal Institute of British Architects in London. His diaries and sketch-books are with the Society for Hellenic Studies in London.
34 The Comte de Choiseul-Gouffier, *Voyage pittoresque de la Grèce* (2 vols., Paris, 1782–1809), vol. 1, pp. 1, viii, ix.

35 Léonce Pingaud, *Choiseul-Gouffier: la France en Orient sous Louis XVI* (1887), p. 179n, Vergennes to Segur; Pierre Duparc, *Recueil des instructions données aux ambassadeurs et ministres de France, Turquie* (1969), p. 477, instruction of 2 June 1784.
36 Max Roche, *Education, assistance et culture françaises dans l'empire Ottoman* (Istanbul, Editions Isis, 1989), pp. 17–18; see also, Abbé Martin, *Voyage à Constantinople fait à l'occasion de l'ambassade de M le Comte de Choiseul-Gouffier à la Porte Ottomane* (1819).
37 Cassas' drawings, signed and dated 1790, of sites in Anatolia hang in Castle Coole, Ireland; others are at Ickworth and Attingham, properties of the National Trust.
38 Constantin-François Volnay, *Voyage en Syrie et en Égypte pendant les années 1783, 1784 et 1785*, seconde édition, revue et corrigée (1787), vii. Another political travel book, very hostile to Choiseul-Gouffier, is *Mémoires Historiques, politiques et géographiques des voyages du Comte de Ferrières-Sauvebœuf faits en Turquie, en Perse et en Arabie depuis 1781 jusqu'en 1789* (2 vols., 1790).
39 C.S. Sonnini, *Voyage en Grèce et en Turquie fait par ordre de Louis XVI* (2 vols., Paris, L'Harmattan, 1801), I, p. 31.
40 Baron de Riedesel, *Voyage en Sicile, dans la Grande Grèce et au Levant* (1802), p. 345: 'la douceur et la bienfaisance forment le caractère des Turcs'; Count Jean Potocki, *Voyage en Turquie et en Egypte fait en l'année 1784* (1788).
41 Countess of Craven (ed.), *Letters* (1814), p. 187, letter of 25 April, 1786; Jeremy Black, *The British Abroad: The Grand Tour in the Eighteenth Century* (London, Croom Helm, 1985), p. 69; *Museum Worsleyanum* (2 vols., 1794), (the collection there described is now at Brocklesby, seat of Worsley's descendant the Earl of Yarborough).
42 Baron de Dedem de Gelder, *Mémoires* (1900), p. 66.
43 *Ibid.*, pp. 20–3; D. Sestini, *Lettere e Dissertazioni numismatiche sopra alcune medaglie rare della Collezione Ainslieana* (1789).
44 Bodleian Library, Oxford, English Mss. c 433 f 180, diary of Lord Guilford (1792): see also, Briony Llewellyn, 'Luigi Mayer – Draughtsman to His Majesty's Ambassador at the Ottoman Porte', *Watercolours*, 5:4 (Winter 1990), 9–13.
45 I.e. Luigi Mayer, *Views in Turkey in Europe and Asia Comprising Romelia, Bulgaria, Wallachia, Syria and Palestine* (1801–6); *Views in Egypt from the Original Drawings in the Possession of Sir Robert Ainslie Taken during his Embassy to Constantinople* (1801–4); *Views in Palestine* (1801–4); *Views in the Ottoman Empire, Chiefly in Caramania* (1803); *Views in the Ottoman Dominions* (1810); *A Series of Twenty-Four Views Illustrative of the Holy Scriptures Selected from Sir Robert Ainslie's Celebrated Collection of Drawings* (1833).
46 Thomas Macgill, *Travels in Turkey, Italy and Russia during the Years 1803, 1804, 1805 and 1806* (1808), vol. 1, p. 2.
47 Colonel Rottiers, *Itinéraire de Tiflis à Constantinople* (Brussels, Tencé Frères Century, 1829), p. 345.
48 J.B.S. Morritt, *A Grand Tour: Letters and Journeys 1794–1796* (London, Century, 1985), pp. 67, 92, 111, 142, 215, letters of 25 July 1794, 12 November 1794, 6 December 1794, 4 June 1795. Albums of Morritt's drawings of the Ottoman Empire are still in his descendants' possession at Rokeby.

49 James Dallaway, *Constantinople Ancient and Modern with Excursions to the Shores and Islands of the Archipelago and to the Troad* (T. Cadell, junr. & W. Davies, 1797), pp. iv–vi, 7.
50 David Watkin, *Thomas Hope 1769–1831 and the Neoclassical Idea* (London, Murray, 1968), pp. 6–10.
51 Cockerell, *op. cit.*, pp. 28–9.
52 Thomas Moore (ed.), *Life and Letters of Lord Byron* (London, 1844), p. 111, letter of 30 July 1810.
53 Henry Holland MD, FRS, *Travels in the Ionian Isles, Albania, Thessaly, Macedonia etc. during the Years 1812 and 1813* (2 vols., London, Longman, Hurst, Rees, Orme and Brown, 1819), I, p. 180.
54 Moore, *op. cit.*, p. 96, letter of 12 November 1809.
55 *Ibid.*, p. 108, letter of 28 June 1810.
56 John Galt was author of, among other works, *Letters from the Levant: Containing Views of the State of Society, Manners, Opinions and Commerce in Greece and Several of the Principal Islands of the Archipelago* (1813).
57 Hugh Tregaskis, *Beyond the Grand Tour: The Levant Lunatics* (London, Ascent Books, 1979), pp. 86, 93, 98, 101. Some of Cockerell's drawings were published in Revd T.S. Hughes, T. D., *Travels in Greece and Albania*, 2nd edn. (2 vols., 1830); see also David Watkin, *The Life and Work of C.R. Cockerell* (London, H. Colburn and R. Bentley, 1974), pp. 7, 9; most are in the Greek and Roman Department of the British Museum.
58 William Turner, *Journal of a Tour in the Levant* (3 vols., London, 1820), vol. 3, p. 344.
59 Mrs Demont, *Voyages and Travels of Her Majesty, Caroline Queen of Great Britain* (London, Jones & Co., 1821), pp. 397, 402, 673; Flora Fraser, *The Unruly Queen* (New York, Knopf, 1996), pp. 284–7.
60 Comte de Forbin, *Voyage dans le Levant* (1820); cf. his gigantic picture in the Musée de Picardie, Amiens, dated 1819, showing Muhammad Ali watching the massacre of the Mamluks in the Citadel of Cairo.
61 John Lewis Burckhardt, *Travels in Nubia* (London, J. Murray, 1819); *Travels in Syria and the Holy Land* (London, Darf Publishers, 1822); *Travels in Arabia* (London, H. Colburn, 1829).
62 Edward Dodwell, *A Classical and Topographical Tour through Greece during the Years 1801, 1805 and 1806* (2 vols., London, Rodwell & Martin, 1919), vol. 1, p. iii. The same year he also published *Views in Greece*. Dodwell had travelled in 1801–2 and 1805–6 with Sir William Gell. Other visitors, excluding those already mentioned, had included Edward Daniel Clarke 1800–1, who gave antiquities from the Ottoman Empire to the Fitzwilliam Museum, Cambridge; Lord Carlisle in 1801; Lord Valentia in 1802–6; Lord Aberdeen in 1803–4; William Purser and John Sanders in 1817–20; Captains Irby and Mangles in 1817–18; Lord Belmore, in Egypt, in 1816–18; William Page in 1816–24; Lewis Vulliamy in 1818; and Frederick Catherwood in 1824. Literary remains of these Ottoman Grand Tours include: Peter Edmund Laurent, *Recollections of a Classical Tour through Various Parts of Greece, Turkey and Italy Made in the Years 1818 and 1819* (London, W.B. Whittaker, 1821); H.W. Williams, *Travels in Italy, Greece and the Ionian Islands in a Series of Letters Descriptive of Manners, Scenery and the Fine Arts* (2 vols., Edinburgh, 1820); Robert Richardson, *Travels*

along the Mediterranean and Parts Adjacent; in Company with the Earl of Belmore during the Years 1816–17–18 (2 vols., London, T. Cadell, 1822); Hon. Charles Leonard Irby and James Mangles, *Travels in Egypt, Nubia, Syria and Asia Minor during the Years 1817 and 1818* (London, T. White & Co., 1823); Sir William Gell, *Narrative of a Journey in the Morea* (London, Longman, Hurst, Rees, Orme, and Brown, 1823); James Edward Alexander, *Travels from India to England in the Years 1825–6* (London, Parbury, Allen, 1827); William John Bankes, *Narrative of the Life and Adventures of Giovani Finati* (2 vols., London, J. Murray, 1830s). Artistic remains include the lithographs of Louis Dupré who, in 1818, accompanied three Englishmen, Messrs Vivian, Hyett and Hay, published as *Voyage à Athènes et à Constantinople* (1825); and Sir William Allan, 'The Slave Market of Constantinople' in the National Gallery of Scotland.

63 The safety of Caroline, Princess of Wales, was challenged by *banditti* in Palestine in 1816, see Demont, *op. cit.*, pp. 604, 667.
64 Hobhouse, *op. cit.*, pp. 110, 550, 588.
65 Tregaskis, *op. cit.*, p. 162.
66 Hobhouse, *op. cit.*, p. 1000.
67 For example, among others, Captain Charles Colville Frankland, *Travels to and from Constantinople in the Years 1827 and 1828* (2 vols., London, H. Colburn, 1829); R.R. Madden, *Travels in Turkey, Egypt. Nubia, and Palestine in 1824, 1825, 1826, and 1827* (2 vols., London, Whittaker, Treacher, 1829); Charles MacFarlane, *Constantinople in 1828* (2 vols., London, Saunders and Otley, 1829); John Carne, *Letters from the East: Written during a Recent Tour through Turkey, Egypt, Arabia, the Holy Land, Syria and Greece* (2 vols., 1830); Olphar Hamst, *Sketches of Turkey in 1831 and 1832* (New York, J. & J. Harper, 1833); John Auldjo, *Journal of a Visit to Constantinople and Some of the Greek Islands in the Spring and Summer of 1833* (London, Longman, Rees, Orme, Brown, Green & Longman, 1835); Alphonse de Lamartine, *Souvenirs, impressions, pensées et paysages pendant un voyage en Orient (1832–1833) ou Notes d'un voyageur* (4 vols., Paris, C. Gosselin, 1835); Revd Vere Monro, *A Summer Ramble in Syria with a Tartar Trip from Aleppo to Stamboul* (2 vols., London, R. Bentley, 1835); Major Sir Grenville Temple Bt., *Travels in Greece and Turkey* (2 vols., London, 1836); Revd R.A. Walsh, *Residence at Constantinople* (2 vols., London, F. Westley & A.H. Davis, 1836); Maréchal Duc de Raguse, *Voyage en Hongrie, en Turquie . . . et en Egypte* (4 vols., 1837); Julia Pardoe, *The City of the Sultans and Domestic Manners of the Turks in 1836* (2 vols., London, H. Colburn, 1837); Adolphus Slade, *Turkey, Greece and Malta* (2 vols., 1837); and the most famous in English, A.W. Kinglake, *Eōthen* (London, John Olivier, 1844), describing a journey made in 1834–1835.
68 Robert Blake, *Disraeli's Grand Tour* (New York, Oxford University Press, 1982), pp. 30–1, 47.
69 Anthony Trollope, *Doctor Thorne*, first published in 1858 (1914 edn), p. 433. I am grateful for this reference to Dr Peter Clark.

3

Dressing Native

John Rodenbeck

E.W. Lane, the great ethnographer and lexicographer, who figures occasionally in the pages that follow, warned that sayings are a bad guide to the morality of a people. I should, nevertheless, like to ponder for a moment the contrasts represented by two pairs of sayings and consider what they suggest as to similarities and differences in attitudes towards clothing in the West and the Arabic-speaking East.

A common Arab saying is *kul mā yiʿjibak wa ilbis mā yiʿjib an-nās* (eat what pleases you and wear what pleases others).[1] At first glance, these words resemble a Western commonplace traceable directly back to St Ambrose (*c.* 339–397): 'When in Rome, do as the Romans do.'[2] But the sentiments expressed in the Arab saying, which emphasises the value of appearances, and in this traditional Western one, which advises one to be flexible in one's habits, are not really identical at all.

The ideas behind another pair of sayings are even more incompatible. 'You can't tell a book by its cover', says a Western proverb of unknown origin, which takes up the familiar theme of discrepancy between appearance and reality. But its equally trite Arab counterpart says, *al-kitāb yuqrā'* [or *yuʿraf*] *min 'inwānih*[3] (a book is known by its cover), suggesting that, in some sense, appearance actually is reality. The ontological and epistemological conflict implied by the contrast between these two banalities may well exemplify an area of unconscious cultural presumption over which the Arab world and the West are profoundly and secretly at odds.

Animosity is certainly evident in some of the comments made by or on behalf of Arabs about Western travellers of the past and about their motives for wearing Eastern clothing when travelling in or living in the Middle East. For example, in *Orientalism*, his most celebrated work, Edward Said takes E.W. Lane to task for wearing Turkish clothing during his first two stays in Cairo and claims that it was a disguise. 'One portion of Lane's identity floats easily in the unsuspecting Muslim sea', he says, while 'a submergent part retains its secret European power, to comment on, acquire, possess everything around it'.[4] Said's assertion that Lane wore a disguise has been echoed and elaborated by Timothy Mitchell, and the wearing of either Turkish or Arab clothes by Westerners in the Middle East is equated, in general, with espionage, schizophrenia or megalomania by Rana Kabbani, who sees no difference either in the costumes or the sartorial motives of E.W. Lane, Sir Richard Burton, T.E. Lawrence or Wilfred Thesiger.[5] Leila Ahmed, one of Lane's best and most useful biographers, goes even further, with a declaration to the effect that, since Lodovico Vartema, all Europeans who have worn Middle Eastern clothes are expressing 'enmity, aggression and rivalry' and must be spies, and that even in the otherwise obviously Arabophile E.W. Lane and Wilfrid Scawen Blunt these hostile attitudes remain 'latencies' that are only 'dormant'.[6]

Such critics I shall refer to as Occidentalists. Certainly their accusations are supported by no evidence and bear no relation to the well-documented realities of nineteenth-century Egypt, in particular, or to the alternatives actually available to travellers in the Middle East as a whole during the past three hundred years. What I hope to do in this chapter is to demonstrate, in fact, that Western visitors and sojourners in the Middle East between 1600 and 1850 wore Eastern clothing for a wide variety of well-attested motives, among which espionage is undoubtedly the least important, in terms of incidence, and 'enmity, aggression and rivalry' do not figure at all.

If Occidentalist allegations are made in something like good faith by people who consider themselves rational, it follows logically that such accusers presume that all Westerners who ever wore Middle Eastern clothes did so entirely of their own volition, not only without compulsion or coercion of any kind from Ottoman, Persian or Arab authorities, but actually in defiance of such authorities, as well as of all Middle Eastern custom and usage. They must presume that every Western visitor to the Arab world has always been permitted to wear whatever he or she liked, either in public or in private, and that those who chose Middle Eastern clothing always did so deliberately, in order to carry out a particular programme of deception.

These presumptions are absurd, no matter what historical context, if any, they may have reference to. Even in the present day, for example, all women of whatever origin in such countries as contemporary Iran or Saudi Arabia are compelled by law to conform to prescribed local norms of dress in public. There is no choice in the matter. And these presumptions of perfect freedom are even more absurd in regard to the past.

Like other contemporary European autocrats, Ottoman sultans issued sumptuary laws prescribing clothing according to social rank. Under Murat IV (1609–40, r. 1623–40), for example, elaborate regulations forbade anyone to wear anything other than the clothing and headgear pertaining to his or her '*millet*, rank, class, occupation and so on'. To ensure enforcement, the Sultan himself patrolled Istanbul in disguise at night and ordered the summary execution of lawbreakers, whose headless bodies were left in the streets as a mute admonition to fellow-citizens.[7] In addition, as Nabil Matar has pointed out, several Ottoman sultans specifically forbade their subjects – including millions of European ones – to dress like 'Franks' either at home or abroad.[8] During the Tulip Period – *Lāle Devri* – coinciding with the Grand Vezirate of Damat Ibrahim Pasha (1718–30) under Ahmet III (1673–1736, r. 1708–30), regulations were relaxed momentarily and Ottoman subjects took to wearing European coats or Indian robes. The old strictures against foreign clothing were vigorously reinstated, however, by Halil Hamit, Grand Vezir between 1782 and 1785 under Abdülhamid I (1725–89, r. 1774–89) and again by Selim III (1761–1808, r. 1789–1807), even as he introduced the *nizam al-jadid*, the New Order that was to transform the Empire.

In Egypt before Muhammad Ali, the ban on foreign clothing was extended to include foreign visitors, whatever their status. Eyles Irwin noted in 1777, for example, that Alexandria was the only town in Egypt in which Europeans could show themselves in European clothes.[9] In 1779, two years later, taking what was then the hazardous Overland Route to India, Mrs Eliza Fay recorded being forced by the Egyptian authorities to put on Egyptian clothing from the skin outward – *shintiyan*, two gowns, *burqu'*, *habarah* and yellow morocco slippers – before she was allowed to enter the city.[10] In 1784, James Capper prescribed Turkish dress as part of the necessary kit for any traveller using the Overland Route.[11] And sixty years later, the ghost of these rules still applied: touring Egypt in 1838–9, David Roberts was allowed to work in mosques only on condition that he wore Turkish clothes and did not use hog's-bristle brushes.[12]

It is obvious, therefore, that one major reason for Westerners to wear Eastern clothing in the Middle East – a motive of which Occidentalist commentators seem utterly ignorant – was official compulsion, pure and simple: they actually had no choice in the matter. But Occidentalists also seem to have no notion that a Westerner might actually like Eastern clothing for its own sake and might even find it beautiful. In one of the first letters Ogier Ghiselin de Busbecq wrote about his embassy to Turkey between 1555 and 1562, for example, he describes the gathering of Süleyman the Magnificent's courtiers at Amasya:

> Take your stand by my side and look at the sea of turbaned heads, each wrapped in twisted folds of the whitest silk; look at all these marvellously handsome dresses of every kind and every colour; time would fail me to tell how all around is glittering with gold, with silver, with purple, with silk, and with velvet; words cannot convey an adequate idea of that strange and wondrous sight: it was the most beautiful spectacle I ever saw.[13]

The aesthetic appeal of Eastern clothing certainly led thousands of Westerners to wear it willingly, even eagerly, for reasons that had nothing at all to do either with disguise or espionage, with enmity, aggression, or rivalry, or with compulsion. Such was obviously the case, for example, when Turkish costume was assumed in parts of the world hundreds of miles beyond the Ottoman borders. In such places, far out of reach of the Sultan's writ, Turkish costume could only be worn for display or advertisement, not disguise. Espionage was physically impossible and the motive that must be presumed is one that had essentially to do with personal pleasure.

Turkish clothing was thoroughly familiar to the upper levels of society in the West well before the end of the fifteenth century. Apart from the reports and souvenirs of Western travellers, many of whom returned dressed as Turks,[14] glimpses of authentic Eastern costume were afforded by visitors and sojourners, such as Cem Sultan (1459–95), rebellious son of Mehmet II (1432–81), the conqueror of Constantinople, and brother of Bayezit II (1446–1512), who spent the last twelve years of his life in France and Italy. Accurate images of Eastern dress were also brought to Europe by agents expert in visual knowledge. Gentile Bellini (c. 1429–c. 1507), for example, spent fourteen months between September 1479 and November 1480 as court painter in Constantinople, where he painted the portrait of Mehmet II now in the National Gallery.[15] The drawings and sketches he carried back to Venice, exemplified by the famous depiction of the Janissary in the British Museum, represent visual ideas that were to be used some 25 years later in one of two huge canvases undertaken by Gentile for the Scuola di San Marco, the *St Mark Preaching in Alexandria*, completed after his death in 1507[16] by his brother Giovanni.

This picture, now in the Brera, shows us a wide city square not unlike the Piazza di San Marco, but identified as Alexandrian by the fact that Pompey's Pillar and an obelisk are visible in the background, along with figures in Eastern clothing, a camel, a giraffe and some fantastic minarets. At the leftmost quarter of the foreground, the saint stands on a stepped podium, preaching anachronistically to an audience of a hundred or so men and women in Turkish costume, while a couple of dozen sober Venetians bear witness behind him. The well-known *Venetian Embassy to Damascus* in the Louvre, which depicts Eastern and Western officials in ceremonial dress, and the idealised portrait of Sultan Qaitbay (r. 1468–1498) in the Uffizi, which shows the aged Mamluk ruler in a fur-trimmed robe of honour, were probably both produced in a Bellini workshop during the same era.

The well-known depictions of Turks or Arabs produced during this period by artists such as Giorgione (1476/8–1510)[17] and Raphaël (1483–1520)[18] are idealised, but show knowledge of Eastern costume. Especially gorgeous, however, thanks to detailed treatment of rich textiles, are the Eastern costumes of several kinds depicted among the frescoes in the Sala dei Santi of the Borgia Apartments at the Vatican, painted for Pope Alexander VI Borgia by Pinturicchio (c. 1454–1515) and his assistants sometime between 1492 and 1494. The fresco of St Sebastian's martyrdom shows a seated Janissary[19] directing the toxophily and the *Disputa di Santa Catarina*, based upon another Alexandrian subject, includes depictions of Mamluks and an equestrian portrait in full Ottoman finery of Cem Sultan, who had been living in the Vatican since 1486 and was to die in Naples a year or so later.

In 1509, the recently crowned 18-year-old Henry VIII wore Turkish dress – a robe of *baldachin* (brocade woven of silk and gold – powdered with gold and a headdress of crimson velvet with rolls of gold) to a banquet at Westminster. His daughter Elizabeth I (r. 1558–1603) frequently wore Turkish clothes, though she preferred to dress *à l'italienne*.[20] She was presented with a Turkish wardrobe by Sultana Safiya, the Venetian beauty of the Baffo family who was captured by corsairs and became not only the chief consort of Murat II (r. 1574–95), but also the mother and regent of Mehmet III (r. 1595–1603), sovereigns with whom Elizabeth sought military alliances against Spain.[21] Nor was Turkish influence confined to the Court during her reign: William Harrison's popular and lively *Description of England* (1587) declares that English fashion was as likely to draw inspiration from Turkish or Moorish modes as from French or German ones.[22] Under James I young gentlemen even sported headgear modelled upon the Ottoman turban.[23]

Western travellers in the Middle East during the seventeenth century therefore felt no inhibitions about dressing in local clothing. Fynes Morrison mentions wearing Turkish clothing in his account of a journey to the Levant made in 1596;[24] and Van Dyke painted the portrait (1609–1610) of Sir Robert Sherley that now hangs at Petworth 'in full Persian dress, which he always wore'.[25] The earliest surviving published engraving of a European in Turkish clothes is apparently the frontispiece added to the 1632 abridged edition of William Lithgow's *Peregrinade from Scotland to the Most Famous Kingdomes in Europe, Asia, and Affricke*, first published in 1614.[26] Sir Henry Blount (1602–82) tells us that he was 'clad in the Turkish manner during his voyage to the Levant in 1634' and Thomas Smith reports the same in 1678.[27]

During the eighteenth century, more Westerners than ever wore Turkish clothing within the Ottoman Empire, then carried Ottoman fashions back to the capitals of the West, where they soon came to feed a mania. In 1699, a young Flemish painter, Jean-Baptiste Vanmour (1671–1737), was included in the entourage of Charles de Ferriol, the newly appointed French ambassador to the Sublime Porte. Vanmour's job was to record Turkish costumes, manners and customs and to document Ferriol's mission. In 1711, Ferriol returned to France where, between 1712 and 1715, he published Vanmour's paintings of Ottoman clothing in a celebrated series of engravings, which was widely pirated and counterfeited.[28]

Vanmour himself remained in Constantinople, however, for the rest of his life. Appointed 'peintre ordinaire du Roi en Levant' in 1725, he meanwhile undertook commissions from other patrons, such as William Sherrard (1659–1728), consul at Smyrna for the India

Company from 1708 to 1715, Sir Edward Wortley Montagu, the British Ambassador from 1716 to 1718, and Cornelis Calkoen, the Dutch Ambassador, who collected the sixty paintings now in the Rijksmuseum. Vanmour painted many of the foreign community in Turkish costume and became the most important visual chronicler of the eclectic hedonism of the Tulip Period (1718–30).[29]

Displayed in the Victoria and Albert Museum is one of the Turkish dresses Lady Mary Wortley Montagu wore daily during her stay in Constantinople, on the eve of the Tulip Period.[30] Among several portraits of her in Turkish attire, painted after her return to England, the best known is the one by Jonathan Richardson in the collection of the Earl of Harrowby at Sandon Hall.[31] Lady Mary's madcap son, Edward Wortley Montagu (1713–76), an Arabist, was converted to Islam, and wore Eastern clothing not only during his stays in Egypt, Syria and Turkey (1762–73) but throughout his final years in Padua and Venice, where he 'lived like a Turk and received visitors sitting on the floor'.[32] So, the portrait of him by George Romney (1735–1802), though painted in Venice during the artist's tour of Italy (1773–5), shows him dressed in Turkish clothes.[33]

The Swiss pastelist, Jean-Étienne Liotard (1702–89), was taken to Constantinople by Lord Bessborough in 1738.[34] His work there is exemplified by the full-length portrait in the Musée d'Art et d'Histoire in Geneva of the Right Reverend Richard Pococke (1704–65), an important traveller, dressed in the Oriental costume he wore during his year-long tour of the Middle East in 1737–8.[35] In the same museum, and dating from the same epoch, are several other portraits by Liotard of subjects in Turkish dress, including a 'Femme franque vêtue à la turque et sa servante.' After his return to Western Europe in 1742, Liotard continued both to wear a beard and Turkish clothing himself, and to paint portraits of royal and noble sitters wearing Turkish clothing, which had come into vogue as part of a general rage for *turquoiserie*.

This Turcomania started in 1721, when the Grand Vezir, Damat Ibrahim Pasha, sent Yirmisekiz Çelebi zâde Mehmet Effendi at the head of a major embassy to the court of Philippe d'Orléans, whose brief regency (1715–23) paralleled the Tulip Period in both time and taste. For the next six decades or so, the polite and cultivated classes of Europe delighted in the Turkish Novel and Turkish Tale[36] (one might recall that the garden in Voltaire's *Candide* [1759] ends his days cultivating is in fact in Turkey), the Turkish Comedy,[37] the Turkish Opera,[38] interior decoration and even architecture *à la turque*, not to mention Turkish picnics and masquerade balls.[39] One of the more lasting influences during this period came from Turkish military bands: they demonstrated the use of cymbals, the triangle and the bass drum to Mozart, Haydn and other makers of Western martial music, in which it has remained a permanent feature.[40]

At the height of the eighteenth-century Turcomania, even untravelled artists, such as Boucher (1703–70), Jean-Baptiste Leprince, Lancret (1690–1743), Étienne Jeaurat, Jacques de Lajoüe and Jacques Aved (1702–66), made portraits of such models as the Marquise de Sainte-Maure, the Marquise de Pleumartin, the Marquise de Bonne and the Comtesse de Magnac in authentic Turkish dress, while Fragonard (1732–1806) would paint a series of erotically idealised sultans and sultanas.[41] In Venice in 1741 or 1742, the Saxon soldier of fortune, Marshal Count Johann-Mathias von der Schulenberg (d.1747), hired Francesco (1712–93) and Giovanni-Antonio Guardi (1699–1760) to paint fourteen new versions of costumes and settings by Vanmour.[42] For his patroness, Mme de Pompadour (who became the Louis XV's *maîtresse en titre* in 1745), Carle van Loo (1705–65) painted three decorative works in which Turkish costumes clothe ideal figures in Neo-Classic settings.[43] Liotard now made portraits in Turkish garb of such highly placed subjects as Maria Gunning, Duchess of Coventry[44] and Princess Marie-Adelaide (1732–1800), fourth daughter of Louis XV and the only one actually to be reared at Court. Meanwhile another generation of artists, such as Antoine de Favray, went to Constantinople (1762) to paint another generation of foreign dignitaries, such as Mme de Vergennes, the wife of the French ambassador, wearing Oriental dress.

In England, likewise, which he visited in 1754–5 and in 1772–4, Liotard painted ladies of the nobility and gentry in Turkish dress. His local rivals and imitators in the same costume portrait genre included major painters such as Joshua Reynolds (1724–92), Romney (as noted above) and John Singleton Copley (1738–1815), as well as minor ones such as Joseph Highmore (1692–1780), Francis Cotes (1724–70) and George Willison, whose portrait of the successful *demi-mondaine*, Nancy Parsons, is based upon Liotard's portrait of a lady presumed to be the Duchess of Coventry.[45]

Equally significant in England as a testament to its familiarity, however, were more ephemeral appearances of Turkish clothing for both men and women, at such occasions as masked balls, routs and receptions. One of the more important was the Oriental Ball given in 1768, at the Haymarket Theatre in London, by Christian VII, the mad king of Denmark, where three-quarters of the guests wore Turkish dress.[46] (Conversation must have touched upon the Danish scientific expedition that Christian's predecessor Frederik V had sent to the Middle East in 1761. Its sole survivor had only recently returned: Karsten Niebuhr, who owed his life to a sound constitution and Arab clothing.)[47] The Turkish reception given by William Beckford in 1781, at Fonthill Abbey, which he had completely transformed for the event, was an occasion so inimitable that it probably marks the end of the era of Turcomania.

To the motive of compulsion as a reason for a Westerner to wear Eastern clothes, we can now add motives that pertained outside the Middle East, but also certainly had their place within the Ottoman world: aesthetics, fashion, personal inclination and the wish to contribute to a spirit of festivity – motives that in the Arabic of Egypt would rightly be ascribed to *mazāg* or a sense of *fantaziyyah*.[48]

When Thomas Hope stood for his portrait for Sir William Beechey in 1799, four years after his return from Istanbul, he was signalling a new and different set of European fashions, attitudes, emotions and aesthetic ideas. Beechey's portrait of Hope (now in the National Portrait Gallery) and likenesses of such celebrities as Byron, painted in Albanian dress by Thomas Philips in 1814,[49] embody the high drama of the Romantic era and testify to motives that have little to do with compulsion, nothing whatever to do with disguise and a great deal to do with a heroic sense of the human ego – with swagger and bravura. In mood and spirit they parallel the great Bonapartist propaganda pieces of Baron Gros, and point to motives of display diametrically opposed to either compulsion or disguise. Certainly neither was the motive of those young Russian officers on service in the Caucasus, exemplified in the careers and writings of Pushkin, Lermontov and Tolstoy, who took so enthusiastically to wearing the *beshmet*, *cherkeska* and *qalpaq* of the Muslim tribes.

'As regards that noble battle garb', writes Pechorin, Lermontov's 'hero of our time', on a fictional date of 16 May, in the 1830s, 'I am an absolute dandy: not one bit of superfluous braid; costly arms in plain setting; the fur of the cap neither too long nor too short; leggings and boots fitted with the utmost exactitude; a white *beshmet*; a dark-brown *cherkeska*.'[50] Stationed in the Caucasus in the early 1850s, Tolstoy noted that for a Cossack 'to be smartly dressed means to be dressed like a Circassian'.[51] Circassian clothing not only became 'typically Cossack', but ultimately displaced the baggy trousers gathered at the bottom that had earlier been the chief visual index of Cossackdom, and were thus historically and ethnically more authentic. Worn by the Cossack troops that occupied Paris in 1814 and 1815, these baggy trousers became an item of French dandyish fashion in the late 1830s. They are thus depicted in the caricatures of Gavarni[52] and figure in the first chapter of Flaubert's *Éducation Sentimentale*, fictionally dated to 14 September 1840. They then re-entered Russia as the latest Parisian mode.

Other armies had meanwhile already been penetrated by Turkish influence in their dress and accoutrements, as they had been earlier by Turkish music, through the mediation of military fashion along the Ottoman Empire's Central and Eastern European marches. New regiments of light cavalry, raised on Eastern models, replaced horsemen in heavy armour; and the Central Asian *qilij*, renamed *szabla* or *sablya* among Slavs and *száblya* among Magyars, made its way westward to become the sabre, their standard weapon. The most dashing and colourful of these new cavalry formations were hussar regiments, a feature of every major European army, whose uniform included a truncated version of the Turkish *dolman*, called by that name and generally worn draped over the left shoulder, like a robe of honour.

The army with which Napoleon Bonaparte invaded and occupied Egypt in 1798 had as its major mission the imposition of European culture upon Egypt, and was therefore never given the option of dressing in the oriental style. A cheap print, made for propaganda purposes, shows the general himself in a robe and turban, but he is said on the unimpeachable authority of Fauvelet de Bourrienne, his private secretary, to have tried the experiment only once and then very briefly. He tells us that Bonaparte had Turkish dress made, with which he surprised his staff one day at breakfast:

> As soon as he was recognized he was received with a loud burst of laughter. He sat down very coolly, but he found himself so encumbered by his turban and Oriental robe that he speedily threw them off, and was never tempted to a second performance of the masquerade.[53]

Bonaparte's invading French, however, were virtually the sole and obvious exception to a long-standing rule. Burckhardt actually arrived in the Middle East in 1809, after the French departure, already wearing Oriental clothing and never wore anything else until his death in Cairo eight years later. In 1815, Burckhardt met the great Belzoni, who is portrayed wearing Egyptian dress in Gauchi's frontispiece to his *Narrative of the Operations and Recent Discoveries within the Pyramids, Temples, Tombs and Excavations, in Egypt and Nubia*.[54] Among the many portraits of early nineteenth-century Western residents in the Middle East reproduced by Sarah Searight in *The British in the Middle East*, virtually none is shown in anything other than the local dress that was customary for foreigners during the period.[55] And even while condemning the practice, Leila Ahmed admits that for Western travellers or residents in Egypt to don Eastern clothing was 'almost a routine practice'.[56]

Among the English travellers in Egypt between 1815 and 1820 who published books during the 1820s, she notes that Charles Irby (1789–1845) and James Mangles (1786–1867), who were in Egypt in 1817–18,[57] and William Rae Wilson (1772–1849), who was in Egypt in 1819,[58] all record that they habitually wore Arab or Turkish clothes in Egypt. So does Dr Robert Richardson (1779–1847),[59] who accompanied Viscount Mountjoy and the Earl of Belmore as their physician during their travels throughout the Middle East between 1816 and 1819 and attended Burckhardt on his deathbed. Not mentioned by Leila Ahmed was an earlier English traveller of the same era, John Maxwell, also portrayed in Eastern dress.[60] An important French arrival in 1817 was Louis Nicolas, Philippe Auguste, Comte de Forbin, accompanied by the 18-year-old Louis-Maurice-Adolphe Linant de Bellefonds, who was destined to stay on in Cairo at the service of several vice-regal governments, to be elevated to the ranks of bey and pasha and to wear Turkish clothing until the day he died in 1883, decades after Western garb had become the upper-class Egyptian norm.

To this list may be added John Madox, who visited Egypt, Nubia and Syria in 1822, 1823, 1824, 1827 and 1829,[61] and Dr Richard Robert Madden, a long-term resident of Alexandria, author of *Travels in Turkey, Egypt, Nubia, and Palestine, in 1824, 1825, 1826, and 1827* (published in 1829 and 1833).[62] Leila Ahmed quotes Dr Madden, 'Arabs despise us more for our apparel than they even hate us for our creed: our tight clothes appear to them not only ridiculous, but indecent; and it is their general impression that our garments make us look like monkeys.' He also remarks that he himself found 'Oriental costume ... decidedly best adapted to the climate.'[63]

Dr Madden customarily dressed in Turkish clothes, as did virtually all foreigners in the Arab world. Resident in Egypt during the years between 1815 and 1840 in anything other than an official diplomatic position, Edward W. Lane would have had to have been quite eccentric not to wear some form of local dress. Jason Thompson has shown that such clothing was normally one of the first acquisitions of any foreign male after his arrival, and has published plates showing Lane's friends, Gardner Wilkinson and Robert Hay, with two of Hay's artists in Turkish dress and two servants in Arab clothing.[64]

Edward William Lane was not obliged by law to dress as an Ottoman during his three stays in Cairo (1825–8, 1833–5, and 1842–9), but did so out of choice, clothing himself in the costume worn by most townsmen throughout the Ottoman Empire, which was 35 per cent Christian, and even beyond its borders; Braudel has observed that, 'wherever the strength and influence of the Osmanli sultans made itself felt the upper classes adopted their costume – in far-off Algeria and in Christian Poland, where Turkish fashions only belatedly gave way (and then imperfectly) to French fashion in the eighteenth century.'[65]

During the first half of the nineteenth century, elements of Ottoman-style formal clothing were thus still worn by the magnates of Eastern Europe – not just the Orthodox *boyars* of Ottoman Wallachia and Moldavia, who have left us their magnificent robed and turbaned portraits, but also their Protestant and Catholic German and Magyar neighbours in Hungarian Transylvania and the Puszta and the great landowners of Croatia, Slavonia, Slovakia, Galicia, Ruthenia, Bukovina, Volhynia, the Ukraine, Bessarabia, the Crimea and the Caucasus. We have also seen that Turkish clothing had been perfectly familiar to the urban inhabitants of Western Europe throughout the previous hundred years and posed no mysteries.

The portraits of Mangles and Irby, painted by Jean-Baptiste Borely in 1819, show them in full formal Turkish dress, with robes of honour, an old-fashioned mode that rapidly disappeared after 1826.[66] Lane and other visitors to early-nineteenth-century Egypt dressed in the simpler everyday costume worn by Christian and Muslim males throughout the

Empire, as common in Saloniki, Sofia, Belgrade, Bucharest or Jassy as in Constantinople, Smyrna, Trebizond, Jerusalem or Damascus and worn by a large non-Egyptian minority in Cairo. In Cairo between 1825 and 1835, such a costume was not native, of course, but it was certainly local and extremely common, since it was worn by the innumerable employees of Muhammad Ali, including his military officers, as well as by Ottoman subjects from Europe and other male foreign residents. It was therefore relatively unobtrusive, which was its primary advantage for foreigners. Lane was quite conscious, however, of the fact that dressing as an Ottoman citizen merely made him a different kind of foreigner in Egypt and could not in any way 'disguise' him as an Egyptian.[67]

The single feature that distinguishes Turkish clothing unconditionally from Arab or Egyptian dress is trousers. In this simple costume, the trousers were not the great billowing bloomers (*caqçir*) that were an official part of Ottoman formal dress until 1826, but the baggy *sirwāl* (Arabic, pl. *sarāwīl*; *shurwal* in Lane's version) or Turkish *shalvar*, gathered below the knee Nizami-style. *Sarāwīl* were still visible in Bulgaria, Palestine and Syria, in the mountains of Lebanon, and on the north coast of Egypt, as well as in Turkey itself, a mere thirty years ago and are still worn in Anatolia and further east to this day, as testified recently in person by the young travel writer William Dalrymple.[68]

We know exactly what costume Lane wore during his final seven-year stay in Egypt because a suit of his clothes was presented to the Ashmolean Museum by a member of the Lane family in 1983.[69] It consists of woollen trousers, a matching jacket, a long-sleeved waistcoat, a cotton shirt, cotton underdrawers, a cotton cummerbund and a cotton skull-cap. One obvious missing element is a *tarboosh* – they are extremely perishable items – and no formal outer robes seem to have survived.

Any outer robes would not have been much used, of course, since Lane devoted himself throughout the entire seven years exclusively to his great Arabic–English Lexicon, and sometimes, according to Jason Thompson, 'did not leave home for months on end. He later boasted to his friend Wilkinson that he took less than half a week of holidays during the entire seven years.'[70] That in such thoroughly sequestered privacy, far from the possibility of any encounter with any unknown Muslim, Coptic or Turkish strangers, Lane should, nevertheless, have chosen to wear Ottoman clothing demonstrates conclusively that his intention in doing so could hardly have been 'disguise'. All Lane's English friends likewise dressed *à la turque*. James Webster, for example, who visited Egypt during Lane's first stay, records being turned away by servants from the house shared by Hay's associates, Charles Humphreys and James Burton, because he was dressed in *afrangi* clothes. Humphreys eventually 'received us, quite in the Turkish fashion', however, says Webster, and a visit was arranged. Of James Burton, who had travelled up the Nile with Lane, Webster observes not only that he was dressed in Eastern clothing, but that he also 'has a beard of great length, wears his feet bare, and is, to all appearances, a perfect Turk'. Spending the same evening with Hay, who lived in the house next door, he there 'met seven Englishmen, all dressed in the Turkish fashion'.[71] A high-handed attempt in 1822 by Henry Salt, British consul general from 1815 to 1827, to curtail the wearing of local dress by British citizens had clearly been ill-advised and was foredoomed to failure.

Champollion's triumphant tour of Egypt took place during the same era, and Nestor L'Hôte records in *Sur le Nil avec Champollion* that he and the great Egyptologist both had their heads shaved, allowed their moustaches to grow and dressed up in Turkish clothing, including the baggy trousers. Diane Harlé has most graciously shown me copies of L'Hôte's accounts, which provide the price paid for each item.[72] Later he observes:

> The gravity of our physiognomy no doubt impresses the Muslims... or more likely they are simply accustomed to seeing Europeans in Oriental dress. So far nothing has happened to us like what happened to some English travellers, who wore the costume with such clumsy inappropriateness that they were believed to be making fun of the inhabitants; and the first time they displayed themselves in it were so roughly handled that they returned home nearly naked.[73]

That such vehement reactions to clothing at this period are, indeed, culturally specific, but have nothing to do with Islam, is demonstrated by the experience of Hugh Clapperton, who explored Muslim West Africa on behalf of the Africa Association during precisely the same decade. In 1824, as Robin Hanbury-Tenison describes it:

> Clapperton found himself about to become the first European to enter Kano. He dressed in his best naval uniform and made himself as smart as circumstances would permit. Then, expecting to make a

tremendous impression on people who had never seen a British officer, he strode into town. 'Alas! I might have spared all the pains I had taken with my toilet; for not an individual turned their head to gaze at me.'[74]

It should also be noted that the further eastward Europeans went, the less they adopted local costume. With the exception of Sir Robert Sherley, few travellers in Persia seem to have taken to Persian dress; and in the Indian subcontinent, Westerners merely added their own styles to a vast repertoire of dress that ranged from near nudity to the regally monumental, and in substance from a cotton string or a garland of flowers to elaborate constructions of the utmost complexity and sumptuousness.

One motive for dressing in local costume was the wish for comfort, though in this respect the flowing cotton of the native *gallabiyya* was far more suitable than the Turkish *fustian* of wool. The *gallabiyya* is still worn by many foreign residents in Egypt in the privacy of their own homes. An additional motive for Lane was, undoubtedly, an intention to remove the most obvious barrier between himself and his neighbours, incidentally forestalling the mutual anonymity that is necessary for the more virulent manifestations of class-hatred and xenophobia. A primary motive among all European travellers and residents, however, including Lane, was the simple hope of securing relative safety and freedom from insult in public places. Henry Blount recorded, in 1634, that unless he wore Turkish clothes on his travels through the Ottoman Empire, he could expect to be treated 'like an Owle among other birds'.[75] Lane's English friends in Cairo two centuries later all knew instances of insult, injury and even murder due directly to someone's having worn Frankish clothes.[76] Sarah Searight rightly remarks that 'adoption of local costume was often essential for reasons of safety'.[77]

Xenophobia is correctly presumed by natives of the Middle East to be an ordinary component of daily life, and, as such, it is thoroughly familiar to every serious student of the region, both from research and from first-hand experience. 'In Egypt', an Egyptian expert on tourism has observed, 'the visitor, irrespective of his position or rank, is always suspect'.[78] Tourist industry propaganda and the myth of 'Arab hospitality' notwithstanding, the reception of unarmed strangers, native or foreign, has traditionally been unfriendly. As late as the 1970s, casual and unprovoked stonings of private motor vehicles were common in Egypt, even along main roads close to Cairo; and in the city itself gangs of schoolchildren were apt to stone strangers, Egyptian or foreign. Nor is it paradoxical that Cairo then was otherwise probably the safest metropolis in the world, as it is now. Many towns and villages – Rashid (Rosetta), Bassatin, Al-Lahun, Bani Suwayf or Armant, for example – still have well-deserved reputations for hostility to strangers.

Egyptian reactions to the murder and mutilation of 58 unarmed foreign tourists by Muslim fanatics at Luxor in November 1997 ignored the suffering of the victims and their families and focused on local damage control. The butchery was deplored by the government as an affront to its dignity and to national prestige, bemoaned by the people of Luxor as a devastating blow to the local economy and denounced by the Egyptian middle class as an appalling demonstration of what happens when the lower orders are not sufficiently repressed; and in at least one working-class area of Cairo it was greeted with glee.[79]

That parts of Egypt were no more hospitable two centuries or so ago than they are today is plentifully recorded by ordinary transients such as Eliza Fay, as well as by seasoned adventurers such as James Silk Buckingham. Passing through Egypt in 1779, Eliza Fay records being attacked by brigands en route from Alexandria to Cairo and threatened with death by the authorities in Cairo, lest she and her compatriots should reveal to the world at large that the most recent Cairo–Suez caravan of Western travellers had been plundered and most of its passengers slaughtered.[80] Buckingham visited Egypt in 1813–14, just a decade earlier than Lane, met Burckhardt and Belzoni, and endured, among other adventures, being attacked, pillaged, stripped and left for dead on the shores of the Red Sea.[81]

The autocratic exertions of Muhammad Ali had made a considerable difference, however, even by as early as 1806.[82] By 1824, Egypt was undoubtedly safer than much of southern Italy, where the indomitable C.T. Ramage declared:

> I cannot say I am sorry I am now to be bidding adieu to Calabria, though I have every reason to be grateful for the kind and hospitable manner with which I have been almost invariably received. Still it is harassing to be constantly in the expectation of being either robbed or murdered, and during several hours of the day I was fully prepared to encounter some such fate.[83]

In 1830, Léon de Laborde could note that 'the Bedouins are so well restrained under the rule of the Pacha [Muhammad Ali] that a Frank may travel without any obstruction in a round hat and frock coat'. He advised the travelling Frank not to try to do so, however, but to 'live after the fashion of the country'.[84] (The Marquis de Laborde's guide was Linant de Bellefonds, now over thirty, who knew every part of the country, spoke its languages, and himself dressed habitually, as already noted, in Turkish clothes.)

By 1835, Syria and the *pashalik* of Adana had been added to Muhammad Ali's enormous fiefdom, which was already larger than any of the several empires recorded throughout five thousand years of Egyptian history. Alexander Kinglake was, therefore, able to travel from Beirut all the way to Cairo and back in European clothes, accompanied only by two dragomans and various drovers, without molestation, if not without consciousness that what he was doing was occasionally still risky. He writes in Chapter 24 of *Eōthen*:

> Nablus is the very furnace of Mohammedan bigotry, and I believe that only a few months before the time of my going there it would have been madly rash for a man, unless strongly guarded, to show himself to the people of the town in a Frank costume, but since their insurrection the Mohammedans of the place had been so far subdued by the severity of Ibrahim Pasha that they dared not now offer the slightest insult to a European. It was quite clear, however, that the effort with which the men of the old school refrained from expressing their opinion of a hat or a coat was horribly painful to them. As I walked through the streets or the bazaars a dead silence prevailed.

In Chapter 27, he writes: 'Until a year or two before the time of my going there, Damascus had kept up so much of the old bigot zeal against Christians, or rather against Europeans, that no one dressed as a Frank could have dared to show himself on the streets.'[85] Kinglake ascribes a good deal of the change in Damascus not only to vigorous intimidation on the part of Muhammad Ali and Ibrahim Pasha, but also to the British consul's refusal to be humiliated, and concludes that 'Damascus was safer than Oxford.'[86]

Kinglake's nineteen-day stay in Cairo, in the spring of 1835, coincided with the height of an outbreak of plague. He met and used the services of the famous Osman Effendi, one of whose wives was to die before the middle of May. He missed meeting E.W. Lane, who had retreated to Upper Egypt to escape the disease and who might have explained that Cairo, the seat of an empire, had already undergone the kind of changes that still lay in the future for its Syrian provinces.

E.W. Lane wrote in the diary of his second sojourn in Egypt, 1833–5:

> Formerly a grandee of Musr, with his retinue of twenty or more well-rounded men, clad in habits of various & brilliant hues, & with splendid accoutrements, the saddles covered with embroidered velvet, & plates of gilt & embossed silver, & the bridles, head-bells and other trappings ornamented in a similar manner, & with rows of gold coins suspended to them, presented a strikingly picturesque and pompous spectacle. Sights of this description are no longer witnessed in the Egyptian metropolis. Even the Ba'sha, when he occasionally rides through the streets, is followed by only three or four attendants, & is not more distinguished by the habits than by the number of his retinue. As dark colours, and particularly black, are now fashionable among the Turks & their dresses are generally embroidered with silk, instead of gold lace, there is much less contrast and variety observable in the costumes of the passengers in the crowded streets.[87]

Though David Roberts records being officially required to wear Turkish clothing in Egyptian mosques in 1839 and 1840, it is clear that he usually dressed in European clothing during his travels through the territories ruled by Muhammad Ali, which included not only Egypt, but also Nubia, Palestine and Syria. He wore Arab dress in Sinai, however, and Robert Scott Lauder's well-known portrait of Roberts 'in the dress he wore in Palestine', painted in London soon after his return, shows him clothed in what appears to be old-fashioned Turkish formal dress, and armed with the *qilij* then standard in the Egyptian army.[88] Sarah Searight observes that 'during his tour of the Levant in 1840–41, David Wilkie refused to paint Europeans in the Middle East unless he could portray them in Oriental costume, which most of them would have owned at that time'.[89] Throughout his decade of residence in Cairo, from 1841 to 1851, John Frederick Lewis wore Turkish clothes. In 1843, touring Egypt to make studies and sketches for 23 paintings, the Venetian painter, Ippolito Caffi, wore Arab rather than Turkish clothing.[90]

The great Egyptologist, Richard Lepsius, wore Turkish dress throughout the Prussian Expedition he led through Egypt and Nubia between 1842 and 1845.

The only photograph taken of Flaubert in Egypt, where he toured in 1849–50, shows him wearing a *gallabiyya* topped with a skullcap and a *tarbush*. The latter was recommended by such authorities as Gardner Wilkinson, and was popular even among those tourists who, increasingly from the 1840s onwards, came pre-supplied with European clothes made of flannel.[91] The *tarbush* retained its status as part of formal dress in Egypt until the Revolution, and was required to be worn on official or formal occasions by all senior government officials, including Westerners.

The fashion for local dress otherwise must have died out among Westerners in Egypt in the 1850s, after the Viceroys 'Abbas and Sa'id, like their sovereigns, the sultans, had adopted Western-style dress as the standard, both formally at court and informally in private. The shift to Western-style clothing throughout the Middle East certainly began in the Egyptian and Ottoman armies. Arif Pasha, the retired field-marshal who assembled a classic work on Ottoman court costume, witnessed personally the beginning of the change at the court of Sultan Mahmud, and pinpoints it quite precisely as taking place from 1825 onward, with Sultan Mahmud's reinstatement of Selim III's innovations as his own *Nizam al-Jadid* and his subsequent series of revolutionary reforms, immeasurably speeded up by what is referred to as the 'Auspicious Event', the destruction of the Janissaries, in 1826.[92]

In Egypt, the Nizami style was adopted almost instantly. In the manuscript diary he kept during his second stay in Egypt, 1833–5, E.W. Lane observed that:

> No change has taken place in the costume of the natives, but the military officers & the Turks in the employ of the Ba'sha, have adopted the Niza'mee dress, which was becoming common among them before I last quitted Musr [i.e., in 1828, three years after the official introduction of the style in Turkey].[93]

Sultan Mahmud II subsequently promulgated a whole series of clothing regulations to promote Western-style dress in the army and the civil bureaucracy, all of which were accepted without fuss until he decreed in 1829 that every civil official should wear the fez. 'The 1829 regulations', one scholar has commented, 'whose drama actually matches that of the destruction of the Janissaries, pushed aside a centuries-old Ottoman tradition in which headgear had provided the crucial and central marker of identity, status, and rank.'[94]

The Nizami style came to be widely imitated, even outside the Ottoman Empire. During the Crimean War (1853–6), for example, the Cossacks in their bandoliered *cherkeskas* would have encountered French regiments of Algerian Spahis (from Turkish *sipāhī*) or Zouaves.[95] The uniform of the Zouaves, an adaptation of Nizami dress, but peculiarly typified by a short, round-fronted jacket, was imitated less than a decade later not only by a unit of Papal Guards, but also by several of the Northern regiments in the American Civil War (1861–5). In action or on parade, these Western soldiers must have looked far more Oriental than the Nubian troops that were sent to Napoleon III by Viceroy Sa'id in 1862 and 1863 to support the French invasion and occupation of Mexico.[96]

In a letter written in October 1846, during his last stay in Egypt, Lane linked the changes he saw taking place in the clothing of the ruling class with changes in political and social structures:

> I told you of some instances of the 'march' of European innovation here; the march has now become a gallop. The officers of the Government . . . following the example of Constantinople, have begun to put themselves into the complete Frank dress: frock-coat, waistcoats and trousers, the last as narrow as any of ours . . . The sheykhs are very angry at all this, which they justly regard as indicating more important changes.[97]

Following the lead of the Viceroy and his suzerain, the Sultan, men among the Egyptian upper classes adopted Western-style clothing wholesale. And it was clearly their vigorous and universal endorsement, not any imagined political or military pressure from one of the Western imperialist powers, that ended the abuse of anyone wearing such clothing hitherto traditional throughout the Arab world. In such cities as Cairo or Istanbul, the wearing of Eastern clothing by Western men must have soon begun to look like an affectation, though still advisable for desert travel.

As late as 1857, even transient Europeans in Egypt still at least wore adaptations of Eastern headgear.[98] Two years later, however, Stanley Lane-Poole, Lane's nephew, observed that Muhammad Ali had otherwise swept away entirely the visual grandeur that had pertained under the Fatimids, the Ayyubids, the Mamluks, and the Ottoman governors. He remarked:

> Every day witnesses the decay of some old custom, to be followed by a bastard European imitation . . . European dress has displaced oriental costume, cloth of gold, and dresses of honour: European architecture elbows the quaint beauty of the old Arab capital: and the cavalcade of fifty horsemen around a grandee is succeeded by an English carriage that profanes the quiet streets of the city, and frightens away both 'Efreets and their memory.[99]

In making such complaints, Lane-Poole was merely echoing sentiments that his uncle had recorded two decades earlier.

In Upper Egypt, older ways doubtless lingered, as they do today. In 1860, for example, Prisse d'Avennes and his collaborator Jarrot wore Turkish clothes as their ordinary dress in Upper Egypt and were sketched in this costume by Willem de Famars as they worked in the temples at Luxor, copying inscriptions for Prisse's *Atlas de l'Histoire de l'Art Égyptien*.[100] In Cairo or in Istanbul, however, even before the accession of Isma'il in 1863, Westerners who wore Eastern clothing had already begun to do so either in privacy, as did Linant de Bellefonds, or in the obscurity of remoter suburbs, as 'Pierre Loti' would at Egypt in 1876–7[101] or Wilfrid Scawen Blunt would at Shaykh 'Ubayd as late as 1905.

Outside the immediate penumbra of Egyptian or Ottoman culture and political power, according to all accounts, lawless violence remained the norm. In light of the dangers that continued to be commonplace in such areas before 1914, it is particularly stupid to blame someone who took the precaution of wearing Eastern clothing there for being 'in disguise'. Jane Digby, for example, was wearing European clothes when she arrived in Jerusalem and Damascus in 1853, but her Arab husband-to-be insisted that she leave them behind when they set out across the desert for the first time to Palmyra, 'for not only were they impractical, but they would create unnecessary danger'.[102] Lord Dalkeith and his party had been attacked on the same route only six months earlier, robbed and held for ransom. The remainder of Jane Digby's life, until her death in 1881, was to be a chronicle of bloody religious strife, official injustice and raids and counter-raids, interspersed with arms-buying expeditions. Travellers in Syria and Palestine were warned by Baedeker to go armed as late as 1898, 'Weapons are unnecessary on the main routes, but indispensable on the others.'[103]

What might be expected in remoter parts of Egypt when there was an absence of viceregal power was exemplified in 1882, the year before Linant de Bellefonds' death, by the fate of E.H. Palmer, the Arabist, and his four companions, Captain William Gill, Lieutenant Harold Charrington, Khalil Atik and Bakhur Hassun. Though certainly charged with a 'secret mission' in Sinai, during the anarchy immediately preceding the British Occupation, they were murdered by *badw* of the Dabur and Tarabin clans for their money and material possessions, not for anything resembling patriotism or for political motives. The three Englishmen all wore Western clothes, rags of which were found with their scattered remains.

Wilfrid Scawen and Lady Anne Blunt both wore Arab clothing throughout their excursions among the *badw* during the years 1876–9. They met Jane Digby in 1878, which was one of the worst years for tribal warfare in the Syrian desert. For safety's sake, Lady Anne dressed as a man, though she rode, in fact, side-saddle. Two decades later, in 1897, Blunt, on his own, made a haphazard and ill-fated trip to Siwah wearing Arab dress, armed with letters of credence describing him as 'Naif ibn al-Hajj Mahmud ibn al-Hajj Batran al-Halabi'. The excursion ended in disaster, chiefly because Blunt allowed himself to be persuaded by a *badawi* shaykh to assume this preposterous 'disguise' among tribes that were traditionally pro-British, a fact humiliatingly pointed out by no less a figure than Lord Cromer. At Shaykh 'Ubayd, this antinomian champion of Egyptian, Indian and Irish nationalism anticipated today's obsessions with sun, sand and recreational sex by a hundred years. In his generally successful campaigns of seduction, he deployed an arsenal of blandishment in which blarney and moonlit nights were backed up by deep cushions, bare feet and Bedouin clothing. At Crabbet or Newbuildings, Blunt continued not only to wear *badawi* robes occasionally himself, but to supply them to such dinner guests as Winston Churchill, until his death in 1922.[104]

Our list of motives that have inspired Westerners to wear Middle Eastern clothes now ranges from official compulsion through aesthetic indulgence and dandyish display to self-defence. With Blunt we can add another: sexual seduction, an activity in which, as centred around

Eastern clothing, Blunt was something of a pioneer, and which was to appear as a cultural motif repeatedly during the generation after his death, from the end of the 1914–18 War until 1948. It is visible as a theme in a wonderful series of Hollywood films, beginning with *Kismet* (1920) and *The Sheik* (1921), and continuing with *The Thief of Bagdad* (1924), the first of four films with the same name, including an excellent British production in 1940, *Son of the Sheik* (1926), another *Kismet* (1930), *Arabian Nights* (1942), *Ali Baba and the Forty Thieves* (1943), still another *Kismet* (1944) and *Sinbad the Sailor* (1947). These films use an idealised Arab world as a setting that couples the glamour of sexual attraction with the positive values of justice and freedom, but the attention paid to authentic cultural detail, including clothing, is often quite impressive. After the creation of Israel in 1948, Hollywood lost interest, however, and in *Exodus* (1960), in which several characters are supposed to be disguised as Arabs, their appearance is so ludicrously off the mark that in real life they could never have fooled anyone.

We have, then, a wealth of reasons why Westerners used to 'dress native' in the Middle East. Even when they wore Eastern dress for their own safety, however, very few Western travellers over the past two or three centuries can be shown to have thought of themselves as 'disguised' or to have been regarded as such. And certainly, among the thousands of ordinary Westerners who toured the Middle East or were resident there, espionage, enmity, aggression or cultural rivalry have figured so minimally as motives for the way in which they dressed as to be worthless for purposes of general explanation and useless for anything but the erection of an anti-Western myth. In any sane, serious, logically conducted and well-founded consideration of the practice, of the era to which it belongs, or of the history of relations between the East and the West, coarse allegations as to the general importance of such bizarre motivation should be dismissed as an insult to average intelligence. What is one to make, then, of such travellers as Ali Bey al-Abbasi, Burton, Doughty, Isabelle Eberhardt and T.E. Lawrence, all of whom are reputed to have disguised themselves successfully as Arabs and so to have carried out espionage? In a sardonic note, Burton observes:

> Ali Bey has not been duly appreciated. In the first place, his disguise was against him: and secondly, he was a spy of the French Government. According to Mr. [William John] Bankes [1786–1855], who had access to the original papers at Constantinople, Ali Bey was a

Catalonian named Badia, and was suspected of being of Jewish extraction. He claimed from Napoleon a reward for his services, returned to the East, and died, it is supposed, of poison in the Haurán, near Damascus. In the edition I have consulted (Paris, 1814) the author labours to persuade the world . . . that he is a real Oriental, but he perpetually betrays himself.[105]

Ali Bey presents himself throughout his narrative as an Arab Muslim;[106] and it should be noted that although Burton derides his ability to pass as an Arab, he does not question either Ali Bey's accuracy as an observer or his religious faith.[107]

Burton may conceivably have been on some sort of intelligence mission and was certainly in 'disguise' when he made his pilgrimage to Madinah and Mecca (1853).[108] But he was also a Muslim,[109] entitled in every respect to make the pilgrimage; and the main purpose of his 'disguise' was not to give him access to places otherwise forbidden to him, but to obviate the humiliations and dangers inevitably consequent on being recognised as a European and thus as presumptively a mere convert, 'an object of suspicion to many and of contempt to all'.[110] Even 25 years later, Burton's apprehensions were confirmed by John F. Keane, who made the pilgrimage in 1877–8 and describes being mobbed.[111]

Doughty spoke fluent Arabic, but advertised the fact that he was a Christian Frank at every opportunity.[112] Consequently, as recorded in *Arabia Deserta* – and much to Burton's disgust – *badawi* Arabs never treated him more civilly than with contemptuous forbearance. The fact that he dressed as a Syrian undoubtedly had no positive influence whatever on them. Thanks both to his own abrasive and uncompanionable nature and to their hostility, for which he sometimes seemed to plead, he barely escaped death by violence or starvation on several occasions.[113]

The Russian Muslim, Isabelle Eberhardt (1877–1904) consciously 'disguised' herself throughout her stays in Algeria and Morocco. Her chief interest, however, was less to be taken for an Arab than to be taken for a man. Her brilliant biographer, Annette Kobak, has shown that Isabelle Eberhardt's assumption of Arab dress was the extension of a deep-seated personal impulse towards transvestism, which appeared first during her adolescence in Switzerland and soon became a habit. Her later assumption of Algerian or Moroccan clothing arose when this impulse coalesced with anarchist ideology, neurosis, poverty, mysticism and a French political programme. As Kobak says:

Isabelle retained a touch of European naivety in failing to realise that the Arabs' acceptance of her disguise often reflected their face-saving tact, rather than the success of her own camouflage. She was certain, for example, that Salah and her subsequent guides took her at face value as Si Mahmoud Saadi, the young Tunisian journeying from *zawiya* to *zawiya*, in the long tradition of students in search of Koranic truth, but the highly realistic Randau [i.e. her friend the Algerian-born writer Robert Arnaud] later maintained (and Isabelle eventually realised) that the Arabs with whom she was in contact for any length of time always knew perfectly well that she was a woman, and a European, but went along out of discretion with how she chose to present herself.

And Kobak quotes Arnaud as remarking:

> All of them knew that this svelte cavalier in her immaculate white burnoose and soft red leather boots was a woman. The innate courtesy of the Arabs is such that in her presence none of them ever made any allusion, even by so much as a wink to a quality she did not want to acknowledge.[114]

The only person ever fooled by Isabelle Eberhardt's disguises, it would appear, was Isabelle herself.

Of T.E. Lawrence it can be said with reasonable assurance that he never wore a disguise except in one instance – an instance, however, that is probably a fiction. As he told John Buchan in 1927, he wore European clothes throughout his walking tours in Syria before the war, though he adds that he wore 'Arab kit on one or two short treks after forbidden antiquities'.[115] His sartorial practice during the war is summarised in Article 18 of the 'Twenty-Seven Articles' he published for the use of British intelligence officers in August 1917. It reads as follows:

> Disguise is not advisable. Except in special areas let it be known that you are a British officer and a Christian. At the same time if you can wear Arab kit when with the tribes you will acquire their trust and intimacy to a degree impossible in uniform.[116]

This advice, for its time, place and circumstances, seems absolutely sound. After the war, in a letter sent to W.S. Sterling on 28 June 1919, Lawrence declared that less than three months after having written this very clear statement of principle against disguise he had deliberately walked out of the Sharifian encampment at Azraq and gone 'into Deraa in disguise to spy out the defenses, was caught', recognised, suffered sexual humiliation, then managed to escape.[117] At a hotel in Paris three weeks later, on 17 July 1919, he repeated the same story to Richard Meinertzhagen.[118]

Lawrence's letter to Stirling a year and half after the alleged fact is the first mention of the famous Deraa incident, the basis of a key episode in *Seven Pillars of Wisdom* that has been invaluable to pop-Freudian dramatists and political propagandists. There is no official evidence of any kind whatever to support Lawrence's personal testimony about the incident, however, which varies in detail from document to document.[119] The fullest version, set in print by *The Oxford Times*, remained in galleys. Its elaborate pacing and detail, involving feats of observation that are anatomically impossible, make it read like sado-masochistic pornography.[120]

Even Jeremy Wilson, Lawrence's most recent 'authorised' biographer, finds the Deraa episode somewhat puzzling. It has been regarded as suspect by George Antonius, Antony Nutting, Philip Knightley and Colin Simpson, while the number of those who have believed that it never occurred at all includes friends and colleagues of Lawrence, such as Meinertzhagen and Bernard Shaw, as well as biographers, such as Soleiman Moussa and the late Desmond Stewart, an admirer of Lawrence whose most important allegations have been denounced by Jeremy Wilson, but not refuted.[121]

From a lengthy conversation I had more than 25 years ago with the late General Sir John Paget Glubb Pasha, I can add two more names to the list of sceptics: those of Glubb himself and his predecessor as head of the Arab Legion, Frederick Peake, who had previously commanded the Egyptian Camel Corps attached to the Sharifian army and was Lawrence's tent-mate at Azraq during the time when the Deraa incident is supposed to have occurred. According to Glubb, Peake met Lawrence after the publication of *Seven Pillars* and challenged his veracity with a remark that during the time in question Lawrence had never left the encampment, to which Lawrence replied, 'Oh, give the public what it wants!'

When Glubb told me this story Peake was still alive, in his nineties, in Scotland, but I was too lazy to verify the tale. Now that Glubb himself is dead, you have only my word for it that he ever said anything to me at all. Even so, I trust I have supplied reasons to suppose that the Deraa episode may never have taken place, and so that Lawrence did, indeed, adhere to his own rule of not adopting a disguise. A welter of photographs has been published showing Lawrence in expensive 'Arab kit'. The motives suggested by them have very little to do with unobtrusiveness, but a great deal to do with underemployed intellectual brilliance, officer-class high jinks, Edwardian theatricality and the clapped-out pageant of imperialist politics.

NOTES

1 Ascribed to the Mashriq in general in Primrose Armander and Askhain Skipworth, *The Son of a Duck is a Floater* (London, Stacey International, 1985), p. 63. The early nineteenth-century Cairene version given by Burckhardt is pithier and more specific: '*kul mā tushtihiyya nafsak wi ilbiss mā tilbis an-nāss*' (eat whatever you like, but dress the way other people do). See J.L. Burckhardt, *Arabic Proverbs, or the Manners and Customs of the Modern Egyptians Illustrated from their Proverbial Sayings Current at Cairo* (London, 1817; repr. London, Curzon Press, 1984), p. 193. Ascribed to South Lebanon in Paul Linde and Justin Wintle, *A Dictionary of Arabic and Islamic Proverbs* (London, Routledge and Kegan Paul, 1984), p. 8.
2 What St Ambrose said is actually something of the order of, 'When you are in Rome, behave in Roman fashion; when you are elsewhere, behave the way they do there': *Si fueris Romae, Romano vivito more; Si fueris alibi, vivito sicut ibi.*
3 Colloquially: '*il-kitāb yitqiri min 'inwānih.*' But cf. '*al-mar'u bi-ādābihi lā bi-thiyābihi*' (One is judged by one's manners, not one's clothes), Armander and Slipworth, *op. cit.*, p. 19.
4 Edward Said, *Orientalism* (New York, Vintage Books, 1979), p. 160.
5 Timothy Mitchell, *Colonising Egypt* (Cambridge University Press, 1988), p. 27; Rana Kabbani, *Imperial Fictions: Europe's Myths of Orient* (London, Pandora, 1994), pp. 47, 50, 89–92, 110, 117.
6 Leila Ahmed, *Edward W. Lane: A Study of His Life and Work and of British Ideas of the Middle East in the Nineteenth Century* (London & New York, Longman and Librairie du Liban, 1978), pp. 95–6. As levelled by Middle Easterners or ex- or pseudo-Middle Easterners who actually live in the West and who customarily wear Western clothes themselves, such allegations can hardly fail to strike a rational reader as deeply hypocritical.
7 Stanford Shaw, *History of the Ottoman Empire and Modern Turkey. Empire of the Gazis: The Rise and Decline of the Ottoman Empire, 1280–1808* (Cambridge University Press, 1978), vol. 1, p. 198.
8 Nabil I. Matar, 'Renaissance England and the Turban', *Images of the Other: Europe and the Muslim World before 1700*, Cairo Papers in Social Science, 19:2 (1997), 46.

9 See Sarah Searight, *The British in the Middle East* (New York, Atheneum, 1970), p. 97; and Eyles Irwin, *A Series of Adventures in the Course of a Voyage up the Red Sea on the Coasts of Aden and Egypt and of a Route through the Deserts of the Thebaid, hitherto Unknown to the European Traveller, in the Year MDCCLXXVIII in Letters to a Lady* (Dublin, printed for W. Sleater, 1780; London, J. Dodsley, 1780). The two-volume London edition of 1787 contains in addition, *A Supplement of a Voyage from Venise to Latichea, and of a Route through the Deserts of Arabia, by Aleppo, Bagdad, and the Tigris to Busrah, in 1780 and 1781*. German edition: *Reise auf dem Rothen Meer auf der Arabische und Ægyptische. Küste und durch d. Thebaischen Wüste* (Leipzig, Weidmann, 1781). French editions (which include translations of the *Supplement*): *Voyage à la Mer Rouge sur les côtes de l'Arabie, en Égypte et dans les deserts de la Thébaîde; suivi d'un voyage Bassorah, etc. en 1780 et 1781*, traduit de l'anglais par J.P. Parraud (Paris, 1790), traduit de l'anglais par Billecocq (Paris, 1793).
10 Eliza Fay tells us about the hazards and hardships of taking the overland route to India in her *Original Letters from India: Containing a Narrative of a Journey through Egypt, and the Author's Imprisonment at Calicut by Hydar Ally, to which is Added an Abstract of Three Subsequent Voyages to India* (Calcutta, 1817). An abridged edition was published as *Original Letters from India (1779–1815)*, ed. E.M. Forster (New York, 1925). See E.M. Forster, 'Eliza in Egypt' in *Pharos and Pharillon* (London, Michael Haag, 1983), pp. 59–72.
11 *Observations on the Passage to India, through Egypt and across the Great Desert with Occasional Remarks on the Adjacent Countries and also Sketches of the Different Routes* (London, printed for W. Faden, Geographer to the King; J. Robson and R. Sewell, 1783), p. xiv. See Sarah Searight, *Steaming East: The Forging of Steamship and Rail Links between Europe and Asia* (London, The Bodley Head, 1991), p. 33.
12 Helen Guiterman, *David Roberts R.A. 1796–1864* (London, Helen Guiterman, 1978), p. 10.
13 Quoted from 'Turkish Letters' in Charles Thornton Forster and F.H.B. Daniell (trans.), *The Life and Letters of Ogier Ghiselin de Busbecq* (London, C. Kegan Paul, 1881); see James Bruce Ross and Mary Martin McLaughlin (eds.), *The Portable Renaissance Reader* (New York, Viking, 1953), p. 254.
14 See Matar, *op. cit.*, p. 41.
15 The portrait drawing in the Library of the Topkapi Saray of Mehmet II, presumably from life, has been attributed to Bellini and Constanzo da Ferrara.
16 A misprint in the Everyman edition of Vasari gives the date as 1501.
17 According to the earliest surviving documentation (1525) Giorgione's *Three Philosophers* with its Arab central figure was completed by Sebastiano del Piombo after Giorgione's death. Its date is thus uncertain, as is the degree to which del Piombo contributed to the final result, now in the Kunsthistorisches Museum, Vienna.
18 To the right of the well-known young Francesco Maria della Rovere, who is distinctively wrapped in a white cloak, in Raphaël's *Scuola di Atene*, executed for Pope Julius II della Rovere in the Stanza della Segnatura (1509–10), an Arab peers over the shoulder of Pythagoras. This figure has been identified as a portrait of Leo Africanus.
19 Traditionally, and incorrectly, identified as a Persian: see Carlo Cechelli, *Il Vaticano* (Rome and Milan, Restetti e Tumminelli, 1927), pp. 40, 116, 125. The

headdress is unmistakable and conclusive, however, and the pose recalls Bellini's drawing.
20 See Matar, *op. cit.*, pp. 41–2.
21 Safiya was also the generous patroness of a foundation in Cairo that still bears her name: the mosque of Malika Safiya (1610), the only royally endowed Ottoman mosque in the city. She inherited the building with the rest of his estate from its original founder, Uthman Agha, chief of the Black Eunuchs, who was her personal slave.
22 Book II, Chapter 7.
23 Matar, *op. cit.*, p. 42, citing T.G. (Thomas Gainsford), *The Glory of England* (1618), p. 23.
24 See Matar, *op. cit.*, p. 43.
25 Christopher Lloyd, *English Corsairs on the Barbary Coast* (London, Collins, 1981), p. 80.
26 See Matar, *op. cit.*, p. 43. Lithgow's account is entitled *A Most Delectable and True Discourse of an Admired and Painful Peregrinade from Scotland to the Most Famous Kingdomes in Europe, Asia and Affricke* (London, printed by Nicholas Okes, and are to be sold by Thomas Archer . . . 1614, 2nd imp. 1616; repr. New York and Amsterdam, Da Capo Press and Theatrum Orbis Terrarum, 1971). Second edn: *The Total Discourse of the Rare Adventures and Painefull Peregrinations of Long Nineteene Years Travayle From Scotland to the Most Famous Kingdoms in Europe, Asia and Africa* (1632; repr. Glasgow, James MacLehose and Sons, Publisher to the University, 1906); New reprint ed. Gilbert Phelps (London, 1974).
27 See Matar, *op. cit.*, pp. 43–4; Sir Henry Blount, *A Voyage into the Levant: a Brief Relation of a Journey Lately Performed by Master H.B. Gentleman from England by Way of Venice, into Dalmatia, Sclavonia, Bosnia, Hungary, Macedonia, Thessaly, Thrace, Rhodes and Egypt unto Gran [sic] Cairo: With Particular Observations Concerning the Moderne Condition of the Turks and Other People Under that Empire* (London, printed by I.L. [John Legatt] for Andrew Crooke, 1636), p. 98; Thomas Smith, *Remarks upon the Manners, Religion and Government of the Turks* (London, 1678), p. 36.
28 *Recueil de cent estampes représentant différentes nations du Levant, tirées sur les tableaux peints d'après nature en 1707 et 1708 par les ordres de M. de Ferriol Ambassadeur du Roi à la Porte et gravées en 1712 et 1713 par les soins de M. le Hay* with new editions in 1714 and 1715. See Jean Michel Casa, 'Art from a distance: Van Mour and Guardi', *Cornucopia*, 5 (1993–4), 16.
29 Lynne Thornton, *La Femme dans la peinture orientaliste* (Paris, ACR Éditions Internationales, 1993), p. 4.
30 See Sarah Searight *op cit.*, p. 21.
31 Thornton, *op. cit.*, p. 12.
32 Sir Leslie Stephen and Sir Sidney Lee (eds.), *The Dictionary of National Biography* (Oxford University Press, 1917–), vol. 13, p. 686.
33 Through the third Earl of Bute, his brother-in-law, this portrait descended to Lord Wharncliffe. See Patrick Conner, 'Travellers and Collectors', *The Inspiration of Egypt: Its Influence on British Artists, Travellers and Designers, 1700–1900*, ed. Patrick Conner (Brighton, Brighton Borough Council, 1983), p. 12.
34 William Ponsonby, Baron Bessborough and the second Viscount Duncannon, who became the first Earl of Bessborough the following year (1739).

35 See Anita Damiani, 'Richard Pococke', *Enlightened Observers: British Travellers to the Near East, 1715–1850* (Beirut, American University of Beirut, 1979), pp. 70–104.
36 The entire sub-genre of the Oriental Letter (e.g. Montesquieu's *Lettres persanes*, Goldsmith's 'Chinese Lettres') was inaugurated by Giovanni Paolo Marana (1640–1693) with his (partially translated from the Italian) *L'Espion des grands seigneurs dans les cours des princes chrétiens ou Mémoirs pour servir à l'histoire de ce siècle depuis 1637 jusqu'à 1682* (6 vols., Amsterdam and Paris, 1684–6). An English version in eight volumes, called *The Turkish Spy*, appeared between 1687 and 1694 and a continuation soon followed, probably by Defoe.
37 For example, the enormously popular *Les Trois Sultanes* (1761), by Charles-Simon Favart (1710–1792).
38 For example, Mozart's *Entführung aus dem Serail* in K. 384 (1789), the best-known of several plays and comic operas on the same subject. Cf. Johann Andre's *Entführung aus dem Serail* (1781), Dieter's *Belmont und Konstanze* (1784) and Justin Knecht's *Belmont und Konstanze* (1787).
39 A set of six French paintings of Turkish masquerade costumes, c.1800, was offered at Sotheby's in October 1993. 'Autumn Windfalls', *Cornucopia*, 5 (1993–1994), 20–91.
40 For example, the second movement of Haydn's 'Military' Symphony, no. 100 in G major, first performed in London in 1794. Cf. the finale, a *rondo alla turca* of Mozart's piano sonata in A, K. 331 (1778), occasional effects in *Entführung aus dem Serail* and the march introducing the tenor solo ('Froh, wie seine Sonne fliegen') in the last movement of the Ninth Symphony. Ottoman originals from the same period may be heard performed twice daily at the Military Museum in Istanbul (Pera).
41 Thornton, *op. cit.*, p. 54.
42 See Casa, *op. cit.*, pp. 16–18.
43 In 1779, his younger brother Amédée was commissioned by the Gobelins works to paint four pictures of 'sultanas' as the basis of design-cartoons for tapestries. See Thornton, *op. cit.*, pp. 7–8.
44 Versions in the Musée d'Art et d'Histoire, Geneva, and the Rijksmuseum, Amsterdam.
45 See Thornton, *op. cit.*, pp. 11–13.
46 *Ibid.*, pp. 10–11.
47 Kathryn Tidrick, *Heart-beguiling Araby: The English Romance with Arabia*, revised edn. (London, Cambridge University Press, 1989), pp. 14–15.
48 That is, humour or whim, fanciful or capricious extravagance. See entries in El-Said Badawi and Martin Hinds, *A Dictionary of Egyptian Arabic* (Beirut, 1986).
49 The full-length original, now in the British Embassy in Athens, shows Byron posed against 'a romanticized Greek landscape complete with swirling mist and ruins'. See Caroline Bugler's excellent catalogue note in Mary-Anne Stevens (ed.), *The Orientalists: Delacroix to Matisse, European Painters in North Africa and the Near East*, Exhibition Catalogue (London, Royal Academy of Arts and Washington DC, National Gallery of Art, 1984), p. 218. Copies by the artist of the upper part of the picture, with the landscape replaced by a dark background, are in the National Portrait Gallery and at the offices of John Murray, Byron's

publisher. Byron purchased the costume in Epirus in 1809, while on the tour that provided raw material for *Childe Harold*. In a letter to his mother, written on 19 November 1809, he observed that such clothes were 'magnifiques' and 'the only expensive items in this country'. Five years later, after Philips had painted his portrait, Byron presented the clothes to Lady Elphinstone to wear at masquerades, and they are now displayed in Bowood House, Wiltshire.

50   Mikhail Yurevitch Lermontov, *A Hero of our Time* [*Geroi Nashego Vremeni*], 1841, trans. from the Russian by Vladimir Nabokov in collaboration with Dimitri Nabokov (New York, Doubleday, 1958), p. 107.

51   *The Cossacks: A Story of the Caucasus* (*Kazaki: Kavkazskaya Povesm*, written 1852–1863), trans. from the Russian and ed. R. Daglish (Moscow, Foreign Languages Publishing House, n.d.), p. 95.

52   For example, *Paul Gavarni*, ed. Georg Pilz (Berlin, Eulenspiegel Verlag, 1971), p. 7 (from *Les Petits Malheurs du bonheur*, 1837) and p. 26 (from *Paris le Soir*, 1840).

53   Louis Antoine Fauvelet de Bourrienne (1769–1834), translated excerpt from *Mémoires de Napoléon Bonaparte* (1829) as published in *Napoleon in Egypt: al-Jabarti's Chronicle of the French Occupation, 1798* (New York, Markus Wiener, 1993), pp. 154, 159.

54   Published in London by John Murray, 1820.

55   See Searight *op. cit.*, plates and captions between pp. 128–9, 168–9.

56   Ahmed, *op. cit.*, p. 88. Ahmed specifically mentions 'Arab robes', however, when in fact travellers generally wore Turkish clothing. Domingo Badia-y-Leblich, (alias Ali Bey al-Abbasi), author of *Voyages d'Ali Bey al-Abassi en Afrique et en Asie pendant les années 1803–1807* (Paris, Didot, 1814), reports that in 1803 the same was true of the Maghrib, 'The dress of the Moors is very little known in Europe, because when they visit it, they generally make use of the barbaric costume of the Algerine Turks.' See *Travels of Ali Bey in Morocco, Tripoli, Cyprus, Egypt, Arabia, Syria, and Turkey, between the Years 1801 and 1807* (London, Longman, Hurst, Rees, Orme, and Brown, 1816; repr. Westmead, Gregg International, 1970), p. 7.

57   Charles Irby and James Mangles, *Travels in Egypt, Nubia, Syria, and Asia Minor in 1817 and 1818* (London, T. White & Co., 1821). *Travels in Egypt, Nubia, Syria, and Asia Minor during the years 1817 and 1818* (London, 1823). See the popular edition of *Travels in Egypt, Nubia, Syria and the Holy Land* (London, 1844), p. 5; Ahmed, *op. cit.*, pp. 88–9.

58   William Rae Wilson, *Travels in Egypt and the Holy Land* (London, printed for Longman, Hurst, Reese, Orme, and Browne, 1823), p. 122; Ahmed, *op. cit.*, pp. 88–9.

59   Dr Robert Richardson, *Travels along the Mediterranean, and Parts Adjacent: in Company with the Earl of Belmore, During the Years 1816–17–18. Extending as far as the Second Cataract of the Nile, Jerusalem, Damascus, Balbec, etc.* (London, printed for T. Cadell, 1822), vol. 1, pp. 6–7. Robert Richardson was a physician who accompanied Viscount Mountjoy and the Earl of Belmore and also attended at Burckhardt's death.

60   Anonymous portraits in Glasgow. See Conner, *op. cit.*, p. 59. Maxwell was accompanied by his servant John Cunningham and John Bramsen, a former officer in the Prussian army, who described the tour in *Letters of a Prussian Traveller, Descriptive of a Tour through Sweden, Prussia, Austria, Hungary, Istria,*

the Ionian Islands, Egypt, Syria, Rhodes, the Morea, Greece, Calabria, Italy, the Tyrol, the banks of the Rhine, Hanover, Holstein, Denmark, Westphalia and Holland (2 vols., London, printed for H. Colburn, 1818); and *Travels in Egypt, Syria, Palestine, and Greece, in the Years 1814 and 1815* (London, H. Colburn, 1818).

61 John Madox, *Excursions in the Holy Land, Egypt, Nubia, Syria, &c. Including a Visit to the Unfrequented District of the Hauran* (London, R. Bentley, 1834).

62 Dr Richard Robert Madden, *Travels in Turkey, Egypt, Nubia, and Palestine, in 1824, 1825, 1826, and 1827* (London, H. Colburn, 1829), vol. 1, pp. 318–82; quoted in Ahmed, *op. cit.*, pp. 88–9.

63 Quoted in Ahmed, *op. cit.*, p. 88.

64 Jason Thompson, *Sir Gardner Wilkinson and His Circle* (Austin, University of Texas Press, 1992), pp. 39, 44–7, with plates between pages 30 and 31.

65 Fernand Braudel, *Capitalism and Material Life 1400–1800*, trans. Miriam Kochan (London, Collins, 1974), p. 208.

66 Displayed by the Fine Art Society in 1980.

67 See Ahmed, *op. cit.*, p. 99.

68 The photograph opposite p. 155 of Dalrymple's *In Xanadu: A Quest* (London, Flamingo/HarperCollins, 1989) shows him wearing a pair. In this book (p. 303), however, Dalrymple defines *charwal* (i.e., *sirwāl*) as specifically meaning 'baggy pyjama bottoms, bottom half of a *charwal chemise*' (*sic*), and defines the latter as 'Pyjama suit; the unofficial national dress of Pakistan.' In *City of Djinns: A Year in Delhi* (London, HarperCollins, 1993), p. 343, he offers us an Urdu version of the same term, *salvar kameez* (i.e. Turkish *shalvar* = Arabic *sirwāl* + Arabic *qamis*) defined as 'Long tunic and matching loose trousers favored mainly by girls in North India and by both sexes in Pakistan and Afghanistan.'

69 See the description in Conner, *op. cit.*, p. 73.

70 Jason Thompson, 'Edward William Lane's "Description of Egypt"', *IJMES*, 28 (November 1996), 574.

71 James Webster, *Travels through the Crimea, Turkey, and Egypt; Performed during the Years 1825–28, Including Particulars of the Last Illness and Death of the Emperor Alexander, and of the Russian Conspiracy in 1825* (London, H. Colburn, 1830), vol. 2, pp. 15, 17–18; Ahmed, *op. cit.*, p. 89.

72 Nouvelles Acquisitions Françaises (NAF) 20395, Département des Manuscrits, Bibliothèque Nationale, fol. 40 verso.

73 NAF 20377, fol. 34 numéroté 14, 'le sérieux de nos physionomies en impose sans doute aux musulmans ou plutôt leur habitude de voir des Européens avec les habits orientaux; toujours est qu'il ne nous est pas encore arrivé d'aventure semblable à celle de ces voyageurs anglais qui portaient le costume d'un air si gauche qu'on crût qu'ils l'avaient pris par dérision, et dès la première fois qu'ils le mirent ils furent si bien houspillés qu'ils rentrèrent chez eux presque nus.'

74 Robin Hanbury-Tenison, 'Keeping up Appearances', *The Geographical Magazine*, 69:9 (February 1997), 69.

75 See Matar, *op. cit.*, p. 44.

76 See Thompson (1992), *op. cit.*, p. 469; see his '"OF THE OSMANLEES, OR TURKS": An Unpublished Chapter from Edward William Lane's Manners and Customs of the Modern Egyptians', *Turkish Studies Association Bulletin*, 19 (Autumn 1995), 21.

77 See Searight, *op. cit.*, caption to portrait of James Silk Buckingham between pp. 128 and 129.
78 Salah Attiya, 'Unscrupulous plan to obtain larger part', *The Egyptian Gazette* (Monday, 17 April 1995), 7.
79 Notable as well was the lack of official expressions of sympathy. The 58 foreign victims came from Switzerland, Britain and Japan. A few days later, as the newly arrived ambassador of one of these countries was being ushered in to present his credentials to the Egyptian President, he informed his Egyptian handlers that he would be unable to do so unless he could be absolutely certain that he would receive condolences on behalf of the people of his country in the course of the ceremony. His insistence, diplomatically quite correct, eventually prevailed and his country remains the only one to have been favoured with any such mark of sympathy. No condolences were directed by the Egyptian government to the families of the victims.
80 Forster, *op. cit.*, pp. 62–3, 69–70.
81 See *Autobiography of James Silk Buckingham, Including his Voyages and Travels, Adventures, Speculations, Successes and Failures, Faithfully and Frankly Narrated Interspersed with Characteristic Sketches of Public Men with Whom he has had Intercourse* (London, Longman, Brown, Green, and Longmans, 1855). H.W. Pickersgill's portrait of Buckingham and his wife in Oriental dress adorns the main stairwell of the Royal Geographical Society.
82 Chateaubriand, who never travelled overland in Egypt and stayed in Cairo for only seven days, under consular protection, came away with the false impression that 'European clothing was no longer an object of insult', *Itinéraire de Paris à Jerusalem* (Paris, Garnier-Flammarion, 1968), vol. 1, p. 385.
83 Craufurd Tait Ramage, *Ramage in South Italy. The Nooks and Byways of Italy: Wanderings in Search of its Ancient Remains and Modern Superstitions*, abridged and edited by Edith Clay, with an introduction by Harold Acton (London, Longmans, 1965; repr. Chicago, Academy, 1987), pp. 138–9.
84 See *Journey through Arabia Petraea, in Mount Sinai, and the Excavated City of Petra, the Edom of the Prophecies* (London, John Murray, 1836), the translation of his *Voyage de l'Arabie Pétrée par Léon de Laborde et Linant de Bellefonds* (Paris, Girard, 1830).
85 Alexander Kinglake, *Eothen* (repr. Marlboro, 1992), pp. 909, 997.
86 This final remark is directed at his English readership, lest they should be so smug as to believe that all bigotry had been banished from Britain forever by the Catholic Emancipation of 1829.
87 Quoted by Thompson (1995), *op. cit.*, p. 27.
88 Helen Guiterman, *David Roberts R.A. 1796–1864* (London, Helen Guiterman, 1978), pp. 10–11, 20. I am indebted to Briony Llewellyn for pointing out an entry in Roberts' *Eastern Journal* (National Library of Scotland) for 15 December 1838, in which the painter describes himself as wearing a straw hat, a 'French blouse' and European trousers.
89 See Searight, *op. cit.*, caption to portrait of 'Mrs. Moore, wife of the British Consul in Beirut' between pp. 168 and 169.
90 Caroline Juler, *Les Orientalistes de l'école italienne* (Paris, ACR Édition, 1994), p. 42.
91 Deborah Manley, *The Nile: A Traveller's Anthology* (London, Cassell, 1991), pp. 95–8.

92　Mahmud Salih Arif Pasha, *Les Anciens Costumes de l'Empire Ottoman depuis l'origine de la monarchie jusqu'à la réforme du Sultan Mahmoud* [*Majmuat tesavir uthmani*] (Paris, Lermercier, 1863–), p. 3.
93　Quoted by Thompson (1995), *op. cit.*, p. 27.
94　Donald Quataert, 'Clothing Laws, State, and Society in the Ottoman Empire, 1720–1829', *IJMES*, 29 (August 1997), 12.
95　Moroccan Spahis demonstrated their prowess ninety years later during the Italian campaign of World War II, when they inspired the creation of a new verb in the Italian language: *marocchinizzare*. They still provide a guard of honour for Spanish kings.
96　William Thayer, the American consul-general, otherwise best known for his friendship with Lucie Duff Gordon, lodged an official protest, invoking the Monroe Doctrine and pointing out that participation in this French adventure implied either that the Ottoman sultan was at war with Mexico or that Egypt was in rebellion against the sultan. A third Egyptian intervention, in support of the puppet Emperor Maximilian, intended to take place in 1865, was thwarted by another American protest and a change of Egyptian foreign ministers.
97　Quoted in Ahmed, *op. cit.*, p. 45.
98　See '"Sketch on the Verandah at Suez", *Illustrated London News*, April 25, 1857' in Nicholas Warner (ed.), *An Egyptian Panorama: Reports from the Nineteenth-Century British Press* (Cairo, Zeitouna, 1994), p. 4. (The man dressed in this picture is possibly a dragoman, not a traveller: one cannot be quite sure.)
99　'The Editor's Preface', *The Thousand and One Nights, Commonly Called in England, The Arabian Nights' Entertainments, A New Translation From the Arabic, with Copious Notes by Edward William Lane*, ed. Stanley Lane-Poole (London, Charles Knight, 1859), pp. x–xi.
100　See *Atlas de l'histoire de l'art égyptien d'après les monuments depuis le temps les plus reculés, jusqu'à la domination romaine* (Paris, 1868–78), exquisitely reprinted by Zeitouna in Cairo in 1991. Prisse is shown in Turkish costume in the frontispiece of this reprint, which also reproduces de Famars' sketch, from the dated original in the Willem de Famas Testas, Teglers Museum, Harlem. The best known portrait of Prisse, also showing him in Turkish costume, was drawn by Achille Déveria in 1844.
101　See Lesley Blanch, *Pierre Loti: The Legendary Romantic* (New York, Harcourt Brace Jovanich, 1983), p. 108.
102　Mary S. Lovell, *A Scandalous Life: The Biography of Jane Digby el Mezrab* (London, Fourth Estate, 1995), p. 159. This important biography includes generous quotations from Jane Digby's diaries, never published before, which give an excellent picture of the lawlessness throughout Greater Syria between 1853 and 1881, the year of her death.
103　Karl Baedeker, *Palestine and Syria* (Leipzig, Baedeker, 1898), p. xxxiii.
104　The remains of the Blunt estate were rediscovered in May 1997 by two students at the American University in Cairo, Mona Kotb Soliman and Nariman Alaywan, in the urbanised district of Izbit al-Nakhl, Matariyya, on the north-eastern periphery of Cairo. What has survived is not the main house, which was demolished some three decades ago, but six or seven rooms of 'al-khayshah' (the tent), a two-story mudbrick honeymoon cottage that Blunt built in 1891. See Elizabeth Longford, *A Pilgrimage of Passion: The Life of Wilfrid Scawen Blunt*

(London, Weidenfeld and Nicolson, 1979), pp. 136–51, 294, 309–15, 327–9, 409. The area is still referred to locally as 'Ginaynit Blunt' (Blunt's Garden) and local legend has it that al-khayshah was built by Lady Anne as a refuge after a rift caused by Blunt's womanising.

105 Sir Richard Burton, *Personal Narrative of a Pilgrimage to Al-Madinah & Meccah*, Memorial Edition (2 vols., London, Tylson and Edwards, 1893), vol. 2, p. 311.

106 Ali Bey al-Abbasi records having been accused of being a non-Muslim only once: 'it was because I was wearing a blue burnous; and in this country [Palestine] that colour is particularly worn by Christian inhabitants', *Travels of Ali Bey*, op. cit., vol. 2, p. 212.

107 His account includes a concise and accurate summary of Muslim belief and practice and a remarkable *encomium* on Islam. See *ibid.*, vol. 1, pp. 81–100 and vol. II, pp. 66–7. Chateaubriand, who met him in Alexandria in 1806 and took him to be a Turk interested in contemporary French literature, corrected his error with a charming note in the third edition of the *Itinéraire de Paris à Jerusalem* (Paris, Le Normant, 1812).

108 Ali Bey al-Abbasi remarks that mere disguise was inadequate without circumcision, *Travels of Ali Bey*, *op cit.*, vol. 1, p. 12. Both he and Burton had undergone this operation.

109 A conclusion supported by his most recent biographer. See Edward Rice, *Captain Sir Richard Francis Burton: The Secret Agent who Made the Pilgrimage to Mecca, Discovered the* Kama Sutra *and Brought* The Arabian Nights *to the West* (New York, Harper, 1990), p. 139.

110 Burton (1863), *op. cit.*, vol. 1, pp. 99–123; see also vol. 1, pp. 41, 233–40. Burton's Afghan persona justified his pronunciation of Arabic, which must have been heavily tinctured – if the English text of the *Pilgrimage* is any guide – by Indo-Persianisms.

111 John F. Keane, *Six Months in the Hejaz: An Account of the Mohammedan Pilgrimage to Meccah and Medinah* (London, Ward and Downey, 1887), pp. 46–51.

112 Doughty's motive for undergoing such hardship was among the strangest ever recorded. Robert Graves reports that T.E. Lawrence told him, 'When I asked Doughty why he had made that Arabian journey, his answer was that he had gone there "to redeem the English language from the slough into which it has fallen since the time of Spenser".' Robert Graves, *Goodbye to All That* (Harmondsworth, Penguin Books, 1957), p. 244.

113 See Tidrick, *op. cit.*, p. 140.

114 Annette Kobak, *Isabelle: The Life of Isabelle Eberhardt* (New York, Alfred A. Knopf, 1988), pp. 88–9, 197.

115 Quoted in Jeremy Wilson, *T.E. Lawrence: The Authorised Biography* (London, Minerva, 1990), p. 995.

116 In the *Arab Bulletin*. See *ibid.*, Appendix IV, p. 963.

117 See Wilson, *op. cit.*, pp. 460–1. The letter was written at the British Residency in Cairo.

118 See Desmond Stewart, *T.E. Lawrence* (London, Paladin, 1979), pp. 231, 329.

119 The 'confirmation' offered by Edward H. T. Robinson in *Lawrence: The Story of His Life* (Oxford University Press, 1933) and *Lawrence the Rebel* (London, Lincolns-Praeger, 1946) rests upon Robinson's false claim to have been among the British participants in the Sharifian campaign. It has also been noted that

Robinson was convicted of forgery in 1929 and theft in 1937, when he sold papers lent to him by A.W. Lawrence in order to pay a blackmailer. See Stephen E. Tabachnick and Christopher Matherson, *Images of Lawrence* (London, Jonathan Cape, 1988), p. 47.

120 For a full text, see Phillip Knightley and Colin Simpson, *The Secret Lives of Lawrence of Arabia* (London, Nelson, 1969), pp. 207–13.

121 Stewart's queries, for example, regarding Lawrence's claim to have met secretly with 'Ali Riza Pasha Rihabi' (i.e. Ali Ridha al-Rikabi) on 13 June 1917, in the course of an epic two-week camel ride are parallelled by official reservations at the time and have remained unanswered. See Stewart, *op. cit.*, pp. 167, 187–8.

4

English Pleasure Travel in the Near East, 1580–1645[1]

John Ghazvinian

Earlier in this century, the history of late Tudor and early Stuart travellers played an ancillary role in the grand histories of conquest, of navigation, of shipping and of that exuberant event, the 'Birth of the British Empire'. Men like Boies Penrose, Sir William Foster, John Parker, G.D. Ramsay and J.H. Parry cobbled together impressive, if starry-eyed, accounts of 'the early days of Empire', but they generally did not feel that it was necessary to separate the pleasure traveller from the merchant, the conqueror or the diplomat. More recently, these Whiggish histories have been displaced by a more critical brand of history, and the emphasis has shifted towards literature and its discursive powers in shaping culture. Unfortunately, the history of travel has benefited little from this shift, since literary scholars have again cast travel in a supporting role in a larger drama – this time of oppression, representation and constructions of the Other. Both approaches have supplied much useful information to the historian, but both have casually used curiosity travel as a handmaiden to a larger project. Travel and travellers deserve a spotlight of their own as social and historical phenomena, out of the shadows of mercantile history or debates over ethnocentrism.

With that in mind, then, the attention of this chapter will be focused on the Englishmen who travelled for nothing but the satisfaction of their daydreams and their curiosities. It will be my argument that two irreconcilable intellectual approaches were used by these men,[2] and that the story of travellers in this period is thus a story of confusion and contradiction.

In an attempt to reflect the travellers' approaches accurately, and not to take their statements at face value, I have examined not only their own writings, but also the writings of those who stayed at home and offered their thoughts on curiosity travel. I hope, therefore, to deliver an examination, not of descriptions and representation, which for me have been of secondary interest, but of a burgeoning new phenomenon in the cultural milieu of early modern England.

Stephen Greenblatt writes eloquently[3] of the sixteenth century as an age of 'wonder' and 'discovery'. He says that Europeans experienced 'something like the "startle reflex" one can observe in infants: eyes widened, arms outstretched, breathing stilled, the whole body momentarily convulsed'. This metaphor works well for the sixteenth century, but, in examining what came next, I would like to replace Greenblatt's startled infant with a curious toddler – finished with 'discovery' and ready for 'exploration'. All the travellers I have looked at exhibited an empiricism born of youthful fascination, a passionate curiosity to explore and a desire to engage in undiluted visual observation and playful, even tolerant, investigation of foreign lands.

Our travellers were, in the first place, very young – generally in their early twenties. They were, of course, well-off – usually the second sons of established gentry. They were recent graduates of Oxford or Cambridge. Some were dropouts. They all exhibited a certain restlessness and wanderlust, even an irritation with the rigidity of their medieval-style educations. 'Confound your Academies all', wrote Thomas Coryate, 'of *Brazen-nose* and *Penbrooke* Hall.' Coryate had dropped out of Oxford, despite showing an 'admirable fluency in Greek'. On his travels, he taught himself Persian, Turkish and Hindustani. George Sandys was the seventh son of the Archbishop of York, and matriculated to St Mary's Hall, Oxford at the tender age of eleven. He appears to have taken no degree. Henry Blount, meanwhile, graduated from Trinity College, Oxford, where he had a reputation for being unusually bright but not very interested in his studies. Blount's 16-year-old mind was occupied elsewhere. He was bored by the academic emphasis on confirming and disputing what was read in the Bible or the classics. Blount wanted to experience things directly:

> Wherefore I desiring somewhat to informe my selfe of the Turkish nation, would not sit down with a booke knowledge therof, but rather (through all the hazard and endurance of travell,) receive it

from mine owne eye not dazled with any affection, prejudicacy, or mist of education.[4]

Such tempestuous curiosity naturally raised eyebrows. 'Rash inconsiderate hot-headed spirits, and vaineglorious brain-sick youths', wrote Thomas Neale in 1643, 'overheated by a furious brain, does skip in forraigne Countries, inflamed with an incessant desire'.[5] Interestingly enough, few of the travellers would have disagreed with this assessment. 'I plead guilty to all the imperfections you can throw upon youth or hast', admitted Thomas Herbert.[6] Coryate, the man John Donne called the 'great Lunatique',[7] was a passionate traveller from birth. 'Some say, when thou wert borne (O wondrous hap)/ First time thou pist thy clouts, thou drew'st a map', wrote an admirer.[8] In a calmer moment, Bishop Hall admitted that he was not opposed to travel per se, rather, 'it is the Travell of curiosity wherewith my quarell shall bee maintained'.[9] Critical elders, such as Neale and Hall, could see that there was something dangerous in the idea of youths who did not have to justify their travels as part of commerce or diplomacy. How unnerving is must have been for such traditionalists to hear a young traveller declare in 1617, 'I say the fruit of travel is travel it selfe.'[10]

Along with youthful curiosity went a rejection of the academic, and of second-hand knowledge in general. Many travellers were so dedicated to empirical investigation that they insisted on learning new languages and avoiding other Englishmen while abroad. 'Let [the traveller] sequester himselfe from the Company of his Country men and diet in such Places',[11] wrote none other than Francis Bacon, and it appears that many of the travellers did just that. Blount craved the opportunity to be 'let into the breasts of many',[12] and Fynes Morrison mocked the man who would 'rather snort in a chimney corner',[13] than travel, or the traveller who used an interpreter, and 'doth only borrow his knowledge, and take it at second hand'.[14] James Howell in his *Instructions for Forreine Travell* noted that 'The *Eare* is not so authentique a wit-nesse as the Eye',[15] but an advice manual of 1633 is most worth quoting for its uncanny resemblance to a latter-day study-abroad brochure:

> It hath bin lately maintained in an Academicall Dispute, That the best travailing is in maps and good Authors: . . . A pleasing opinion for solitary prisoners, who may thus travell over the world, though confinde to a dungeon . . . Our sedentary Traveller may passe for a

wise man, as long as hee converseth either with dead men by reading; or by writing, with men absent. But . . . ability to treat with men of several humours, factions, and Countries; . . . is not gotten onely by reading of books, but rather by studying of men. Yet this ever holds true; The best scholler is fittest for a Traveller, as being able to make the most useful observation: Experience added to learning, makes a perfect Man. He, that never travelled but in his Books, can hardly shew his learning, without manifestation of his want of experience.[16]

Out of this empirical emphasis on observation and experience grew a fair degree of tolerance, the best exemplar of which was Henry Blount. Blount insisted on receiving an 'ocular view', because:

> The eye [has] the most immediate, and quick commerce with the soule . . . so that an eye witnesse of things conceives them with an imagination more compleat, strong, and intuitive, then he can apprehend by way of relation . . . For relations are not only in great part false, out of the relaters mis-information, vanitie, or interest; but which is unavoidable, their choice, and frame agrees more naturally with his judgement whose issue they are, then with his readers . . . But a traveller takes with his eye only such occurrents into observation, as his owne apprehension affects, and can digest them into an experience more naturall for himselfe, then he could have done the notes of another.[17]

In a fascinating turn, Blount continues in this emphasis on first-hand observation, and then turns it into a statement of what today we would call postmodern relativism:

> Most men judge things by their owne silly education, and received opinions guided by sublimities, and moralities imaginary . . . I, in remembering the Turkish institutions, will only Register what I found them, nor censure them by any rule, but that of more or less sufficiency to their ayme . . . for the just censure of things is to be drawn from their end whereto they are aymed, without requiring them to our customes and ordinances, which they acknowledge not for their touch-stone . . . [they cannot] comply to a rule, by which they were not made.[18]

Blount asked whether 'the Turkish way appear absolutely barbarous, as we are given to understand, or rather another kinde of civilite, different from ours but no lesse pretending'.[19] Blount's fascinating open-mindedness grows directly out of his desperate desire to satisfy curiosity and to observe things first-hand, without recourse to the medium of old books.

On the other hand, of course, our young traveller was not as impetuous as one might be led to believe from what I have said. He was, after all, a recent university graduate, and had patiently spent two or three years being put through the classical curriculum. He had, doubtless, read some of the myriad travel advice books, as well as having received written or oral advice from his fathers' friends, all of which urged him only to leave England's shores armed with centuries of biblical, classical and medieval knowledge about the lands in which he was about to embark.

He set sail, therefore, not only as a curious youth, desperate to record the discoveries of his own eyes, but also as a learned young man. Not surprisingly, though, he often saw nothing but bane and waste and the overwhelming non-existence of the Near East of Herodotus, Pliny or the Bible. Though he had travelled to record what his eyes would show him, his eyes were lodged firmly in a head crammed with the ponderous authority of ancient texts. The explanation that was normally given for this, however, was the presence of Islam and the Turk, whose recent activities had obliterated a mighty past. The remainder of this paper, therefore, deals with the process by which the English traveller tried to resolve contradictory approaches and reconcile his eyes to his education.

Travellers sought out locations mentioned in Classical sources and subjected them to a rigorous empirical scientific investigation. The putative Tower of Babel was measured, and John Cartwright noted that it was 'a quarter of a mile in compasse', made of 'burnt bricke cimented and joined with bituminous mortar . . . The brickes are three quarters of a yard in length, and a quarter in thikcnesse.'[20] The exact location of the garden of Eden was debated by several travellers, and Fynes Morrison suggested a form of intellectual carbon dating for the buildings of Jerusalem.

There was a sense that a new scholarly enterprise was underway. An anonymous poet,[21] praising Coryate, wrote:

> The like of things as thou hast noted,
> nor is, nor was, nor shall be quoted.
> Nor in the chanting Poets theames,
> Nor in the wisest sickmens dreams:

Nor in the books of Bacon Friar:
Nor in Herodotus the lyar.[22]

Several writers and travellers brazenly mocked the errors of Abraham Ortelius, perhaps the last of the medieval-style geographers popular at the time, and the accounts were filled with statements such as that of William Lithgow, 'Although Josephus witnesseth, that in his time . . . [a golden apple grew on the banks of the Jordan] . . . yet I affirme now the contrary'.[23]

Even as the authority of old books was being subjected to empirical investigation, there was sometimes a fair amount of optimism that the two approaches would yield complementary results. James Howell wrote:

> Books are likewise good teachers . . . yet the study of living men, and a collation of his own Optique observations and judgement with theirs, work much more strongly . . . where these meet (I mean the living and the dead) they perfect. And indeed, this is the prime use of Peregrination, which therefore may be not improperly called a moving Academy, or the true Peripatetique Schoole.[24]

But such triumphant accord was the exception and not the rule. More typical was Thomas Herbert's remark at Persepolis, 'how time has demolisht her glory, as most of all the Wonders of the World, how she lies now subjected';[25] or that of Henry Timberlake in Jerusalem, 'Terra sancta è no mais'.[26] And for most travellers, there was only one explanation for the glaring discrepancy: the inhabitants of Persepolis, exclaimed Herbert, 'so little know or value memory, that they daily teare away at the monument, for Sepulchres and benches to sit upon'.[27] Lithgow had no doubt why the famed cedars of ancient Lebanon were not to be seen: they were 'destroyed by Sheepheards, who have made fires thereat, and holes wherein they sleepe'.[28] And George Sandys spoke of the land

> where God himselfe did place his owne Commonwealth, gave lawes and oracles, inspired his prophets, sent Angels to converse with men; above all, where the Sonne of god descended to become man; where he honoured the earth with his beautifull steps, wrought the worke of our redemption, triumphed over death, and ascended into glory.[29]

This land, says Sandys, is now filled with

> the most deplored spectacles of extreme miserie: the wild beasts of mankind having broken in upon them, and rooted out all civilitie; and the pride of a sterne and barbarous Tyrant possessing the thrones of ancient and just dominion.[30]

There was an inherent contradiction in the two approaches that the travellers imposed on their subjects, a contradiction that could only be explained by the barbarity of the Turks and Persians.

Of course, it was only a contradiction so long as young men – boys, really – were torn between their classical education and their passionate desire for exploration, investigation and observation. And, lest I be accused of imposing an overly reified, anachronistic and analytical reading to people who would never have seen things this way, I should draw attention to one summer's night in the sands of Mesopotamia, when Sir Anthony Sherley found himself in an anguished state of indecision:

> To tell wonders, of things I saw, strange to us, that are borne in these parts, is for a Traveller of another profession then I am, who had my end to see, and make use to of the best things; not to feed my selfe, and the world, with such trifles, as either by their strangeness, might have a suspition of untruth: or by their lightnesse adde to the rest of my imperfections, the vanity, or smallnesse of my iudgement. But because I was desirous to certifie my selfe truly of the estate of the Turke in those parts, through which I passed, understanding, where wee lodged one night, that the Campe of *Aborisci*, King of those *Arabies*, which inhabite the desert of *Mesopotamia*, was a mile off; I hazarded myselfe in that curiosity, to go into it; and saw a poore King with a ten or twelve thousand beggerly subiects, living in tents of blacke haire-cloth: . . . we passed . . . through them all in such peace . . .[31]

Given Sherley's tiresome heavy-handedness throughout the *Relation*, one has to pause at this arrestingly revealing moment in the text. We can genuinely feel the temptations and obligations that are coursing through his head as he battles his own 'curiosity', and reminds us (and probably himself) that he is a gentleman, not interested in the strange 'trifles' that might reveal the 'smallnesse' of his judgment. Sherley knew what he was supposed to write about and what he wanted to write about. It is this tension between the two, which I think comes through brilliantly in this passage, that I have tried to make the subject of my paper. One can only imagine Sherley's feeling of naughty excitement as he secretively indulged himself, and tiptoed through the Arab encampment unnoticed.

While the aim of my study has manifestly not been psycho-history, I have tried hard to look at these travellers as travellers and not merely as texts. I have attempted to see travel as a socio-historical phenomenon, best understood by an examination not only of the texts, but also of the personal histories of the travellers, and the commentaries of those who stayed at home.

The picture that I think emerges is undoubtedly one of tension and confusion, between two irreconcilable epistemological approaches: an older, affirmation-based medieval approach; and a more visual, empirical (one might even say 'modern') approach, of which the traveller seemed instinctively more fond.

Notes

1 This paper is a much-distilled version of a master's thesis written at the University of Oxford under the supervision of Cliff Davies, to whom I should like to extend my gratitude.
2 I have yet to come across any indication of a female traveller in this period.
3 Stephen Greenblatt, *Marvellous Possessions: The Wonder of the New World* (Oxford, Clarendon Press, 1991).
4 Henry Blount, *A Voyage into the Levant* (London, printed by John Legatt for Andrew Crooke, 1636), p. 4.
5 Thomas Neale of Warneford, *A Treatise of Direction How to Travell Safely and Profitably into Forraigne Countries* (London, 1643), p. 13.
6 Thomas Herbert, *A Relation of Some Yeares Travaile* (London, W. Stansby & J. Bloome, 1634), pp. 1–2.
7 *Coryates Crudities, Hastily Gobbled up . . .* (London, W. Stansby, 1611), f. D3^r.
8 John Scory in *Crudities, op. cit.*, f. G2^v.
9 Joseph Hall, *Quo Vadis? A Just Censure of Travell as it is Commonly Undertaken by the Gentlemen of our Nation* (London, E. Griffin for F. Butter, 1617), p. 5.
10 Fynes Moryson, *An Itinerary* (London, J. Beale, 1617), vol. 1, p. 1.
11 Francis Bacon, *Essays* (London, John Haviland for Hanna Barret, 1625), p. 103.
12 Blount, *op. cit.*, p. 5.
13 Moryson, *op. cit.*, vol. 1, p. 4.
14 *Ibid.*, I, p. 14.
15 James Howell, *Instructions for Forreine Travell* (London, 1642), pp. 3–4.

16 Robert, Earl of Essex, Sir Philip Sidney, and William Davison, *Profitable Instructions* (London, printed for Beniamin Fisher, 1633), ff. A1^r–A3^v.
17 Blout, *op. cit.*, pp. 2–4.
18 *Ibid.*, pp. 2–4, 61.
19 *Ibid.*, p. 2.
20 John Cartwright, *The Preachers Travels* (London, for Thomas Thorppe, 1611), pp. 99–100.
21 Probably Coryate himself.
22 *Crudities, op. cit.*, ff. G1^v–G2^r.
23 William Lithgow, *A Most Delectable, and True Discourse, of an Admired and Painefull Peregrination from Scotland, to the Most Famous Kingdomes in Europe, Asia, and Affricke* (London, N. Okes, 1614), f. P2^r.
24 Howell, *op. cit.*, pp. 7–8.
25 Herbert, *op. cit.*, p. 57.
26 Henry Timberlake, *A True and Strange Discourse of the Travailes of two English Pilgrimes* (London, Thomas Archer, 1603), p. 24.
27 Herbert, *op. cit.*, p. 60.
28 Lithgow, *op. cit.*, F. A2^r.
29 George Sandys, *The Relation of a Journey* (London, W. Bartlett, 1615), dedication.
30 *Ibid.*
31 *Sir Anthony Sherley his Relation of his Travels into Persia* (London, N. Butter & J. Bagfet, 1613), p. 19.

5

Egypt in 1615–1616 as seen through the Eyes of the Armenian Simeon of Poland

Angèle Kapoïan

Simeon was born around 1584 in Zamosc, near Lvov, which was then in Poland but is today in the Ukraine. His parents were Armenians who had emigrated from the Crimea.

The oldest traces of Armenian emigration to Poland and the Ukraine[1] date back to the capture of Ani, the medieval capital of the Bagratid kings of Armenia, by the Seljuk Turks in 1064. Later, the stream of emigrants increased following the Mongol invasions of Armenia in the thirteenth century, and after 1375, when the Armenian kingdom of Cilicia fell into the hands of the Mamluks of Egypt.

Simeon received an Armenian religious education and became a deacon and a scribe. During his extensive travels, which lasted more than a decade, his ability to copy Armenian manuscripts helped him earn his living wherever he went: Constantinople, Rome, Cairo, Jerusalem and so on. As a result, he is known both as Simeon of Poland (Simeon Lehats'i in Armenian) and as Simeon the Scribe (Simeon Dpir).

Anxious to make the pilgrimage to Jerusalem, he left his birthplace in 1607, at the age of 23 or 24, to undertake a voyage that took him, in chronological order, to Constantinople, Western Asia Minor, the Balkans, Italy, the Greek Islands, Eastern Asia Minor, again Constantinople, Egypt and finally to the Holy Land and Syria. He returned to Poland in 1618, via Constantinople once again. These itineraries included most of the cities of the Ottoman heartland.

Simeon completed his *Travel Account* in 1635 at Lvov, after having gathered and edited all the notes he had taken on his trip. He pleaded:

> I beg you not to get bored during the reading and not to be critical, since I sometimes wrote on a ship, sometimes riding a

mule, sometimes in an inn or a caravanserail. While others were eating, drinking and having fun, I was trying to finish this diary which is intended for the use of other pilgrims.[2]

The unique manuscript of Simeon's work was kept in the University Library of Lvov until 1944-5, when it disappeared with other manuscripts and rare books during the German occupation. Fortunately, Father Nerses Akinian, of the Mekhitarist Order of Vienna, had copied it in 1932, and published the complete text four years later.[3] This *Travel Account* is especially replete with carefully organised information on the population and the customs of each town and city that Simeon visited in almost all the eastern Mediterranean countries. Furthermore, Simeon appended to his journal a brief autobiography, a detailed report on the attack of the Ottoman Sultan Osman II against Poland in 1622 and a political commentary on the wars involving Poland, Russia, the Ottoman Empire and Persia from 1623 to 1635. The work has not yet been fully translated into a western European language. We have only a Russian translation, published by M.O. Darbinian, and partial ones in Turkish, Italian, Polish and French.[4] I am working on complete translations in both English and French.

Simeon's description of Egypt starts with his arrival in Alexandria in 1615 from Constantinople:

> It is a large and fortified city . . . Here we drank the water of the third river of Paradise[5] and along the sea, we saw the ruins of the Basilica of the 72 Translators [who rendered the Old Testament from Hebrew to Greek]. Four western Consuls had their residence in Alexandria. There was a Greek church and a large caravanserai. Greeks, Copts and Europeans were living here, but no Armenians. There was the miraculous stone church of St Sava [St Catherine] who had great power over the sea, that is why sailors implored her help . . . We had to make a contribution of one gold coin to visit it, even the priests had to pay but monks were exempt . . . We saw the deep underground cisterns made of stone and with arcades, filled with fresh water because there is neither water nor reservoir of rain water . . . A very small canal coming from the Nile was running through the city. It is said that King Alexandre had this water brought here by undertaking great construction works.[6]

After a two-day journey on the Nile, Simeon reaches Bulaq, the port of Cairo. Upon entering the capital, which he finds as large as Rome – a city he visited in 1611 – but more populated, he seeks out the Armenian quarter, as he does everywhere he goes, in order to find a lodging. He discovers two Armenian priests in a Coptic church. Seemingly, the Armenians did not have their own church at that time as they did in earlier periods, and especially the eleventh and twelfth centuries under the Fatimids, when there were several Armenian churches and monasteries, according to Abu Salih, an Armenian who wrote in Arabic in the first years of the thirteenth century.[7] Simeon notes that about two hundred Armenian families had sought refuge in Egypt from the chaos caused in Anatolia by the insurrectional movement of the Jelalis against Ottoman authority, at the end of the sixteenth and the first decade of the seventeenth century.[8]

As an Armenian living in the diaspora, he is not only interested by his compatriots but also by other minorities, such as the Copts, whom he presents as follows:

> According to the defters [official registers] there are 40,000 Coptic families, most of them rich . . . They hold all the administrative posts of the city. They own houses made in stone. They wear silk turbans, and attend the *Divan* of the Pasha because they are, by tradition, the secretaries of the *Divan* and keep the defters . . . Their churches are in dark places . . . Their patriarch has his seat in Alexandria . . . When the Copts celebrate mass, they cover their face and their head, and they sing in Greek 'Kyrie Eleison' and other hymns . . . The women sing a sort of chant, like a murmur, vibrating their lips with their fingers. They do this not only at church but also at weddings and other festivities. Their priests are married. Their monks wear a black hair-shirt. They do not eat any meat, and during Lent they do not use any oil and do not drink any wine . . . They wear a large black cap in felt as the Jews in Poland; the laymen do the same . . . Like the Greeks, they use plain bread instead of the host, and everyone makes and sells it. They circumcise not just the boys but also the girls . . .[9]

Our traveller is much concerned about the great poverty of the Egyptian peasants, the fellahin:

> Though the country is fertile, some of its inhabitants are famished, poor, unhappy, naked, always searching for a piece of bread because they never have enough food . . . They eat smelly, molded and wormy cheese as if it were sugar . . . They are the servants, the

slaves of foreigners [the Ottomans] . . . There is no people more unfortunate since they are deprived of everything: food, clothes, house, possessions of any sort. They sit, eat and sleep on the ground.[10]

On another occasion he speaks rather bluntly, though with picturesque language, of the dirtiness of the fellahin, 'Their noses are always snotty; a yellowish pus runs out of their ears; one could plant vegetables on their feet; their knees are like those of a camel . . .'[11]

Though Simeon is a devout Christian, he cannot hide his admiration for the religious fervour of the Muslim Egyptians. For example, when he describes the ceremony when a caravan departs for Mecca, transporting in great pomp the *kiswa*, the black brocade cover for the Ka'ba sent each year from Cairo,[12] he exclaims:

We admired their ardent love for their prophet. The Christians do not have such a love for Christ. To go to Mecca, the Muslim pilgrims are willing to endure all the torments of a difficult journey of 40 days through the desert . . . They are exposed to many accidents and difficulties, but those things do not bother them. They go barefoot, beating their chests, crying and murmuring prayers and finding themselves unworthy.[13]

Simeon, like all travellers to Egypt, visits the Khan al-Khalili, the great bazaar of Cairo, where he marvels, of course, at the world's finest cotton, edged with silk. There he meets many Muslim and Armenian merchants from Constantinople, Diyarbekir and Aleppo, as well as traders from Ethiopia and India. He is struck by the quantity and variety of goods from all corners of the globe, and is reminded of the Bedestan, the central bazaar of Constantinople,[14] which he had visited in 1608, 1611, 1615 and 1618.

He also mentions, as did al-Maqrizi in the first half of the fifteenth century and Jean Palerne, Samuel Kiechel and Villamont in the sixteenth century and George Sandys in the seventeenth, the way the Egyptians transform the muddy water of the Nile into a pure liquid:

I am going to tell you another miracle: this turbid water is poured into big urns and jars, the rims of which are rubbed with bitter almonds and apricot stones, and soon the water gets clear and drinkable; if not it is just mud.[15]

The well-known artificial hatcheries also attract his attention, 'Here the hens do not hatch their own eggs which are [instead] buried by the thousands in dunghills. Twenty days later, the new-born chicks are removed and sold.'[16]

Our author then gives a description of Matariyya in the following terms:

> One day, Father Maghakia [an Armenian priest who lodged Simeon] took me to Matariyya . . . On the way we saw the Monastery of Saint Sargis [Sergius] where the Armenians buried their dead. At Matariyya there was a large reservoir filled with water by an hydraulic wheel. It is said that, during their flight to Egypt, Christ [the Holy Family] stopped in this village; Jesus was thirsty, so his mother went to fetch water but no one gave her any. Thus the Holy Mother of God struck a malediction: 'May your water be [forever] salty!' and it was so. As she was sadly returning to her son, she saw a spring gushing forth at his feet. Glory to God! It is still the same today because the water of the village is salty everywhere except at this spot. Every day someone brings this water to the Pasha because he does not drink any other water. In front of the reservoir there was a circular niche like an altar, with benches and tables where we offered animals in sacrifice and lit candles. From there we entered a vast garden and, while walking around, we saw many lemon trees. In Egypt the lemons are small, the size of a walnut, very juicy and acid. They covered the ground like hail. We also saw balsam trees which were dried up. It is said that in the past four men used to guard them.[17]

Among the other subjects that occupy Simeon's narrative on Egypt are the markets of horses, donkeys and camels, the main diseases, the agricultural production, the monasteries and the celebration of the annual rise of the Nile. But Simeon's inquisitive eye is perceptibly more attracted by the social and economic conditions of the country and its customs than by its architecture or its flora and fauna. After spending almost a year in Egypt, he speaks rather laconically about a few Islamic monuments and does not even mention the Pyramids.

On slave markets Simeon has the following to say:

> Farther along [from the Khan al-Khalili] are two slave markets: one of white Turks and the other of Arabs. We entered and saw black male and female Ethiopians lined up. The walls seemed black

because of their darkness. There were young virgins, naked and shameful, whose intimate parts were exposed. The Blacks have no value here... One could buy three Blacks for the price of a White... The Turkish slaves were dressed and were wearing belts while the Blacks were naked. A young black girl or boy was sold for only two piastres.[18]

In the summer of 1616, Simeon departs from Cairo for Jerusalem by journeying as far as Ramla with the caravan transporting the *khazina* – that is, the annual tribute of Egypt to the Ottoman sultan. At this point he leaves the caravan to go on his separate way.

The few translated excerpts I have presented cannot render fully the vivid colour and frank expressiveness of Simeon's language: a mixture of classical and vernacular Armenian interspersed with Turkish, Persian, Arabic and Polish words and phrases. Among other Armenian works of this genre, Simeon's *Travel Account* stands out, both for its original form and rich contents. Furthermore, while most seventeenth-century Western accounts are written by well-educated travellers of means, anxious to discover and describe exotic lands and usually sent on diplomatic, military, scientific, religious or commercial missions, Simeon, a modest pilgrim, does not try to impress his readers with romantic adventures or by his knowledge. He judges everything directly and simply as a representative of the lower-middle class rather than of the establishment, and as a member of a minority community in his own country. This is the most striking difference between his travel notes and those of most West European travellers. Finally, Simeon's work is unusual for being among the rare accounts of Egypt and the Near East written by a traveller born and raised in Europe, but ethnically a Middle Easterner.

Notes

1 On the Polish-Ukrainian Armenian diaspora, see especially the series of articles by Ya. Dachkévytch published in the *Revue des Études Arméniennes*, starting in 1964.
2 Nerses Akinian, *Travel Account, Annals and Colophons of Simeon the Scribe of Poland* (in Armenian) (Vienna, 1936) [Hereinafter Akinian]; French translation of the section on Egypt by Angèle Kapoïan-Kouymjian, *L'Égypte vue par des Arméniens (XIe–XVIIe siècles)* (Paris, Fondation Singer-Polignac, 1988) [Hereinafter *L'Égypte*], p. 29.

3 See the previous note.
4 For details on the various translations, see *L'Égypte*, p. 29 and notes 30–2. The more recent excerpts in Polish have been translated by Zbigniew Kosciow, *Symeon Lehacy (Szymon z Polski). Zapiski Podrozne* (Warsaw, 1991).
5 Of course, Simeon is referring to the Nile. We read in Genesis 2:10–14 about the four rivers of the garden of Eden: the Pison (Ganges?); the Gihon (Nile?); the Hiddekel (Tigris); and the Euphrates. Other travellers have also put the source of the Nile in Paradise, since this was an accepted notion in the Middle Ages; see, for instance, Emmanuel Piloti, *L'Égypte au commencement du XVe siècle d'après le Traité d'Emmanuel Piloti de Crète (Incipit, 1420)*, ed. P.-H. Dopp (Cairo, 1950), p. 3, or Joos van Ghistele, *Le Voyage de Joos van Ghistele, 1482–1483*, trans. from the Flemish, introduced and annotated by Renée Bauwens-Préaux, Institut Français d'Archéologie Orientale du Caire (Cairo, 1976), p. 61, or Ibn Battuta, *The Travels of Ibn Battuta, A.D. 1325–1354*, trans. H.A.R. Gibb with revisions and notes from the Arabic text ed. C. Defrémery and B.R. Sanguinetti (Cambridge University Press for the Hakluyt Society, 1958), I, p. 49.
6 Akinian, *op. cit.*, p. 213; Kapoïan-Kouymjian, *op. cit.*, pp. 32–3.
7 *The Churches and Monasteries of Egypt and Some Neighbouring Countries Attributed to Abu Salih, the Armenian*, trans. from the original Arabic by B.T.A. Evetts, with added notes by Alfred J. Butler (Oxford, 1895), pp. 1–6, 10–13, 143–4, 249. See also Th[orgom] E[piskopos] G[ushakian], *Ancient and Modern Armenian Churches in Egypt* (in Armenian) (Cairo, 1927), *passim*, and Ardashes H. Kardashian, *Material for the History of the Armenians in Egypt* (in Armenian, additional titles also in English and Arabic) (Cairo, 1943), vol. 1, *passim*.
8 On the Jelalis, see Mustafa Akdag, *The Origin of the Great Jelali Disorders* (in Turkish) (Ankara, 1963), or M.K. Zulalyan, *The Jelali Movement and the Condition of the Armenians in the Ottoman Empire* (in Armenian) (Erevan, 1966), and Halil Inalçik, 'The Heyday and Decline of the Ottoman Empire', *The Cambridge History of Islam*, ed. P.M. Holt, Ann K.S. Lambton, Bernard Lewis (Cambridge University Press, 1970), vol. 1, pp. 347–50.
9 Akinian, *op. cit.*, pp. 217–19; Kapoïan-Kouymjian, *op. cit.*, pp. 34–5.
10 Akinian, *op. cit.*, pp. 219–20, 226–7; Kapoïan-Kouymjian, *op. cit.*, pp. 35–6, 39–40.
11 Akinian, *op. cit.*, p. 219; Kapoïan-Kouymjian, *op. cit.*, p. 36.
12 For more details, see, for instance, J. Jomier, *Le Mahmal et la caravane égyptienne des pèlerins de La Mecque (XIIIe–XXe siècles)* (Cairo, 1953).
13 Akinian, *op. cit.*, p. 236; Kapoïan-Kouymjian, *op. cit.*, p. 46.
14 Akinian, *op. cit.*, pp. 222–4; Kapoïan-Kouymjian, *op. cit.*, pp. 37–8.
15 Akinian, *op. cit.*, pp. 220–1; Kapoïan-Kouymjian, *op. cit.*, p. 36.
16 Akinian, *op. cit.*, p. 222; Kapoïan-Kouymjian, *op. cit.*, p. 37. Most voyagers were struck by this practice; for a partial list see Kapoïan-Kouymjian, *op. cit.*, p. 27, n. 28 and for a detailed discussion for the practice see Rozière and Rouyer, 'Mémoire sur l'art de faire éclore les poulets en Égypte par le moyen des fours', *Description de l'Égypte*, 2nd edn by Panckoucke (1822), vol. 11, pp. 401–27.
17 Akinian, *op. cit.*, pp. 230–1; Kapoïan-Kouymjian, *op. cit.*, pp. 42–3.
18 Akinian, *op. cit.*, p. 223; Kapoïan-Kouymjian, *op. cit.*, p. 38.

6
Adam Olearius's Travels to Persia, 1633–1639

Elio Brancaforte

The story of Adam Olearius begins at the midpoint of the Thirty Years War. Duke Frederick III, ruler of the small northern German duchy of Holstein-Gottorp, agreed to sponsor a commercial venture that would eliminate all its debts, by convincing Shāh Safi I of Persia to export his country's silk via the Volga, through Russia and the Baltic States, to Gottorp. From there the silk would be sold throughout northern Europe. The war had blocked off the traditional routes through southern Germany by which northern Europe obtained its silk, and the Turkish monopoly of the trade had led to exorbitantly high tariffs. Duke Frederick decided to send an embassy to the Shah's capital in Isfahan. Otto Brüggemann, a Hamburg merchant whose brother-in-law was the Shah's personal watchmaker, was to lead the three hundred members of the expedition, accompanied by the doctor and poet Paul Fleming and by Adam Olearius, who was to chronicle the mission as its official secretary. Olearius, born Adam Öhlschlegel in 1599, had distinguished himself as a student of theology, philosophy and the natural sciences at the University of Leipzig. He also had a great facility for learning languages, mastering the basics of Persian, for example, during his first three months there. The entire mission lasted from 1633 to 1639 and resulted in Olearius's magnum opus,[1] the *Vermehrte Newe Beschreibung der Muscowitischen und Persischen Reyse* (*The Extended, New Description of the Journey to Moscow and Persia*) of 1656. It is this text, the only major German baroque non-devotional work to have been translated from German into other foreign languages during the seventeenth century, that will be the focus of my discussion.[2]

Olearius's travel account is truly a baroque text, since it bridges the gap between Renaissance/humanist thought (with its overdependence on ancient classical authorities) and the scientific, enlightened spirit of the

[119]

eighteenth century. The text is not a simple compendium of information gathered from a journey. For a number of reasons, it may be regarded as the work of a comparatist.

First, as a scholar and humanist, the author often refers to classical and Renaissance authors, but with the critical attitude of a scientist, for he corrects his sources when the statements do not correspond to his own experience as an eyewitness. One of the best-known examples of this methodology occurs during a storm in the Baltic, near the beginning of the journey. Olearius notes that seasickness cannot be caused by saltwater, as the humanist Pontanus maintained, but that the motion of the waves is responsible, since the crew felt the same effects later on the freshwater Caspian Sea. Also, after a discussion with two Samoyeds (a Siberian tribe), Olearius speculates that what sailors have claimed were 'monsters' living along the Siberian coast were actually natives. During the winter, the indigenous people wore big furs over their heads, making it appear that they were 'headless'; and their 'huge feet' were, most probably, snowshoes. The existence of 'acephalous' (or headless) beings, had been reported since the time of Pliny and Augustine.

Second, Olearius's methodology is concerned with juxtaposing the customs and social structures of the people he meets with those of his native land, and at times he even expresses admiration for some of their traits. Olearius's favourite Persian poet, Sa'dī, 'speaks about God and his works, and how man should relate to God as well as a Christian might, often his thoughts are so spiritual as to put a Christian to shame'.[3] Olearius does not claim to possess all the answers, and consults with scholars and native informants of the lands he visits, in the interest of science. The most practical effect of the trip was the superior cartography that Olearius produced; it enabled him to correct previous maps, many of which were considerably flawed. It also led him to dismiss the Ptolemaic system of the world, which still prevailed officially during his lifetime. The *Newe Reisebeschreibung* includes large, detailed, fold-out maps describing Moscow, the course of the Volga and Northern Persia, which so impressed Tsar Mikhail by their accuracy that he later attempted to enlist Olearius into his service. These maps also maintained their validity until well into the eighteenth century.

Third, the very structure of the work is evidence of its multiplicity, for it is many texts at once. It is both a travel account and an advisory, and alternates between first person accounts of the journey itself and third person descriptions of the landscape. For example, one section might deal with the adventures that befell the expedition – such as a shipwreck, or an attack by Cossacks or Tartars – and the next section discusses a region's flora and fauna and the history of the peoples who are encountered from the past to the present (using classical sources as well as accounts from legend or folklore). Next, one might find a description of the natives and what the author terms their 'nature'. In short, the reader of modern texts, who is used to studying disciplines such as geography, linguistics, biology, or ethnography, in separate, compartmentalised forms, is taken aback when confronted with the excess of information contained within this eight hundred-page folio text.

I will now discuss a few of the illustrations relating to the expedition's stay in Persia. The engravings, most of which were drawn by Olearius himself, are an integral part of the work. They not only contributed greatly to the financial success of the work, but also underscored the author's claim that the descriptions were drawn from life.

The reader encounters the first Persians on the frontispiece (fig. 1). Two Persian men (a servant and a nobleman, who is distinguished by feathers on his turban) are placed on the left-hand side, while their Russian counterparts are situated on the right. The men are on display, facing the viewer and standing within an architectural framework supported by neo-classical pillars. Just above their heads rests an emblematic cartouche bearing a religious message: a man standing on the earth is attached to the sun. 'In consilio tuo ducis me', reads the motto hovering above Olearius's entire enterprise, indicating that the traveller, led by the true God, is walking toward the true light. The emblematic message is a necessary component of the representation, and displays the piety not only of the author but also of his patron. The stance, gestures, costumes and demeanour of the figures in the frontispiece all point to the theatricality of the depiction, yet the exotic figures are contained within imposing Western-style architecture; the control of the Other is thus assured. One may recall Edward Said's point, in his work *Orientalism*, that the Orient is like a theatrical stage affixed to Europe, on which the whole East is confined. 'On this stage will appear figures whose role it is to represent the larger whole from which they emanate.'[4] In this, the age of *theatrum mundi* (in which all the world is a stage), the frontispiece serves merely to open the curtain on the subject, while assuring the Western reader of the dominance of the author, who has God on his side.

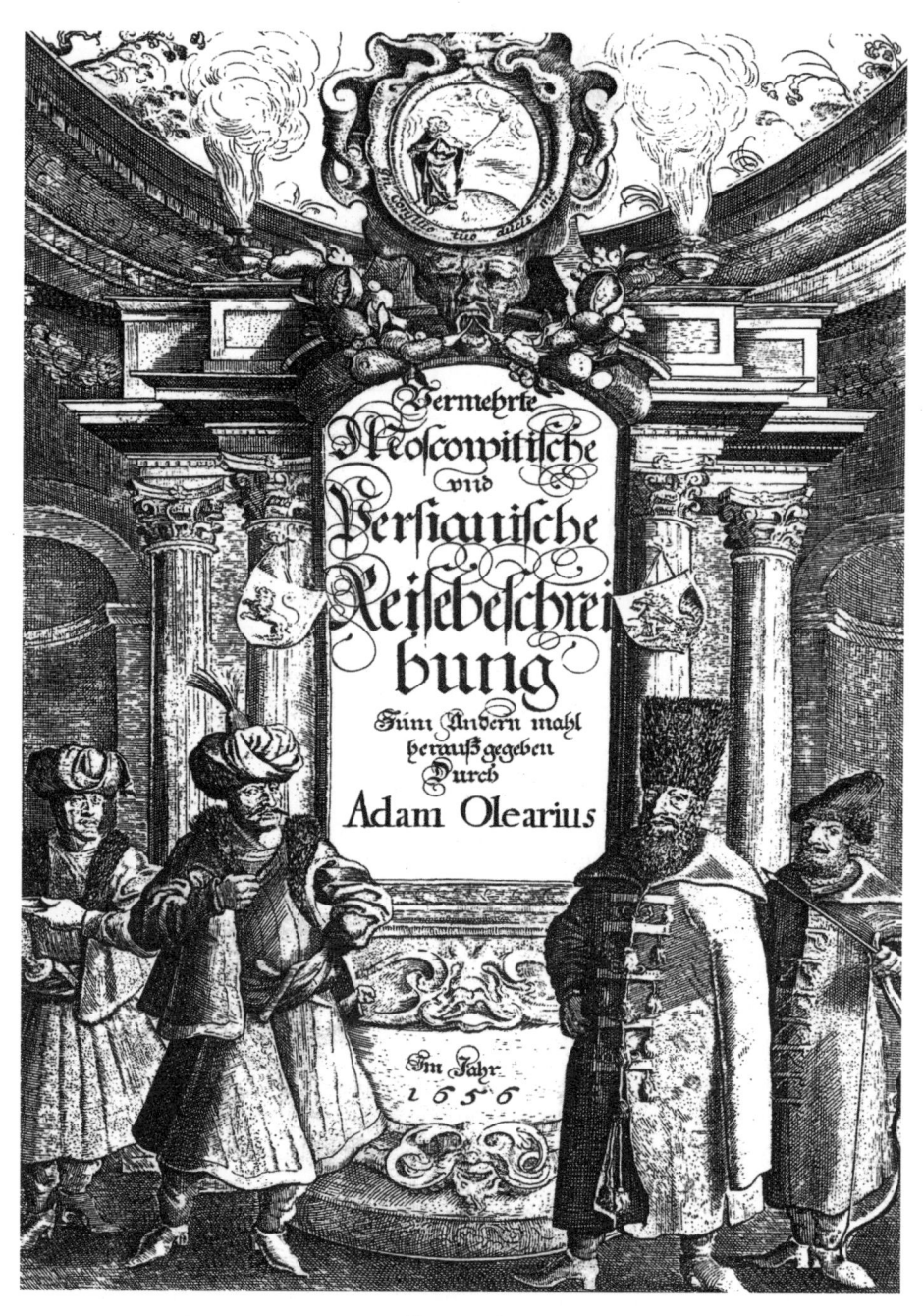

FIGURE 1
Frontispiece of Adam Olearius's *Reisebeschreibung*
(by courtesy of Max Niemeyer, Publisher)

In another depiction we see that even a relatively innocuous subject, such as a cityscape, is not what it seems (fig. 2). The Persian city Kāshān is characterised by the prominent front and back view of a tarantula in the bottom left-hand corner. The five to six scorpions hiding on top and alongside the cartouche are not so readily identifiable – the viewer who does not notice these creatures at first is, in a way, invited to confront in a pictorial representation the danger that the author himself experienced in real life. Olearius notes that he alone, out of the entire entourage, was bitten by one of these scorpions, and describes the symptoms that he experienced. He then advises that a victim should try to kill the animal that inflicted the bite and place it against the wound. According to the law of 'sympathies', the poison in the human would be attracted back to the creature and a cure would follow. Olearius notes that a specimen scorpion, which he took back to Gottorp, is in the Duke's *Kunstkammer* (cabinet of curiosities): the Oriental danger is thus immobilised and tamed, on display.

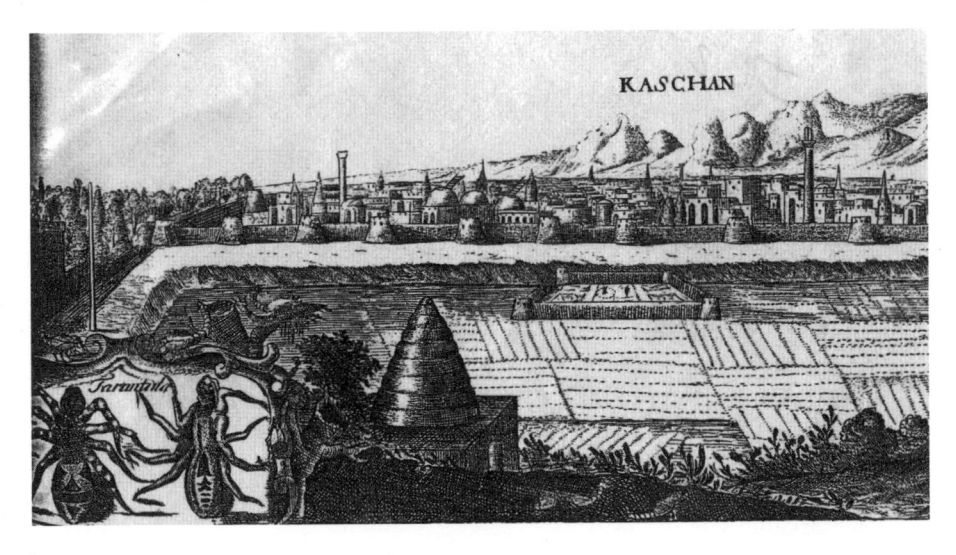

FIGURE 2
An illustration of Kāshān
(by courtesy of Max Niemeyer, Publisher)

After a description of Persian fauna, Olearius goes on to codify his human hosts (fig. 3). On the one hand, our author is impressed by the curiosity and intelligence of the Persians he meets:

FIGURE 3
An illustration of Persian clothing
(by courtesy of Max Niemeyer, Publisher)

> By nature the Persians are gifted with remarkable perspicacity and a good mind; they are sharp-witted and good teachers, therefore there are many excellent poets among them who write reflective poetry; in general they have a high regard for the liberal arts. They are very friendly toward each other, especially toward foreigners, their speech is remarkably polite and kind . . . The Persians are also known to be fierce warriors; they are very clean, and the streets are remarkably safe (p. 589).

On the other hand, in spite of his admiration for certain traits, Olearius, a Protestant, cannot but attack Persian character traits, especially those concerning religion, morality, and sexual behaviour. When discussing the latter, he goes into some detail. Already the outward appearance of his subjects is suspect, because cross-dressing indicates moral confusion in the European context. In describing Persian men, he observes:

> Their clothes hang on their bodies loosely and sloppily. From afar they look like women and they walk and move to and fro like geese, whereas the clothes of the women are even more delicate than those of the men, they don't tie them around their bodies and they wear their pants and shirts like men (p. 586).

Sexual identity is thus unclear. Women's outdoor apparel also leads to confusion:

> The women, when they go out into the streets don't show their faces; they are covered with long white cloths that hang down over their calves and only at their faces is there a slit through which they can barely see. Under those clothes one finds often very beautiful images, and often under beautiful clothes are hidden very ugly images (p. 588).

With regard to sexual conduct, he regards Persian males as abnormal. They are too sexually promiscuous: they take many wives; they frequent brothels; and they are perverse, since the greatest sin, sodomy, is rampant among them. This corporeal licentiousness is only to be expected, since their leaders (both worldly and spiritual) are depraved. Olearius notes that Shāh Safī, his host, was not only a typical Oriental despot, but was suspected of engaging in homosexual acts. In addition, Muhammad ... even proclaimed that carnal relations would play a large part in the afterlife, in order to convert simple folk to Islam.

Olearius also tells the amusing story of a woman who filed for divorce, on the grounds of her husband's impotence (actually, Olearius uses the term *impotentiae* – when dealing with risqué subjects Latin is used for the sake of women and young people who read his work): 'when the judge asked the man why he had taken a wife if he knew about his condition, the man answered: he wanted her to scratch his back. She replied: I've scratched your back long enough, but have never been scratched in return' (p. 610). Sexual deviance is often aroused by dancing, which is loved beyond measure, and enhanced by hashish, which 'strengthens nature in preparation for the games of Venus' (p. 594). On the other hand if one drinks too much *kahwae* (coffee-water), carnal desires are completely extinguished.

The German embassy held its own sexual entertainments while in Persia, which fully conformed to traditional Western stereotypes of exotic eroticism. The visitors were invited to a banquet held in a setting that corresponded to a European's notion of what an Oriental feast should entail (fig. 4). In the middle of the banquet room hundreds of large and small mirrors were set into the walls; a fountain shot water upward; and musicians played in the background, while the Shah's female dancers performed acrobatic, sexually arousing feats for the guests. The evening did not end just with visual stimulation, however (note the three seated German ambassadors on the left side of the engraving, one of whom is watching the entertainment). The dancers were expected to perform sexual favours for the foreign guests in specially prepared rooms. By characterising it as a *Thorheit* (foolishness) Olearius seems to show that he was not interested in acceding to his host's invitation.

FIGURE 4
An illustration of Eahtemad döwlet's banquet
(by courtesy of Max Niemeyer, Publisher)

The last representation I wish to consider in detail portrays Shāh Safi's audience for the Holstein embassy, the highpoint of the *Newe*

Reisebeschreibung in terms of Oriental drama (fig. 5). The gaze of the viewer is raised, as if in a private box at the theatre, commanding the entire scene. At the centre of attention, in a closed space, is the Shah's *Diwankhaneh* (house of judgement): a 'stage' raised off the main courtyard by three steps and equipped with red velvet curtains, which could be raised or lowered by means of ropes which control the spectacle. The foreground, partitioned into three sections by two walls, contains, on the left, the monarch's horses. The right-hand side depicts the ruler's 13, sumptuously dressed dancers, whose faces are uncovered, seated next to the lesser members of the German embassy (the woman alongside the right wall seems to be flirting with a German looking in her direction).

FIGURE 5
An illustration of Shāh Safī's banquet for the Holstein Embassy
(by courtesy of Max Niemeyer, Publisher)

The centre foreground includes servants, guards, dogs and wrestlers, located between the two small walls. If one extends the axes of these walls, the eye is led to the alcove in which the Shah is to be found. Exotic profusion is everywhere. European paintings and costly tapestries hang from the walls; in the fountain at the monarch's feet are found all varieties of flowers, as well as lemons, apricots, pomegranates, apples and other fruit; and the table settings are all of gold. Yet our author maintains his critical stance, in spite of being surrounded by such opulence. In short, this scene of Eastern excess and decadence corresponds exactly to a seventeenth-century (or even a twentieth-century) Westerner's conception of an Oriental court. It is a necessary representation, necessary for the simple fact that it confirms and repeats the stereotypical elements of the Oriental 'stage'. The reader/viewer is comforted by the fact that in spite of Olearius's 'scientific' observations and attempts to correct long-held views regarding Persia, the fundamental picture still corresponds to established views.

After the embassy returned to Germany in 1639, a Persian delegation was sent by Shāh Safī to Gottorp. It seems that it, too, had to contend with the inexplicable customs of the people they met. The Shah's ambassador, for example, was very distressed by the curiosity displayed by the inhabitants of Narva, a Baltic city, and inquired whether the women there were all whores, since they let themselves be seen so openly. When the Persian embassy arrived in Holstein, the few bales of silk that it offered to Duke Frederick as a present from the Shah were the only amounts of the precious material that Gottorp would ever obtain from the entire mission. The long, dangerous route, and the high tariffs required by the Tsar, as well as the fact that Persia did not produce enough silk, made the venture unprofitable.

Finally, when the Persian delegation made ready to leave Gottorp, a number of delegates defected, including the secretary, Haqq-werdi. This was to prove most fortuitous for Olearius, since he was able to perfect his knowledge of Persian, as well as check the information he had acquired abroad with a cultured, native informant. Together the men prepared a – never published – Persian-Turkish-Arabic dictionary. Most importantly, Haqq-werdi helped Olearius translate the celebrated Persian poet Sa'dī's *Golestān*,[5] under the title *Persianisches Rosenthal* (1654), which helped introduce the German literary public to Persian poetry. This translation, along with the travel account, influenced Jakob Grimmelshausen (author of *Simplicissimus*), Montesquieu's *Persian Letters* and Goethe's *West-östlicher Diwan*. Olearius was appointed court librarian by Duke Frederick, and charged with developing the Duke's *Kunstkammer*, made up, in large part, of mementos from the trip to Russia and Persia. This carefully assembled collection, the forerunner of our museums, consisted of bizarre objects (scorpions preserved in oil, minerals, fossils and stone relics), which were organised and presented in a controlled environment. It has long been dispersed, but Adam Olearius's textual curiosities remain.

NOTES

1. Adam Olearius, *Vermehrte Newe Beschreibung der Muscowitischen und Persischen Reyse* (1656), ed. Dieter Lohmeier, Deutsche Neudrucke 21 (Tübingen, Max Niemeyer, 1971). See also [*Vermehrte Newe Beschreibung der Muscowitischen und Persischen Reyse*] *Moskowitische und persische Reise: die holsteinische Gesandtschaft beim Schah, 1633–1639*, ed. Detlef Haberland (Stuttgart, Thienemann, 1986).
2. Quotations in my paper refer to the reprint of Adam Olearius's *Vermehrte Newe Beschreibung der Muscowitischen und Persischen Reyse* [1656], ed. Dieter Lohmeier, Deutsche Neudrucke 21 (Tübingen, Max Niemeyer, 1971). All translations of the text are my own. This, the second edition of the voyage, incorporates information from subsequent trips to Russia, and is considerably longer than the first edition, the *Offt begehrte Beschreibung der Newen Orientalischen Reyse* (1647). Accounts of the journey were soon translated into Dutch (1651), French (1656), Italian (1658), and English (1662). A modern scholarly translation into English, translated and edited by Samuel Baron entitled *The Travels of Olearius in Seventeenth-Century Russia* (Stanford University Press, 1967) is limited to the Russian section of the journey.
3. Cited in Lohmeier, *op. cit.*, p. 35.
4. Edward Said, *Orientalism* (New York, Vintage Books, 1979), p. 63.
5. Mosleh al-Din Sa'di-ye Shirazi, *The Gulistan or Rose Garden of Sa'di*, trans. by Edward Rehatsek (London, George Allen & Unwin, 1964).

7

The British in Oman since 1645

Sir Terence Clark

As in so many other parts of the world during the period of British overseas expansion in the seventeenth and eighteenth centuries, the flag followed trade in establishing contact between Britain and Oman. The East India Company led the way, as it penetrated the Gulf in its drive to seek new markets for its goods, but the initiative came in this case from the Omani side.

In 1645, the Imam Nasir bin Murshid wrote to the East India Company offering them trading facilities at Sohar, to which the Company responded in February 1646 by sending their representative from Surat, Philip Wylde, to negotiate a treaty with him.[1] This document gave the British remarkably generous exclusive trading rights at Sohar, as well as the freedom to practise their own religion and extraterritorial jurisdiction. When the British ship *Fellowship* called at Muscat in 1650, shortly after the Omanis recaptured the town from the Portuguese, the captain was offered 'the best house in the town' if the Company would settle a trading 'factory' there.[2] So well disposed was the then Imam, Sayyid Sultan bin Saif, that in 1659 he negotiated a treaty with the Company's representative, Colonel Henry Rainsford, providing that the English should have one of the forts dominating Muscat town, Jalali or Mirani, be given part of the town for residence, provide a garrison of one hundred soldiers and share the customs. Colonel Rainsford, however, died and by the time a successor had arrived to renegotiate the treaty – apparently a diplomatic necessity in those days – the Imam had had second thoughts, possibly because of the influence of the Dutch, who were then strong and successful rivals for trade in the area. The English were, nonetheless, invited to trade in Muscat and did so from visiting ships without setting up a factory there. By the late eighteenth century, British interests were being looked after by a local merchant who acted as 'Consul for the English'.

It took a further century and Napoleon's threat of invading British India for the British to consolidate their position in Muscat. In 1798, the East India Company's representative in Bushire, Mirza Mahdi 'Ali Khan, was despatched to Muscat to conclude a *qaulnameh* (treaty) with the Imam Sayyid Sultan bin Ahmad, granting the British an even more generous exclusive position vis-à-vis the French and their Dutch allies but, requiring the British to defend Muscat, its trade and its shipping.[3] The Governor General of India thought it prudent to confirm this treaty and despatched Captain (later Sir) John Malcolm to sign with the Imam on 26 April 1800 an equally remarkable treaty, establishing that 'an Englishman of respectability shall always reside at the port of Muscat' and that the friendship of the two states should 'remain unshook till the end of time, and till the sun and the moon have finished their revolving career'.[4]

British enthusiasm was short-lived, discouraged in large part by the high mortality rate of the British Residents appointed there. In the course of ten years, four Residents died in Muscat, and in January 1810 Captain Malcolm, then on his third mission to Persia, recommended that the Residency in Muscat should be abolished because 'English constitutions were unequal to withstand the baneful effects of the climate at Maskat'[5] and that the representation of British interests should be entrusted to the Resident at Bushire. However, the Resident there reported in May 1810 that 'the pernicious effect of the climate of Muscat obliged him to resign all further charge of the duties of that station'. For the next thirty years, until 1840, Britain was content to leave British commercial and consular interests in the hands of a native agent. Robert Binning, who passed through Muscat in October 1850, described the British Agent, Khoja Ezekiel, as 'an indolent and nonchalant rascal'![6]

Once again in response to a perceived external threat – intelligence that the Egyptians in Eastern Arabia might invade Oman – the Muscat Residency was reopened at the beginning of 1840, under Captain Atkins Hamerton of the Bombay Army. But Sayyid Sa'id bin Sultan preferred to live in Zanzibar, and when he transferred his court there in 1843 the Resident accompanied him. The Residency remained in Zanzibar until Sayyid Sa'id died in 1856, when Oman and Zanzibar became separate sultanates.[7] The separation was a complicated matter, and was resolved by arbitration under British auspices in the Canning award of 1861. In the process, it was felt that the Sultan in Muscat was at a disadvantage compared with his brother in Zanzibar, who had the benefit of advice from the British Resident, and that for this and other commercial reasons the post at Muscat should be reopened. Lt W.M. Pengelley of the Indian Navy was appointed in 1861, and the post has remained occupied in one form or another virtually ever since.

Much of the early detailed work on the exploration of Oman was done by visitors from British India, from where British commercial, political and consular representation in the Gulf was administered. Among such travellers, one of the most notable was Lt James Wellsted of the Indian Navy, who toured much of Northern Oman in 1834–5 in execution of the East India Company's commission that he should explore the interior of the country, discover as much as possible of conditions there and evaluate the position of the ruler, Sayyid Sa'id bin Ahmad. He was assiduous in collecting political and economic information as well as in drawing more accurate maps on the two circular tours he made from Muscat, first via the Sharqiyya up to Nizwa and the Jabal Akhdar, and, second, along the Batina and through the mountains to Ibri in an unsuccessful attempt to persuade the Wahhabis to allow him to visit Buraimi. He subsequently published a highly readable account of his experiences.[8] He was accompanied on the second tour by Lt Whitelock, also of the Indian Navy, whom he had met by chance at Samad. Whitelock had been sent to Oman as a language student. Wellsted was later criticised for not giving Whitelock any credit for the journey. Wellsted attempted suicide by shooting himself in the mouth in a fit of delirium and died a lingering death in India. Captain Arthur Stiffe of the Indian Navy, who in 1860 carried out a survey of Muscat and its environs, which was published much later with a full description of Muscat and its recent history,[9] also made a notable contribution to the still fairly rudimentary knowledge of this area. His survey map of Muscat and Matrah shows the British consulate in its historic position on the waterfront below Fort Jalali, which it occupied for over a hundred years until 1995.

With its debilitating climate, its inhospitable deserts and mountains, inhabited by warring tribes or fanatical Wahhabis, and the limited prospects for trade, Oman in the nineteenth century must have seemed less attractive to travellers than many other parts of the then emerging world, and it is hardly surprising that much of the exploration of the interior of the country was left to the British political agents in Muscat.

Among the most notable of these was Colonel Samuel Miles. Himself the son of an Indian Army officer, Miles entered the East India Company and served as a soldier in India. He subsequently joined the Political Service, and served first in Aden and later in Makran before being appointed as political agent and consul in Muscat, a post which he held from 1872 to 1886 with only short breaks for leave and temporary postings elsewhere – a remarkable record considering the unhealthy living conditions there. He clearly made a considerable impression on Grattan Geary, editor of *The Times of India*, a casual visitor to Muscat in March 1878. He wrote, 'Colonel Miles, sitting alone in the Residency, and the beautiful little gunboat at anchor in the harbour preserve Muscat and its prince from the ravenous prowlers who long to sack the one and depose the other.'[10] Miles' greatest legacy is his monumental work *The Countries and Tribes of the Persian Gulf*, but he also wrote a number of detailed reports of his travels all over Oman, some of which were published in learned journals.[11] He travelled frequently by camel, a mode of transport more suited to familiarisation with the country than the motor car of today, which is obliged to follow roads, and took the time to sit and talk with the people along the way. He meticulously recorded what he saw and heard and took exceptionally good photographs, so that when visiting these places today you can still trace where he went. Some changes, however, have been profound, and many of the traditions he described have gone forever. For example, when visiting Semail in 1876, he noted[12] the weaving industry there:

> The creaking of the loom may be heard in every hamlet. Lungies, puggries, and khodrungs are the chief articles produced, the cotton of which they are made, both white and brown varieties, being extensively grown in the valley. The loom is somewhat heavy and clumsy in construction, and is horizontal . . . And the weaver sits and works at it in a shallow pit, with his body half below the surface.

Today cotton is not grown in the Wadi Semail, and no loom is heard there. The sole remaining traditional weaver is in Sur, manufacturing expensive lungies for the shaykhs.[13]

The discerning traveller would have seen from such detailed reports that Oman was much more attractive than it appeared, and was, in fact, a treasury of surprises awaiting discovery by the curious visitor. Let us look at some of these more unusual aspects of Oman. Miles recorded[14] the presence of gypsies in his report on his visit to Buraimi in 1875. He describes them as *zaṭṭ* (plural *zaṭūṭ*) in Arabic, and at once distinguishable from the Arabs there. He quotes the German Dr Sprenger's *Alte Geographie Arabiens* as his source for identifying them with the Jats of India and writes:

> They are taller in person and more swarthy, and they have that cunning and shifty look stamped on their physiognomy so observable in the gypsies of Europe. The Zatt are spread over Central and Eastern Arabia from Muscat to Mesopotamia and are very numerous in Oman.

Like gypsies elsewhere, he said:

> They are accomplished handicraftsmen, being farriers, smiths, tinkers, carpenters, weavers, and barbers. They also manufacture guns and matchlocks; indeed most of the trades and manufactures seem to be in their hands, and they are to the natives of the interior what the Banians and other Indians are at the sea-port towns.

But where are they today? Gypsies are never spoken of, and the very crafts that they once practised are today in the hands either of Arab Omanis or of recent immigrants from the Indian sub-continent.

Miles' reference to the Banians or Hindus is noteworthy, as there is hardly a report by any traveller that does not mention their presence in virtually every settlement of importance. Stiffe and others relate the role of a Banian merchant in the recapture of Muscat by the Omanis from the Portuguese in 1652, which suggests their involvement in Oman for a very long time. It seems that the Portuguese governor had fallen for the merchant's daughter, but rather than marry her to a Christian the merchant devised a cunning scheme to deplete the town's reserves of water, grain and gunpowder under the pretext of renewing them, whereupon he promptly advised the Omani rebels of this advantageous moment to attack Muscat. The town fell to them and the merchant's daughter was spared a fate worse than death! Nearly two centuries later, Wellsted noted that the Banians controlled the lucrative coffee trade in Muscat and much of the business of Sur. Pengelley noted in 1861[15] that Banians of Barka on the Batina held all the ready cash there, which they obtained not so much from trading as 'in advancing money on arms, ornaments, wearing apparel, etc or in other words as "pawnbrokers"'. Miles observed that in the interior the peripatetic vendors were Makrani Balouch, who acted as agents or travellers for the Hindu and Khoja merchants of Muscat and Kuryat who never ventured to penetrate the interior themselves. He also noted that the Banians bought up wholesale the frankincense produced in Dhofar. Sir Percy Cox, political agent in Muscat from 1899 to 1904 and a great traveller in Oman, recorded that along the Batina 'are to be found small communities of British Indians: partly Hindu Bunnias, and partly Muhammadans of the Khoja persuasion, descendants of immigrants from Sind and disciples of H.H. the Agha Khan or recent seceders from his faith'. The Khojas, or Lawatiyah as they are more usually called today, have become fully integrated into Omani society under the present Sultan and enjoy the same rights as other Omanis.

Of greater interest to anthropologists today are two distinct groups of Omanis who are unique to Oman, and whose presence and special characteristics were first noted by British travellers. They are to be found at the two extremities of the country – the Hamitic Qara, Shahara, Mahra and Harsusi tribes in Dhofar and the Shihuh and Kumazara in the Musandam peninsula – where they probably owe their existence to the remoteness and defensibility of their tribal areas. One of the earliest reports[16] on the Qara (or Gara) people of Dhofar was written by Captain Haines, whose survey ship, *Palinurus*, visited the Dhofar coast in 1834. He described them thus:

> ... a fine athletic race of men, dressed in a blue, glazed waistband, which is in general their only covering ... They allow their hair to grow long and it is then gathered behind, like the Mahrahs, which gives them a wild appearance ... Their faces are much longer than Arab faces generally are, their eyes are large and bright ... They are much fairer than the Arabs of the coast and they were apparently pleased to see men stouter and fairer than those of their own tribe. Indeed they were frequent onlookers at my crew when playing at cricket.

One can think of other reasons why they should be amazed at the sight of cricketers! However, Bertram Thomas, who spent much longer in Dhofar on visits between 1927 and 1930, during his time as Minister of the Council of the State of Oman or the Sultan's Wazir, saw the Qara slightly differently.[17] He described them as 'Men of big bone, they have long faces, long narrow jaws, noses of a refined shape, long curly hair and dark brown skins.' Both were agreed that they were of Hamitic origin, and to this must be attributed their differences as regards languages and customs to those of the neighbouring Arabs. In some cases their customs are quite the opposite. For example, the circumcision of boys is delayed until incipient adolescence, whereas among Arab Omanis it is at the age of six years; and girls are circumcised at birth or on the second day, whereas Arab girls are circumcised at about ten years. Moreover, the Dhofari tribes practise clitoridectomy, whereas the Arabs incise the top of the clitoris. Both of these practices are slowly dying out with the spread of better health education. Certainly the performance of male circumcision is no longer the public spectacle it was in Thomas' day. Another example of different customs relates to milking cows: no Arab man would dream of demeaning himself by milking one, whereas the Dhofaris believe it is shameful for a woman to milk one. As the languages or dialects of the Dhofari tribes are not written, it seems inevitable that they will gradually disappear under the all-pervasive pressure exerted by Arabic, as the sole medium of education and entertainment through television and the means of advancement and wider job opportunities. There were sound political reasons after the end of the insurrection in Dhofar, in 1976, for the homogenisation of the country and its peoples, but today it might be time to consider how to conserve the rich diversity of Oman's cultural heritage by encouraging the survival of these tribes' languages and folklore.

At the opposite end of the country, in Musandam, reside the equally different Shihuh and Kumazara tribes in their mountain fastnesses. Bertram Thomas made a detailed survey of these tribes and reported[18] that the Shihuh were primarily shepherds in the interior and fisherman, boatbuilders and, to a limited extent, date-gatherers along the coast. He thought they were by far the most primitive tribe in all Oman. He said, 'The traveller who wishes to penetrate this country must do so on his own flat feet, and be prepared to climb three thousand feet to reach small inhospitable settlements, where water is scarce, food is unobtainable, and he is unwelcome.' As if this were not enough to discourage most visitors, he noted also that their dialect, though unmistakably Arabic, was virtually unintelligible to outsiders. He speculated interestingly on their origins, questioning whether they might have been the 'Shuhite' mentioned in the Book of Job and therefore Jewish. He rejected the notion that they might have been a Persian relic. That they are different from other Omanis is nowhere more pronounced than in their custom, observed to this day, of the *nadaba*, performed after a meal. As Thomas said:

> Following an Arab feast of princely proportions, the Shihuh shaikh rose, and, standing a little aside with hands still unwashed – this I gathered was a necessary observance – placed his left arm across his chest and his right arm bent above and behind his head; then, straightening and bending the raised arm, he set up a curious howl not entirely unmusical, ascending and descending the scale over a compass of perhaps an octave . . . Meantime, a dozen or so tribesmen standing close together in a ring about him with their hands to their mouths, *muedhdhin* fashion, broke in at intervals with a curious dog-like bark.

I have heard this sound at a distance, and very eerie it was, too.

The *nadaba* is also practised by the neighbouring Kumazara, living in Kumzar at the tip of Musandam, who regard themselves as Shihuh and are regarded by the latter as Shihuh. However, they are distinguished from the Shihuh by their language. As Thomas said, 'It is a compound of Arabic and Persian, but is distinct from them both, and is intelligible neither to the Arab nor to the Persian nor yet to the bilinguist of both.' In Musandam, too, the spread of educated Arabic through children at school seems likely to obliterate these local dialects, unless an effort is made to keep them alive.

Almost the last of the great travellers in Oman was Captain (later Sir) Percy Cox. He had been hand-picked by Lord Curzon when Viceroy of India to be Political Agent and Consul in Muscat, where he served from 1899 to 1904 before going on to be Political Resident in the Persian Gulf and High Commissioner in Mesopotamia. Some 25 years after he left Muscat, he read a paper to the Royal Geographical Society[19] on some of his excursions. In particular, he travelled by camel from Ras al-Khaima to Buraimi and the Batina, one section of which – from Ras al-Khaima to Dhank – had not been covered by a European before. He found that he was not always welcome because of the imagined consequences of visits by previous travellers. For example, when at Tanuf he recorded:

> The shaikh did not come in to me again during the day, but was busy making every sort of ridiculous difficulty, including the old

chestnut which I had so often heard, that as a result of Col Miles' visit five and twenty years before, a blight had fallen on their fruit. Also that the people were alarmed at my camera and prismatic compass – all bunkum.

Cox did not always travel by camel, but sometimes availed himself of passing British warships. The problem was getting ashore from them, particularly on the exposed Batina coast. As he recorded:[20]

> Unfortunately most of this coast is liable to heavy surf when the wind is off the sea, and landing from boats is then very difficult and often impossible. It was consequently always my habit . . . to wear a bathing suit under my clothes; and I have several times . . . had to wade and swim in with my clothes on my head. On one or two of these visits I have reached the beach in this undignified garb under a ceremonial salute of two or three guns from the local Arab Governor.

I know how he must have felt, having once had to swim ashore years ago to visit Tiwi near Sur and appearing dripping in the village – to the amazement of the locals.

Cox and his long-suffering wife, Belle, were clearly undaunted by the rigours of the climate or the general difficulties of living in Muscat, as can be seen from his affectionate description of where they lived:

> The harbour and approaches to Muscat from the sea form an extremely attractive picture, and for me possess a charm entirely of their own. The first indication a traveller gets of the place as the steamer comes up the coast from the southward is a glimpse of the old Portuguese fort at the south-eastern corner of the harbour, now known as Fort Jalali. Then passing on towards the eastern arm of the harbour, or cove, as it really is, and rounding the island promontory you see on your port how the barren rocks bearing a time-honoured record of the ships which visited the port of old and painted their names on the barren rocks. Then you have before you the front and entrance of the same old fort, Jalali, with its battery of antique cannon directed from their embrasures at random across the harbour. While the closely-packed town lying at the toe of the horseshoe opens out to view as the ship passes between the points. The picture now before us includes the Sultan's custom house and palace on one side with the British Agency at the eastern end of the foreshore, its foundations forming the sea wall at that point. It will be realised that when as often happens in winter a strong breeze from the

north drives breakers into the harbour, their constant thud against the walls of the building is somewhat trying, but as is the case of most chronic noises one gets used to it after a bit.

Having lived in the British Agency for four-and-a-half years, I can certainly endorse that! He went on:

> At the other or western extremity of the foreshore lies Fort Merani, the other of the two old Portuguese forts built to command the sea approaches. Though the older of the two, it is neither so solid nor so picturesque as Fort Jalali, and the old cannon located on an emplacement halfway down the rock are now relegated to saluting purposes.[21]

Sadly, the Cox' residence is no more, but before it was demolished I had the honour of receiving there on a long-delayed return visit the last of the great travellers in Oman – Sir Wilfred Thesiger, together with his surviving companions. His epic traverses of the Empty Quarter by camel in 1946 and 1947 are beautifully recorded in *Arabian Sands*.[22] When I took him to revisit Izz, near Nizwa, where he had been nearly fifty years earlier, we were astounded when an old man came to us in the shaykh's *majlis*, greeted Thesiger like a long-lost brother and recounted how as a boy he had seen him ride in on his camel. What is more, the man even remembered the name of the camel! Thesiger is the stuff legends are made of! But it is a sad reflection on the times that when his biographer, Michael Asher, attempted a few years ago to retrace Thesiger's route by camel across the sands, he could not find any bedouin willing and able to undertake such hardships.

Finally, to show that Oman has not yet revealed all its secrets to the foreign traveller, let me recall briefly the most recent expedition to explore a different kind of legend – the lost city of Ubar. In 1991, Sir Ranulph Fiennes, who had previously become interested in Ubar when serving as a soldier in the Sultan's Armed Forces, returned to Oman to carry out a reconnaissance of potential sites of 'the Atlantis of the Sands', as Bertram Thomas called it. He was sufficiently convinced to return the following year to lead an expedition, concentrating on the oasis of Shisr on the edge of the Empty Quarter. The expedition certainly uncovered there a site of great antiquity, but discovered no firm evidence that it was 'Iram of the columns, the like of which has not been created in the (other) cities', as it is described in the Holy Qur'ān.[23]

This enigma and others still await a solution, and add to the many attractions of Oman for the intrepid traveller.

NOTES

1. Ian Skeet, *Muscat and Oman* (London, Faber & Faber, 1974), p. 65 and Annex 1.
2. J.G. Lorimer, *Gazetteer of the Persian Gulf, Oman and Central Arabia* (4 vols., Calcutta, Government of India, 1908–1915).
3. Skeet, *op. cit.*, Annex 2.
4. *Ibid.*
5. J.A. Saldanha, *Précis of Correspondence Regarding the Affaires of the Persian Gulf, 1801–1853* (possibly Calcutta, 1908).
6. Robert B.M. Binning, *A Journal of Two Years' Travel in Persia, Ceylon, etc.* (London, W.H. Allen, 1857).
7. Penelope Tuson, *Records of the British Residency and Agencies in the Persian Gulf* (London, India Office Library Records, 1978), pp. 151–3.
8. Lt J.R. Wellsted, *Travels in Arabia* (2 vols., London, 1838).
9. Capt. Arthur W. Stiffe, 'Ancient Trading Centres of the Persian "Arabian" Gulf: Muscat', *Geographical Journal* 10:6 (December 1897), 608–18.
10. G. Geary, *Through Asiatic Turkey* (London, 1878).
11. Philip Ward's *Travels in Oman* (Cambridge, Oleander Press, 1987) reproduces these reports.
12. S.B. Miles, 'Across the Green Mountains of Oman', *Geographical Journal*, 18 (1901), 465–98.
13. The editor took photographs of weavers in the Batina weaving cotton *lungis* as recently as 1976.
14. Samuel B. Miles, 'On the Route between Sohar and el-Bereymi in Oman', *Journal of the Asiatic Society of Bengal*, 46:1 (1877).
15. W.M. Pengelley, 'Remarks on a Portion of the Eastern Coast of Arabia between Muscat and Sohar', *Transactions of the Bombay Geographical Society*, 16 (1860–1862), 30–9.
16. Capt. S.B. Haines, 'Memoir of the South and East Coast of Arabia', *Journal of the Royal Geographical Society* (1845).
17. Bertram Thomas, 'Among some Unknown Tribes of South Arabia', *Journal of the Royal Anthropological Institute*, 59 (January–June 1929), 97–111.
18. Bertram Thomas, 'Musandam and its people', *Journal of the Royal Central Asian Society* (1929).
19. P.Z. Cox, 'Some Excursions in Oman', *Geographical Journal*, 63:3 (September 1925).
20. *Ibid.*

21 *Ibid.*
22 Sir Wilfred Thesinger, *Arabian Sands*, (London, Longmans, 1959).
23 Qur'ān, Al-Fajr (The Dawn), verse 7.

8

Ruins and Landscapes from Sardis to Stowe: The Work of Giovanni Battista Borra

Jane Ayer Scott

Until the last two decades, the identity of the architect who accompanied the party of Englishmen whose travels in the East in 1750 resulted in Robert Wood's magnificent publications about Palmyra and Baalbek was unclear. In fact, the man who accomplished the surveying, drafting and topographical recording was Giovanni Battista Borra, architect to Carlo Emanuele III, Prince of Savoy and King of Sardinia.[1] He was responsible for the illustrations in the published volumes,[2] and for a series of drawings of sites in Asia Minor, Greece and Egypt that were never published. The record of the tour is preserved in the autograph notebooks of the participants and Borra's sketchbook in the Joint Library of the Hellenic and Roman Societies in London. Selections from the sketchbook, with quotations from the diaries, were published in 1927 by C.A. Hutton, who traces the group's itinerary.[3]

The magnificent set of finished but unpublished drawings is numbered in plate sequence, and some are gridded and ready for transfer. That they were intended for publication on the same scale as the books about Palmyra and Baalbek is clear from Wood's preface to the latter (p. 16):

> Should health and leisure permit us to give the public that more classical part of our travels, through those countries which are most remarkable as the scenes of antient fable, we may illustrate by some instance what is here only hinted at.

Wood credits James Dawkins for the accuracy of the work 'by having finished drawings made under his own eye by our draughtsman, from the sketches and measures he had made on the spot'.[4] Wood became Undersecretary to the Prime Minister William Pitt in 1756.[5] Dawkins died in 1757, and without his presence or Wood's concentration the project languished.[6]

The finished drawings prepared by Borra fell into oblivion until a great number of them were discovered in a private collection in the early 1970s, and were purchased some years later by Paul Mellon for The Center for British Art, at Yale University, in New Haven, Connecticut.[7] These drawings show a rich variety of architectural ornament, ruins in their settings, a great interest in reconstruction and topographical studies, all of which bear on Borra's subsequent practice in England.

The tour was initiated by James Dawkins and John Bouverie,[8] both Oxford graduates, with whom Wood had travelled in France and Italy. They invited Wood to join them in this ambitious new endeavour to record distant monuments both because of his strong background in the classics and the fact that he had already travelled in the Middle East.

The three spent the winter of 1749–50 in Rome and there engaged Borra. It is significant that, on the threshold of the transition from Palladianism to neoclassicism, the Englishmen engaged the services of an architect who had an active and distinguished practice, who understood the methodology of measuring buildings and making topographic studies and who was an outstanding draftsman. Neoclassicism demanded first-hand study of the monuments of the past, as opposed to reliance on literary descriptions. Architects were looking beyond the Roman works and Palladian ideals to their ultimate source, the architecture of the ancient Greeks. The tour was undertaken to provide a record of their monuments and their settings at a time when architecture and design were founded on actual antique examples rather than on theory.[9] In this regard, the focus of the Englishmen is in contrast to that of Piranesi, who claimed Roman sources as the primary ones.[10]

Borra was born in Italy in 1713.[11] He was a pupil of Vittone in Turin and prepared the plates for Vittone's *Architecture civile* published in 1737. Through this and similar projects he was thoroughly versed in the classical orders and their baroque variants.[12] Borra himself published an engineering treatise, *Trattato della cognizione pratica delle resistenze geometricamente*.[13] He had a strong background in the theory of architectonics, and his views of Turin show the high quality of his draftsmanship and his ability to use a grey wash to render landscape. In addition, his writing shows that he looked back to ideals of the great architecture of Greece and of Egypt which he perceived were lost when the barbarians invaded Italy.[14] This background made him an ideal choice to record the antiquities of the great ancient cities of the East.

In the preface to *The Ruins of Balbec,* Wood wrote, '... descriptions of ruins, without accurate drawings, seldom preserve more of their subject than its confusion ... [and thus it] shall ... be our principal care to produce things as we found them, leaving reflections and reasonings upon them to others'. The publication of his books about Palmyra and Baalbek provided the first measured drawings of ancient buildings available to architects and scholars in England, who led in the rediscovery of classical antiquity and the development of architecture as a science. The volumes were not intended to present merely a compendium of isolated, measured architectural members and decorative motifs, but to include plans, views and surveys to show the setting of the sites and to identify the geographical features described by ancient historians and poets, especially Homer. To quote Wood:[15]

> Circumstances of climate and situation, otherwise trivial, become interesting from that connection with great men, and great actions, which history and poetry have given them: The life of Miltiades or Leonidas could never be read with so much pleasure, as on the plains of Marathon or at the streights of Thermopylae; the Iliad has new beauties on the banks of the Scamander, and the Odyssey is most pleasing in the countries where Ulysses travelled and Homer sung ... Where we thought the present face of the country was the best comment on an antient author, we made our draftsman take a view, or make a plan of it. This sort of entertainment we extended to poetical geography, and spent a fortnight with great pleasure, in making a map of the Scamandrian plain, with Homer in our hands.

Wood was anxious to set the record straight about the accuracy of Homer's geography, which had been thrown into confusion by translations – notably that of Pope, whose alterations 'produced a new map of his own, and deprived us of that merit of the original which he called upon us to admire'. The map that Wood devised, drawn by Borra, was published in 1775 with his essay, *A Comparative View of the Ancient and Present State of the Troad,* to which is prefixed an *Essay on the Original Genius of Homer.*[16] Later scholars respected Wood as a topographer on the basis of this map. George Huxley confirms that Wood is correct in saying that Homer's description of the winds matches the practices of modern – i.e. eighteenth-century – navigation and marks him a 'conspicuously successful topographer'. The information about the winds that was gained by sailing from Troy to Tenedos and 'his topographical criticism show the poems to have their own historical context in the real world'.[17] The great scholar of the Troad, J.M. Cook, wrote in 1973 that, 'it was research of this sort that was needed to confront the geographers with the geographical fact and expose the futility of the prevalent armchair cartography'.[18] In addition to the map and a view of the ruins of Alexander Troas, published in 1775, Borra prepared a remarkable topographic study of the shore (Yale no. B1977.14.994). Other outstanding examples of topographical recording are a plan of the Maeander valley from as far east as Hierapolis to the Aegean coast, and plans of the harbours at Halikarnassos (Bodrum) and at Knidos (Yale nos. B1977.14.997, 941, 956).

Wood gives the following criteria for recording ancient cities and their buildings (*The Ruins of Palmyra . . .*, p. 35):

> In the following works we not only give the measures of the architecture, but also the views of the ruins from which they are taken, as the most distinct as well as the most satisfactory method. For as the first gives an idea of the building, when it was entire, so the last shows its present state of decay, and (which is most important) what authority there is for our measures.

During the segment of the tour that passed through the great Hellenistic and Roman cities of Asia Minor, Wood and his colleagues adhered to this scheme. In most cases, a view precedes the record of the ruins and the measured drawings of the architectural fragments. Great care was taken in recording the topographical setting. The drawings of individual sites and buildings provide the earliest known measured drawings of Hellenistic and Roman architecture in Asia Minor.

The party left Naples on 5 May 1750 and on 18 May landed at Smyrna, of which there is a charming view of the harbour filled with trading vessels, with the town rising above to the castle and Mount Pagos in the background (Yale no. 1977.14.930).[19] The party found Smyrna disappointing in respect of antiquities and on 25 May, having obtained supplies and horses as well as local guides, they rode through the pass of Mount Sypilos into the plain of Nymphi, sweet with the bloom of almonds and apricots and rich in olives, and through the Hermos (modern Gediz) river valley[20] to Sardis, the site most thoroughly recorded.

They passed over the ancient bridge spanning the river Pactolus (Sart Çay), the river whose gold brought legendary wealth to King Croesus and in which Midas bathed to rid himself of the golden touch. Borra made views and renderings of the extant Roman and Late Antique ruins along the highway, and of the Temple of Artemis and the large Lydian burial mounds in the cemetery to the north, known as Bin Tepe.

In studying the record of Sardis we can appreciate the value and assess the accuracy of Borra's work, because extensive survey and excavation have been undertaken there by two American teams: the first was led by Howard Crosby Butler, of Princeton University (1910–14; 1922); the second was the Harvard-Cornell Expedition initiated in 1958 by George M.A. Hanfmann and directed by him until 1978 and thereafter by Crawford H. Greenewalts Jr.[21] Borra made a remarkably accurate plan of the existing ruins. The team identified the temple of Artemis, the bridge, the bath-gymnasium complex and bath ('CG'), the unexcavated bath ('Building C') and Justinianic basilica ('Building D'), the theatre and stadium as well as segments of the city wall. A panoramic view shows the standing remains of these buildings and others, giving an invaluable picture of the remains of ancient Sardis. The accuracy of the plan falls down only in respect of some exact measurements and in the orientation of the buildings, partly as a result of the variance between magnetic and true north.[22]

Borra comes closer to achieving the level of accuracy that Wood claimed for him in the plan for the building they took for a palace, but which is now known to be the Roman bath-gymnasium complex. Borra's plan of the bath block can be compared with that of Fikret Yegül (figs. 1–2). The proportions of the two rooms flanking the Imperial Court (MC in fig. 2) are generally correct, and the details of the alternating rounded and squared niches around the pool (BE–H) are very precise. However, the presence of niches in BSH and BNH is incorrect, and it is unclear what evidence Borra had for them. The sketch plan shows that Borra found evidence for the columns of the screen colonnade on the east façade of MC, which were not above ground when the building was excavated. This valuable evidence was omitted from the finished drawing.[23]

The standing remains of the temple of Artemis, six columns of the east portico, five with capitals, bearing a section of the architrave still in place and a portion of the *anta*, are charmingly illustrated and precisely

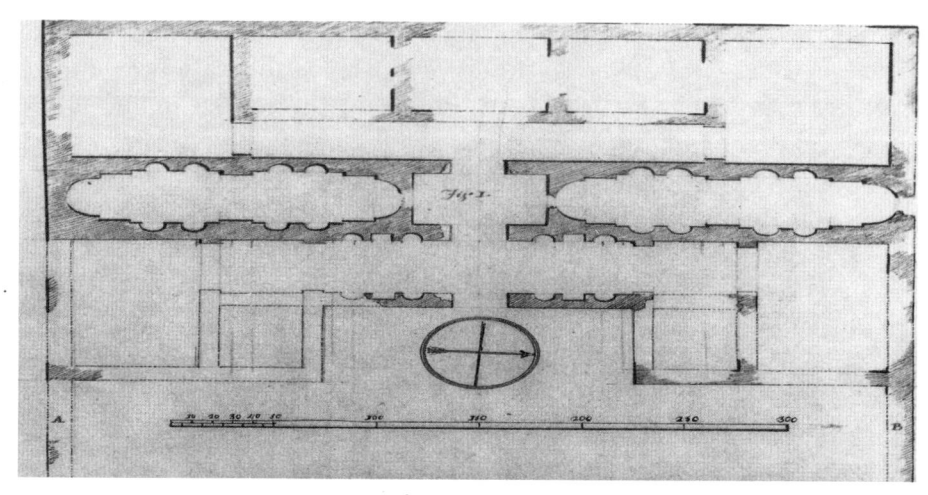

FIGURE 1
A plan of the bath-gymnasium complex at Sardis by Giovanni Battista Borra
(by courtesy of the Yale Center for British Art)

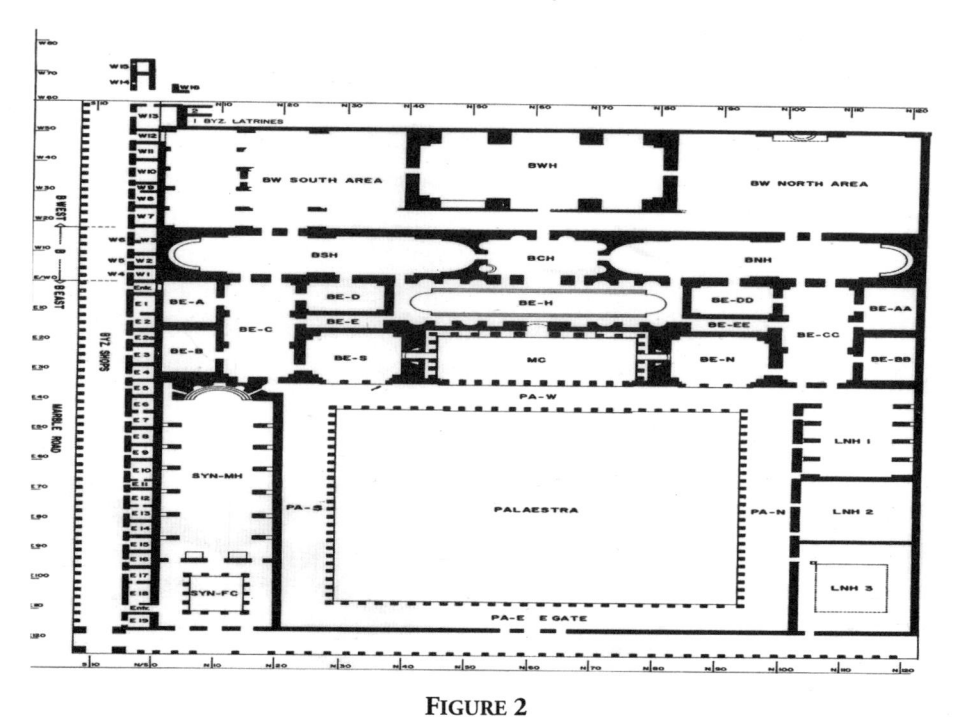

FIGURE 2
A plan of the bath-gymnasium complex at Sardis as excavated
(with minor restorations) by Fikret K. Yegül
(by courtesy of Archaeological Exploration of Sardis)

documented by a single-point perspective looking to the south against a faithful description of the surrounding landscape. The drawing is inscribed in brown ink, 'View of the ruins of an Ionick temple at Sardis taken from the 44º E^s with the Tmolus behind.' The value of this record may be appreciated when compared with the standing remains before Butler began his excavations (fig. 3). Wood made his men dig to the base of one column, and Borra's sketches show its foliate pattern and measurements but no finished drawing of the base or the capitals is extant.[24]

FIGURE 3
A view of the temple of Artemis at Sardis by Giovanni Battista Borra
(by courtesy of the Yale Center for British Art)

When they left Sardis, the travellers proceeded northwest, through the cemetery of Lydian royal burial mounds, toward Thyateira. Borra 'took a view' north toward the Hermos valley. He emphasises the largest of the royal burial mounds, that assigned to the Lydian ruler, Alyattes.[25] Our surveyors then completed the picture by a view south from Alyattes' mound, showing the temple, the Roman buildings and wall and the Acropolis and Necropolis peaks against the magnificent range of the Tmolos [modern Boz Dağ] mountains, a topographical setting that is accurate, albeit conceptual as compared with a photograph.[26]

As remarkable as Wood's determination to record was his interest in reconstruction. His intent was to provide as accurate a sense of the complete building as could be determined from the remains. In this regard the drawings succeed in some instances, but Borra's exuberant enthusiasm for ornament, his Piedmontese heritage, is evident in some of his reconstructions. His plan and measured architectural details of the large theatre at Laodicea are accurate, but in the reconstruction drawings 'the scenes are greatly helped by Borra's fancy without solid authority from the ruins'.[27]

Borra returned to England with Wood and Dawkins (Bouverie died during the voyage) in 1751, after visiting Stuart and Revett in Greece. The volumes on Palmyra and Baalbek, with text by Robert Wood, were published quickly and had an immediate impact, both on decorative taste and on architecture. Robert Adam, in the unpublished draft of his *Ruins of Spaltro*, gives Wood credit for 'that rise of Taste and Love of Antique Architecture' that 'so happily' inspired British design and lauds the effort 'to bring from obscurity neglected or poorly represented remains'.[28]

While in England, Borra contributed to the interior decoration of several great houses – among them Norfolk House in London, Stowe and Stratfield Saye[29] – as well as helping to redesign the gardens at Stowe House in Buckinghamshire. The placement of ruins in their settings, and the plotting of entire river valleys, must have contributed to Borra's versatility as a landscape designer and made him sensitive to the iconography of gardens desired by his British patrons at the time when classical forms were included in gardens to evoke historic and literary associations. This, combined with the exposure to mannerist gardens in Italy, which were designed for vistas, made Borra a logical choice to open the gardens at Stowe to a more natural configuration graced with temples and ruins. He completed the Temple of Concord and Victory, and redesigned the twin pavilions on the crown of the hill, the so-called 'Boycott Pavilions', originally by James Gibb; everything in that area of the park except the Temple of Concord has been ascribed to Borra. He also redesigned Vanbrugh's Rotunda, leaving it with the most distinguished of his temples in a picturesque rolling landscape.[30]

Borra's decorative schemes include baroque and rococo elements developed during his practice in Turin, and specific elements from Baalbek and Palmyra, along with emphasis on the Ionic order, studied at first hand in Asia Minor. The state bed chamber and ceiling at Stowe are attributed to him, with the frieze and ceiling ornaments adapted from the 'Temple of the Sun' at Palmyra.[31] Adam drew on the same ceiling ornamentation at Osterly Park. Legitimised by Adam, all hint of the East disappears and the pattern enters the 'neoclassical' decorative repertoire.[32] When compared with the actual ceiling (difficult to see and doubtless coated with soot then as now), it is clear that it was not the original architecture in Syria or Asia Minor that was influential but the drawings themselves. This is especially true in the drawings of architectural ornament at Palmyra and Baalbek, which the artist (doubtless reflecting the wishes of his patrons) classicised, rendering it with more solidity and substance than the Eastern examples.[33]

Desmond Fitz-Gerald's study of the Norfolk House Music Room, which is now installed in the Victoria and Albert Museum, attributes much of the redecoration to Borra. The trophies on the staircase are his. They are compared with the trophies shown in the *Trattato* published before his classical journey. The trophies on the ceiling may also be after Borra's design. The torso is reminiscent of the helmeted torso in a capital drawn near Priene.[34]

Borra's eclecticism had the intellectual dimension demanded by the times – the enrichment of the present by inquiry into the past that had been nurtured through his travels in classical lands and the recording of ancient buildings under the guidance of Wood, Dawkins and Bouverie. The variety of architectural decoration he recorded was itself eclectic, and included with severe Doric and gracefully simple Ionic the rococo strains in Augustan decoration, revitalised in the surviving Hadrianic buildings and the Severan baroque that enriched Roman decoration of buildings throughout Asia Minor.

Notes

1 See Olga Zoller, *Der Architekt und der Ingenieur Giovanni Battista Borra* (1713–1770) (Bamberg, Wissenschaftlicher Verlag Bamberg, 1996), the first complete study of the work of this many-sided architect/engineer undertaken, to explore the Piedmontese baroque and the generation following the best-known architects of the Settecento there, Filippo Juvarra, Benedetto Alfieri and Bernardo Vittone, to which Borra belonged. This work was not available to me until the

draft of my paper was nearly complete, but I have added references to it, and especially to the illustrations.
2 Robert Wood, *The Ruins of Palmyra, Otherwise Tedmor, in the Desart* (London, A. Millar, 1753); *idem*, *The Ruins of Balbec, Otherwise Heliopolis in Coelosyria* (London, 1757); both published in facsimile, reduced, following the original pagination (Westmead, Farnborough, Gregg, 1971). The original drawings for *Balbec* are in the Royal Institute of British Architects, London.
3 C.A. Hutton, 'The Travels of "Palmyra" Wood in 1750–51', *Journal of Hellenic Studies*, 47:1 (1927), 102–29, with valuable information about the diaries themselves.
4 *Ibid.*
5 Wood was a travelling tutor and scholar, said to have been at Oxford but his name does not appear in Foster's *Alumni Oxonienses*. He was elected a member of the Society of Dilettanti in 1763; he wrote the 'Address to the Reader' in *Antiquities of Ionia* I (London, Society of Dilettanti, 1769). He held office under Pitt and his successors until 1763, and then became M.P. for Brackley, in Northamptonshire, until his death in 1771, which occurred in the house where Gibbon was born. *Dictionary of National Biography*, vol. 21, s. v.
6 Dawkins was born in 1722 in Jamaica, son of the Chief Justice of Jamaica, hence his name, 'Jamaica Dawkins', for which see James Boswell, *The Life of Samuel Johnson*, ed. Birkbeck Hill (5 vols., London, G. Routledge, 1885), vol. 4, p. 130. He funded the trip and endowed the Society of Dilettanti on his death in 1757. He served briefly as envoy to Frederick the Great in Berlin and as M.P. for Hindon Borough in Wiltshire. *Dictionary of National Biography*, vol. 22, Supplement s. v.
7 The Paul Mellon Collection, accession numbers B1977.14.922–1019. Most are executed in black with brown ink and pencil and grey wash on paper, sheet size *c.* 53.5 x 36.8 cm. See Francis Russell, 'Breaking Fresh Ground', *Country Life* (4 November 1976), 1292–4, published before the collection went to Yale. Abstracts of papers given by the writer appeared in *XI International Association for Classical Archaeology Abstracts of Papers* (London, 1978), p. 126; and *72nd Annual Meeting of the College Art Association Abstracts of Art History Papers* (Toronto, 1984), p. 45. For the drawings of Pergamon, see Max Kunze, 'Pergamon in Jahre 1750: Reisetagebücher von Giovanni Battista Borra', *Antike Welt*, 26 (1995), 177–86, with careful analysis and comparison to the excavated buildings; also Russell, figs. 2–3. For the drawings of Sardis, see below. See Zoller, *op. cit.*, figs. 18.6–7, 18.9, 18.11–14, 18.16–17, 18.19–22; see 11–12 for other collections and archives. The sequence also includes views of Italy (*ibid.*, fig. 18.2=Russell, fig. 1), Mediterranean islands, the Holy Land (Russell, fig. 8) and the Pyramids at Giza and Saqqara, of which the publication by the late I.E.S. Edwards is forthcoming. I am grateful to Mr Mellon for his permission to publish the drawings of Sardis and for arranging to have photographs sent to me.
8 Bouverie had made the Continental Tour and visited Rome many times. He collected drawings, coins, gems and cameos, and was well versed in art and archaeology. For his drawings, see N. Turner, C. Plazzotta, *Drawings by Guercino from British Collections,* exhibition catalogue (London, British Museum Publications, 1991), pp. 8, 21ff.
9 For a summary of this transition and its immediate effect on British architecture and landscape design, see Michael Bevington, 'The Development of the Classical

Revival at Stowe', *Architectura: Journal of the History of Architecture*, 21:2 (1991), 136–61. John Harris cuts off the Palladian era in 1750, 'a convenient terminating point when architecture was still neo-Palladian rather than neo-Classic', *The Palladians*, Royal Institute of British Architects Drawings Series (New York, 1982), p. 9.
10 I am grateful to N.H. Ramage for her comments in this regard. She points out that Piranesi's views of Paestum came later (private communication).
11 Zoller, *op. cit.*, pp. 19–24 for biography.
12 Bernardo Antonio Vittone, 1702–70, *Corso d'architettura civile sopra li cinque ordini di Giacomo Barozzio da Vignola, disegnato da Giambatista Borra* . . . (Turin, 1737); see also Accademía delle Scienze di Torino, *Bernardo Vittone e la disputa fra classicismo e barocco nel Settecento* (Turin, Academy of Science, 1972); Zoller, *op. cit.*, pp. 28–9.
13 Published under the name Gianbatista Borra, *Trattato delle cognizione pratica delle resistenze geometricamente* . . . (Turin, 1748). The two forms of his name caused considerable confusion and delayed recognition of Borra as the architect who worked in England later in the century. See Zoller, *op. cit.*, pp. 39–58.
14 Wood, *The Ruins of Balbec, op. cit.*
15 Wood, *The Ruins of Palmyra, op. cit.*
16 Robert Wood, *An Essay on the Original Genius and Writings of Homer with a Comparative View of the Antient and Present State of the Troade* (London, 1775); reprint to which the 1769 privately printed edition, a valuable bibliographic note and correspondence between Wood and Michaelis are appended (Hildesheim and New York, George Olms Verlag, 1976). The edition also contains a view of Alexander Troas by Borra.
17 George Huxley, 'Homer's Perception of his Ionian Circumstances', *The Maynooth Review*, 3:1 (June 1977), 73–84. For a general description of the topography and the winds, see M. Korfmann in *Troy and the Trojan War*, ed. M. Mellink (Bryn Mawr, Pa., Bryn Mawr College, 1986).
18 However, Wood, as J.-B. Le Chevalier (*Voyage de la Troade fait dans les années 1785 et 1786* [Paris, 1799]) notes, believed Troy to be situated at the source of the Scamander and did not recognize the Scamander in the stream that flows from the Pinarba springs; J.M. Cook, *The Troad: An Archaeological and Topographical Study* (Oxford, Clarendon Press, 1973), pp. 20–1. Although Wood used Lisle's map as a basis he took his own bearings, and Cook considers the map Wood's own work, 'Though inadequate for the Trojan plain, Wood's map renders the physical relief with a fair degree of verisimilitude', *ibid.*, p. 46.
19 Hutton, *op. cit.*, pp. 102–4.
20 They made a plan of the course of the river, Yale no. B1977.14.927, captioned 'Pianura dell'Hermo in Faccia á Sardes'; R.L. Vann, *The Unexcavated Buildings of Sardis*, BAR International Series 538 (Oxford, B.A.R., 1989), pp. 6–7, fig. 4, which also shows the Gygean Lake and other topographical features.
21 Hutton, *op. cit.*, pp. 105–9 gives excerpts from the diaries and shows the sketch of the bridge (pl. XVI), of which the finished drawing is Yale no. B1977.14.958. For a volume that summarizes the excavations at Sardis, see George M.A. Hanfmann, *Sardis from Prehistoric to Roman Times* (Cambridge, Mass., and London, Harvard University Press, 1983); for reports of excavation thereafter,

see C.H. Greenewalt, Jr. and others, *Bulletins* and *Annuals* of the American Schools of Oriental Research.

22 For an analysis of these drawings compared with the measurements taken by the excavators, see Vann, *op. cit.*, pp. 6–7, figs. 6–7 (city plan and panorama, Yale nos. B1977.14.928, '*Pianta della città di Sardes con alcuni vestigi di più fabriche antiche ancora esistenti nell anno 1750*' and 924); pp. 23–39, figs. 33–34 (bath 'C', Yale no. B1977.14.923); pp. 47–9, fig. 89 (theatre and stadium, Yale no. B1977.14.929A, black over brown ink with water colour and traces of body colour – one of the few in which colour is added). See Hutton, *op. cit.*, for sketches for the city plan (pl. XV) and bath 'C' (pl. XVII, captioned 'Court of Judicature').

23 Fikret K. Yegül, *The Bath-Gymnasium Complex at Sardis*, Archaeological Exploration of Sardis Report 3 (Cambridge, Mass., and London, Harvard University Press, 1986), p. 3, fig. 5 (Borra's sketch), figs. 7–8 (building plans as excavated and restored).

24 See Hutton, *op. cit.*, pp. 108–9, fig. 1 for a comparison of the sketch plan for the east portico with Butler's plan, Howard Crosby Butler, *Sardis*, Publications of the American Society for the Excavation of Sardis I, *The Excavations* Part I *1910–1914* (Leiden, E.J. Brill, 1922), pl. II. The finished version of the plan, Yale no. B1977.14.929B, is inscribed on the verso, 'the pillars mark'd black are standing as in ye view, those mark'd with lines not so black just appear above ground and those dotted are supposed.' Borra removed two columns shown in error in the south aisle (the temple is a *pseudodipteros*) but he mistakenly also removed two columns opposite the portal (Sardis nos. 11 and 12); he firmly locates the south anta and the portal, and he shows which column was excavated, 'E' = Sardis no. 16. For the sketch of the elevation and architectural details, see Hutton, *op. cit.*, pls. XVIII and XIX and compare Butler, ills. 106 (anta capital), 112 (torus), 115 (capitals). Borra's drawings had been forgotten when *Antiquities of Ionia* IV (Society of Dilettanti, 1881) was prepared: James Ferguson wrote that the temple had not been explored and had no knowledge of the carving on the bases (p. 15).

25 Yale no.1977.14.942, 'Mausoleo d'Haliatte in faccia a' Sardes'. Three mounds actually dominate the horizon; Alyattes' mound is perhaps the only one shown because Herodotus (I:93) wrote that it was the only marvel to be seen in Lydia. See also the commentary by Vann, *op. cit.*, pp. 6–7, fig. 5. For the cemetery, see Hanfmann, *op. cit.*, pp. 54–8.

26 Yale no. B1977.14.958A, Vann, *op. cit.*, fig. 7.

27 Yale no. B1977.14.990, Zoller, *op. cit.*, fig. 18.9 showing a plan of the theatre, measurements of steps and risers, column and pilaster capitals and decorative carving of the arcade. These elements appear in a fanciful reconstruction drawing of the smaller theatre, showing delightful vignettes of sculpture and landscape through the arcades of the *scena frons*, Yale no. B1977.14.925 (Zoller, *op. cit.*, fig. 18.11); also published by Russell, *op. cit.*, fig. 6 with a similar reconstruction of the theatre at Hierapolis (Yale no. B1977.14.987), in which the plan, the carved detail and the spiral columns are based on actuality but the trophies that crown the arches bear closer resemblance to those in Borra's *Trattato* than to Roman theatre decoration.

28 Quoted in D. Wiebenson, *Sources of Greek Revival Architecture* (London, A. Zwemmer, 1969), p. 33.
29 John Conforth, 'Stratfield Saye House, Hampshire. The Seat of the Duke of Wellington, I–II', *Country Life* (April 10 and 17, 1974), 899–902 and 982–5; Zoller, *op. cit.*, pp. 157–8.
30 Borra's contribution to the garden buildings is traced and analysed by Bevington, *op. cit.*, p. 8; see David R. Coffin, *The English Garden: Meditation and Memorial* (Princeton University Press, 1994) index, s. v. Stowe; Zoller, *op. cit.*, pp. 117–28.
31 Wood, *Palmyra, op. cit.*, pl. xix, monolithic slab ceilings of the north and south adytons of the temple of Bel.
32 Iain Browning, *Palmyra* (Park Ridge, N.J., Noyes Press, 1979), pp. 90–6, figs. 36–38 show the dining room ceiling at Stratford Saye and drawing room ceiling at Osterly Park with Borra's plate of the south adyton ceiling. Zoller, *op. cit.*, figs. 25–26 traces further dissemination of the Palmyra motif in England, France and Germany, including a book of designs by M.-J. Peyre, 'after an Italian sketchbook'.
33 See Paul Coullart and Jacques Vicari, *Le Sanctuaire de Baalshamin à Palmyre* II *Topographie et architecture* (Neuchâtel, Institut Suisse de Rome, 1969), pl. LXII, fig. 2, engraving of architrave and capital from *Palmyra*. Compare the animated Syrian style of the original capitals, pls. LXXXIII–LXXXVII. Iain Browning points out that the fallen fragments were made more orderly and 'artistically visible in Borra's views', 'Rescue from Oblivion', *London Archaeologist*, 6:16 (1992), 32–4; see Browning (1979), for many comparisons with the actual remains.
34 Desmond Fitz-Gerald, *The Norfolk House Music Room* (London, Victoria and Albert Museum, 1973); Zoller, *op. cit.*, pp. 147–57. See Yale no. B1977.14.937. Borra's interiors in England were subdued compared to the exuberance of his rooms at Racconigi. Cf. Axelle de Gaigeron, 'Racconigi, un château européen, *Connaissance des arts* (February 1982), 84–9.

9

Ottoman Women through the Eyes of Mary Wortley Montagu

Mary Ann Fay

In 1716, Lady Mary Wortley Montagu accompanied her husband, Edward, to Istanbul, where he took up his post as English ambassador to the Sublime Porte. From the time she arrived in the Ottoman Empire until she left Istanbul, in the spring of 1718, she wrote a series of letters to friends and family in England. The letters are remarkable for several reasons: because they display Lady Mary's wit, empathy and sense of adventure; because they are a description of upper-class Ottoman women and the *haramlik* by an eighteenth-century European who actually visited the palaces and harems of the elite; and because her accounts of elite women's lives and their position in society contradict those of male travel writers of the period.

In this paper, I shall confront the question of why Lady Mary's accounts of Turkish women and opinions about them were so startlingly different from those of male writers of the time. In a letter of April 1718, Lady Mary criticised male writers who 'lament the miserable confinement of the Turkish ladies who are (perhaps) freer than any ladies in the universe . . .'[1] How can we explain such contradictory points of view?

An Englishwoman in Istanbul

When Lady Mary arrived in Istanbul, four years after her marriage to Montagu, she was already a prolific letter writer and diarist. She continued writing letters from Istanbul that reveal not only her empathy with Turkish women but also show how she was able to construct a narrative that challenged and contradicted that of her male contemporaries.

Lady Mary was well aware that her representation of Turkish women was defiantly different from the way in which European male writers of the same period viewed women in the various parts of the Ottoman Empire. In one letter, she remarked:

> You will perhaps be surprised at an account so different from what you have been entertained with by the common voyage writers who are very fond of speaking of what they don't know.[2]

Lady Mary made this comment in a letter describing the palace in Adrianople set aside by the sultan for Ambassador Montagu and his retinue. Her letter included descriptions of the interior, including the harem, and the gardens. Whereas men saw the harems of the elite as sites of unrestrained sexuality, in which women were kept as virtual prisoners, Lady Mary focused on Turkish women's right to own property and described the harem as what it was; the private or family quarters of an upper-class household. She even considered the veil as a useful device that gave women opportunities for sexual adventures.

Lady Mary, by virtue of her gender and her class, had access to the women's baths[3] and was often invited to the homes of high-ranking Turkish women, such as the wife of the Grand Vizier,[4] the Sultana Hafisa, widow of Sultan Mustafa II (1695-1703), and Fatima, wife of the Grand Vizier's deputy. This privilege would not be extended to European men, for whom the harem would be strictly off-limits. As Lady Mary knew, the female or family quarters of an upper-class household, known as the *haramlik* during the Ottoman period, were prohibited to men unrelated to the females of the house. The European men who wrote with such apparent knowledge about the harem, therefore, had almost certainly never entered one.

In the same letter in which she commented on the ignorance of 'common voyage writers', Lady Mary noted:

> It must be under a very particular character or on some extraordinary occasion when a Christian is admitted into the house of a man of quality and their harems are always forbidden ground. Thus, they can only speak of the outside, which makes no great appearance; and the women's apartments are all built backward, removed from sight, and have no prospect than the gardens, which are enclosed with very high walls.[5]

Lady Mary also differed from male travel writers on the meaning of the veil, which European men saw as a sign of the subjugation of women.

Lady Mary, who donned the dress of an Ottoman lady, including the veil, on her forays into the centre of Istanbul, disagreed. In her opinion, the veil gave women sexual opportunities because

> tis impossible for the most jealous husband to know his wife when he meets her, and no man dare either touch or follow a woman in the street . . . This perpetual masquerade gives them entire liberty of following their inclination without danger of discovery.[6]

Although European men almost certainly never saw an elite woman unveiled, or spoke to her or visited her in the *haramlik*, they confidently described them as not truly beautiful, or, as Karsten Niebuhr did during his voyage to Arabia and Egypt in 1761, as 'excessively ignorant and merely great children'.[7] On the other hand, C.S. Sonnini, a naturalist who visited Egypt between 1777 and 1780, described the women of the Mamluks thus:

> Perpetually recluse, or going out but seldom, and always with a veil, or, to speak more correctly, with a mask which entirely cover their face . . . And for whom are so many charms thus carefully preserved: For one man alone, for a tyrant who holds them in captivity.[8]

Consider also the description of the Comte de Volney, a French savant, who visited Egypt and Syria between 1783 and 1785 and described women as

> rigorously sequestered from the society of men. Always closed up in their house, they communicate with their husband, father, their brother and their first cousin; carefully veiled in the streets, scarcely daring to speak to a man, even on business.[9]

Volney blamed what he considered the miserable condition of women on Muhammad and the Qur'an, for not doing women the honour of treating them as part of the human species. He also claimed, incorrectly, that the government deprived women of all property and personal liberty and made them dependent on a husband or father, a state that he described as slavery.[10] European men, such as Volney and Sonnini, described upper-class Egyptian women as confined to their harems, even though they also reported seeing them travelling through the streets on donkeys, visiting the cemeteries on Fridays and participating in wedding processions or public events such as the opening of the canal in Cairo.

The only exception among the male writers that I have discovered in my survey of eighteenth-century travellers is G.A. Olivier, a French physician who was sent to the Ottoman Empire, including Egypt and Persia, on an official mission by the new republican government of France in 1792.[11] Not only was Olivier well-informed and knowledgeable about such matters as Islamic law, but he was possibly the only eighteenth-century European man to have been invited into the women's quarters of an upper-class home.

The invitation came from a Turkish official who wanted Olivier to treat his sick mother. Olivier described the salon in which he examined the mother and reported that she remained veiled throughout the examination, as did the two female slaves who attended her.[12] Not only did Olivier gain entry to the sacrosanct precincts of the harem, but he is the only European to comment on the ability of harem women to exert influence on public affairs, on the nomination of government officials and on the distribution of favours.[13] Olivier stands alone among the 'common voyage writers' as an uncommon observer who was able to escape the confines of the emerging Orientalist discourse on women and Islamic society.

In contrast, Lady Mary's understanding of and appreciation for Ottoman women, at the beginning of the eighteenth century, were particularly due to her ability to penetrate the sacrosanct precincts of the *haramlik*. As an empathetic woman and an astute observer, Lady Mary was quick to realise that Ottoman women possessed something that Englishwomen of the eighteenth century did not – namely, financial independence. Lady Mary was aware that Turkish women, while married, retained control of their own money, and in the event of a divorce the husband was obliged to pay support to his former wife. This explains in part why Lady Mary described Ottoman women as 'the only free people in the Empire' and '(perhaps) freer than any ladies in the universe'.[14] Lady Mary would be keenly aware of the advantage Ottoman women had over their English counterparts because of her own circumstances and her recognition of the link between property ownership and independence.

Early influences on Mary Wortley Montagu

What were the particular circumstances of her marriage to Edward Montagu and the events surrounding them? Lady Mary reveals them and relates her reactions to them in a series of letters written before her stay in Turkey.[15]

Lady Mary was born into the English aristocracy in 1689, as the daughter of an earl, Lord Dorchester. Unusually for women of the time, she was an avid reader and moved in intellectual circles. At her father's home she met people such as Joseph Addison and Richard Steele, as well as William Congreve. As an adult she corresponded with the poet Alexander Pope, until they fell out for reasons that remain unclear.

When she was 14-years-old, Lady Mary met Edward Montagu, also a member of a titled, aristocratic family, who was then 25. They corresponded for seven years before Montagu asked for her hand in marriage. Lady Mary's father agreed, but the engagement foundered on the issue of the marriage settlement. Although Montagu was prepared to make provisions for his wife, he refused to accede to Dorchester's demand that he entail his property to his eldest son.

Montagu's views on the subject of marriage settlements were published in the *Tatler* of 12 September 1710. In his essay, Montagu compared the settlement of property on a woman by her prospective husband to 'robbery' undertaken by the father who uses his daughter's beauty as a means of coercing her lover into making a large settlement. Montagu ended his essay with the hope that the legislature would remedy this situation by fixing a marriage price depending on whether the woman was a maid or a widow, so 'that there should be no frauds or uncertainties in the sale of our women'.[16]

Like Montagu, Lady Mary believed that marriage among members of their class was tantamount to the sale of women, and she used the word 'slavery' to express her sentiments. In a letter to Montagu dated November 1710, Lady Mary wrote:

> Since I am so unfortunate to have nothing in my own disposal, do not think I have any hand in making settlements. People in my way are sold like slaves; and I cannot tell what price my master will put on me.[17]

Although Lady Mary wrote to Montagu breaking off all relations with him, he refused to stop corresponding with her or planning to marry her. In the early summer of 1712, she agreed to accept a suitor chosen by her father, but refused to go through with the marriage at virtually the last minute. Her father threatened to exile her to his estate in the north of England and, further, promised that he would not approve her marriage to any other suitor, make another settlement or leave her anything but a small annual income in the event of his death.[18] Alarmed at the prospect of her exile to a remote corner of England and failing to receive Dorchester's consent to the marriage, the pair decided to elope.

In a plaintive letter to Montagu before their marriage, Lady Mary said:

> Tis something odd for a woman that brings nothing to expect anything; but after the way of my education, I dare not pretend to live but in some degree suitable to it. I had rather die than return to a dependency upon relatives I have disobliged. Save me from that fear if you love me.[19]

In the end, Lady Mary would be disappointed: Montagu was remote, seemingly uncaring, absent for months at a time and because increasingly miserly as he grew older. Eventually, she and Montagu would live apart from each other, she on the continent and he in England.

Legal position of women in England and the Ottoman Empire

Lady Mary's predicament was due to the fact that the law in eighteenth-century England did not accord women property rights or even a separate legal personality. Under English common law married women could not own property, and, therefore, could not make contracts on their own. Once she was married, a woman's personal property (chattels) became her husband's absolutely, to use or dispose of as he chose without her consent.[20] W.S. Holdsworth, in *A History of English Law*, described the law's concept of marriage as 'a gift of the wife's chattels to her husband'.[21] As Sir William Blackstone, the noted eighteenth-century English jurist, said:

> By marriage the very being or legal existence of a woman is suspended, or at least it is incorporated or consolidated into that of the husband, under whose wing, protection and cover she performs everything and she is therefore called in our law a *feme covert*.[22]

As a feme covert, a married woman could not own any personal property except clothing and personal ornaments, could not control her real estate and could not make a contract in her own name. The law placed the wife under the guardianship of her husband and made him legally responsible for her. The only way a woman could be recognised as a feme sole or a separate legal person was by remaining a spinster or becoming a widow.

Since changes in women's legal status were not possible under common law, they began to be made through equity jurisprudence in the Chancery Courts. From the sixteenth century onwards, equity law and Chancery provided the propertied classes with the legal means to settle property on women that would be for their separate use, with the consent and approval of the husband.[23] This, of course, is what Lady Mary would have received if Montagu had not quarrelled with her father, or if she had accepted the suitor chosen for her by her father.

By contrast, there is nothing in Islamic law that is comparable to the notion in English common law that a woman's legal personhood and identity are conflated into her husband's after marriage. Islam accords to women's legal standing not only through property rights, but above all through a woman's right to execute a contract. Indeed, property rights are contingent on the right to make contracts. Among Muslims and under Islamic law, marriage is a contract to which a woman who has reached her legal majority must give her consent either orally or in writing.[24] Islamic law does not make a distinction between a feme covert and a feme sole. Only minors, both boys and girls, had legal guardians, or *walis*, usually the father or grandfather of the child. However, the guardian's authority to act for his son or daughter ended when the child reached his or her majority. Tucker, in her study of two eighteenth-century jurists, pointed out that Hanafi judges agreed that a woman in her legal majority had the right to arrange her own marriage contract or to hire a *wali* to arrange a marriage for her.[25]

Women's right to property in Islamic law is derived from a verse in the Qur'an, which Muslims believe is the word of God as revealed to the prophet Muhammad in the seventh century AD. The Qur'an also became one of the sources of Islamic law. The particular revelation relating to women's property ownership is found in *surah* 4:8:

> From what is left by parents
> And those nearest related

> There is a share for men
> And a share for women,
> Whether the property be small
> Or large – a determinate share.[26]

Under the law, a woman has the right to own and manage her own property, to will it to her heirs after her death and to endow it as *waqf*. The only legal restriction on women's property ownership is the same as that on that of men, namely, that the property of the deceased is subject to division according to the law. The Qur'an stipulates the relatives who have an interest in the property of the deceased and the size of the share each should receive. Female children are entitled to half the share of their brothers. The Qur'an says:

> God (thus) directs you
> As regards your children's
> (Inheritance): to the male,
> A portion equal to that
> Of two females . . .[27]

Both men and women can evade the division of property stipulated by the Qur'an by making a will, which allows the testator to divide the property as he or she pleases. However, only a third of the testator's estate can be willed and is, therefore, not subject to Islamic inheritance law. Additionally, the dowry or *mahr* is paid directly to the woman, not to her family or to her husband, and she maintains control of it after her marriage. The Qur'an makes this explicit by saying, 'And give the women (on marriage) their dower as a free gift.'[28]

A woman retains possession of her property after her marriage, and neither spouse has a legal claim to or interest in the property of the other because of the marriage. The woman does not have the legal responsibility or obligation to use her personal wealth or property to support her husband or family. Maintenance, providing food, clothing and lodging, is the primary responsibility of the husband. In return, a woman gives her husband faithfulness and obedience. According to the Qur'an:

> Men are the protectors
> And maintainers of women,
> Because God has given to one more (strength)
> Than the other, and because

They support them
From their means.
Therefore the righteous women
Are devoutly obedient[29]

Islam, therefore, while expanding the legal and property rights of women, did not overturn the patriarchal order of seventh-century Arabia. It did, however, restructure the gender system by expanding the rights accorded to women.

Conclusion

Throughout her writings, Lady Mary's personality is writ large, not just in her ability to empathise but also in her spirit of adventure and her insatiable curiosity, which propelled her into the streets, mosques and bazaars of Istanbul with her face veiled like an upper-class Ottoman lady. And Lady Mary's gender allowed her the access to the women's quarters that was denied to men. However, gender is not a sufficient explanation for her attitudes in itself. As we know from the writings of nineteenth-century women in British India and imperial Africa, European women often shared with their male counterparts Orientalist views of 'native' women and societies in general.[30]

Lady Mary's personality and gender undoubtedly played a role in shaping her attitudes toward Turkish women. However, her letters from Istanbul are more than descriptive essays about Turkish women and the customs and mores of their society. In writing about Turkish women, Lady Mary was also writing autobiographically about and, by extension, other Englishwomen of her class. So, for example, Lady Mary could describe Turkish women as 'free' because she knew that they controlled their own property, and, further, she understood the link between property ownership and autonomy for women. This is in contrast to the situation of eighteenth-century Englishwomen such as herself, who had no property rights under English common law. Such insights about Turkish women were possible, I argue, because while Turkish women were the objects of her writings, she herself was the subject. In the case of Lady Mary, we can only conclude that her writings are free of Edward Said's 'essence of orientalism': 'the distance between Western superiority and oriental inferiority',[31] that is, the discourse in which women in Islamic societies were represented as the dominated Other.

NOTES

1. Christopher Peck (ed.), *Embassy to Constantinople: The Travels of Lady Mary Wortley Montagu* (New York, New Amsterdam Books, 1988), p. 189.
2. *Ibid.*, pp. 125–6.
3. Fanny Davis, *The Ottoman Lady: A Social History from 1718 to 1918* (New York, 1986), pp. 132–3.
4. Fatma, daughter of Ahmed III, widow of Ali Pasha and married to the Grand Vizier, Ibrahim Pasha. She was 14 when Lady Mary visited her in 1718; see Philip Mansel, *Constantinople: City of the World's Desire, 1453–1924* (Harmondsworth, Penguin, 1997), p. 167.
5. *Ibid.*
6. *Ibid.*, p. 111.
7. Carlsten Niebuhr, *Travels through Arabia and Other Countries in the East*, trans. Robert Heron (Edinburgh, R. Morison, 1792; repr. Beirut, Librarie du Liban), p. 123.
8. C.S. Sonnini, *Travels in Upper and Lower Egypt* (1799; repr. Westmead, Gregg International Publishers, 1972), p. 164.
9. Comte de Volney (Constantin François Chasseboeuf), *Voyage en Syrie et en Égypte pendant les années 1783, 1784 et 1785* (2 vols., Paris, Volland et Desenne, 1787), vol. 2, p. 441.
10. *Ibid.*, pp. 441–2.
11. G.A. Olivier, *Voyage dans l'empire Ottomane, l'Égypte et la Perse* (3 vols., Paris, H. Agosse, [1801]–1807). Olivier travelled throughout the Ottoman Empire between 1790 and 1795.
12. *Ibid.*, pp. 150–2.
13. *Ibid.*, p. 170.
14. Peck, *op. cit.*, p. 111.
15. For biographies and collected letters, see Lewis Saul Benjamin, *Lady Mary Wortley Montagu, Her Life and Letters 1689–1762* by Lewis Melville (pseud.) (Boston and New York, Houghton Mifflin, 1925); Robert Halsband, *The Life of Lady Mary Wortley Montagu* (Oxford, Clarendon Press, 1956); Robert Halsband, *The Complete Letters of Lady Mary Wortley Montagu* (3 vols., Oxford, Clarendon Press, 1965–7); Malcolm Jack (ed.), *Turkish Embassy Letters* (Athens, Ga., University of Georgia Press, 1993); Peck, *op. cit.*; *The Letters and Works of Lady Mary Wortley Montagu*, ed. by her great grandson, Lord Wharncliffe (2 vols., London, Swan Sonnenschein, and New York, Macmillan, 1893).
16. Benjamin, *op. cit.*, pp. 51–52.
17. Wharncliffe, *op. cit.*, vol. 1, p. 178, letter to Montagu dated November 1710.
18. *Ibid.*, vol. 1, p. 187, letter to Montagu dated 'about July 4'.
19. *Ibid.*, vol. 1, p. 192, letter to Montagu dated August 1712.
20. Lee Holcombe, *Wives and Property: Reform of the Married Women's Property Law in Nineteenth-century England* (University of Toronto Press, 1893), p. 22.
21. W.S. Holdsworth, *A History of English Law*, 3rd edn (Boston, Little, Brown, 1923), vol. 3, p. 531.
22. Cited in Holcombe, *op. cit.*, p. 25.

23 *Ibid.*, p. 10; Holdsworth, *op. cit.*, p. 533; and Susan Staves, *Married Women's Separate Property 1660–1833* (Cambridge, Mass., and London, Harvard University Press, 1990); in Staves, see her discussion of the jointure which allowed property to be settled on a married woman, pp. 95–7.
24 Judith Tucker, 'Muftis and Matrimony: Islamic law and gender in Ottoman Syria and Palestine', *Islamic Law and Society*, 1:3 (1994), 266; and John Esposito, *Women in Muslim Family Law* (Syracuse University Press, 1982), p. 16.
25 Tucker, *op. cit.*, p. 275.
26 *The Holy Qur'an*, translated with a commentary by A. Yusuf Ali (Brentwood, Maryland, Amana Corporation, 1983), p. 180.
27 Sura 4:2 (*ibid.*, p. 181).
28 Sura 4:4 (*ibid.*, p. 179).
29 Sura 4:34 (*ibid.*, p. 190).
30 See Nupur Chaudhuri and Margaret Strobel (eds.), *Western Women and Imperialism, Complicity and Resistance* (Bloomington and Indianapolis, Indiana University Press, 1992).
31 Mansel, *op. cit.*, p. 214.

10

James Silk Buckingham (1786–1855): An Anecdotal Traveller

Peta Rée

Described at different times in his life as a swindler, a villain, an artful adventurer and as one whose energies were generally devoted to useful and benevolent objects, it would clearly take a biography to explore, with justice, the character and deeds of James Silk Buckingham. I cannot attempt to do so here. I will look only at a very short period of his life, when he was in friendly contact (to begin with) with many of the travellers relevant to our theme.

What can be said with certainty of Buckingham is that he attracted those he met by a boundless enthusiasm for whatever he was engaged in at that moment, and a conversational style that was voluble, lively and indiscreet. In short, he was an accomplished gossip.

Others of our travellers certainly enjoyed a good gossip too, but usually only in private conversation or letters; of all the travellers who wrote of their experiences, few but Buckingham carried a gossipy style into their published work. He reveals many details about the people and the way of life of the Europeans in Egypt – details that the intelligentsia of his own day might brush aside with contempt as trivia, but that can put flesh on the bones of history for us.

In 1813, Buckingham was 27-years-old, and, as a seaman, and later the captain of merchant vessels, had spent most of the last 15 years engaged in trade with America, the West Indies and latterly with the countries around the Mediterranean. He had long hoped to visit Greece, Palestine and Egypt, and now, he says:

> [I] applied myself with more than common ardour, to the reading of every book within reach that was likely to extend my knowledge of the interesting countries by which I was on all sides surrounded;

and unfavorable as the incessant duties, and the hardy life of a sailor are to such studies, every moment that I could spare from the vigilant watch which squalls, and storms, and pirates, and more open enemies, constantly demanded, and from all the complicated claims which commerce and navigation forced on my attention, was given to study.[1]

A devoted husband, he decided to give up seafaring and establish himself as a merchant in Malta in order to have his family with him – a decision that, in the event, was to lead to his being parted from them for ten years. When he reached Malta there was plague in the island, and he sailed on to Smyrna, arriving on 30 June 1813. Only a few weeks later, he learned that all his stores had been destroyed by a fire in Malta, leaving him but £100 in the world.

Financially ruined, he was persuaded by friends in Smyrna to go to Egypt, where the Pasha 'was known to desire the aid of Europeans of talent and character in his service'.[2] This was clearly an opportunity that an enterprising man should seize. Carrying letters of recommendation to the British consul in Egypt, Colonel Missett, he landed at Alexandria on about 9 or 10 September 1813.

Missett was at Cairo, but, like many another British traveller, Buckingham was kindly and hospitably received into the home of the Levant Company's vice-consul in Alexandria, Peter Lee. He, Buckingham tells us, was the brother of John Lee of Smyrna and of Edward Lee, 'the head of the house', in London. His wife, Emma, had been one Miss Arboyne.

Buckingham describes consular social life in Alexandria as follows:

> We had most agreeable reunions every evening; as each Consul, as a matter of duty, kept open house for an evening reception once in the week; and on Sunday evenings the parties were still more numerous. After an hour devoted to the reception, from 7 to 8, music was usually introduced, and pleasant chamber concerts given . . . and from half past 9 to 11 the evening was wound up by a dance. No other refreshment than coffee, *eau sucre*, and lemonade was produced for the visitors, so that the entertainments were inexpensive and therefore easy to be often repeated, and as the houses were large, there were always rooms or balconies to which those who did not join in the music or dance might retire for conversation.[3]

James Silk Buckingham (1786–1855)

The comment of another traveller suggests there may have been a further reason for the temperance of the consular parties. 'The supply of wine was precarious', wrote Captain Light of the Royal Artillery, on leave from Malta in 1814; 'the only wine I tasted there was the commonest red Cyprus, bitter and disagreeable'. Also, heavy duties levied by the Pasha discouraged the importation of wine.[4]

Buckingham had a charming anecdote to tell about Captain Light, regarding an occasion when they had gone together to a village near Cairo:

> As the captain was short-sighted, he always wore spectacles; and at his appearance we observed, that instead of running away, which was the usual course of the women especially, they stood bolt upright with their legs as close together as they could put them; and with both arms extended downwards, holding fast their garments as if afraid they would fly upward . . . on inquiring we found that someone in the village had once looked through an English night glass or sea telescope, which reverses the objects seen through it, or turns them upside down; and had proclaimed to the women that the Frank had put on these spectacles for the express purpose of reversing their figures. Not supposing the possibility . . . of such a reversal . . . could possibly happen without the inevitable consequence of their clothes falling over their heads, and thus exposing their bodies in a state of nudity, they did their best to prevent this . . .[5]

As the men were beginning to gather threateningly, the Franks abandoned any attempt to persuade them of their error and 'cut short our excursion'.

Buckingham soon tore himself away from the delightful social life of Alexandria, departing for Cairo on 22 September, via Rosetta, where he was received by the British consular agent, Mr Lenze. He was a Levantine, but always dressed himself as he thought appropriate when visitors from France or England arrived. With the greatest politeness he showed Buckingham the points of interest in what Buckingham described as a 'prettily situated, and in many respects agreeable little town'. He wrote:

> Wherever we went, however, our European dress attracted attention; the men gazing in silence – the women and children setting up a shriek either of surprise or alarm, and the dogs . . . following at our heels with their yelling and howling bark. It must be confessed,

however, that the costume of the vice-consul was such as would have drawn a crowd around him in any town in England. His stature was at least six feet six inches; his form remarkably slender, and his legs so thin as to seem quite inadequate to the support of even his attenuated trunk. His dress consisted of a pair of white kersemere pantaloons as tight as the skin, and carried up to within six inches of the arm-pits, for the sake of displaying a profusion of dark braiding in front, after the Hungarian fashion, with a pair of Hessian boots and gold tassels. The waistcoat was not more than 8 inches in depth . . . and the flaps of the coat, which was bright scarlet, were equally short, leaving an immense length of coat-tails, descending to a sharp point, and covered, wherever possible, with gold embroidery . . . his head was crowned with one of those lofty pyramidical cocked-hats which rise to a great height in the centre and being worn at right angles presented a most imposing front . . . he seemed like a man sewn up in garments never intended to be taken off.[6]

In Cairo, Buckingham stayed in the residency of Colonel Missett, and gives a description of the group of friends with whom he now travelled:

Colonel Missett was a distinguished officer of the Enniskillen dragoons, and a perfect specimen of an Irish gentleman; courageous and chivalrous to the last degree, an ardent admirer of the fair sex, a bon vivant of great refinement . . . an admirable recounter of anecdotes of military and diplomatic life, an excellent singer of after-dinner songs . . . and though, from paralysis of all his extremities, he was quite unable to use either his legs or arms – being wheeled to table in a chair, and his food cut up for him by his valet – his trunk, heart and head were perfectly sound; for though he lived freely or generously, he had excellent digestion, good sleep, and his benevolence and high spirits were both constantly overflowing. On the whole, I have never met . . . a more fascinating man than Colonel Missett.

Also of the household was 'a merry and light-hearted officer of dragoons from Piedmont, Major Taberna, whose feats of arms and camp adventures formed endless materials for conversation', and 'Mr Thurburn, the colonel's secretary, a more quiet but more intelligent and instructive companion and full of the gentlemanly qualities by which the colonel himself was so much distinguished.'

'Nothing could surpass the pleasure of our lives', wrote Buckingham. There were sumptuous breakfasts and dinners, 'composed and prepared by the ex-*chef-de-cuisine* of the King of Naples'; there were morning rides to see the sights, 'on the most tractable Arabs'; and there were evening parties, 'often graced' by the local European and Levantine ladies, sometimes ending with a ball, to which 'handsome Turkish women from the harems of distinguished men came as visitors and spectators'.[7]

At the end of October, Buckingham sailed up the Nile, as far south as Dukka, where an attack of ophthalmia turned him back, and, after an abortive journey across the desert from Qina to the Red Sea, he was back in Cairo at the end of December.

On the way upriver, at Esna, he met John Lewis Burckhardt – he called himself Shaykh Ibrahim and passed himself off as a Muslim merchant who was waiting there for a caravan to the Red Sea, his ultimate destination being Mecca. This is how Buckingham described him:

> He came aboard and introduced himself, speaking excellent English. He was dressed . . . with a blue cotton blouse, covering a coarse shirt, loose white trousers, and a common calico turban round his head; he had a full dark beard, was without stockings, wearing only the slip-shod slippers of the country, and looked so completely like . . . a Syrian, having a fairer complexion and lighter eyes than the Egyptians, that few would have suspected him to be a Swiss, as he really was, but have taken him to be a native of Antioch or Aleppo, the dialect of Arabic he spoke being of that region also . . . We spent the evening together at the house of the Turkish Governor of Esne, with whom we supped.

Next morning, before sunrise, Burckhardt came to share Buckingham's breakfast of coffee and rice-pilau; 'we were so intensely and mutually interested in each other's conversation' commented Buckingham, 'that we continued together, seated in the boat in an uninterrupted talk till sunset, with scarcely an interval of pause between, for at our noon-day and sunset meals our conversation still continued in unabated volubility'.

> The truth is, that the meeting of two Europeans in so remote a spot from their respective homes, makes them friends and brothers at once; and as each is sure to have a large amount of sympathy, bottled up as it were, for want of reciprocal exercise, it is sure on such occasions to overflow . . . [and] in the frankness of unlimited confidence, each narrates the leading incidents of his own life and adventures, and both parties are mutually gratified.

So remarked Buckingham – and how much truer this was of Burckhardt, starved for many months of European companionship.[8] Burckhardt told his friend Renouard that he 'opened his heart' to Buckingham as he had done to only three other men in the East.[9] He was to repent it, but that was still in the future when he wrote the letter that awaited Buckingham's return from the south, regretting he would miss him, for 'on my part, I beg you to rest assured, that the memory of the two days you kindly granted me . . . shall never be obliterated from my mind and heart'.[10] In the event, he had not yet left when Buckingham arrived, and they spent a few hours together before parting on 14 December 1813.

Buckingham had not yet met the Pasha of Egypt, who was away waging war against the Wahhabis, but at some time in August 1814, the Pasha was in Cairo, and Buckingham had an audience that lasted from seven o'clock until midnight, talking of commerce and navigation – 'subjects his usual European visitors were ignorant of'.

Many travellers described the Pasha, but Buckingham's remarks are particularly free:

> His aspect was that of a worn-out and exhausted person, but with an eye of a penetrating nature, and a general recklessness of spirit that seemed to care very little about the means to accomplish his ends, provided they could be successfully employed . . . his principal enjoyment was in his harem . . . and . . . there was no present that would so effectually prepare the way for the grant of any favour as that of a young and beautiful virgin. Whatever were the imputed heresies of which he was accused, as departures from the Moslem faith, or lapsing into infidelity, in this he was a perfect Mohammedan.[11]

Before their meeting, Buckingham had been commissioned by the Pasha to survey the Isthmus of Suez, with the idea of opening a canal to facilitate trade between the Mediterranean and India. The Pasha now recounted to Buckingham how, as he had been told, the British had gradually taken over India: first they came as traders, then they established stores to keep their goods safe, then they asked permission to fortify them against thieves; next, only extra land would suffice for security – and so, little by little, they took over the country. It would be chiefly English ships which would use the canal – would they not practise the same tricks in Egypt? Buckingham could only say it was not impossible.

Then, said the Pasha, would not building the canal 'be sharpening the knife by which our throat was to be cut?' And so, guessed Buckingham correctly, 'I considered this question of the canal to be settled in the negative, during his lifetime at least.'[12]

The Pasha gave Buckingham a commission to purchase some ships for him at Bombay, whither Buckingham was bound on behalf of Peter Lee's mercantile house, to persuade the Bombay merchants to open up trade with Egypt. So, in October 1814, Buckingham set sail from Suez for Jeddah, where, having lost most of his possessions and all his money in a storm, his 'plight was a pitiable one', not least because he was ill with fever and exhaustion.

Araby Jellany, the English agent at Jeddah, took him in, but he was soon visited by a young Scotsman: William Thomson, who, as a soldier in the 78th Highland Regiment had been taken prisoner at Rosetta in 1807, and was now known as Osman.

> Though he preserved all his northern peculiarities of light complexion, sandy hair and moustaches, face, light blue eyes, and yellowish eyebrows and eyelashes, his dress, air, and manners were completely those of a Turk. He preserved, however, all his veneration for his native country, and his sympathies for all who came from thence.[13]

Osman arranged for Buckingham to stay on an English ship that was in harbour. Here Burckhardt, down from Mecca, came to visit, and again, 'perfectly free from intrusion or interruption, we enjoyed to the full the "feast of reason and the flow of soul"'. At dinner, wine was served, and Burckhardt, 'though professing to be a Mohammedan ... took a glass without hesitation'. Osman, however, had scruples of conscience about 'disgracing his Moslem faith' and declined:

> Being rallied, however, by his brother Moslem, his resistance gave way, and he took a single glass ... Whether it was the motion of the ship, though at anchor, or the long disuse of wine, or both combined, perhaps ... he became sick; and he gravely and seriously attributed this to divine wrath, as a punishment for his infringing the precepts of the Koran![14]

Buckingham departed for India in January 1815, but found that the Bombay merchants were not prepared to enter into trade with

Egypt without a fixed treaty to insure protection and light duties. As Buckingham was prevented from setting up in business for himself, because he had no licence from the Court of the East India Company in London, he had no choice but to leave, and was back in Cairo by the middle of November.

The entire expedition, to India and back, had taken 11 months; his next journey there, one way only, was to take nearly a year, and to be one reason for his losing the goodwill of most or all of his acquaintances in the East. He was sent again to Bombay by the business house of Lee & Briggs, this time with a trading treaty from the Pasha, and 'clothed with the authority of Mahomet Ali's envoy'.[15]

Leaving Alexandria on Christmas Day, 1815, he was in Jerusalem by 17 January, and was put up in the best room at the convent of Terra Santa, that 'generally appropriated to travellers of distinction . . . every part of the door of which is crowded with names' including 'Edward Clarke and companion, Captain Culverhouse, Dr Wittman, John Gordon (1804), whose name is everywhere in Egypt, Colonel Maxwell and Captain Bramsen, Mr Fiot, William Turner 1815.'[16]

On 20 January, the wealthy and erudite William John Bankes arrived, and whatever Buckingham's intentions may have been to journey directly east, he joined Bankes, first in a week of sightseeing in Jerusalem, then in a trip to Jordan and Jerash and then travelled to other places on his own.

It was from this time that his actions caused him to cease being everyone's favourite friend and instead come to be considered 'the most artful of adventurers'.[17] 'I possessed', he wrote, 'an ardour in the pursuit of enquiry and research which all my previous sufferings had not in the least abated', and he visited 'the greater part of Palestine, the country beyond Jordan, eastern parts of Moab, Bashan, Gilead and the Auranites: crossed Phoenicia and the higher parts of Syria, in various directions from Baalbek by . . . Lebanon to the sea coast, from Antioch to Aleppo'.[18]

His ardour for enquiry was viewed differently by those who had paid for his journey. 'This man who has a most prepossessing manner', wrote Henry Salt, now British consul general in Egypt, 'made many friends, whom he afterwards lost by a transaction which can scarcely be termed otherwise than that of a swindler'. With money paid by the house of Briggs, he had, instead of 'making the best of his way' to India, 'travelled to and fro throughout Syria, with an evident view to collect materials for the press. The consequence was that he did not arrive in India within the twelvemonth, to the great prejudice of Briggs' affairs.'[19]

For a few weeks in Palestine, Buckingham had enjoyed the friendship and trust of William Bankes, but by the date of this letter, in 1819, Salt had been told by Bankes that 'the most interesting part' of the book Buckingham had 'so pompously announced' he was to publish were 'pilferings from Mr Bankes who was kind enough to take him in his company'.

Through his father, Henry Bankes, William persuaded John Murray not to publish Buckingham's *Travels in Palestine*, but two years later it was brought out by Longman. By this time, Buckingham was well aware of Bankes' actions against him; despite this, the book is still complimentary about Bankes' 'known talents, pure taste and extensive erudition'.[20]

But was this passage added after 1819? The two men had been exploring Jerash in a downpour of rain so heavy that 'it became difficult to walk from the weight of our garments' (they were in Turkish dress). Returning to their inn, Buckingham stripped naked and huddled between two straw mats for warmth, but Bankes was 'better provided', with dry clothes. Observing Bankes' 'shirt and drawers, which were of fine calico' being dried at the fire, the locals became suspicious, with nearly fatal results. Indeed, observed Buckingham, Bankes' 'lack of the language and manners of the country meant we were driven to subterfuge and evasion, for only an uncertain safety at best'.[21]

Did these remarks add an extra dose of vitriol to the critique that appeared in the *Quarterly Review*, described with justice by Buckingham as 'one of the most ungentlemanly, bitter and slanderous articles that ever disgraced the critical literature of the country',[22] which was penned (anonymously) by none other than William Bankes? Legal actions taken by Buckingham against John Murray, William Bankes and his father Henry Bankes were to drag out over many years – but that, as they say, is another story.

NOTES

1. James Silk Buckingham, *Travels in Palestine* (London, Longman, Hurst, Rees and Brown, 1821), p. viii.
2. James Silk Buckingham, *Autobiography of James Silk Buckingham* (London, Longman, Brown, Green and Longman, 1855), p. 123.
3. *Ibid.*, p. 130.
4. Henry Light, *Travels in Egypt, Nubia, the Holy Land, Mount Lebanon and Cyprus in the Year 1814* (London, printed for Rodwell and Martin, 1818), p. 9.
5. Buckingham, *op. cit.* (1855), p. 157.
6. *Ibid.*, p. 140.
7. *Ibid.*, pp. 152ff.
8. *Ibid.*, pp. 179ff.
9. Mss Renouard, British Museum Add Mss 27620: 29.
10. Buckingham, *op. cit.* (1855), p. 186.
11. *Ibid.*, p. 267.
12. *Ibid.*, p. 277.
13. *Ibid.*, p. 291.
14. *Ibid.*, p. 293.
15. *Ibid.*, p. 421.
16. Buckingham, *op. cit.* (1821), p. 178.
17. James Silk Buckingham, *Travels among the Arab Tribes* (London, Longman, Hurst, Rees, Orne, Brown & Green, 1825), p. 639 (quoting Burckhardt).
18. Buckingham, *op. cit.* (1821), p. xiv.
19. British Museum, Department of Egyptology, Salt Ms., Document 6.
20. Buckingham, *op. cit.* (1821), p. xxii.
21. *Ibid.*, p. 403.
22. James Silk Buckingham, *Travels in Mesopotamia* (London, H. Colburn, 1827), appendix.

11

Lord Belmore proceeds up the Nile in 1817–1818

Deborah Manley

In 1797, Armar Lowry-Corry was created first Earl of Belmore and his family moved into their new house at Enniskillen, in County Fermanagh, Ireland. The architect, James Wyatt, had created in lush parkland at Castle Coole the finest neoclassical house in the country. The new earl lived only another five years, and died at Bath in 1802. His son, Somerset Lowry-Corry, then 28, inherited the title and the estate, and it was he and his cousin Juliana, who was also his wife, who were responsible for the outstanding Regency interior and furnishings that were planned to outdo his in-laws' pretensions at nearby Florence Court. The family also had a house in Dublin and another at Cowes, on the Isle of Wight, where the Earl was an important member of the Royal Yacht Club.[1]

In 1791, at the age of 17, Somerset Lowry-Corry had journeyed to Spain and Morocco and acquired a taste for travel. With the Napoleonic Wars over and building work disrupting Castle Coole, the Belmores set off in the summer of 1816 on a journey that would take them to the Near East and Egypt.

The party consisted of the Earl, then 42, and in the prime of life, his countess, Juliana (and probably her lapdog, Rosa),[2] and their two sons: Armar, born in 1800; and Henry, three years younger. The Earl's chaplain, the Reverend Holt, acted as the boys' tutor and his doctor, Robert Richardson, became the party's chronicler. Richardson was an experienced traveller, having accompanied Viscount Mountjoy, later husband of the famous Countess of Blessington, on the Grand Tour.[3] The Earl's ship, the *Ospray*, was commanded by Captain Armer Corry RN, the illegitimate son of the first earl. Corry was described by Henry Salt as a man of fine natural spirit and agreeable manners, 'absolutely formed for travelling'.[4] It is through his enthusiasm for carving his name – or having the sailors carve it – that we can follow their stopping places along the Nile. The Belmores' names appear only on top of the pyramid and at Abu Sir; the boys carved their names at Abu Simbel, too, and the Reverend Holt added his at Philae. Dr Richardson was very disapproving of this custom, and, as far as we have discovered, did not follow it. Youngest of the party was Miss Juliana Eleanor Brook, then about ten or eleven years old, the daughter of a liaison between the Earl and Lady Brook while her husband was absent at the Peninsula Wars. The Earl's two manservants cared for his domestic needs and carried his gun when he went shooting; the countess had her personal maid.

The Earl had purchased the 232-ton *Ospray*, reputedly a former American privateer, and fitted her out completely for the purpose of the voyage. Her crew of 32 able-bodied seamen was under the command of Captain Corry. There were a number of British sailors, including the ship's carpenter, attached to the cavalcade. Their names and wages survive on lists in the logbook of the voyage in the Castle Coole archives. The sailors left their own mark, for it was not 'Mr O'Spray' who was in Egypt but the crew of the *Ospray*.

The *Ospray* sailed from Southampton on 21 August 1816. The party spent ten days in Gibraltar, ten in Malta and wintered in Naples, where Richardson found the contrast between rich and poor and the hypocrisy on view a disgust – with 'pimps at every corner, priests in every café, and miracle-mongers in the Cathedral'.[5] They left Naples on 30 March 1817 and drifted eastwards slowly, visiting Albania and the Greek islands and reaching the Bay of Saide by late August.

The Earl was undecided as to whether to go to Jerusalem before Egypt. His correspondence with Lady Hester Stanhope, now in the Castle Coole archives, decided him. She was firmly of the opinion, and the firmness of her opinions is well known, that they should go to Egypt for the winter and return to Jerusalem in the spring. She added several pages of advice about how they should dress and conduct themselves in Egypt and who they should meet. She had been in Egypt for a few months several years before, but her advice was as detailed as any I have read. It resides in the Castle Coole archive with the correspondence about the voyage. Lady Hester was not renowned for her enthusiasm for her fellow countrymen, but the Belmores intrigued her:

> There is something so novel, so interesting, in this degenerate age in a father travelling for the instruction of his children, and in a woman accompanying her husband upon hazardous journeys, instead of devoting her time to folly and dissipation, that for once I feel no sort of apprehension of my motives being misconstructed if I take the liberty of giving you my candid opinion upon your plans, which you can always act upon or not, as you like.

They did as she suggested and the *Ospray* sailed into Alexandria on 7 October 1817.

In Egypt their paths crossed those of many travellers. Their host in Cairo and companion up to Luxor was Consul General Henry Salt – who Lady Hester had rightly said would show them every attention. In Cairo they met, and later mourned, Salt's friend and colleague, John Lewis Burckhardt, the Swiss explorer. How far, one wonders, was their appreciation of him marred by Lady Hester's words? She wrote:

> There is also another man who might be useful to you, but whom I think vastly ill of . . . He is very plausible, but very false, very envious and with the mask of sentiment and high feelings . . . I detest a man full of low intrigues and who wears half a dozen faces as he thinks best suits his purpose.

Also in Cairo were two delightful naval captains on half-pay, Charles Irby and James Mangles; and in Luxor they would meet Giovanni Belzoni, at a moment of triumph and fury, and Salt's secretary Henry Beechey. All four men had not long returned from Abu Simbel. Count Forbin, later Director-General of French museums, Frédéric Cailliaud, the French mineralogist and the Tuscan doctor and draughtsman, Alessandro Ricci, were also in Luxor, as were the former French Consul General, Colonel Bernadino Drovetti and his agent, the sculptor Jean-Jacques Rifaud. Less grand, but also present, were Giovanni Finati, Salt's janissary; the young Greek, Yanni d'Athanasi, soon to become Salt's agent; and Sarah, Belzoni's wife and their young Irish servant, James Curtin. When they travelled on to Jerusalem they met William John Bankes and Thomas Legh. The Earl was also received by Muhammad Ali and spent a happy day with his son-in-law, the Deftardar Bey, at Asyut. The list reads like *Who was Who in Egyptology*.[6] What makes the years 1817–18 especially interesting is that so many travellers wrote about their experiences, and it is possible to refer from one to another and check each observation and record.

In 1822, the *Quarterly Review* would comment deprecatingly on Richardson's book:

> As a writer of travels, he is neither entertaining nor so instructive as might be wished, mistaking frequently cant and vulgar phrases for wit, and uncouth words for learning. That he has told the truth we cannot for a moment doubt; but that he has told it, as he says, 'in as few words, and an agreeable manner as possible', we can by no means concede to him.[7]

These are harsh words, and not very fair. His book is an important record of a moment in the history of European travel in Egypt. Richardson discussed current ideas about the discoveries being made that reflect ideas shared by the travellers that would be reasonably acceptable to modern archaeologists. His employer Lord Belmore, however, would nowadays be considered to be one of the 'rapists of the Nile'. Dr Richardson's record of the journey reads as if it was a pleasant experience enjoyed by all. The truth may have been rather different. How often do the private records of travellers vary from the published version? In the Castle Coole archives is a letter from Henry Salt, dated 18 October 1818:

> Your account of Dr Richardson did not in any way surprise me – the rudeness of his character was too evident and as I felt no (need) of bearing with it led me I fear once or twice to express myself more strongly than I ought to have done in your and Lady Belmore's presence, but it really was at times unbearable. Your patience I am sure must have been long exhausted before you parted, but it was far better, under all the circumstances to bear with rudeness than have been deprived of his medical skill.

The doctor must have been irritating indeed, for Salt was very long-suffering on the whole – as can be clearly seen in his relations with the troublesome Belzoni. Salt and the Earl obviously shared some concerns about what the doctor would say when he published. Salt felt that, 'he was neither a profound observer nor by his shortness of sight capable of forming any judgement of the superb monuments of antiquity which he had so good an opportunity of visiting'.[8] He underestimated Richardson. His book is both more sympathetic and more interesting than they feared.

Through Richardson we learn a great deal, both about travellers and about the great discoveries of those significant months. Just two months before the Belmores arrived in Egypt, Belzoni, Beechey, the two captains and Finati entered the great temple at Abu Simbel, in August 1817. Belzoni had discovered the tomb now known as that of Seti I, but colloquially known as 'Belzoni's tomb', on 18 October 1817. Belzoni, with the important but usually not acknowledged aid of d'Athanasi, entered the Second Pyramid on 2 February 1818. Each time, the Belmores were among the first Europeans to enter after him. Henry Salt had financed Belzoni's first two ventures, and it was while the Belmores were in Egypt that Salt and Belzoni fell out over their individual contributions to these achievements. There was a furious row in Luxor at the end of November, and Belzoni and Sarah went north ablaze with righteous indignation. It was some months before Salt and Belzoni met again and signed the agreement about their dual responsibility for the finds. Later, Belzoni still argued about this, but on 18 April 1818, he wrote a most revealing letter in his own inimitable style to Lord Belmore in Jerusalem, 'I have the honor to acquint your Lordship that on the arrival of Mr Salt in Caira My Affer with him took the Good Tourn I most hapely could wish we mad arangements satisfactory to both parties and all ended in most frendle tremes.'[9]

When the Belmores arrived in Egypt, the Earl was suffering from a lengthy attack of gout that would have made a man of even the most equable temper difficult company. Alexandria was a disappointment. 'It is in rubbish,' said the doctor, 'the enemy has levelled its towers, and broken down its walls, and the wind from the desert has laid it under a load of sand.' He made a thorough tour of the sights, nonetheless, stumbling on Cleopatra at every turn – or so the local guides assured him.[10]

On 22 September they moved from the comforts of the *Ospray* onto a *djerm* that took them along the coast to the Nile proper, where they transferred to a two-masted *maash* that carried them to Cairo. They arrived at Bulaq on 28 September and Henry Salt himself came to welcome them, bringing the Pasha's carriage for Lady Belmore – one of the very rare wheeled vehicles in Egypt and described as being rather like the Lord Mayor's coach – and a horse for his lordship. The rest of the party found that the asses, which were almost as common as hackney cabs in London, provided rapid transport.[11]

At the consulate they met Captains Irby and Mangles, full of the excitement of their involvement in opening the great temple at Abu Simbel, and the burly Swiss traveller, John Lewis Burckhardt.[12] Dr Richardson thoroughly enjoyed himself in Cairo, and gives enthusiastic descriptions of the people and places he saw. It was some days before the Earl was recovered sufficiently from his gout – 'which had greatly checked his perservering zeal in antiquarian pursuits' – for Salt to take the men to Muhammad Ali at his summer residence by the Nile. The Earl and the Pasha conversed about their respective climates, the making of ice and the Earl's plans in Egypt, and shared anecdotes about petty larcenies.[13]

Lady Hester's letter may have been taken out and studied to guide their behaviour in Egypt:

> Allow me to hint that the more Lady B. covers her face and acts unlike Mrs Gambier [a relative of the Pitts] the more she will be admired and considered the wife of a great Pasha, for it is quite impossible to say how the Turks in Syria are *horrified* with European costume . . . [In Cairo] your son also ought not to be allowed to jump about when out of doors like an English boy, for it is not only unlike the conduct of children of distinction here, but it is that of *dancing boys* in this country and he might be insulted.[14]

On 10 October, Salt arranged for the whole party to go to the Pyramids. The countess, having donned Turkish dress, reached the summit – where she carved her name and, according to the Captain Fitzclarence, who was there not long after, that of her lapdog Rosa – although it seems unlikely that Rosa achieved these heights.[15] It was a most successful outing, but bad news awaited them on their return to the consulate. Burckhardt, whom Dr Richardson had treated for an attack of dysentry before their departure, was much worse and had sent a message for help. Dr Richardson went to him and was with him until his death.[16]

Salt was desolated. He and Burckhardt had known each other since their London days with the Africa Association; they had shared in the enterprise when Belzoni collected the head of the young Memnon from Luxor and every afternoon they had walked and talked in the gardens near the consulate. But there was little time to mourn. The Belmores were ready to leave Cairo and Salt was to go with them – on his first tour of Upper Egypt. He had been looking forward greatly to the journey, as for weeks every new courier from Luxor had brought him an account of some valuable discovery.[17]

There were several boats in the flotilla, but everyone dined communally – Salt being a guest at the Earl's table. Again, they had probably turned to Lady Hester's advice, 'All of you should cover your eyes at night particularly going up the Nile, for the night air causes ophthalmia more than any thing . . . Check of perspiration, the general cause of more illness in this part of the world.'[18]

At Dendera there was an interesting discussion on the question of whether travellers should remove the antiquities of Egypt. Could this have been a matter upon which Salt and Richardson (and his employer) fell out? It certainly would not have done for the doctor to comment adversely on the Earl's desire to collect trophies and souvenirs. They were able to compare the monuments with their depiction in the *Description d'Égypte*, which Salt had with him. His copy had been loaned by the British Museum, so that he could compare the work of the French artists with the actual monuments. Sadly, the whereabouts of this annotated copy is not known. Richardson commented on the *Description*, 'It is extremely elegant, and well executed; but it is perfectly foppish, and not the least Egyptian in its style or manner – and extremely incorrect.'[19]

On the evening of 16 October, their boats moored at Gurna under the great sycamore tree. The next morning, Salt's secretary, Henry Beechey (son of the artist Sir William Beechey) and Giovanni Belzoni came down from their residence in the tombs of the Valley of the Kings to welcome them. The whole party set off in joyful anticipation to see the new discoveries. The valley's dismal appearance, with the tomb entrances 'like so many mines', depressed Richardson. But one of these 'mines' was that discovered by Belzoni only a week before. Belzoni pronounced it, 'a new and perfect monument of Egyptian antiquity – superior to any other in point of grandeur, style and preservation'.[20]

Richardson must have spent many long hours there, for, despite his short sight, he described the tomb in very great detail. 'It is impossible', he wrote, 'adequately to describe the sensations of delight and astonishment that by turns took possession of the mind as we moved along the corridor, and examined the different groups and hieroglyphics that occur successively in every chamber of this most perfect of all ancient relics'.[21] There, too, was the sarcophagus of minutely sculptured alabaster that would cause Salt and Belzoni such grief. Four days later they led Colonel

Drovetti into the tomb. Drovetti was overwhelmed. He was the only Frenchman whom Richardson had ever seen run out of the small change of compliments and admiration. Eventually – after many exclamations – Drovetti stood in speechless astonishment.[22]

Salt and Beechey soon set to work recording, by candlelight, the find in a series of wonderful watercolours now in the British Museum. Of these Salt wrote – proudly and correctly – to his friend Earl Mountnorris, 'I assure you they begin to make a show.' And anyone who has seen the originals in the British Museum cannot but agree. Still lying in the tomb was the magnificent sarcophagus of white alabaster, almost as translucent as crystal. Salt observed, with his artist's eye, that the colours used are 'generally pure and brilliant, but intermixed with each other nearly in the proportions of the rainbow, and so subdued by the proper introduction of blacks, as not to appear gaudy, but to produce a harmony that in some designs is really delicious'. Beechey wrote, 'One would think it was in Egypt that Titian, Georgiano and Tintoretto had acquired all that vigour and magic of effect.'[23] The Deftardar Bey had been to visit the tomb in state, and Salt suspected that 'the Pasha himself will not rest long without seeing it'. To secure the marvellous find against vandals, he arranged for a door with iron bolts and bars to be fixed, in the hope of keeping the tomb 'open and entire for the inspection of travellers'.[24]

On 22 November the lordly party continued up river to Aswan, leaving Salt at Luxor. At Aswan they spent a few days preparing for their journey into Nubia. They changed from their spacious *maash*es to 'small, open, miserable-looking cock boats', that Richardson thought 'the *ne plus ultra* of low accommodation'. They stocked up with bread, plenty of livestock, two milch goats, eggs and melons and 'the noble traveller had taken care to be well provided with a due assortment of the juice of the grape'. After a farewell dinner under the stars they were due to set off but they were delayed. The colours had been forgotten. The Earl could not sail without them at the masthead. Two sailors were sent back to retrieve them.[25]

At Kalabsha, where other travellers sometimes met awkwardness, the Earl, with his sword, pistols and Turkish costume, quelled all demands for *baksheesh* and so humbled the locals that he felt able to take Lady Belmore ashore. There was then some trouble about the eventual payment of the locals by the interpreter. The Earl had to lay down the rules to him very firmly: 'Keep faith with all men, and scrupulously so with savages among whom you travel. The master's word is sacred and never ought to be compromised . . . whatever.'[26]

The flotilla tied up at Abu Simbel in the early evening of 20 December. The temple had been first opened only four months before, but the sand had drifted down to close it again. They went into the temple of Nefertari, where, later, Captain Corry carved his name. The next day the sailors opened up the great temple, and they entered what Richardson described as 'a perfect stove'. This visit was brief, and they shut up the door with large stones to keep out the sand until their return. On 23 December they reached the second cataract and the limit of their journey south, and that night they celebrated the 17th birthday of Lord Corry, the Earl's heir, with plenty of French wines and porter and a bumper of the best Irish whiskey. The next day, they clambered about the rocky terrain, set the ship's carpenter to work with his chisel and mallet to carve all the party's names and noted on the great rock the names of their English friends.

On Christmas Day, Lord Belmore took a final reading of the latitude and caused it to be engraved on the rock, and then, with his boat leading the way, the party set off north. The current was with them now, and the Nubian sailors – who had had to track the boats southwards – donned yellow turbans and sang songs of love and war as they glided along.[27]

At Kalabsha, Lord Belmore discovered a small Grecian temple and carried away from it a small sphinx. They spent a long day at Philae, which the doctor describes in great detail and where even the Earl's chaplain, Reverend Holt, carved his name. They were soon back at the first cataract. They had visited 18 ruined temples as well as those at Philae, had counted 85 villages on the west bank and 74 on the east bank and travelled well over four hundred miles since they were last there.[28]

At Aswan, on 4 January 1818, all was in order with their *maash*es, except that rats had gnawed the Earl's stuffed crocodile and some possibly two-legged rats had drunk the spruce-beer that he was looking forward to enjoying. They left Aswan on 7 January, with eight oarsmen rowing the *felucca*s and towing the *maash*es. They stopped at Kom Ombo, at the quarry at Hadjr Silsil (where they noted many Greek inscriptions), at Edfu (where Dr Richardson described the local method of threshing), at Esna (where a fair had drawn together an immense crowd of well-dressed country people to a somewhat dull occasion) and went 'joyfully on their way to Thebes'.[29] The mountains of western Thebes 'loomed like a smiling friend', and in the afternoon of 13 January, Mr Salt and Mr Beechey welcomed them ashore.

In the Belmores' absence, a 'diligent and faithful Greek' had been collecting for the Earl. Awaiting him was a huge door (which he gave to Salt who sold it to the British Museum), various stone jars, statues, *scarabei* and stones covered with hieroglyphics. In the days that followed, the noble traveller 'set an example of most commendable industry' directing labourers at his excavations. Modern archaeologists must blench at the description of his activities. All that can be said in his favour is that, eventually, most of the objects he discovered went to the British Museum and that to many of them he gave some sort of provenance.[30] He discovered a stone mummy case above Medinet Habou that he presented to the Museum in 1820, and many tablets that were reproduced in the same size as the originals in 1842, in *Tablets and Other Egyptian Monuments from the Collection of the Earl of Belmore, now Deposited in the British Museum.*

While the Earl was thus occupied, Lady Belmore wandered intrepidly around the sites. Her progress was watched by others with interest. Drovetti's agent, Jean-Jacques Rifaud, was so overcome by her charm that he gave her permission to excavate at Karnak – an area usually under Drovetti's dominion. Chance, reported Rifaud, immediately smiled on the Countess. She found a beautiful black granite boat, five feet long with a little temple surmounting each end. The boat is now in the British Museum, and Rifaud profited from his generosity to the Countess by selling several sculptures found by him to her husband.[31]

Another French traveller was less amenable. The dapper Comte de Forbin, the Director General of Museums, was renowned as the best-dressed man in Paris. He had been travelling in the Middle East with his brother, the Abbé Forbin, and had recruited a 19-year-old midshipman, Linant de Bellefonds, to join them as a draughtsman. The Comte was in Luxor during the Belmores' second visit. He did not approve of them – or so he said. He had intended to go further up the Nile – even 'to penetrate as far as the island of Meroe' – but, in a statement that has become famous, he declared: 'I no longer experienced a wish to ascend the Nile from the moment I observed an English family arrive at Thebes on their return from the Cataracts.' Here there were:

> husbands, wives, children, chaplains, surgeons, nurses, cooks, all babbling of Elephantine. From this moment the illusion vanished for me – there was an end of the matter. I even set off from Thebes sooner than I had intended, finding it quite impossible to support the perpetual appearance among the venerable ruins of an English lady's maid in a pink camisole.[32]

In 1820, when Forbin's account was published, Salt wrote to Lord Belmore:

> The work of Forbin must have amused you – a poor return for the kind attentions he received during his short stay at Thebes, and the falsity of pretending to have run away from that place on account of your suite is too evident when we recollect that he stayed one day longer on purpose to spend it on board your boat.

But it was not only the English who had been upset by Forbin. He had not, wrote Salt, 'one partizan in Egypt . . . his work being universally pronounced superficial, silly and woefully incorrect'. He so damaged the French interest by his comments on Muhammad Ali and Mr Boghos that their consul had to go to great lengths to make people forget his visit.

Other Frenchmen saw matters at Thebes quite differently to Forbin. Frédéric Cailliaud, a young French mineralogist in the employ of the Pasha and Drovetti, returned in January from the Eastern desert with a bag of emeralds and settled down at Gurna. There he was impressed both by the grandeur and the kindness of Salt and the Belmores. He thought Lady Belmore 'showed courage far superior to her sex' in her daily explorations. He had praise, too, for Richardson for his attention to those who implored help with their infirmities.[33]

The Belmores left Luxor on 10 February, 1818, leaving Salt there until early April. They had one further historic adventure. Belzoni, after his row with Salt, had not returned to Upper Egypt, but had been turning his attention to entering the Second Pyramid. On 2 March, with the help of Salt's young Greek employee, Yanni d'Athanasi, he had achieved this great feat. The Belmores arrived ten days later and so were again among the first Europeans to admire his achievement.[34]

The Belmores left Cairo on Thursday 26 March. At Castle Coole there is a fragment of a journal kept by the Earl, recording that they had between them two mares, seven asses and a number of camels, and that Belzoni accompanied them for the first leg of the journey and stayed with them at the first night's camp.[35] When they arrived in Jerusalem they renewed their acquaintance with Irby, Mangles and Sarah Belzoni, and met John William Bankes and Thomas Legh.

The Earl's collection of antiquities was shipped from Egypt on the *Ospray*, but in Malta the cargo had to go through customs and quarantine as it left the Ottoman Empire, and many of the more fragile items were destroyed by zealous customs officials who tipped everything out of their cases. Salt wrote offering the Earl a replacement papyrus as a gift, but we do not know whether this momento of their happy time in Egypt ever arrived.[36]

Four decades later, in February 1859, the fourth earl followed his grandfather and father to Egypt in company with a Reverend Hughes and a Mr Morrissey, but they had no Dr Richardson with them to chronicle their journey, and we know little about them apart from how many piastres they spent.[37]

Notes

1. *Castle Coole*, National Trust Guide (London, National Trust, 1988).
2. Fitzclarence, *Journal of a Route across India, through Egypt to England* (London, John Murray, 1819), p. 447.
3. *Dictionary of National Biography* (Oxford, Oxford University Press, 1967–8), vol. 26, p. 1128.
4. Castle Coole Archives, Egyptian manuscripts (hereafter 'CC, Egypt mss').
5. R.R. Richardson, *Travel around the Mediterranean, and Parts Adjacent: In Company with the Earl of Belmore, during the Years 1816, 1817, and 1818, Extending as far as the Second Cataract of the Nile, Jerusalem, Damascus, Balbec, etc.* (2 vols., London, printed for E. Cadell, 1822), vol. 1, p. 5.
6. M.L. Bierbrier, *Who was Who in Egyptology*, 3rd revised edn (London, Egyptian Exploration Society, 1995).
7. *Quarterly Review*, (London, John Murray, October, 1822).
8. CC, Egypt mss (25 August 1817).
9. *Ibid.*
10. Richardson, *op. cit.*, vol. 1, p. 15.
11. *Ibid.*, vol. 1, p. 47.

12 *Ibid.*, vol. 1, p. 52.
13 *Ibid.*, vol. 1, p. 97.
14 CC, Egypt mss (25 August 1817).
15 Fitzclarence, *op. cit.*
16 J.J. Halls, *Life and Correspondence with Henry Salt, Esq.* (London, R. Bentley, 1834), vol. 2, p. 16.
17 *Ibid.*
18 CC, Egypt mss (25 August 1817).
19 Richardson, *op. cit.*, vol. 1, p. 204.
20 Giovanni Belzoni, *Narrative of the Operations and Recent Discoveries within the Pyramids, Temples, Tombs, and Excavations, in Egypt and Nubia, etc.*, 3rd edn (London, John Murray, 1822), p. 230.
21 Richardson, *op. cit.*, vol. 1, p. 304.
22 *Ibid.*, vol. 1, p. 306.
23 'Egypt', *Encyclopaedia Britannica* (1824), vol. 4, part 1, p. 38.
24 Halls, *op. cit.*, vol. 2, p. 54.
25 Richardson, *op. cit.*, vol. 1, pp. 343–65.
26 *Ibid.*, vol. 1, pp. 373–7.
27 *Ibid.*, vol. 1, p. 424.
28 *Ibid.*, vol. 1, p. 505.
29 *Ibid.*, vol. 1, pp. 514–33.
30 EA 39, presented 1820; EA 9906, 10000, 10030, 10043–4. The bulk of collection was purchased in 1843 by the British Museum and the remaining items sold in Sotheby's November 20 and December 4, 1972, according to Bierbrier, *op. cit.*, p. 262.
31 Jean-Jacques Fiechter, *Le Moisson des dieux* (Paris, Éditions Julliard, 1994), p. 14.
32 Louis Nicholas de Forbin, *Voyage dans le Levant en 1817 et 1818* (Paris, Imprimerie Royale, 1819), pp. 1–50.
33 Frédéric Cailliaud, *Voyages à l'oasis de Thèbes et dans les déserts situés à l'orient et à l'occident de la Thèbaide, fait pendant les années 1815, 1816, 1817 et 1818* (Paris, Imprimerie Royal, 1821), p. 82.
34 Richardson, *op. cit.*, vol. 2, p. 154.
35 CC, Egypt mss.
36 *Ibid.* (27 October 1818).
37 Captain Corry assured a traveller he met on the return journey that, 'it is perfectly safe travelling in Egypt and very easy . . . Provisions are amazingly cheap, a sheep not costing above a dollar. It is, however, necessary,' he reported, 'to go armed and in Oriental costume and to let your beard grow'. (Letter from John Bowes Wright who met the Belmores in Naples in 1818, private collection.)

12

From Cairo to Petra: Léon de Laborde and L.M.A. Linant de Bellefonds, 1828

Pascale Linant de Bellefonds

Nowadays, the thousands of tourists who visit Petra every day must find it very difficult to imagine that the magnificent pink sandstone façades remained unknown to the Western world until the early nineteenth century, and even more difficult to realise that simply entering the area was an amazing achievement in itself.

This achievement was first realised by a Swiss, Johan Ludwig Burckhardt. In 1812, after spending three years in Syria on behalf of the Africa Association in London, Burckhardt, who called himself Shaykh Ibrahim and passed himself off as a Muslim merchant, left Aleppo to take the road to Cairo. On the way, he came to hear about some fabulous ancient ruins located in the region of Kerak, and managed to convince his guide to take him to Wadi Musa, the valley of Moses, pretending that he had to sacrifice a goat to the prophet Aaron. He knew that the prophet's tomb stood on a peak at the far end of the valley and that the only way to reach the place of sacrifice was through this valley. This is how, on 22 August 1812, Burckhardt entered the Sīq, the narrow gorge leading to the ruins of Petra. He was thus the first European to discover this grandiose sight. However, his guide was watching him constantly, so he was unable to show any curiosity, let alone take notes or draw sketches, without risking his life. He only glanced at the Khazneh, the site's most famous monument, but could not resist the temptation to take a closer look at the only free-standing building, the Nabataean temple, Qasr al-Bint. At this point, his guide reprimanded him. Burckhardt did not insist and went on to Aaron's tomb to sacrifice his goat. Nevertheless, he had seen enough to conclude his short stay with this decisive remark: 'It appears very probable that the ruins in the Wadi Mousa are those of ancient Petra.'

Burckhardt's brilliant intuition had a certain impact even before he released the account of his journey, which was published in 1822 by the Africa Association in London.[1] As early as 1818, two Royal Navy captains, Charles Leonard Irby and James Mangles, ventured on his trail together with William John Bankes and his Janissary, Giovanni Finati, and a fifth man, Thomas Legh. Leaving Jerusalem on 6 May 1818, the travellers reached Petra on 24 May. Although they were able to spend only two days on the site, we know that Bankes had sufficient time to draw a number of monuments, including the famous Khazneh. But these drawings, currently kept at Dorchester's County Record Centre, were never published,[2] and, oddly enough, the story of this journey, published in 1823 under the names of Irby and Mangles,[3] does not include a single one of Bankes's drawings.

It was therefore left to two Frenchmen, Léon de Laborde and Linant de Bellefonds, to reveal the fascinating world of Petra to the European public. In 1828, they managed to spend almost a week on the site and produced many drawings, maps and plans; two years later, in 1830, in Paris, a beautiful folio book, comprising 88 pages and 69 lithographs, called *Voyage de l'Arabie Pétrée par Léon de Laborde et Linant* was published.

The success of their enterprise was probably due to two main factors: first, both men, in spite of their youth, were already quite familiar with Oriental journeys and had prepared this expedition with great care; in addition, they had picked a new itinerary that allowed them to secure the protection of a powerful local tribe, the Alaouin. There was also a chance factor: we shall see that once in Petra they took advantage of a totally unexpected event, to which I shall return later.

To begin with, we should briefly assess the personalities of our two travellers, who first met in Cairo late in 1827. Léon de Laborde was only twenty years old, but he was already knowledgeable about Oriental antiquities. During his studies at Göttingen University, he had familiarised himself with biblical sources and Greek and Latin authors, as well as travellers' stories and historical books. In 1826, his father, the Marquis Alexandre de Laborde, a politician fascinated by the arts, took the young Léon on a mission to the Levant. From Italy they went to Smyrna and Constantinople and crossed Anatolia, then, in the spring of 1827, they reached northern Syria, followed the Levantine coast and crossed Lebanon, Syria and Palestine, visiting a great many historical sites along the way. Léon de Laborde learnt how to observe, to describe landscapes and monuments and to copy inscriptions, and to draw locations, buildings and people. Leaving Jerusalem, the travellers went to Jerash and Amman; they intended to go to Petra, but the region's dangers forced them to abandon their plan. Then they went to Egypt, again travelling overland after which, feeling unwell and anxious to return to politics, Alexandre de Laborde decided to go back to France, leaving his son behind in Cairo.

Léon de Laborde spent nearly a year in Cairo, using the time to take part in excavations near the Pyramids and endeavouring to learn Arabic before setting up an expedition to the Sinai and Arabia Petraea. After shortlisting various Englishmen as companions, he eventually settled on Linant de Bellefonds, a more experienced man with a better knowledge of the area; this encounter proved crucial to the organisation of the expedition and its achievement. At this point we should note that, as far as Laborde is concerned, this journey only marked the beginning of an exceptionally fruitful career. As soon as he returned to Europe, he became a diplomat: he started as secretary to Chateaubriand at the French Embassy in Rome, then became a deputy and finally a senator, but he will always be better known in his multiple roles as archaeologist, archivist and art historian. His book, *Voyage de l'Arabie Pétrée*, is but the first of an impressive series of works and essays relating to all types of subject. Laborde became curator of the Louvre Museum, then, in 1857, General Director of the Archives. He died, covered in glory, in 1869.

I do not propose to discuss the personality of Louis Maurice Adolphe Linant de Bellefonds, as I have already covered this in a previous publication.[4] When Laborde met him in Cairo, Linant had been living in Egypt for about ten years, and had made several journeys through Nubia and and Sudan, taking notes and drawing monuments, mostly on behalf of the London Africa Association. He had also visited the Sinai several times, with, among others, the Italian Alessandro Ricci, so he had taken the opportunity to establish relationships with local people – a great asset, as it turned out, for his expedition with Laborde.

The preparations took several months. The book does not mention how the trip was financed, but it is likely that Laborde drew on his family's fortune, while Linant appears, once again, to have been granted funds by the Africa Association. Unlike Burckhardt, who travelled alone or with small caravans, Laborde and Linant decided to travel, in their own words, 'like lords'. Their entourage was indeed large. Laborde was accompanied by his dragoman, Mr Bellier, and Linant by a Mr Petit-Jean, an ex-soldier of the Napoleonic armies based in Cairo. In addition, each man had his own manservant, as well as an Arab guide already known to him: Linant took with him a member of the Oualed Said tribe whom he had met in the Sinai – this was a major advantage for the first part of the journey, since the travellers' protection was guaranteed up to Aqaba as a result. After Aqaba they had to enrol the help of Alaouin guides, so the caravan consisted of eighteen people and sixteen camels in all. The two men decided to adopt Arab costume, but, contrary to Burckhardt, this was more for practical reasons than to hide their identities. They chose to travel light, with no tent, no mattresses and a minimum of supplies: they planned to hunt and buy food from local people. On the other hand, they took great care over their drawing materials. During the many hours spent riding their camels, these items were carried in a small bag tied to the pommel of the saddle, but when they travelled on foot, the men found an ingenious way to keep their hands free: they put paper, pencil, penknife and compass in their tarboosh, under their keffiyeh.

The success of the expedition is probably due to the travellers' choice of itinerary, as well as to their thorough preparations. Until then, the few westerners who visited Arabia Petraea had come via the north and the town of Wadi Musa, just as we do today. But Laborde and Linant decided otherwise. From Cairo they took the southern route along the Sinai valleys, to take advantage of the element of surprise. Thanks to Linant's travel notebook, we can follow the main stages of the journey. After leaving Cairo on 23 February 1828, they followed the path of the old canal from the Nile to the Red Sea, reached Suez on 27 February and left two days later to cross the Sinai. Their main stops were at Moses' Fountains, Hammam Firaoun and Sarbout el-Khadim, where they drew the stelas (fig. 1). Then they went past the foot of St Catherine's Mount and reached the eastern coast of the peninsula near Dahab on 8 March. They continued along the coast toward the north, and arrived in Aqaba on 11 March. This marked the limit of the territory under the influence of the Sinai Bedouins, who until then had given them protection, and the start of the Alaouins' territory. Our travellers sent a messenger to the chief of this tribe, asking for protection on their way to

Petra. They had to wait in Aqaba for about 12 days; during the whole of this period they were the guests of the fortress governor, to whom they had been recommended by a letter from Muhammad Ali.

FIGURE 1
Sarbout el-Khadim, drawn by Léon de Laborde
(by courtesy of the Linant de Bellefonds family)

Laborde's drawing (fig. 2) shows what this residence looked like. Built in the early sixteenth century, the fortress was also used as a caravanserai for the pilgrims on their way to Mecca, and Laborde found it amusing to liven up his drawing by showing the arrival of the Pilgrimage Caravan. The two men did not waste their time while in Aqaba; they made the most of their enforced wait to explore the area and to go to Graie Island[5] and visit its fortress which dates from the Crusades. They did not hesitate to take risks to get there, and Linant was more than happy to use his sailing skills to build a raft out of palm tree trunks, propelled by date palms instead of oars. In a fit of chauvinism, they also took a French flag with them, intending to plant it at the top of the highest bastion of the fortress. They believed themselves to be the first Europeans to visit the island since the Crusades, being unaware at the time that the German traveller, Rüppel, had been there in 1822.

FIGURE 2
The fortress of Aqaba, drawn by Léon de Laborde
(by courtesy of the Linant de Bellefonds family)

Eventually, the Alaouin guides arrived in Aqaba. On 25 March, our travellers were able to resume their journey to the north. For three days they followed the long valley of the Araba up to the latitude of Petra. Soon they sighted Aaron's tomb, a small white dot on the summit of a mountain, and, on the morning of 28 March, came across the first Nabataean tombs, carved into the rock. As expected, they entered the site by means of a south-western valley. This was to their advantage: the Wadi Musa fellahin who kept a watchful eye over the ruins were ensconced at the other end of the narrow ravine called the Sīq, which is the usual route into the site. But an additional and quite unexpected danger proved to be a decisive factor in giving them peace of mind. Shortly before reaching Petra, they learnt that the plague was rife in Wadi Musa, and that the fellahin, dismayed by the violence of an epidemic that had already killed several dozen of them, were staying safely in their tents.

After quickly setting up camp in a tomb carved into the rock, probably somewhere near the present museum, the travellers went off to explore the site. They crossed the ancient city and entered the gorge of the Sīq, which they followed all the way up to the usual point of entry. There they saw a few people from Wadi Musa who tried to approach them; to keep them away, the two men shouted, from a distance, that they came from Gaza, where the plague was raging. Thanks to this stratagem, Laborde and Linant were able to get down to work and carried out their task methodically over the following six days. The amount of work that they completed in such a short time can only fill us with admiration.

Their first achievement was to produce, *in situ*, the first near-accurate plan of the Petra site, since Burckhardt could only draw his from memory. A comparison with a recent map shows that they had already understood the orientation of the various valleys and the ancient city, and noted the position of the main buildings: the Qasr al-Bint, the Temenos Gate, the series of great tombs hollowed into the cliff of the Jabal al-Khubthah, the theatre and the Khazneh.

As the two men did not know how long they would be able to remain on the site, they did not waste a single moment and coordinated their efforts. They always stayed together, not only for obvious safety reasons but also for greater efficiency. For example, one of them would draw the façade of a tomb while the other would note its plan or copy an inscription. The two men tackled the major monuments by each working from a different angle. Take the Qasr al-Bint temple, which may have been dedicated to Dusares, the great Nabataean god: while Laborde drew a general view from the bed of the Wadi Musa, where he could see the decorations of the façade and the platform of the altar in front of the temple (fig. 3), Linant drew the rear of the building, which clearly shows its structure and details of the cornice (fig. 4). We see a similar division of work nearby, with the monument they called the 'triumphal arch', which is, in fact, the massive gate giving access to the sacred compound of the Qasr al-Bint. Linant drew this from the west, showing the ornaments inside the gate and its engaged columns. Meanwhile, Laborde drew the main frontage of the building with the Qasr al-Bint esplanade in the background. His engraving reveals the sculpted decorations of the central bay, with alternating blocks of floral motifs and busts of people, and, on top, a Nabataean capital. The Khazneh, the monument that, in itself, would have been enough to ensure Petra's fame, was also shown from two different viewpoints. Linant drew the façade from the corner of the esplanade, where one can stand

FIGURE 3
The Qasr al-Bint, drawn by Léon de Laborde from the bed of Wadi Musa
(by courtesy of the Linant de Bellefonds family)

FIGURE 4
The Qasr al-Bint, drawn by Linant de Bellefonds from the rear
(courtesy of the Linant de Bellefonds family)

FIGURE 5
The Khazneh, drawn by Linant de Bellefonds
(by courtesy of the Linant de Bellefonds family)

back a little (fig. 5) – this is a favourite spot for tourists who try to fit the entire monument in their viewfinder without the benefit of a wide-angle lens. The engraving includes the amusing detail of two figures pointing their rifles towards the stone urn; for a long time, this urn, which is now riddled with bullet holes, was used as a target by the citizens of Petra who believed that the treasure of an Egyptian king was hidden inside; hence the name of *khaznet firaoun*, 'the Pharaoh's treasure', which is still given to this monument today. In fact, this local belief partly explains why the people of Petra were so suspicious of the first foreign visitors: convinced that these magnificent monuments were bound to hide fabulous treasures, they thought that western travellers came with the sole intention of robbing them. Laborde, for his part, drew the building from the front, positioning himself at the mouth of the Sīq (fig. 6). Today, the façade differs slightly from the 1828 drawings: the column to the left of the entrance was restored in 1960, but, more importantly, the drawing gives the impression that the sculptures were in a much better condition than they are now. In fact, it could be that the drawing was over-interpreted. For example, it is likely that the

FIGURE 6
Léon de Laborde's view of the Khazneh
(by courtesy of the Linant de Bellefonds family)

central decor of the gable never showed an eagle but rather a head; and, above that, the statue of Isis is fully dressed, while Laborde showed her half-naked. Strangely enough, we can notice the same mistakes on the lithograph of the Khazneh executed by David Roberts some years later.

Continuing their trek along the Sīq, Laborde and Linant were much impressed by a great arch bridging the gorge at a height of about fifty feet. The drawing Laborde made of this arch (fig. 7) is especially valuable, because this monument, which marked the entrance to the gorge, collapsed in 1895; today, all that remains are the abutments, which are very eroded. A little further up, the two men spent time copying a long Greek inscription in a tomb drawn by Laborde; once again, this drawing is of documentary value as the sculpted façade of this tomb collapsed in 1847. Today, all we can see is the bottom right-hand side of the tomb – everything else, including the inscription, has disappeared.

The two travellers were not content with drawing the monuments dotted along the Sīq gorge. They did not hesitate to explore secondary

FIGURE 7
The arch at the entrance to the Sīq, drawn by Léon de Laborde
(by courtesy of the Linant de Bellefonds family)

*wadi*s and discovered many more tombs. In the south, they stopped in a particularly charming and shaded spot of the Wadi Farasa, where they came across the so-called 'Garden Tomb'. On his drawing, Linant made a point of showing the terrace in front of the tomb, and, on the right, the wall supporting the upper terrace (fig. 8). In the same area, the so-called 'Tomb of the Roman Soldier' caught their attention. Here again they shared the viewpoints. Linant drew the front of the monument, with the vast esplanade once surrounded by colonnades linking the tomb to its triclinium, in the foreground. Laborde, for his part, drew the inside of the triclinium, showing clearly the engaged columns crowned with pseudo-Ionic capitals.

The travellers devoted nearly two days' work to the series of great tombs carved into the cliff of al-Khubtha. They each started by drawing a general view, again from different angles, Laborde from the north-west, Linant from the south-west; then they reproduced the façades they considered the most spectacular. The 'Corinthian Tomb' was of particular

FIGURE 8
The 'Garden Tomb', drawn by Linant de Bellefonds
(by courtesy of the Linant de Bellefonds family)

interest, and they were very conscious of the damage caused to monuments by water seeping up into the rock, a problem that is currently of great concern to UNESCO; they also noticed that parasitic plants were growing on the cornices. Regrettably, the façade has deteriorated considerably since 1828.

Finally, the two men devoted a whole day to the most impressive of Petra's monuments, already called the Deir, or monastery. Right on the middle of the mountain, this building could only be reached after a long and arduous climb. Burckhardt was unaware of its existence, while Bankes and his companions saw it from afar through a telescope, but were unable to get any closer. Laborde and Linant were, therefore, the first Europeans to visit it. We can compare Linant's original and unpublished drawing[6] with the engraving made from Laborde's drawing (fig. 9): in the latter, the addition of overly large figures distorts the colossal proportions of the building.

Six days had gone by. Our friends would happily have stayed longer if the plague epidemic had not reached alarming proportions. With

FIGURE 9
Léon de Laborde's view of the Deir
(by courtesy of the Linant de Bellefonds family)

the Alaouin guides urging them to leave, they packed up on the afternoon of 3 April. The return journey followed a different route, using valleys running to the east of the Araba depression. This gave them the chance to discover the ruins of Sabra, two hours' walk south of Petra, which they identified as those of a small ancient city. They took note of its layout and paid special attention to the theatre, which they drew (fig. 10). From there, they crossed the mountain chain south of Petra and arrived at the Aqaba fortress on 11 April. They left Aqaba again on 16 April and, on 20 April, parted company after stopping at the Oualed Said camp, in the heart of the Sinai. Linant was keen to return to Cairo: he took only three days to reach Suez, then travelled for a day and a half by the direct route from there to Cairo, and arrived at midday on 24 April. Laborde chose to stay a little longer in the Sinai and visit St Catherine's Monastery, of which he made a few sketches. Finally, he returned to Cairo in the early days of May.

All in all, this relatively short journey – two months for Linant, approximately ten weeks for Laborde – was accomplished with much enthusiasm and without any great mishap. Throughout the whole trek,

FIGURE 10
The theatre at Sabra, drawn by Léon de Laborde
(by courtesy of the Linant de Bellefonds family)

the two men enjoyed a good relationship and worked in true partnership. Before leaving Cairo, they agreed upon specific terms: they would each work on their own and would be free, after one year, to publish the account of their travels, Linant in England, through the Africa Association, and Laborde in France. Unfortunately, immediately upon his return to Cairo, Linant found himself fully occupied with his responsibilities as an engineer for the Viceroy, and his publication never materialised. Fortunately, he left us his journal and numerous drawings that are currently kept in the Louvre.[7] So Laborde undertook the publication of the journey on his own, obtaining permission from the Africa Association to include some of Linant's drawings. Laborde chose a sumptuous and expensive format that was common at the time for this type of book. Its title, *Voyage de l'Arabie Pétrée*, could be that of one of the simple travel stories which were so popular during the nineteenth century. But the earnest tone of the introduction left no doubt as to the seriousness of the subject: Laborde wanted, first and foremost, to act as a historian. Admittedly, his description of the Sinai, while picturesque and enlivened by quality engravings, told little that was new. In fact, he made a point of keeping it short and avoided repeating what had already been written by his predecessors. The book's novelty was to be found in the section devoted to Petra and the Nabataeans – truly a revelation to the educated public of the times. Laborde compiled all the available facts on this subject, assembling biblical sources and excerpts from ancient authors. His account was necessarily fairly basic, because Nabataean epigraphy and the other sites of the Nabataean kingdom were still unknown at the time. But we must be grateful to our two travellers for having opened the way to further research by bringing to light a considerable amount of information in this field.

Supported as they are by numerous illustrations, Laborde's descriptions of monuments are deliberately superficial. He was perhaps too influenced by aesthetic preconceptions to appreciate the originality of Nabataean art, and we often find the word 'decadence' applied to the architecture of certain buildings that would commonly be described as 'baroque' nowadays. At this time, however, these descriptions and reflections did as much as the illustrations to attract the interest of scholars. The work was also very well received outside scholarly circles: the quality of the illustrations ensured a wide success, and it is fair to say that Laborde and Linant's drawings actually revealed Petra to many of their contemporaries. For at least ten years, until the publication of David Roberts' lithographs, these illustrations were the one and only graphic representation of Petra available to the educated western world. They were much admired and widely copied. Before setting off on his great journey to the East in 1838, David Roberts himself reproduced Laborde's view of Petra's theatre to illustrate a book on biblical landscapes.[8] And after his visit to Petra, in 1836, John Lloyd Stephens did not hesitate to 'pirate' the illustrations of our travellers to complement his own work, *Incidents of Travel in Egypt, Arabia Petraea and the Holy Land*, published in 1837.[9] That was only the beginning of a long series of reproductions that continues to this day, still without due credit being given to the authors of the drawings.

Notes

1. J.L. Burckhardt, *Travels in Syria and the Holy Land* (London, John Murray, 1822).
2. On J.L. Burckhardt and W.J. Bankes in Petra, see R.A. Stucky and N.N. Lewis, 'Johan Ludwig Burckhardt und William John Bankes' in Th. Weber and R. Wenning (eds.), *Petra* (Mainz, Ph. Von Zabern, 1997), pp. 5–12 (with, for the first time, a reproduction of a drawing of the Khazneh by Bankes, fig. 5).
3. C.L. Irby and J. Mangles, *Travels in Egypt and Nubia, Syria, and Asia Minor, during the Years 1817 and 1818* (London, T. White, 1823).
4. Marcel Kurz and Pascale Linant de Bellefonds, 'Linant de Bellefonds: Travels in Egypt, Sudan and Arabia Petraea, 1818–1828' in P. and J. Starkey (eds.), *Travellers in Egypt* (London, I.B. Tauris, 1998), pp. 61–9.
5. Known today as Jeziret Firaoun, or Pharaoh Island.
6. This drawing has recently been reproduced in *Jordanie, sur les pas des archéologues*, catalogue of the exhibition in Paris, Institut du Monde Arabe, 13 June–5 October 1997 (1997), p. 31 (the caption wrongly indicates the 'Qasr al-Bint').
7. Bibliothèque des Musées nationaux, ms 266 (notebook) and ms 268 (drawings). Ample excerpts from Linant's unpublished notebook have been included in the recent re-edition of Laborde's book, *Pétra retrouvée. Voyage de l'Arabie Pétrée, 1828. Léon de Laborde et Linant de Bellefonds* (Paris, Pygmalion, 1994), preface and notes by Chr. Augé and P. Linant de Bellefonds.
8. Briony Llewellyn, 'Petra and the Middle East', *The Connoisseur* (June 1980), 123.
9. Before he left, Stephens had the good fortune to meet Linant, who encouraged him in his intention of visiting Petra and gave him some advice. Stephens reports a humorous anecdote from that meeting: 'Mr. Linant has been twenty years in Egypt, and is now a bey in the pasha's service; and that very afternoon, after a long interview, had received order from the great reformer to make a survey of the pyramids, for the purpose of deciding which of the gigantic monuments, after having been respected by all preceding tyrants for three thousand years, should now be demolished for the illustrious object of yielding material for a petty fortress or scarcely more useful and important bridge.' Stephens adds in a note: 'On my return to Alexandria, I learned that Mr. Linant had reported that it would be cheaper to get stone from the quarries. After all, it is perhaps to be regretted that he had not gone on, as the mystery that overhangs the pyramids will probably never be removed until one of them is pulled down, and every stone removed, under the direction of some friends of science and the arts.'

13

James Burton and Slave Girls

Neil Cooke

In 1832, the Tory government suffered the humiliation of defeat when the Liberal Party was elected on the basis of a manifesto that challenged a fifty-year political malaise and reversed indifference to worsening social conditions throughout England. In its first year of office, the new government ended child labour in mines and factories and introduced an Education Act to provide reading and writing skills that would help children to achieve a better future. In 1833, the government passed another of its far-reaching pieces of legislation, the Abolition of Slavery Act.

Although the Abolition movement had been strong in England for over a quarter of a century, many English travellers in Egypt still bought slaves, right up to 1833. This was curious, as most travellers were educated gentlemen engaged in scholarly pursuits and inclined to vote Liberal at home in England. Yet, in Egypt, they bought slaves without a second thought, the result perhaps of having servants around the house during their childhood. James Burton's father recorded in his journal that 'Jane Black, servant' was present at the birth of his children, William Ford and Eliza; that 'Margaret' was present at the birth of Emma and 'Priscilla (Cilla) Jones' at the birth of Septimus, Octavia, Decimus, Alfred and Jesse (Jessy). It is likely to be this familiarity that led Burton's son to write in his journal when in Egypt: 'The slave, if good, becomes a son of the family – in youth he is the playmate of the mistresses children – in age their faithful, humble friend.' In his letters home, James Burton often sent 'best wishes' to his old nanny 'Cilla', indicating that she was still living with the family many years after his birth.

The Abolition of Slavery Act, however, was not really concerned with slaves in places such as Egypt. Its focus was on slaves taken across the Atlantic to work on plantations. Throughout the Middle East, as in Egypt, slavery was linked with religious laws. The Qur'an allowed polygamy and made the ownership of slaves acceptable, and slavery was seen as a way to prevent infanticide of a surplus of female babies by their parents. Slaves were often captured for sale and slavery was a useful way of dealing with the remnants of a conquered army. Children were also sold into slavery by their parents, if these were poor or had a surplus of girls to look after. But such slaves were not thought of as a substitute for paid labour, and were often well treated and had recourse to the law in all types of dispute. For many centuries, the rulers of parts of the Ottoman Empire were the sons born to slaves in the harem. 'The Mahometan is allowed by the Koran 4 wives and as many concubines slaves as it is in his power to keep – the Pasha has 500 – he has no son. His wife's son by a former husband is the second great man – his only son died of the plague owing to his over fondness for a woman who had it. He has left one son who is a great favourite of the old murderer.'[1]

In his Egyptian journals, James Burton indicates that he owned at least three slaves – an Abyssinian bought in May 1822, a second person of unknown nationality and a Greek whom he may have bought at the slave market in December 1824, during a visit in the company of Robert Hay, Joseph Bonomi and Osman Effendi from the British Consulate. On his arrival in Cairo from England, in 1822, Charles Sheffield mentions two slaves being in Burton's house – the Abyssinian and another – but one may have belonged to Charles Humphreys, his secretary and travelling companion. In November 1824, a Mr Hicks also noted: 'On coming near Mr Burton's house I saw one of his ladies looking out of the window, for he lives like the Turks in that respect, but he is not singular.'[2]

Among Burton's fellow travellers, many professed a nobler reason for slave ownership and bought Greek and Cretan girls to save them from abuse by the Turks following the Battle of Navarino. Hay took the lead in encouraging his friends to marry their purchases, as he planned to do. His girl, Kalitza, was, however, 'ill-tempered' and 'as passing for a boy at Thebes'[3] – which is how the girls were often disguised when away from Cairo. Bonomi kept a slave girl named Fatima for several years, and she bore him two sons, the second of whom died. On returning to England, Bonomi ignored the letters that she sent regularly asking for money to help support his child.

The English appear to have looked upon buying slaves as being part of the lifestyle of an upper-class Turk. Copying the practice, they believed, would help their assimilation into Egyptian society by maintaining the higher rank associated with ownership. Burton clearly enjoyed the idea of slave ownership; otherwise, he would not have made his purchase so soon after his arrival in the country. Humphreys expressed a different view initially, but he too soon fell under the spell of ownership and the ready availability of young girls for nights of passion. In June 1826, he wrote to Bonomi: 'I discovered yesterday a very pretty little girl who is content to do business (not a commoner) she is very willing but her principal holds out and (she) makes many objections in order to gain more money, but with the assistance of Venus and [?Plutus] I seize my prize tomorrow night. It will be very expensive work but hunger will break down stone walls.'[4]

It is also Humphreys who provides a contemporary description of the slave market into which 'no Christian could properly enter':[5]

> I am to become a Turk for my dress consisting in a large pair of trousers a yard and a half wide, a waistcoat with loose sleeves large enough to cover over my hands and reach down to my instep, a large cloak, a pair of yellow slippers and a pair of red over them, a large sash round my waist and a turban made of seven yards of white muslin and I carry a pipe of two yards in length. I also have a pair of mustachios and not short ones. In this dress I parade the streets of Qahirah, beat whatever poor devil comes in the way of my donkey, and then am a complete Turk. My head is shaved as is the custom. In this dress I visited the slave market and purchased a young Abyssinian girl for Mr Burton, but do not mention this to my mother. £20 was the sum paid for her but she is ugly as the devil. A most disgusting place is the slave market. The boys and girls exposed for sale here (for men and women are seldom brought down by the caravans) are questioned as to their faith, whether Moslem or infidel and undergo a complete examination according to the intentions of the purchasers. Their limbs are looked at – their skin examined, their teeth, eyes, head – in fact every part undergoes a scrutiny.
>
> Osman came about 9 o'clock to go with Mr B(urton) to complete the purchase of a female slave (from the country of the Gallas, a province of Abyssinia) but he being obliged to go to the Citadel to fuse some metals, I was ordered to go. We went to the slave market and when arrived there a most horrible sight presented itself. The slave market is a large square surrounded by ruinous buildings. In the square sat a number of blacks, male and female for sale, several children of 4 or 5 years old were there to be sold, they

came round me for money and Osman said these young slaves sold for more than those who had arrived at a greater age as it was in the power of purchasers most probably to form their minds to his wish. There were but a few light coloured ones and these were all from Abyssinia (a kind of upper colour) one of which was selected for our fellow traveller [and companion, Mr Burton] . . . I seated myself on the ground with Osman and the slave merchant and we counted our twelve thousand Egyptian piasters the sum agreed upon for their buying and selling of a fellow creature. My blood crawled in my veins. When the purchase was completed the poor girl was called from her miserable companions who all seemed callous to every feeling of friendship for their companion whom they were now about to lose, she was measured for clothes as she was to appear as a boy [to be named Ahmed]. We then left the slave market and went to the Bazaar where we purchased the necessary clothing to the amount of eight hundred and seventy six piasters. We returned and she was stripped of her clothing which consisted of nothing more than a shift and a handkerchief . . . and we took her home. A duty of four piasters is paid for every slave bought at the market besides a certain sum paid to the government when the slaves are brought into the country. The slave purchased was not more than twelve years old at most and she was not sold as a virgin . . . The poor girl . . . Much has been said about the state of slavery in the East. The market on [?Okilit] el Djilal, as it is termed, does not materially give a favourable idea of the condition of those offered for sale . . . At the tents without Qahirah boys and girls may be had with equal facility. The Priests prefer the former on the ground of the prophecy that when Mahomet returns he is to be born of a man.[6]

Seven months later, Sheffield, a mining engineer sent by Greenough to assist Burton in finding coal, arrived at Burton's house in Cairo:

It was Humphreys' birthday and a party was assembled at Burton's house to celebrate it – they all looked such thorough Turks that I could hardly be persuaded there were any Englishmen among them. They were already far advanced in the protestations – which of course brought the host and his new guests more readily acquainted. Burton told me of his harem and offered his black slave for the night as he now had never occasion for her himself. This offer, however, made in his cups, was forgotten next morning, and he did not at all like being reminded of it.[7]

On his return to England, a disillusioned Sheffield informed on Burton and his lifestyle during an interview with Greenough about his visit to Egypt:

> Besides his black slave . . . he has a young Greek purchased for him by a Scots heretic of the name of Osman – she was a mere child when she came to him, little more than twelve years old, dumpy and not handsome. Christians are not allowed by the law to purchase slaves – and if they transgress may be required to marry the girl and turn Mahometan on pain of death – but this law is not enforced by the tolerant government of the present Viceroy. Salt had a slave girl whom he got with child and then made her over to a Musselman – abandoning his progeny. Wilkinson also has a slave – but she refused to have any connection with him till he had satisfied her that he was a Mahometan though an Englishman – James's Greek had similar scruples and it was very difficult to get her into his house. As neither he nor Charles (Humphreys) could speak Turkish and no Christian man can be admitted to the Slave Market as a purchaser, the purchase was made by Osman who received £10 for his pandership. That the slave should object was natural enough not only because the presumption would be that a Christian who violated Christian duties would be a bad master, but because a harem of one or two women only promised to be exceedingly dull. However, finding herself well treated the girl by degrees got reconciled. James keeps his girls locked up and lets no one approach them but himself. I saw the Greek only twice though I lived for some time in the same house with her, and then but for two minutes – (Dehl) Ibrahim cooks for his harem and Vincenzo Rosa carries in the meals. The girls go out now and then to the baths on an ass muffled up under the convoy of a Janissary, but this happens very rarely. Osman also lives upon him and when he is away from Qahirah takes charge of the two girls, whom he removes to his own harem in which there are not less than ten, so he is thought not likely to commit a breach of trust. Charles is very anxious to return (to England), he stipulated for two years absence only and it requires all James' management to detain him. He (James) talks of making over one of the girls to Humphreys and purchasing another for himself.[8]

Greenough expressed concern that James might have a family by one of the girls, but Sheffield assured him there was no chance of it. 'He is from ill health quite impotent. In 2½ years he has done nothing.

Indeed, what should he do with a mere child and he keeps his harem so close that none are likely to father him progeny not his own.'

By 1826 Burton was bored with his first purchases. Humphreys wrote to Bonomi, 'Mr Burton is behaving very well to Blackey, has bought a house for her, furnished it, found her a husband and gives her a sum of money – very expensive work this, paying dear for his pleasures, but it does him much credit.' In 1830, he also tried to repatriate one of the others. He confessed as much in a letter to Greenough:

> You will know of my having purchased a Greek slave. This may sound harsh . . . This individual I cannot desert. There are many ways for me to act. To find some worthy man, a Greek, to whom I can marry her. To deliver her into the hands of her father or friends. To carry her to Europe and find some means there of providing for her happiness. I have taken advantage of an opportunity Mr Hay has given me to send into Crete to find her relatives. Upon the report made to me I shall be better able to decide, but the natives are still at variance with the Turks and she may again be made a slave. During the time I wait your letter I shall be able to come to some decision.[9]

In November 1833, Burton was on his way home to England, accompanied by Humphreys, Vincenzo Rosa, several male servants and Dudu [Mr B's mistress]. A year later, Humphreys wrote to Bonomi from their temporary lodgings in Bordeaux:

> I do not know that Burton will be foolish ever to marry her. She is neither handsome or clever and as she cannot be introduced in those circles which he frequents, or indeed in any other, there is little chance of her ever improving, she will never learn a European language, she will never be a conversable being, she has no mind . . . I cannot imagine what he will do with he, she is a terrible clog.[10]

Burton arrived in England in December 1835 with the male servants and Dudu. Whether he was aware of the Abolition of Slavery Act is not known, but his attitude appears to have changed. He wrote to Hay:

> My mercantile speculation in zoology – or scheme of converting wild beasts into gold failed when on the point of realising my sanguine hopes and instead of putting several thousand pounds in my pocket I have lost. My giraffe died suddenly, when within five days of

England after all the trouble and anxiety and expense of the animals being low spirited and unwell – and fearful of the climate of England – the poor fellow Mohammed had his right arm horribly lacerated by one of the animals [Jackal]. Amputation was first decided upon by the surgeons but I persuaded them to let nature try her powers to preserve the limb. Every artery, vein and tendon [except for that of the little finger] were torn apart and the joint of the wrist laid open so that the hand hung by the fleshy part towards the little finger only. The goodwill of nature and the good blood of the Arab succeeded and I preserved the tombstone of an arm although without the use. The accident besides loading me with very heavy account for surgeons and apothecaries [for the keep of his bed and room four or five months (in Bordeaux)] has left a cripple on my hands for support and brought me to the end of another year and here I am, at length arrived, in the depth of the worst winter or rather what your vile English climate has lowered upon you for many years.[11]

Now in England, Humphreys' conjecture that Dudu might be an illiterate turned out not to be so. As Burton resurrected a correspondence with Hay, he often included 'A letter from Doodoo also' – for Kalitza. 'Poor Dudu is very desirous of writing to Mrs Hay and I have promised to mention it and send her letter.'[12] Whether the two women wrote to each other in Greek or English is not known.

Exactly when and where Burton married Dudu remains to be discovered, but the event caused a rift between them and the rest of his family. Although this was to last for the remainder of their lives, to his credit, Burton did not abandon Dudu. In 1840, he wrote to Hay:

I have been confined to the house latterly and much to my bed, though I am now again near my common mark of good health – for such it should be, since the doctors say so who have been examining me before assuring my life for poor Dudu's eventual benefit in case of my death, as, in spite of all my rights, I am certain she would be left for a long time in absolute want in that case, till legal interference obliged my brothers to pay attention to my will.[13]

It is in their last years together that Dudu's real name is revealed – Adriana Garofalaki. Burton's younger brother, Decimus, mistakenly named her Andrea in his will of 1870, but did refer to her as the wife of his late brother. As a married couple they moved in the 1850s from either

London or St Leonard's on Sea to Newhaven, a village near Edinburgh overlooking the Firth of Forth, where Burton set about organising his will. 'Second, I direct my said Trustees to pay to Adriana Garofalaki or Haliburton my wife as soon as possible after my death the sum of £40 for mournings and interim aliment and as soon as they shall have realised a sufficient sum for that purpose to pay her an annuity of £100 a year free of all taxes and deductions whatsoever.'[14] In his will, Decimus left her a further £100 and £25 a year, although she did not receive any money until 1881. Adriana was given these further sums of money in return for relinquishing any claim on the Burton family estate – the same conditions that had been attached to her husband's bequest.

Following the death of her husband in 1862, Adriana moved to Stoneyfield Cottage, Morningside, Edinburgh. With a reducing income, she moved in 1866 to a smaller house at 8 Gladstone Terrace. A last entry for her, in the directories of 1883, is from this address, where she had presumably died, taking with her the last remaining memories of Burton's time in Egypt. If she was the girl purchased just before Christmas 1824 aged about ten years, she would have been seventy when she died. If, however, she is the second girl mentioned by Sheffield in 1822 as being twelve years old, she would have died aged seventy-three. With so few details known about her life in Egypt or Britain, it is difficult to assess whether Adriana's life was better in one country or the other. Deprived of local customs learned in her childhood and teenage years, she may have found life in a cold northern city somewhat depressing, especially during the twenty years spent living without the husband she had been with for four decades. Whether she would have preferred remaining in Egypt as a slave is impossible to assess. It was certainly a choice she was never offered.

NOTES

1 Letter from Charles Humphreys to William Ward (8 July 1822), University College, London (UCL), Greenough Papers 35/4.
2 Quoted in Selwyn Tillett, *Egypt Itself: The Career of Robert Hay, Esquire of Linplum and Nunraw, 1799–1863* (London, SD Books, 1984), p. 18. Tillett incorrectly identifies Burton's secretary as being Osman, when it should have been Charles Humphreys.

3 UCL, Greenough Papers, loose note.
4 Quoted in Tillett, *op. cit.*, p. 38.
5 UCL, Greenough Papers, loose note.
6 *Ibid.*
7 UCL, Greenough Papers, 35/4.
8 *Ibid.*
9 UCL, Greenough Papers, 35/2.
10 Quoted in Tillett, *op. cit.*, p. 38.
11 Letter from James Burton to Robert Hay (1 January 1836), British Library (BL), Department of Manuscripts, Add Ms 38094 ffs 93+94. James sold all his animals except the giraffe to the Jardin des Plantes, in Paris, in order to raise the money needed to pay the doctor's bills and for the period of convalescence.
12 Letter from James Burton to Robert Hay (19 February 1840), BL Add Ms 38094 ffs 134+135.
13 Incomplete letter from James Burton to Robert Hay (25 January 1840), BL Add Ms 38094 ffs 126+127.
14 James Burton's will, Wills and Probate Office, Edinburgh.

14

The Reverend Jolliffe's Advice to Travellers[1]

Patricia Usick

Not knowing that it was necessary to be provided with every thing in order to travel in Egypt, we had forgotten the article of candles; so that we were in the midst of the most profound darkness in the cabin . . . (E. de Montulé, Cairo, 28 October 1818.)[2]

How did travellers in Egypt and the Near East manage during the early years of the nineteenth century, before the later proliferation of guidebooks advising on sightseeing, on what clothing to take and on more esoteric points, such as the necessity of first sinking your Nile boat to exterminate the vermin?[3]

There was a 'Complete Guide'[4] to India by 1810, because one was needed by the gentlemen intended for employment in the Honorable East India Company, but little material to consult about Egypt. Few published travel journals had much in the way of useful information, as they tended to eschew the practical in favour of the 'brilliant' and 'fictitious glory' of travel as the Comte de Forbin[5] points out when he tells us how sick he was on the sea voyage home. He found the fatigues and dangers to be exaggerated but the 'enormous expense' meant that, 'A voyage to the Levant will be a real and almost destructive waste of money to a private individual'. Nevertheless, for every rich gentleman travelling for pleasure and interest there was also one who travelled to make his fortune, so clearly needs differed.

William John Bankes' 1818–19 voyage up the Nile was ridiculed by Belzoni, who commented sarcastically on Bankes and his companions' luxurious mode of travel. What really irked him were the exaggerated travellers' accounts of hardship and starvation, when they were actually living 'like Sir John Falstaff'.[6]

What we might call 'networking' for on-the-spot advice began with the circle of consuls at Alexandria and Cairo, if not earlier among other travellers at Rome or Constantinople. According to Fagan,[7] the duties of the consuls general were 'far from arduous'; the political issues were 'hardly of major importance' and 'few foreigners resided permanently in Cairo'. This left plenty of time for antiquarian interests and the collection of ancient Egyptian objects, so advice on these matters was not hard to come by.

James Silk Buckingham[8] is a good witness to the social role of the consuls in the 'round of pleasure' at Alexandria in 1813. He was received by Peter Lee, the British consul, and other guests included a wealthy European merchant and a traveller from Rome. '. . . each consul, as matter [*sic*] of duty, kept open house for an evening reception once in the week; and on Sunday evenings the parties were still more numerous'. There were receptions, concerts and dances, and there were always rooms or balconies for conversation for those who did not wish to dance. During the day Mr Lee took him around the sites of interest. At Cairo, Buckingham spent his first night in the house of the Armenian vice-consul, and next day presented his letters of introduction from Smyrna and Alexandria. He was given apartments in the residency 'containing every domestic convenience, indeed luxury', since Colonel Missett, although extremely disabled,[9] was a bon vivant. 'Nothing could surpass the pleasure of our lives.' There were sumptuous breakfasts, gourmet dinners and morning rides on Arab steeds to different parts of the city.

William John Bankes, who arrived in Egypt in 1815, was fortunate in meeting and later travelling with the next consul in Cairo, Henry Salt, who, together with his secretary, Henry Beechey, made agreeable companions with similar scholarly interests in ancient Egypt. Bankes also met the celebrated explorer, Burckhardt, who furnished him with a list of sites to visit on his Nile journey and gave him a detailed list of necessary items of dress, including prices,[10] when he, like others, decided to don Oriental costume – primarily to blend in for reasons of security, but also, perhaps, for comfort and to indulge their Orientalist spirit. To travel from Jerusalem to Jericho in 1816, Bankes chose to dress as a Turkish soldier, while Buckingham, his companion, adopted the clothes of a Syrian Arab.[11] The consequences of leaving Bankes' underclothes drying at the fire were almost fatal; the 'peasants regarded the shirt and drawers, which were of fine calico, as proofs of some difference between our real character, and that which we endeavoured to impose upon them by our outward appearance'.[12] Local dress had other useful advantages. Under cover of his robes, Burckhardt was able to take notes on his journey without alerting the suspicions of the rest of the caravan party.

The Reverend Jolliffe visited Egypt and Syria in 1817, and was thoughtful enough to provide advice to other travellers in the form of a question and answer session, together with a list of various consuls' names, in the appendix to his journal, which was published in 1820.[13] He and his friends had benefited from obtaining these answers to their queries from an (anonymous) Artillery officer they had met at Rome. (The list, incidentally, tells us a great deal about the Reverend's character. He was obviously not the type of traveller who might forget his tickets, passport, visas or travellers cheques today.) The questions were:

1. On embarking at Naples for Alexandria, what are the chief requisites respecting baggage, letters of credit, &c?
2. What description of bed is preferable?
3. If a firman must be procured from Constantinople, to enable us to proceed from Cairo to Jerusalem, will it be proper to write from Rome? and, if so, to whom should application be made?
4. What steps are to be taken on landing at Alexandria?
5. What wages should an interpreter receive?
6. What are the ordinary charges per day at inns?
7. Is it absolutely necessary to appear in the costume of the country? [Presumably Jolliffe is not the type to jump at the chance.] In that case, what is the best mode of procuring a dress, and the probable cost of a complete equipment?
8. What is the first object on arriving at Grand Cairo, and the mode of proceeding from thence to Jerusalem?
9. To whom will it be proper to apply for lodgings on arriving at Jerusalem?
10. What is the best route from Jerusalem to Constantinople, the time it would require, and the method of travelling?

The answers were as follows:

1. There is no difficulty in transporting baggage from place to place; every thing that can add to your comfort, I should recommend you to take. I had a portmanteau, capable of containing twelve shirts, and other things in proportion; a pair of canteens, containing dinner and breakfast conveniences for two; a saddle

and bridle, and small cloak case, similar to that which Dragoons have, to carry a change of linen, on the horse I rode. *By all means carry tea.* Coffee and sugar are to be purchased in every part of Syria. Take letters of credit on Constantinople or Smyrna. *Calculate your expences at two guineas per day.* Herries' bills are payable at Cairo; but if you draw on Cairo from any other place, the loss is very great.

2. A common camp paillasse, a single blanket, and a pair of sheets, render you independent, though at Alexandria, Jaffa, Ram[l]a, Jerusalem, Acre, and Nazareth, beds will be provided for two or even three persons; your beds should roll up, and be carried in a canvas cover. [Jolliffe adds in a footnote here that he himself found a blanket quite unnecessary and had invented a type of sleeping bag with, 'two pair of linen sheets sewed up at each side and at one extremity, as a defence against vermin. These were placed in a leathern case, previously steeped in a preparation used at Naples for resisting contagion.']

3. Write from Rome immediately, taking the precaution to speak to the English Consul here, that he may certify you are English. Your application must be made to the English Ambassador at Constantinople, requesting the *firman* for self and suite, may be sent to Cairo, and addressed to the Consul-General. The communication from Constantinople to Cairo is one month.

4. Call on the British Consul, and do not land your baggage (at Alexandria) till he has sent his attendants to pass it through the Custom House. He will give you the necessary assistance to get to Cairo. I went by land to Rosetta, (30 miles distant from Alexandria, one day's journey,) and thence embarked in a boat for Cairo, a distance of about four days.

5. [Interpreter's fees] A Spanish dollar a day.

6. *There are no inns,* except *one,* at Alexandria, and there it cost for myself and servant nearly a guinea a day. Wherever you go there is a Convent or Consul, to whom you should resort.

7. The Consul-General will be informed of your arrival at Alexandria. Send your letters of introduction to him through the British Consul at Alexandria, and mention when you propose leaving the last mentioned place. Cairo is a mile and a half from the Nile; it will therefore be necessary to call on him before you land your baggage at the port, called Boulac. Of course he will provide you lodgings, either at his own house, or elsewhere; if at the Convent, you should pay about *half a dollar a day for each person,* if you are furnished with a lodging only; but if supplied with necessaries for the table, &c. I should regulate the present as the drogoman of the mission, Monsieur Haziz,

will direct you, and whom you may trust in every thing relative to your movements.

8. [Stops *en route* from Cairo to Jerusalem and modes of travel are here specified; the acting Consul at Jaffa will provide you with mules for the last part of the journey and send notice to your next stop Ramla, and to Jerusalem.]

9. [At Jerusalem, you will stay at the Roman Catholic Convent where you will be 'furnished with every thing you want.' Jolliffe specifies the payments to be made to the treasurer, dragoman and to servants and Janissaries at the holy places, on leaving Jerusalem.]

10. [Jolliffe recommends a route taking six weeks to travel overland from Jerusalem to Constantinople.]

11. [Regarding costume: and yes he *knows*, 'This seems more properly to be an answer to the enquiry, No. 7.'] Whether this is 'absolutely necessary' is not addressed, but Jolliffe advises, 'Take a fine cloth for your benish [a greatcoat] – jacket and waistcoat may be of any colour but green; the benish is generally of a gay colour, and different from the rest. The breeches, called sharroweel, are of great size, almost always blue, requiring about four times as much cloth as common pantaloons. The only advantage of buying the cloth in Europe is, that you get it finer and much cheaper. At Cairo the coarse cloth is dearer than the fine in Europe. Cairo will be the best place to have the dresses made up. I calculated 50*l.* for the dress of myself and servant.'

In addition, Jolliffe adds the times of year of the plague and a final piece of advice given to him by an experienced traveller, who noted his overeager examination of a collection of coins and medals. He switches here into Italian; my rough translation of which follows:

> Remember that you are in Arabia. Everything is done by means of money, and they always try to rob Europeans, especially the English. Use a recommended dragoman and you will pay him less. Antiquities are the means of taking your money off you; you will find better ones in Egypt and they will be cheaper.

He ends on the following intriguing note, '*Keep your eyes open when dealing with everyone, and in particular, with the vice-consuls.*'

NOTES

1. T.R. J[olliffe], *Letters from Palestine, Descriptive of a Tour through Galilee and Judea, with Some Account of the Red Sea, and of the Present State of Jerusalem*, 2nd edn, to which are added, *Letters from Egypt* (London, James Black, 1820).
2. Cairo, 28 October 1818 in E. de Montulé, *Travels in Egypt during 1818 and 1819* (London, printed for R. Phillips, 1821), p. 6.
3. This was common practice but Belzoni's experience was that it merely refreshed the rats. G. Belzoni, *Narrative of the Operations and Recent Discoveries within the Pyramids, Temples, Tombs, and Excavations in Egypt and Nubia; etc.* (London, John Murray, 1822), vol. 1, pp. 255–6.
4. Capt T. Williamson, *The East India Vade-Mecum or Complete Guide to Gentlemen Intended for the Civil, Military or Naval Service of the Hon. East India Company* (London, 1810).
5. Comte de Forbin, *Travels in Egypt, Being a Continuation of Travels in the Holy Land, in 1817–18* (London, printed for R. Phillips and Co., 1819), pp. 74–5.
6. Belzoni, *op. cit.*, vol. 2, pp. 105–6.
7. B. Fagan, *The Rape of the Nile* (New York, Mcdonald and Jane's, 1975), p. 89.
8. J.S. Buckingham, *Autobiography of James Silk Buckingham* (2 vols., London, Longman, Brown, Green, and Longmans, 1855), pp. 130–58.
9. According to Buckingham (*Ibid.*, p. 152), his arms and legs were paralysed.
10. Bankes Mss, Dorset County Archive, Dorchester. HJ1/191.
11. J.S. Buckingham, *Travels in Palestine, etc.*, 2nd edn (2 vols., London, Longmans, 1822), II, p. 50.
12. *Ibid.*, pp. 236–7.
13. Jolliffe, *op. cit.*, pp. 372–7.

15

Italian Travellers in Egypt

Marta Petricioli and Barbara Codacci[1]

A quick look at the volumes written by Italian travellers to Egypt that we have been able to examine reveals how meagre is the sum of Italian travel books compared to that of other European nations in the same period. Unlike France, Britain and Germany, Italy had no great writers such as Flaubert, Chateaubriand or Lamartine, who departed for the East and then wrote reminiscences of their travels. There were only a few exceptions and they did not concern themselves with Egypt. Certainly, there was Edmondo De Amicis and his two volumes on Constantinople[2] and one on Morocco, not to mention Luigi Barzini, who wrote about the Holy Land.[3] But few diplomats and politicians, or other important figures from Italian society, wrote their memoirs. Last, few Italian women had the courage or the opportunity to travel to the East. Unlike the indomitable English and French women who went abroad, Italian women who travelled and wrote about it are rare. It is, however, worth recalling here Cristina Trivulzio di Belgioioso, whose book, published in Paris in 1858, was recently reissued in Italian,[4] and Amalia Nizzoli, whose *Memorie sull'Egitto*, published in 1841,[5] deserves to be better known by the reading public; nor should we forget Matilde Serao, author and journalist, who travelled at the end of the century and Carla Serena, whose books on Persia were published in Paris in the 1880s.[6]

A trip abroad was seldom undertaken for the cultural benefit of the traveller, though an exception to this rule was the young Salvago Raggi's trip to the East before he started his brilliant career as a diplomat.[7] Others went abroad for their work, or to visit relatives. Most people, however, went on a pilgrimage to the Holy Land and took time off to rest or to amuse themselves in other Eastern places. At the turn of the century, for some Italians the reason had become mere tourism, but the tourists did not write their memoirs.

Few of the books reviewed here were brought out by large publishing concerns or ran to more than one edition. Many were published by printers in small provincial towns. Several authors wrote for their own pleasure or for that of a small circle of friends; others, especially the men of God, who went to Turkey, Syria or Egypt either on their way to or returning from the Holy Land, wrote for their superiors or for their parishioners.

Both among Italian writers and among those of other European countries, there is a marked difference between those who travelled at the beginning of the nineteenth century (1815–40) and those at the end of the nineteenth and the beginning of the twentieth century. In the early period, the travellers were far more open to new experiences, more tolerant of diversity and less irked by discomfort, which was far worse than later on. As the century wore on, intolerance and indifference grew, not to mention the complaints of noise, dirt and heat. Stereotypes and 'Orientalist' myths also proliferated. Obviously, the spread of nationalist and imperialist doctrines in Europe, on the one hand, and the reading of more and more books on Egypt, on the other, had an overall negative effect.

In the texts we use here a trip to Egypt refers almost exclusively to Lower Egypt, usually touching on the large cities of Alexandria and Cairo, the pyramids of Giza and, after the opening of the Suez Canal, Port Said, Ismailia and Suez. Rarely do Italian travellers venture further south. What interests them most is the scenery and social life, rather than political events or the economic condition of the country they are visiting. There are long descriptions of the views, detailed topographies of the towns, exact accounts of the monuments, general opinions on the population and precise sketches of this or that social type. These pages contain all the enthusiasm of the travellers, together with their satisfied or disappointed expectations.

The cities

Alexandria was usually the first Egyptian city that Italians visited after crossing the Mediterranean. However, the city's profound transformations during the nineteenth century are interesting, and it is, therefore, worth comparing accounts from the beginning and the end of the last century. For Amalia Nizzoli, who arrived there in 1819, the city was caught between the blue of the sky and the lapis lazuli of the sea, in clear contrast to the yellow of the arid, sandy coast with its sporadic palm trees. Her first description is emblematic, because it contains all the details that help us to appreciate the beauty of the buildings, including the new ones Muhammad Ali had just built.[8] Having disembarked, she is struck by the jubilant chaos of voices, sounds and colours. 'The continuous movement and tumultuous toing and froing in those very narrow streets, embarrassed by long queues of loaded camels and many donkeys and mules',[9] she writes, obviously impressed by the Oriental charm of the city. Yet, when she returned a few years later, she noted how Alexandria had been transformed by its contacts with Europeans involved in the increasing trade between the two, and it was now 'easy to forget for a moment the distance separating us from our own countries'.[10]

In the pages of later authors this modern, Western aspect is emphasised and the city is said to lack the charm of the rest of the country. The authors are almost disappointed. Indeed, Muhammad Ali and his successors had ripped out the centre of the city to give it better infrastructures, and the British bombardment had laid low most of the remaining Arab buildings, including the ancient walls. One of the authors knew he should not expect much. 'A traveller visiting Alexandria today will not find many of the ancient monuments, unlike Cairo, Memphis and Thebes. He will look in vain for majestic ruins.'[11] In 1887 there was not much Oriental flavour in Alexandria for Colocci, either:

> If it were not for the inhabitants' clothes and the odd minaret, nothing would reveal Egypt or Africa to our eyes. The city is too European, too similar to other Mediterranean ports, too despoiled of real monuments to satisfy, when we disembark in the land of the Pharaohs, our desire to stand beneath wonderful examples of Egyptian art.[12]

As for the Arab quarters, their greatest defect is that they have no local colour, and, if it were not for the 'heavy grilles of the windows, the houses look like the ones in ugly villages in the South of Italy'.[13]

Our travellers are somewhat contradictory: they long for the colourfulness of the Orient, they are disappointed when they find none, but then they prefer the modern quarters of the cities they visit. This is true of Augusto Cesana, who writes that in Alexandria, 'The most beautiful part and the one one should visit is Mehmet Ali's square . . . It is a section of the Paris Boulevards, it is a copy of the Corso Vittorio Emanuele in Bari.'[14]

Cairo made a completely different impression. 'Cairo is a city that attracts and charms you',[15] 'all my old impressions vanished, crushed by reality, which won hands down even against my very dreams'.[16] Three civilisations, Ancient Egypt, Coptic Christianity and Islam, are embodied in the city, but our authors were most impressed by Muslim culture. Starting with the legend of how Amr pitched his tent at Fustat, as Nizzoli noted,[17] and which is celebrated in the nearby mosque, the various dynasties are listed by mentioning the main buildings that each left behind, from Ibn Tulun's mosque to that of al-Azhar, from the Citadel to the so-called 'tombs of the Caliphs' from Hasan's *madrasa* to the new mosques built by the Ottomans. The travellers are also impressed by Muhammad Ali's mosque, even though it is not as elegant as the Mamluk mosques, on account of its gigantic proportions and rich decorations: alabaster walls, the golden vault and the precious carpets.

According to the travellers, the city had two faces, and they wrote extensively about the new city built in European style, which 'has lovely, grandiose streets, flanked by luxuriant trees, numerous gardens and fountains'.[18] Old Cairo was the object of rather unflattering comments, which we also find made by these very authors, and by others, when they wrote about the old quarters of Smyrna, Stamboul and Jerusalem. As Minghelli remarked, 'However beautiful, rich, sumptuous is the new Cairo, the other is dirty, poverty stricken, and reveals signs of its decrepitude in every part.'[19] Ten years later Buselli agreed, adding, 'the narrow streets twist and turn, no wider than two metres – a labyrinth – full of every kind of rubbish. The Arab shops and the small innumerable bazaars are no more than hovels and rat-holes, dark, dirty, and so filthy they turn your stomach.'[20]

Any tour of Cairo, after a look at the main streets and the crowded bazaars, ended inevitably at the Egyptian Museum, a prelude to the visit to the pyramids, to which all travellers went as if on a pilgrimage. 'I have seen them! And now that I have seen them I feel I have grown several inches taller; I feel I have become a big shot, so that on going home people will point me out as being worthy of their envy,' was the enthusiastic comment of one of our authors.[21] Unfortunately, most of these travellers only went to see the pyramids of Giza and the Sphinx; very few went further afield. All the pages dedicated to the pyramids, though often excessively flowery, are full of genuine enthusiasm. The writers spend several pages on the origins of these monuments, which are still surrounded in mystery, looking for clues in ancient literature: they quote from Herodotus, Diodorus and Strabo; they recall that not only must the Holy Family have seen them during the exile in Egypt, but also Moses, Joseph and Jacob.

Occasionally the description is amusing, as when Buselli refused indignantly to crawl down the tunnel leading into the pyramid, or to climb to its top while other members of his group flung themselves intrepidly into this adventure.[22] At other times it is claustrophobic, as when Chicco, the most courageous of them all, after a romantic nocturnal excursion 'to the spacious top of that mountain of stone' from which he saw the sun rising, visited the heart of the pyramid, crawling and squeezing down tight, slippery tunnels, hung about with clouds of bats.[23]

Nature and landscape

During the trip from Alexandria to Cairo, or on the rare occasions when travellers went further afield, they took time to observe the landscape. Most of our authors made the journey by train, with only a fleeting view of the panorama, the desert on the horizon and the villages passing rapidly by through the train window. But nature in Egypt is so different from previous experiences that all these authors are obliged to face the issue. Each one approached the problem in a different way, so descriptions vary from attempts to give as scientific an explanation as possible of the phenomena to the most extravagant flights of fancy. At one extreme, Forni, whose book examined the question of humidity with great seriousness, offered a detailed analysis of what he observed, from dust and rain to attempts at a rational explanation of the *khamsin* and the mirage; at the other are accounts full of superficial sensations based on the briefest of trips.

In every description the main subject is the Nile, 'the soul of Egypt', the river that 'is the very essence of all riverine landscapes, and of all their manifold expressions'.[24] Whether they looked down on it from the heights of the pyramids or the Citadel in Cairo, whether afloat in a boat, all the travellers listed its manifold beneficent effects on the lives of the Egyptians, as the main source of the necessary water for the cities and as the cause of the country's prosperous agriculture. The contrast between the irrigated fields and the rest of the land was obvious. 'Where the Nile extends its floods all is green, everything flourishes; where its beneficent effects stop, there the desert begins', wrote Cesana, who went further, with the typical positivist faith in technology of nineteenth-century writers. 'If by huge hydraulic works one could spread this blessed water to the whole vice-kingdom, it could feed all of Europe . . . And this is possible! And perhaps one day it will be accomplished.'[25]

Other, more romantic writers saw the majestic landscape through the prism of cultural associations. Faced by the spectacle of the river, Colocci confessed he forgot his task and felt, 'more inclined to compose a hymn rather than the usual arid reports'.[26] In the same vein were the almost lyrical pages of Matilde Serao, who wrote, 'All rivers inspire an almost ineffable sense of poetry: yet no one can express that of the Nile', and went on to use such expressions as 'strength and power', 'melancholy grace', 'widespread serenity, loving peacefulness', finishing off with a night scene on the river, in which, 'the Nile keeps vigil alone, only it has a soul; and all things vegetable and human are transfused in it, and you yourself exist only for it.'[27] Let us conclude, however, with a description that is less impregnated with the spirit of late Romanticism, and which sums up this vision of the Egyptian landscape:

> Egypt is merely a valley, shut off to the west by the Libyan and to the east by the Arabian chain of mountains; . . . here you have the simplicity of two walls of naked stone, in the midst of which green fields, the fiery heat of sand, the majestic bed of the Nile and the flaming sky compose a majestic, enchanting whole.[28]

Society

Italian travellers showed considerable interest in Egyptian society, mainly because the city dwellers were so varied, but also because of the religious fervour of the Muslims, the extreme poverty of the fellahin and, obviously, the myth of the harem.

Descriptions of the large cities are full of the well-known colourful crowds, noisy and variegated and incomprehensible for some authors. In writing about Alexandria, Bonomelli says of its population, 'it is a mixture of Catholic Christians and schismatic Christians, Greeks, Armenians, Muslims and so on';[29] as in the case of Egyptian Arabs, the distinction between townsfolk and peasants is immediately evident. The first interaction travellers have with the townsfolk is the somewhat frightening experience of arriving in Alexandria, when the ship is boarded by hoards of people offering their services. 'The steamer', wrote Buselli, 'is besieged on the side of the companion-way by a swarm of Egyptian boats, with two or three Arabs per boat, waving and gesticulating, bumping one another and yelling their heads off'.[30] These visions, common to almost all the texts, unleash the usual fear of the unknown, but, once the travellers realise that the Arabs have come to earn their daily bread, fear is replaced by the pleasure of observing their features, their clothing and studying their habits. As for the cities, these habits are compared unfavourably to those of Europeans; one author goes so far as to write, 'To appreciate the superiority of European to the Mahomedan civilisation, one has only to pass, as we did ourselves, from new Cairo to old Cairo. It is the other side of the coin, the negation of all civilisation.'[31]

When writing about the Arab personality, the Italian authors present a very shabby stereotype. The Arabs are, 'a colourful people who move slowly, silently, with nonchalance, as if absorbed in some great thought . . . if the world were to fall they would not shift a foot to move off'. At the same time, 'no people seem colder and more indifferent than the Muslims and no people is as quick to turn fanatic, or more terrible in its explosions of fury'.[32] Expressions of slight admiration alternate with others that reveal great contempt. Though for some, despite their uncouth manners, Arabs are considered to be faithful and to possess great strength,[33] others observe, 'these are people who take no care of their person and have no self-respect; they live like beasts and are dressed in rags'.[34]

In the countryside the fellahin caught the imagination of all travellers. Most saw them only in the distance from the windows of the train from Alexandria to Cairo or to Suez, but they could easily guess their extreme poverty. Those who got a closer look were struck by the miserable dwellings and remarked that, 'in our own countries, the pigs and the chickens are better housed'.[35] In these houses, built of sun-baked bricks with mud as mortar and dried branches for roofs, only the door belonged to the fellah family, which at any moment could be forced to go elsewhere, either because the season had changed or because of the corvée (unpaid labour) The corvée was much criticised and doubts were expressed as to its usefulness. Some authors censured the heavy toll in lives, mentioning that 30,000 fellahin had lost their lives during the building of the Mahmoudieh canal and recalling, 'the cruel treatment, the diseases and all the miseries that killed off this multitude of unhappy souls';[36] others defended the practice by explaining that the *corvée* was the only way in which Egypt could build up its infrastructure.

All authors seemed very interested in the religion of the Egyptians, especially that of the Muslims, but virtually ignored the Copts, 'the aborigines of Egypt, descendants of those Egyptians who were so highly civilised when Greece and Italy were inhabited by a few wild, nomadic shepherds',[37] as well as the Catholics and Protestants of European descent. In the case of the Muslims, their attention was riveted by the practices and duties imposed by that religion, especially the ones that apply to the moral sphere. All those travelling to Egypt at the time of Ramadan, which 'is in fact the Muslim Lent, which lasts one month and varies in period within the course of thirty years', were deeply impressed. However, it was also pointed out that most of the faithful 'use expedients to trick Mahomet, and avoid obeying his laws in gross fashion' by sleeping all the day, when they should be fasting, and living through the night 'when they can fill their bellies to their hearts' content'.[38] On the whole there is an underlying scorn for the rigidity of certain religious practices that seemed to be all external show. The same scorn was reserved for the Muslim holy text, the Qur'an, described by Ghislanzoni as 'a wretched mixture of Buddhist error, Mosaic monotheism, and of a few Christian traditions that have been substantially mutilated and misrepresented, with the addition of sanctions on the senses and false miracles attributed to the Prophet by the compilers'.[39] Despite the prejudice, no one could doubt the deep religious feeling of the Muslims, as proven by their faithful observance of their religious duties and by the presence of numerous religious buildings.

As the main stereotype of travel writing about Muslim countries, the harem is also tackled by Italian travellers. Since these are usually men, their knowledge is indirect and their imaginings titillating, though they usually adopt a high moral tone. Amalia Nizzoli has quite a different approach, because she was invited several times to visit the harem of Muhammad Ali's son-in-law, the Defterdar Bey, one of the most powerful men in the country; she also visited that of the Turkish general, Abdin Bey. Obviously the scene depicted by Nizzoli cannot be compared with that in a poor harem, nor with those of the harems visited a few years later by another Italian traveller, Princess Belgioioso, who visited the houses of lesser Ottoman notables in Anatolia. Nizzoli gives an interesting picture of the domestic life of the ruling class in Egypt, of the world of women, with its coquetry, its pleasures, its amusements and of how the women saw themselves and what they thought. Nizzoli was very struck by the inviolability of the place, protected as it was by guards, eunuchs and odalisques; by the luxury that surrounded the Pasha's daughter, the rich refreshments offered to her and the precious vessels in which these were served, and also by the fact that the princess and her companions smoked all the time from pipes that were changed regularly to show off the entire collection and by the great quantities of coffee consumed. She found the life of the harem boring, though she kept returning, and felt that boredom also affected its inhabitants, since they were so delighted to receive her, bombarding her with questions, and flocked joyfully to the baths wearing their best outfits. However, her impression was that these women did not suffer from being shut away and were not opressed by mental affliction. These were proud women, who flaunted their feminine privileges and whose only worry was to convert their guest because it pained them not to have her pray with them.[40]

Politics

Egypt's political life seemed to interest these travellers more for its mythical qualities than in terms of the everyday facts. This helps to explain why so much space was given to Muhammad Ali compared to his successors. Only travellers from the early nineteenth century had direct experience of the facts they described and met the Pasha in person. The others saw him as a mythical figure, and called him 'the benefactor and saviour of Egypt'[41] or else 'the Garibaldi of Egypt'.[42] They all mentioned his humble origins and sudden rise to power, right up to his definitive move against the Mamluk Bey, who 'infested' the country: 'since he could never be sure of their submission or alliance, he had recourse to a terrible coup d'état which eliminated them all in one stroke'.[43] The fate of the Mamluks excited the pity of some writers, but was justified both in the light of the different mentality of orientals, 'since Muslim ideas are very different from Christian ideas',[44] and because 'the life of peoples crosses grievous periods, that require prompt and violent action, whose results make it easy to forgive the brutality of the causes that provoke them'.[45]

A very positive portrait of Muhammad Ali ('pleasant face', 'penetrating eyes', 'superior instinct') was given by Forni, who knew him personally and spent the central period of reform policies in Egypt.[46] It is these reforms, whether military, or in agriculture and trade, that attract most praise from our authors. Virmarcati summarised the Pasha's work by observing that, 'yet the characteristic by which Mehmed is distinguished from other men of state, is that he is a great agriculturist and a very able trader'.[47] Both Forni and Nizzoli watched the first parades of the new army, made up of Arab recruits, and appreciated its progress; Virmercati listed the new crops introduced into Egypt and also into Syria, but he also mentioned the difficulties these innovations encountered.

The successors of Muhammad Ali received far less attention, though Abbas was much criticised and regarded as the worst of calamities for Egypt, whereas Sa'id, the first of the Princes to have received a completely European education, was the object of unanimous praise. On the other hand, the controversial figure of Isma'il is only mentioned by Cesana, one of the Italian journalists sent to cover the inauguration of the Suez Canal. The special audience that he and his colleagues received gave him an opportunity to sketch some of the aspects of the Khedive's policy, including his desire to modernise the country by abolishing in the future two ancient institutions: the public beatings and the corvée, and, above all, the Capitulations, which he regarded as more urgent than any other reform of justice. But only by reading Cesana's book can one gain an impression of some of the characteristics of Isma'il's policy, such as his prodigality. Cesana himself discovered on setting foot in Egypt that the magic words 'invited by the Khedive' gave him the right to travel, sleep and eat for nothing.[48]

None of these writers mentioned the reasons for the British occupation of Egypt, but they all said the situation seemed rather confused. This confusion is apparent in what Bonomelli wrote: 'The English have real dominion, leaving appearances to the Viceroy, who is said to be the Sultan's vassal, and is subject to Great Britain.'[49] Ghislanzoni wrote in similar vein, concluding, 'The Khedive or Viceroy is apparently a sovereign, though vassal of the Sublime Porte in Istanbul and England's humble subject.'[50] Buselli considered Lord Cromer to be 'the governor, or rather, the true king of Egypt'.[51] This would seem to imply a negative view of the British occupation. On the contrary: opinion was entirely favourable to 'the wise government of the English authorities'.[52] Bonomelli summarises the first 12 years of successful English administration: putting the country's finances in order, public safety and great attention to the infrastructure, and concludes that it 'is of great benefit for Egypt in every way'.[53] Stoppani's genuine enthusiasm for the progress made by the British administration ('there is an overall improvement in all fields') may have deeper roots, however, for Stoppani believed, 'that it is a step forward for civilisation each time a civilised power takes over from the Turkish government'.[54] Perhaps he was already dreaming of Italy's conquest of Libya!

Conclusion

To conclude this brief analysis of what Italian travellers felt and wrote about Egypt, let me underscore that the texts we have examined, though often quite interesting and more balanced than equivalent books written by other foreigners, do not give a realistic picture of the situation in Egypt, and in no way reflect Italian knowledge of or interest in Egypt during that period.[55] Regarding this point, it is sufficient to recall the role played by the large Italian colony in helping to modernise the country, as well as the important posts occupied by Italians in the Egyptian administration up to the last decades of the nineteenth century. A second point is the interest that Italy had in the opening of the Suez Canal, of which it became one of the major beneficiaries. There was also the strong link between the house of Savoy and the Egyptian dynasty, and the great attention paid by the government in Rome to political developments in this neighbouring African country. Even the work of Bernardino Drovetti in collecting Egyptian finds, which led to the founding of the Egyptian Museum in Turin, as well as the work of Giovanni Battista Belzoni or of Ippolito Rosellini, who worked with Salt and Champollion, not to mention the founding of the Graeco-Roman Museum in Alexandria by Giuseppe Botti, barely receive a mention.[56] It is curious to note that the authors we have discussed make frequent use of stereotypes in describing their experiences in Egypt, quite forgetting that very similar stereotypes were used by travellers from northern Europe when they recorded their travels through Italy!

16

Nile Notes of a *Howadji*: American Travellers in Egypt, 1837–1903

Martin R. Kalfatovic

During its relatively short existence, of just over 150 years, the Smithsonian Institution has amassed a collection of more than 150 million objects, ranging in size and scope from microscopic insects to the Space Shuttle *Enterprise*. The Smithsonian's collection of Egyptian artefacts, though small, does have a number of interesting pieces. Of more interest are the supporting materials in various archival units and in the collections of Smithsonian Institution Libraries. The National Anthropological Archives (NAA, part of the Museum of Natural History) has an extensive collection of photographs, postcards, stereoscopic views and other images of Egypt. The National Portrait Gallery (NPG) has photographs, prints and paintings of many of the more well-known travellers. Access to these collections, as well as the Libraries' online catalogue, is available through the Internet.[1]

The Libraries' collections are particularly strong in literature about travel and voyages from around the world. Among the many works related to Egypt are: Pietro Martire d'Anghiera's *Petri Martyris ab Angleria* (1533); the *Description de l'Égypte* (1809–28); James Bruce's *Travels to Discover the Source of the Nile* 1790, also French and German editions; William George Browne's *Travels in Africa, Egypt, and Syria* (1799); Vivant Denon's *Monuments des arts . . .* (1829); Richard Robert Madden's *Travels in Turkey, Egypt, Nubia and Palestine . . .* (1833); David Roberts' *Egypt & Nubia* (1846–9); and William Henry Bartlett's *The Nile Boat* (1850). Additionally, the Smithsonian Institution Libraries has a large collection of ancillary material in support of research into travel (such as Baedeker guides and others that will be discussed later).

In March 1997, I mounted a small exhibition, *Nile Notes of a Howadji: American Travellers in Egypt*, at the Smithsonian. The exhibition was based on the Libraries' fine collection of American travel accounts of Egypt. This paper will focus on books displayed in this exhibition, but makes some digressions to discuss other American travellers.

American travellers in Egypt: 1837–1869

Among the first Americans to visit Egypt was John Ledyard (1751–1789). An adventurous traveller, who counted Thomas Jefferson and the Marquis de Lafayette among his friends, Ledyard went to Egypt at the suggestion of Sir William Banks. Arriving in Alexandria, he travelled on to Cairo, where, unfortunately, he died before he could leave an extensive account of his visit.[2]

In the early decades of the nineteenth century, Egypt and the adventures of travellers, archaeologists, and, of course, Giovanni Belzoni, captured the interest of the American reading public. What follows are but two of many journalistic examples.

In the 'Foreign Articles' of *The American Daily Advertiser* (Philadelphia), of 11 February 1824, a note reprinted from the *Cambridge Chronicle* recounts the latest exploits of Belzoni in North Africa. A few years later, a brief note in the 26 April 1827 issue of *Poulson's American Daily Advertiser* (Philadelphia) comments that a subscription is underway for the support of Sarah Belzoni 'widow of the celebrated traveller' and 'partner in the arduous undertakings of her husband' who is now living in Brussels.

Among the first Americans to leave full accounts of their Egyptian experience were George Bethune English (1787–1828) who travelled in 1820; George Rapelje (b.1771), travelling in 1822; George Jones, the chaplain aboard the USS *Delaware*, which visited Egypt in 1834; and John Lowell, Jr. (1799–1836) travelling in 1834–5.[3]

George Robbins Gliddon (1809–1857), born in Devonshire, was taken to Egypt at an early age by his father, John Gliddon (later United States consul at Alexandria). The younger Gliddon is perhaps best known for his Egyptological works (including *Otia Ægyptiaca*) and for his extensive speaking tour of the United States in the 1840s, which was illustrated with objects collected by Colonel Cohen of Baltimore. For those interested in travellers to Egypt, however, it is Gliddon's reprinting of the Consular Register of Americans who travelled to Egypt during 1832–42 – many of whom would later write on Egypt – that is more interesting (see Appendix I).

This register is appended to one of the more interesting documents related to travel to Egypt. Gliddon's *'Appendix'* to the *American in Egypt* (1842) was published in response to James Ewing Cooley's *The American in Egypt* (1842). Cooley (1802–82), a New York State senator, book dealer and minor poet, wrote a witty and satirical account of his trip to Egypt. Unfortunately, he sometimes played loosely with the facts and lifted many illustrations from other sources. Cooley caricatures David Bushnell (called 'Nebby Daoud' by Cooley), an American living in Alexandria, and goes on at length with a scurrilous parody of the British in Egypt (calling characters the 'Wrinkelbottoms', 'Mr. Sneezebiter', the 'Rev. Dunderlix' and the like). Meeting with John Gliddon, Cooley says, 'He put on an air of great pomposity, and appeared conceited, insincere, and vain' (p. 366). Gliddon, or 'Baron Pompolino', as Cooley calls him, though living in Egypt for twenty years, is 'as ignorant as an old Egyptian mummy, just pulled out of the tombs' (p. 367) of what would be of interest to a traveller such as Cooley. In his *Appendix*, Gliddon vigorously defends the honour of his father and others mentioned by Cooley.

It was, however, John Lloyd Stephens (1805–52) who became the first American to write a truly popular account of his travels in Egypt. By the 1850s, Americans were beginning to visit Egypt and western Asia in greater numbers than ever before. For much of this early period, a trip to Egypt and up the Nile aboard a native *dhahabiyeh* (river-boat) was an experience for most adventurous traveller, or *howadji* – a Turkish word originally meaning 'merchant' or 'shopkeeper'. *Howadji* soon became a term applied by local inhabitants to all foreign travellers. In 1851, George William Curtis popularised the term in his work, *Nile Notes of a Howadji*. Said Curtis, '. . . we played only the part of Howadji, which is the universal name for traveler – the "Forestiero" of Italy' (p. 19).

From this first period of travel, I would like to touch on a few specific travellers whose accounts are in the collections of the Libraries.

John Lloyd Stephens's works stand foremost of those in the Libraries' collection. As his work is suitable for the subject of many papers, I will simply note that Stephens is represented in our collection by four editions of *Incidents of Travel in Egypt, Arabia Petræ and the Holy Land* and numerous copies and editions of his later travels in Central America.

Our next traveller is George William Curtis, who, as a youth, spent two years at Brook Farm, Massachusetts, the Utopian community founded by members of the Transcendentalist Movement, and became influenced by Ralph Waldo Emerson. In 1846, at the age of 22, Curtis left for four years of travel in Europe, Egypt and western Asia. Publishing travel letters in the *New York Tribune*, upon his return, they were worked into two travel books, *Nile Notes of a Howadji* (1851) and *The Howadji in Syria* (1852).

Curtis spent the 1849–50 season in Egypt. Sailing aboard the *dhahabiyeh Ibis*, he travelled as far south as the temple complex of Abu Simbel. Of the colossal figures of Ramesses he noted, 'The face of one of these Aboo Simbel figures teaches more of elder Egypt than any hieroglyphed history which any Old Mortality may dig out' (p. 209). Narrating his travels in the third person, Curtis refers to himself as the *Howadji* throughout the work. Less interested in antiquities than contemporary Egypt, Curtis revels in the exotic elements of the country.

The Libraries' copy of his work is inscribed by Curtis: 'The Howadji's Aunt Eleanor from Himself – March 1851.'

Next is Bayard Taylor. He is represented in the Libraries' collections by *A Journey to Central Africa* (1854). As a side note, I will also mention that the delightful oil on canvas portrait of Taylor by Thomas Hicks, 'Portrait of Bayard Taylor in Oriental Costume' (1855), is in the collection of the National Portrait Gallery, Smithsonian Institution.

Our next traveller is William Cowper Prime, a New York City lawyer. He and his wife, Mary Trumbull Prime, were keen collectors of art. Travelling widely in pursuit of items for their collections, Prime wrote accounts of their travels in such works as *Owl Creek Letters* (1848) and *The Old House by the River* (1853).

The Primes travelled to Africa and West Asia in 1855–6, with Mr and Mrs J. Hammond Trumbull. This trip resulted in *Tent Life in the Holy Land* (1857) and *Boat Life in Egypt and Nubia* (1857). In the latter, Prime recounts his voyage from Alexandria to deep into Nubia. He also includes advice for those contemplating a winter visit to Egypt:

> You will need in Egypt ordinary clothing, such as would be worn in New York in May or the latter part of September, with overcoats for cold changes. No special provision in this respect need be made (p. 497).

In his preface, Prime thanks the Smithsonian Secretary, Joseph Henry, for providing 'such introductions as enabled me to prosecute my explorations in Egypt with satisfactory success' (p. vi).

Prime's brother, the noted Presbyterian clergyman and author, Samuel Irenæus Prime, also travelled to Egypt and wrote of his experiences in *Travels in Europe and the East* (1855).

Our next traveller is Henry Martyn Harman, a professor of ancient languages and literature at Dickinson College, Carlisle, Pennsylvania, also travelled to Egypt in 1869 by way of England, France and Italy. Upon his arrival in Egypt, Harman was struck by the Alexandrian entrepôt and commented:

> What a strange city this Alexandria is! The European or American, who for the first time lands at Alexandria, seems to be in another world. The transition from Naples to Alexandria is sudden. What a mixture of inhabitants you see! (p. 72)

Interspersing quotes from other authors, Harman's account includes his own measurements of various monuments and meticulous notation of his movements and expenditures:

> On Monday morning, quarter to nine, December 6, I left by railroad for Cairo. The fare, second class, was about seventeen and a half francs, and I had to pay two and a half rupees (about 75p) for my trunk (pp. 77–8).

The Libraries' copy of this work is inscribed, 'with the high regards of the author', to Spencer F. Baird, then Assistant Secretary (later Secretary) of the Smithsonian Institution.

American travellers in Egypt: 1870–1903

What began as a small trickle of American travellers to Egypt in the early part of the nineteenth century became a steady stream by the first years of the twentieth century.

By the late 1860s, Thomas Cook and Son began offering Nile excursions on steamers and luxurious *dhahabiyeh*s, reducing much of the hardship of earlier travel. These conveniences brought more American visitors to Egypt, ranging from noted public figures to Midwestern businessmen and their families. Soon, the exotic locales of Nubia and the oases of the western Sahara Desert were offered as de rigueur stops on the Grand Tour for American travellers.

In 1867, Samuel Langhorne Clemens, in the guise of Mark Twain, made a tour of Europe, Egypt and the Holy Land and described them in his book *Innocents Abroad* (1869). Americans who later travelled through these same regions liked to retell Twain's witty anecdotes and observations, and compared them to their own experiences.

A number of other Americans who published books based on their own journeys to Egypt, including Lincoln's Secretary of State, William H. Seward, and his daughter, Olivia (1871); essayist and poet, Ralph Waldo Emerson (1872–3); industrialist, Andrew Carnegie (1879); journalist, Richard Harding Davis (1892); illustrator, Charles Dana Gibson (1897–8); and writer, Henry Adams (1898).[4]

Among the other Americans visiting Egypt at this time, but with a much different purpose, were hundreds of Civil War veterans who joined the army of the khedive Ismail and served in his Ethiopian wars. Among those who wrote accounts of their adventures were William Wing Loring, Charles Chaillé-Long and William Dye.

After a brief career in law, Charles Dudley Warner joined the staff of the *Hartford Evening Press* in 1860. Joining forces with his fellow Hartford resident, Samuel Clemens, Warner co-wrote the novel, *The Gilded Age* (1873). Clemens' *Innocents Abroad* (1869) set an example for Warner, who brought his own keen humour to bear on Egypt when he published his own account, *My Winter on the Nile: among the mummies and Moslems* (1876), after his trip in 1874–5. Apologising for his own addition to the literature, Warner comments:

> I suppose that volumes enough have been written about Egypt to cover every foot of its arable soil if they were spread out, or to dam the Nile if they were dumped into it, and to cause a drought in either case if they were not all interesting and the reverse of dry (p. 18).

Warner's extensive visit included a trip to Alexandria and Cairo, where he stayed at Shepheard's Hotel. For his Nile cruise, he engaged William Cowper Prime's dragoman and sailed aboard the *dhahabîyeh Rip Van Winkle* as far south as Wadi Halfa.

Ulysses S. Grant, the former United States president, began his round-the-world trip in 1877. Grant's trip captured the fancy of the

American public and no fewer than six accounts were written by journalists who covered it, making it one of the earliest 'media events'.[5]

Travelling with his wife, Julia, and son, Jesse, Grant stopped off in Egypt in 1878. He met a number of dignitaries during his visit, including the Khedive and Henry Stanley. After visiting Cairo, Grant and his party sailed up the Nile as far as the temple of Philae.

John Russell Young, a noted journalist who had worked for the *New York Tribune* under Horace Greely, and, beginning in 1872, for the *New York Herald*'s European editorial office in London, was sent to cover Grant's trip. Commenting on Grant's impressions of Cairo, Young noted:

> He [Grant] takes no interest in the ruins, believing Cairo to be more interesting because of the cafés, which remind him of Paris, than the Pyramids, which he regards as entirely useless.[6]

Other notable accounts of Grant's trip include Elbert Farman's *Along the Nile with General Grant* (1904). Farman, the American Consul General at Cairo, gave ex-President Grant and his entourage the royal treatment. After a brief stop in Alexandria, Farnam recounts Grant's visit to Cairo (including that to the Pyramids, which the General declined to climb) before sailing up the Nile to Luxor; during his progress he was hailed by the local people as the 'king of America'. Even with all this attention, however, Grant seemed a bit grouchy:

> On another occasion, just after we had started out, the General on a horse and Mrs Grant and myself on donkeys, Mrs Grant, looking back and not seeing her son asked, 'Where is Jesse?' The General quickly replied, 'If we wait for stragglers, we shall never get there'.[7]

Jesse Grant himself wrote of the trip in his *In the Days of my Father General Grant* (1925). Jesse writes a brief but entertaining account of the stop in Egypt:

> All of the older American officers in the Khedive's army proved to be old friends. General Loring and most of the others had fought on the side of the Confederacy, but their greeting of father showed only genuine friendship and admiration.[8]

Charles Edwin Wilbour, whose collection formed the basis of the collection of Egyptian antiquities in the Brooklyn Museum, travelled throughout Egypt on numerous expeditions between 1880 and 1891. Meeting with famous people from the world of Egyptology, such as Gaston Maspero and Emile Brugsch, his letters give an intimate account of life in Egypt for the archaeologist. He also mentions the Smithsonian in a few letters:

> On learning that the English are raising money for digging in Egypt, he [the American consul] proposes to get the Smithsonian Institution to do so too and I am to take him to see M. Maspero about it to-morrow (from Cairo, 11 November 1881) (p. 77).

And another: 'Aly gave Cox two mummies which he will send to the Smithsonian or somewhere else' (from Luxor, 2 March 1886) (p. 373). Initial research as to whether the mummies in the collections of the Smithsonian are those referenced by Wilbour or from another source has been inconclusive.

Martin Brimmer was a traveller with a different agenda. He was a noted Boston businessman and one of the founders of the city's Museum of Fine Arts. Brimmer travelled to Egypt around 1890 with his close family, as well as his niece, Minna Timmins Chapman.

Brimmer and Chapman's *Egypt: Three Essays on the History, Religion and Art of Ancient Egypt* (1892) deals almost exclusively with the title subject, though there is some description of their travels in Egypt. In the preface, Brimmer notes:

> When the traveller on the Nile has recovered from his first impression of astonishment at the vast remains of monumental art about him, he is moved to inquire into their history and significance (Preface).

Brimmer's interest in Egypt stretched back to 1863, when he purchased the American artist Elihu Vedder's well-known work, 'The Questioner of the Sphinx', which Brimmer later donated to the Museum of Fine Art, Boston. Though Vedder painted this in 1863, the artist did not visit Egypt until 1879–80. Vedder's brief notes on Egypt – recounted in his unusual autobiography, *The Digressions of V.* (1910) – reflect his unique literary style.

Moving from the museum to the stage brings us to Maude Adams, America's most popular actress in the early twentieth century. Her starring roles included Joan of Arc, Chanticleer and the popular Peter Pan. In

1903, Adams made a trip to Egypt[9] that was later related as 'On the Dessert with Maude Adams' in *The Ladies' Home Journal*, by Lucy Leffingwell Cable. The actress relished the active life of an American tourist in Egypt, as Cable describes in this highlight from Adams's visit, 'Then Miss Adams – or was it "Peter Pan" – was eager for a real camel ride, a long one just for the sake of riding' (p. 7). Adams later penned her own version of her travels for *The Ladies' Home Journal* in 1926. From this account, Adams comments on the Nile, 'wonder upon wonders – the Nile; older than the Pyramids, yet always young; the mother of Egypt' (p. 22).

Charles Lang Freer (1854–1919), a Detroit industrialist, founded the museum that houses the Smithsonian's collection of Asian art, the Freer Gallery. In the Gallery's archives is the correspondence relating to Freer's five trips to Asia. Travelling by sea, he often passed through Egypt on his way east. While in Egypt, Freer wrote to his good friend, Colonel Frank J. Hecker; in addition to discussing his acquisition of various Egyptian ceramics and manuscripts, he made some interesting comments on contemporary Egypt, such as this one on Shepheard's Hotel, in a letter from 1909:

> Tell Louise that old Shepheards remains as dirty and attractive as ever, but new hotels and buildings have sprung up like toad stools since her time, and now, in summer, are empty and ghostly as the ancient ruined mosques.[10]

American travellers in Egypt: guides and handbooks

The first American visitors to Egypt used accounts of the region written by Herodotus and other classical writers as their travel guides. By the mid-nineteenth century, American travellers were supplementing these accounts with travel narratives by British and French writers. Publishers, travel operators and hoteliers soon began to provide a wide variety of guides and handbooks for travellers. Egyptologists and Biblical scholars were commissioned to write works about antiquities and Egypt's place in biblical history. Novelists wrote fictionalised accounts of life in Egypt that many travellers carried with them to while away the time spent aboard their *dhahabiyeh*.

The Smithsonian Institution Libraries has a large collection of this ancillary material. A complete collection of Baedeker's little red

'Handbooks' is notable, as is a well-worn but complete copy of William Pembroke Fetridge's *Harper's Hand-book for Travellers in Europe and the East* (1871). Of particular interest is a copy of *Cairo and Egypt: A Practical Handbook for Visitors to the Land of the Pharaohs* (c. 1897–1917), published by Shepheard's Hotel. This small guidebook to Egypt was published for guests staying at the hotel.

Conclusion

In an issue of *The North American Review* from 1839, Egypt was described by the anonymous reviewer of John Lloyd Stephens' *Incidents of Travel in Egypt* as:

> a quarter of the world, where comparatively few [Americans] have travelled, but where we anticipate they will soon penetrate, with all their characteristic ardor and enterprise (p. 184).

As the century progressed, travel became easier and the reviewer's prediction became a reality. So, in 1895, we find Agnes Repplier's (1855–1950) account of 'Christmas Shopping in Assuân' in *Atlantic Monthly* where she notes, 'shopping on the Nile is a very different matter from shopping on Chestnut Street or Broadway' (p. 681).

By 1908, travel accounts were no longer tales of adventure and hardship, but of the tongue-in-cheek travails described by Lillian C. Gilpin in 'To the Pyramids with a Baby Carriage' appearing in *Harper's Weekly*:

> The wheels of the baby's 'Desert Schooner' cling sorrily, so we halt, rig up a sort of awning over the little one's head by means of a cotton sheet brought for the purpose, and a couple of maize sticks pulled at the foot of the great monuments to Time (p. 30).

For some, more bored than awed, this new traveller's Egypt had lost the sense of wonder that earlier travellers experienced. Travellers, such as the woman quoted in Constance Fenimore Woolson's (1840–94) *Cairo in 1890*: 'I have spent nine long days on this boat, staring from morning till night. One cannot stare at a river forever, even if it is the Nile! Give me a thimble' (p. 665).

The American experience in Egypt has left an important and fascinating record in a wealth of travel accounts though perhaps they lack the scope and grandeur of European accounts. As Woolson noted later, the American experience is still in its infancy compared to that of the European nations:

> In connection with the pyramids, the English may be said to have devoted themselves principally to measurements. The genius of the French, which is ever that of expression, has invented the one great sentence about them. So far, the Americans have done nothing by which to distinguish themselves; but their time will come, perhaps. One fancies that Edison will have something to do with it. (pp. 670–1)

In retrospect, we can now see it was not with Edison, but with rather the collected volumes of travel accounts that Americans made their mark.

APPENDIX I
List of Americans Travelling to Egypt, 1789–1915[11]

*Gliddon (see Appendix II).
**[12]

1789
John Ledyard.

1820
George Bethune English.

1822
George Robins Gliddon, George Rapelji.

1832
Col. M.J. Cohen,* The Family of the late Dr Kirkland,* Rev. Eli Smith.*

1833
John W. Hammersley,* Ralph J. Izard,* J.L. Stackpole.*

1834
William B. Hodgson,* George Jones, John Lowell, Jr., The Family of the late Commodore D. Patterson, U.S.N.*

1836
Horatio Allen,* W. McHenry Boyd,* James Augustus Dorr,* Richard K. Haight,* Sarah (Rogers) Haight, Richard Randolph,* John Lloyd Stephens.

1837
Lewis Cass.*

1838
Henry Bard,* Dudley M. Haydon,* Dr Jackson,* H.P. Marshall,* Valentine Mott, Henry McVickar,* Rev. Dr Edward Roberson,* Samuel Waring,* Rev. George Whiting.*

1839
William J. Bennett,* Rev. S.H. Calhoun,* James Ewing Cooley, H.A. Cram,* F.R. Fleming,* Rev. S.R. Houston,* Col. H.A. Ireland,* Rev. Dr C. Lowell,* Stephen Olin, George Sumner,* C.R. Swords,* J.I. Tucker,* S.H. Whitlock,* Aaron Smith Willington.*

1840
Fairfax Catlett,* Thomas Dehone,* Rev. J.H. Hill,* H.B. Humphrey,* George Lewis,* Daniel Lowe,* Rev. J. May,* John S. Miller,* Prof. N. Moore,* Edward Joy Morris, Daniel Paine,* Thomas M. Preston.*

1841
J.O. Colt,* Gen J. Harlan,* C.W. King,* David Millard, F. Oliver,* Alexander Van Rensellaer,* Clemuel Green Ricketts.

1842
Rev. C.W. Andrews,* John Cooke,* Daniel Giraud,* Jacob Giraud,* John Guy Vassar.

1844
John Price Durbin, Francis Schroeder.

1848
William Furniss, Jesse Ames Spencer, Jonathan Mayhew Wainwright.

1849
Howard Crosby, George William Curtis, Matthew Flournoy Ward.

1850
Caroline Paine, Jerome Van Crowninshield Smith.

1851
John B. Ireland, Bayard Taylor.

1852
William Cullen Bryant, Horatio Black Hackett, Randal William MacGavock, Joseph Thomas.

1853
David F. Dorr, Benjamin Dorr, Jane Anthony Eames, John Beasly Greene, Joseph Parrish Thompson, Thomas Cogswell Upham.

1854
Samuel Irenaeus Prime, Andrew Watson.

1855
Samuel Wheelock Fiske, William Cowper Prime.

1856
Warren Isham, Herman Melville, George Francis Train.

1857
Benjamin Bausman, George Leighton Ditson.

1859
William Mason Turner, Aaron Ward.

1860
William Hoffman, Gulian Lansing.

1861
David Austin Randall.

1863
Edward Lord Clark.

1864
Harriet Trowbridge Allen.

1865
Elizabeth Rundle Charles.

1866
Samuel Langhorne Clemens, Charles Carleton Coffin, Harry Harewood Leech, Sylvanus Dryden Phelps, William Wilkins Warren.

1867
Emily (Allen) Severance, Alvan S. Southworth, Eugene Vetromile.

1868
Henry Whitney Bellows, Clara (Erskine) Clement Waters.

1869
Edwin De Leon, William McEntyre Dye, Henry Martyn Harman, William Wing Loring.

1870
Emerson Andrews, Charles Chaill-Long, Louise M. (Roope) Griswold, Frederick W. Holland,** Edward Dorr Griffin Prime.

1871
James Brooks, Olive Risley Seward, J.J. Smith.

1872
Thomas Applegate, Ralph Waldo Emerson, Jacob R. Freese.

1873
Samuel Colcord Bartlett, Orville Justus Bliss, Augustus Warren Edward, Augustus Hoppin, Thomas W. Knox, James Martin Peebles, George Albert Smith, John Vanderslice, Henry White Warren.

1874
Thomas Gold Appleton, William Perry Fogg, Henry Bascom Ridgaway, Bayard Taylor, Charles Dudley Warner.

1875
Mary E. (Galloway) Giffen, Sarah Furnas Wells.

1876
Mrs L.L. Adams, Benjamin Robbins Curtis, Harriet Elizabeth (Tucker) Francis, Mrs L.C. Lane, Charles Warner Stoddard, Ellen Hardin Walworth, G.E. Winants.

1877
Eugene Russell Hendrix, Enoch Mather Marvin.

1878
Elbert Eli Farman, Jesse Root Grant, Ulysses S. Grant, James Dabney McCabe, Joseph Moore, Jr., John Russell Young.

1879
Andrew Carnegie, Henry H. Gorringe, Sullivan Holman M'Collester.

1880
Lucy S. Bainbridge, William Potter Davis, John A.J. Kending, George B. McClellan,** Charles Edwin Wilbour.

1881
De Robigne Mortimer Bennett, Samuel Sullivan Cox, Theodore Ledyard Cuyler, Simon Wolf.

1882
Joseph A. Boll, Walter Harriman, George Robert Salisbury.

1883
Maturin Murray Ballou, John W. Greenwood.

1884
Hiram Francis Fairbanks, Mary Louise (Ninde) Gamewell, John B. Gorman, Anna P. Little, John Henry Paynter, Henry Frederic Reddall, Susan Arnold (Elston) Wallace.

1885
J.J. Escher, T. Holmes, Osmun Johnson, Lillian Leland, George Moerlein, George Edward Raum, Agnes Repplier.**

1886
Jesse Milton Emerson, Philip Phillips, D.N. Richardson.

1887
Isaac Newton Lewis, Milton Stewart, Zachary Taylor Sweeney.

1888
Lenamay Green, Carter Henry Harrison, Edward Herbruck, Sullivan Holman M'Collester, Clara Moyse Tadlock, Edward L. Wilson.**

1889
Daniel F. Beatty, Nathan Hubbell, James Pfeiffer, Charles McCormick Reeve, Peyton L. Stanton, Thomas de Witt Talmage, Elihu Vedder, Thomas Wallace, Walter Andrew Whittle.

1890
Martin Brimmer, Beverly Carradine, Charles J. Gillis, Robert Pollok Kerr, Robert Meredith, Caryl S. Parrott, Milton Henry Stine, Constance Fenimore Woolson, Louisa (Stephens) Wright.

1891
Edwin Holland Blashfield,** Charles Thomas Walker.

1892
Richard Harding Davis, Harry Clay Palmer.

1893
Mary Thorn Carpenter, Eliza McMillan, Daniel Long Miller, Frederick Courtland Penfield, Edward Griffin Read.

1894
James Henry Breasted, Francis Edward Clark, John F. Floyd, William Baxter Godbey, William Henry Jackson, Florida E. (Watts) Smythe, Thomas De Witt Talmage, George Cydus Tenney, Edward Stansbury Wilson.

1895
George Lambert, Emilie Jane (Butterfield) Meriman Loyson, Robert Stuart MacArthur, Archibald McLean, Daniel Long Miller, Charles Parsons, Seneca Roy Stoddard, Anthony S. Underhill.

1896
Mary S. Allen, John Henry Barrows, Margaret (McDonald) Bottome, Francis Edward Clark, Sarah Diodati Gardiner, Mary Perkins Quincy.

1897
Lillian Lida Bell, Charles Dana Gibson, Thomas Skelton Harrison, Lucia A. Chapman Palmer, James M. Peebles, Walter Scott Perry, Delight Sweetser.

1898
Henry Adams, William McMahon.

1899
Finley Acker, Mrs Lee Bacon, Nellie Sims Beckman, Harry Westbrook Dunning, Abraham Van Doren Honeyman, Chalmers Roberts,** Amos Daniel Wenger.

1900
John Fisher Anderson, Suemma Coleman, Elmer Ulysses Hoenshel, Isabella H. Mathews, Minnie Stuart Crawford Ross.

1901
Maltbie Davenport Babcock, William Eleazar Barton, Nahum Harwood, Sigmund Krausz, Francis I. Maule, A. Mellander, Gulian Lansing Morrill, Thomas Nelson Page, Arthur Francis Pennock, John Collinsworth Simmons.

1902
Henry Fuller, James M. Loring, Harry Steele Morrison, Anthony Zurbonsen.

1903
Maude Adams,** George John Blatter, Mary Gorman (travelled with Maude Adams), Edward C. Horn, Miss Ray Rockman (travelled with Maude Adams), George Aaron Barton, Charles Chilton Moore, Mary D. (Richardson) Rosengarten.

1904
William Sampson Brooks, Enoch Edwin Byrum, Frederick Carleton Chamberlin, William Eleroy Curtis, Thomas Medary Iden, Henry Cunningham Rew, Elliott Francis Studley, Charles Gallaudet Trumbull, Robert William Van Schoick.

1905
Harry Alverson Franck, William Baxter Godbey, Jerome Alfred Hart, Edgar Watson Howe, Allie Irick, James C. Oehler, William Webb Wheeler.

1906
George Ade, William Jennings Bryan, George Lister Carlisle, Patrick Cudahy, James E. Kendall.**

1907
Blanche Mabury Carson, Frederick Norton Finney, C. Henry Forster, Ellen Mary (Hayes) Peck, Horace A. Taylor, Marshall Pinckney Wilder.

1908
Leander Adams Bigger, John Milton Gardner, Lillian C. Gilpin,** Amasa Stone Mather, Mrs Frances Elizabeth (Morgan) Matthews, Edwin William Stephens, Grace Maxine Stein, Christopher C. Young.

1909
Daniel Doane Bidwell, Harriet White Fisher, Benjamin Lee Gordon, Lydia Ethel Farmer Painter, Irene Simmonds, William Spooner Smith.

1910
George Hoyt Allen, George Tome Bush, Albert Charles Cosman, William Givens Frizell, Annabelle Kent, Peter August Mattson, William Ford Nichols, Theodore Roosevelt, William Webb Wheeler, Mrs Helen Parker (Wilson) Willard.

1911
Lydia Dunford Alder, Alfred Charles Benson Fletcher, Henrietta Bennett Freeman, Solomon Johnson, Angie Villette (Warren) Perkins, Milton Henry Stine, Alma (Bridwell) White.

1912
Frances Gordon (Paddock) Alexander, Nettie Fowler Dietz, Charles William Elsey, George Hamlin Fitch, Arthur Wellington Hart, Gulian Lansing Morrill, Lewis Parkhurst, Howard Stelle Fitz Randolph, Charles C. Royce, C.B. Struthers, Flavel Benjamin Tiffany.

1913
Acken Gordon Bradt, Mary Elizabeth Crouse, Carlton Danner Harris, Minnie Tising Norfleet, Sophie A. Poe, Frederick George Smith, Sidney J. Thomas, David Snethen Warner, Mary Frances Willard.

1914
Sarah Robb Congleton, Kate Eldridge Glaspell, Joseph M. Rowland, George Fletcher Oliver.

1915
Archie Bell.

APPENDIX II
American Travellers to Egypt, 1832–1842

As recorded in the United States Consular Register reprinted in George Robin Gliddon's *'Appendix' to the American in Egypt*, 28–30.

1832
The Family of the late Dr Kirkland, Boston, Col. M.J. Cohen, Baltimore, Rev. Eli Smith, Boston, 1832-7-8.[13]

1833
John W. Hammersley, Esq., NY, J.L. Stackpole, Esq., Boston, Ralph J. Izard, Esq., S. Carolina.

1834
The Family of the late Commodore D. Patterson, U.S.N., William B. Hodgson, Esq., Virginia,[14] The Family of the late John A. Lowell, Jr., Esp., of Boston, who travelled in Egypt in 1834 and 1835.[15]

1836
John L. Stephens, Esq., NY,[16] James Augustus Dorr, Esq., Boston, R.K. Haight, Esq., New York,[17] Richard Randolph, Esq., Philadelphia, Horatio Allen, Esq., New York, W. McHenry Boyd, Esq., Baltimore.

1837
The Honorable Lewis Cass, Paris.[18]

1838
Rev. Dr Edward Roberson, New York, 1838-41, Henry McVickar, Esq., NY, _____ Bard, Esq., New York, Dr Valentine Mott, New York,[19] Dr Jackson, New York, Samuel Waring, Esq., NY, Dudley M. Haydon, Esq., Kentucky, H.P. Marshall, Esq., New York, 1838–9, Rev. George Whiting, NY.

1839
Wm. J. Bennett, Esq, New York, C.R. Swords, Esq., New York, A.S. Willington, Esq., Charleston,[20] J.I. Tucker, Esq., New York, S.H. Whitlock, Esq., New York, F.R. Fleming, Esq., New York, H.A. Cram, Esq., New York, Col. H.A. Ireland, New York, Rev. S.H. Calhoun, S. Carolina, Rev. Dr C. Lowell, Boston, George Sumner, Esq., Boston,[21] Rev. S.R. Houston, Virginia.

1840
H.B. Humphrey, Esq., Boston, Edward Joy Morris, Esq., Philadelphia,[22] Fairfax Catlett, Esq., New York, Prof. N. Moore, New York, Daniel Lowe, Esq., New York, _____ Paine, Esq., New York, John S. Miller, Esq., Philadelphia, Thomas M. Preston, Esq., Charleston, _____ Dehone, Esq., Charleston, George Lewis, Esq., New London, Rev. J.H. Hill, Athens and NY, Rev. _____ May, Philadelphia.

1841
C.W. King, Esq., Canton and N.Y., Gen J. Harlan, Philadelphia, F. Oliver, Esq., Baltimore, J.O. Colt, Esq., Baltimore, Alexander Van Rensellaer, Esq., Albany.

1842
John Cooke, Esq., Philadelphia, Rev. C.W. Andrews, Virginia, Daniel Giraud, Esq., New York, Jacob Giraud, Esq., New York.

NOTES

1. The NAA and Libraries catalogue is available via SIRIS (the Smithsonian Institution Research Information System), via the World Wide Web at http://www.siris.si.edu or telnet at telnet://siris.si.edu. The National Portrait Gallery collection is available at http://www.npg.si.edu.
2. See Jared Sparks, *The Life of John Ledyard, the American Traveller* (Cambridge, Mass., Hilliard and Brown, 1828) for more details of his life.
3. See Appendix II to the present chapter for a fuller list of American travellers to Egypt.
4. See http://www.cva.edu/kalfatovic/egypt.htm for bibliographic citations. for works by these travellers.
5. The six accounts are: Hicks (1879), Keating (1879), McCabe (1879), Packard (1880), Palmer (1880), Young (1879). Two additional accounts of Grant's trip are: Farman (1904) and Grant (1925).
6. Young (1879), I, p. 232.
7. Farman, E.E. *Along the Nile with General Grant* (New York, The Grafton Press, 1904), pp. 72–3.
8. Jesse Grant, *In the Days of my Father General Grant* (New York and London, 1925), p. 267.
9. Additional information on Adams' trip to Egypt can be found in *Maude Adams: an Intimate Portrait* by Phyllis Adams (New York, G.P. Putnam's Sons, 1956).
10. Letter to Colonel Hecker, dated Shepheard's Hotel, Cairo, 28 July 1909.
11. Extracted from Martin R. Kalfatovic, *Nile Notes of a Howadji: American Travellers in Egypt*, exhibition material at the Smithsonian Institution (Washington, DC, 1992), except where noted.
12. See http://www.cva.edu/kalfatovic/egypt.htm for bibliographic citations.
13. Smith (1801–57) was co-author with Edward Robinson (1794–1863) of *Biblical Researches in Palestine, Mount Sinai, Arabia Petræa, and Egypt* (3 vols., London, John Murray, 1841).
14. William B. Hodgson (1800–71) is the author of *Notes on Northern Africa, the Sahara and Soudan, in Relation to the Ethnography, Languages, History, Political and Social Conditions, of the Nations of Those Countries* (New York, Wiley and Putnam, 1844) and *Remarks on the Recent Travels of Dr Barth in Central Africa, or Soudan: A Paper Read before the Ethnological Society of New York, November, 1858* (New York, s. n., 1858?), 18 pages.
15. Lowell's travels in Egypt are recounted in Edward Everett, *A Memoire of John Lowell, Jr.* (Boston, Charles C. Little and James Brown, 1879).
16. Author of *Incidents of Travel in Egypt, Arabia Petrae and the Holy Land*.
17. Richard K. Haight is the author of the poem, *Not the 'Burden', but the Glory of Egypt: Not the Pharoahs, but the Hierophants, Kings and Priests 'After the Order of Melchisedeck'* (New York, printed for private circulation only, 1843), 12 pages. See also 'Sarah (Rogers) Haight' in Kalfatovic (1992).
18. James Ewing Cooley dedicated his *American in Egypt* to Cass (1782–1866). Cass was US minister to France (1836–42) and an important figure in US politics and government, serving in the US senate, the cabinets of various administrations, and as presidential candidate.

19 Dr Valentine Mott (1795–1865) is the author of *Travels in Europe and the East* (New York, Harper & Brothers, 1842).
20 Aaron Smith Willington would later write an account of his European travels in *A Summer's Tour of Europe, in 1851: In a Series of Letters, Addressed to the Editors of the* Charleston Courier (Charleston, Walker & James, 1852).
21 George Sumner (1817–63) would later write *Memoirs of the Pilgrims at Leyden* (Cambridge, Metcalf, 1845), 35 pages.
22 Morris (1815–81) was the author of *Notes of a Tour through Turkey, Greece, Egypt, Arabia Petræa, to the Holy Land: Including a Visit to Athens, Sparta, Delphi, Cairo, Thebes, Mt. Sinai, Petra* . . . (Philadelphia, Carey and Hart, 1842).

17

Romances and Realities of Travellers

Nadia El Kholy

This paper is not a historical survey of all the travel literature about Egypt written in the nineteenth century. I have been selective rather than exhaustive in my choice of texts. I have concentrated in my research on the makings of a literary Orient by looking at Muhammad Ali, Egypt's Viceroy from 1805 to 1849, and the major Cairo mosques that represent architectural monuments that are alien to the West and yet are indigenous to the Muslim people of the East and their culture. I will be discussing the following travellers: Ali Bey al-Abbasi, Augustus James St John, Georgiana Dawson Damer, Sophia Poole, John Petherick and Elliot Warburton. All were English except for Ali Bey who was a Spanish secret agent working for Napoleon Bonaparte and whose real name was Domingo Badia-y-Leblich.

The defining factor in my selection is that these individuals fictionalised the world they described. In fashioning a scene certain details were augmented and others carefully omitted. Travellers became less concerned with the task of conveying information and were more inclined to express their own personal impressions and experiences. The traveller's perspective is more prominent in their narratives than it was in previous accounts of the late eighteenth and early nineteenth centuries, which were primarily concerned with collecting information and presenting the Western reader with a 'repository of facts'. The earlier desire to inform seems to have passed; it was replaced by a desire to describe. Warburton, in his preface to *The Crescent and the Cross*, says: 'I have pursued no settled plan of writing or classification, but have spoken of each matter as it seemed to suggest itself in the course of a sort of imaginary conversation with the reader.'

Travellers to Egypt had a tendency to perceive in the reality the world that legend had painted. They came with inherited romantic and exotic ideas that were essentially derived from the world of the *Arabian Nights*. The Orient appeared to them as a system of representations framed by a whole set of meanings, beliefs and clichés that brought it into Western learning and Western consciousness. As a result of these pre-conceived ideas, the travellers' interpretations were sometimes a form of romantic restructuring of a reality that did not necessarily conform to their beliefs.

The nineteenth century produced travellers who had begun their voyage long before they actually embarked. They had absorbed many of the ideas and influences that they were to transmit to the East from their education and the books that they had read during their youth.[1] In some cases they were unable to transcend their cultural preconditioning in the process. The idea of penetrating the East preoccupied the British travellers of the Victorian period. Many thought that living as similar a life as possible to that lived by Easterners was the best way to unravel the mysteries of their society. Many of the disguised travellers – Ali Bey, for example – also changed their names. A disguise permitted its wearer to move from one racial category to another as if by magic. Moving from one racial category to another, shedding European clothes for Oriental garb, became a pleasant pastime for the traveller. Wearing a disguise, then, came to serve as leisured play-acting for the wealthy. Doing so appealed to a jaded Victorian/Western imagination by making a journey to the East more exotic, and seemed to allow the traveller closer access to a cloistered world that appeared to guard its secrets closely; the disguised person was playing at being Arab. Disguise was also used as a political weapon, since it was a means of infiltrating a society in order to gain information. The disguised travellers did not merge with the culture they were parodying. They felt themselves to be mentally, as well as physically, superior to those among whom they travelled.

Travel-writers' imperatives changed as a result. They no longer faithfully described objects, but rather gave the impressions made upon their imaginations by the ones they observed. They also began to identify and to describe scenes as 'picturesque'. Responses became stylised – for example:

> sailing on the moon-lit Nile has an inexpressible charm: every sight is softened, every sound is musical, every air breathes balm. The pyramids, silvered by the moon, tower over the dark palms, and the

broken ridges of the Arabian hills stand clearly out from the star-spangled sky. Distant lights, gleaming faintly among the scarce seen minarets, mark the site of Cairo, whose voices come at intervals as faintly to the ear . . . All nature seems so tranced, and all the world wound in such a dream, that we can scarcely realise our own identity.[2]

Instead of trying to convey an aspect of reality, as in the late eighteenth century, the travellers were now concerned with giving their own views.[3] Travellers were always tempted to 'render interesting' the matters they related, and sometimes fell into the trap of choosing and selecting to stress what would interest a Western reader.[4] Consequently, they could draw a picture coloured by Western bias for Western consumption. The emphasis shifts from description to impression, and subjective feeling has the upper hand. When confronted with reality, the travellers constantly searched for the appropriate metaphor. They were only too eager to catch a glimpse of a legendary world and to colour it with their own impressions:

> The graceful garb, the flowing beard, and the majestic appearance of Orientals, are very imposing to a stranger s eye. The rich colouring, the antique attitudes, the various complexions, that continually present themselves, form an unceasing series of tableaux vivant in an Eastern city.[5]

As a result, the Oriental world became established as the metaphor for the realities of dream, of imagination and, eventually, of unreality.

Contemporary Egypt was also part of the world that the traveller knew through the *Arabian Nights*, and so part of another world that also was imaginatively vivid and familiar. The *Arabian Nights* so well known to Western readers was widely accepted as a true portrait of the East. Walking in the streets and gardens of Cairo, travellers saw scenes that echoed the sensuous brilliance and dreamlike quality of the *Arabian Nights*:

> I never saw anything to be compared to the beauty of the Schoubra garden. It is quite an illustration of those described in the Arabian nights. It is formed in the original Grecian plan of garden: straight rows, but thickly planted, and covering three square miles in extent. The lemon, orange, myrtle, and pomegranate succeeded to and

touched each other, and below these, hedges of geranium in bright and full flower; the whole garden appeared to have been just watered, and produced the most refreshing and yet not overpowering fragrance.

We felt quite revived and enchanted, and might be excused for our constant and repeated terms of admiration, of 'Oh! how sweet! – Oh! how charming!'[6]

Descriptions of Cairo became fuller than they had been; the city's appearance and its most salient features: the citadel, the bazaar, the slave-market and the individual mosques – are described in some detail. With the help of their Arab disguise, travellers visited the more grand and famous mosques and gave detailed and accurate descriptions of them. Despite their efforts to catch the ethereal and mercurial quality of the fantasy world of the *Arabian Nights*, this occasionally evaded them. The contrast between the fantasy and the reality brought about a completely new view of the Orient – in certain cases a disappointing one:

> On entering the mosque I was much surprised at the scene which presented itself in the great hall, or portico . . . there was a confusion of noises, like what may be heard in a large school-room where several hundred boys are engaged in play; there were children bawling and crying; men and women calling to each other; and amid all this bustle, mothers and children were importuning every man of respectable appearance for the alms of the ashr . . . The mats, which are usually spread upon the pavement, had been removed; some pieces of old matting were just put in their stead, leaving many parts of the floor bare; and these, and every part, were covered with dust and dirt, brought in by the feet of many shoeless persons . . . I had not been many minutes in the mosque before my feet were almost black, with the dirt upon which I had trodden, and with that from other persons' feet which had trodden upon mine. The heat, too, was very oppressive.[7]

As passages such as this one show, travellers who had anticipated an Oriental world characterised by vivacity, light and mystery experienced an anti-climax. Gradually, however, the fantasy images became blurred and obscure, and others were superimposed in which the reality and not the mental image was dominant. This constant juggling of the romantic and the real is a common thread in the writings of nineteenth-century travellers. Their descriptions swing from the realistic to the impressionistic, and from the appealing to the disagreeable. Augustus St John visited al-Azhar Mosque and wrote:

> On arriving at the gateway, we doffed our slippers, and entered a marble-paved court, surrounded by an elegant colonnade, the entablature of which is adorned with arabesques of a bright red colour. Contrary to the ideas commonly prevailing in Europe, a large portion of the votaries consisted of ladies, who were walking to and fro without the slightest restraint, conversing with each other, and mingling freely among the men. The pulpit, constructed entirely of stone, adorned with slender pillars, and beautifully carved, greatly resembles the suggesta of Catholic churches, and stands at the extremity of the building, directly opposite the entrance. Numerous rows of marble columns, about two feet in diameter, extend the whole length of the edifice, supporting the roof, and creating an idea of grandeur: the pavement, likewise, is of marble.[8]

St John tells the Western reader about the discipline observed inside the mosque and conveys how he had been pleasantly surprised by the 'mingling' of the sexes, which was contrary to what had been understood previously about Muslim manners in relation to the behaviour of men and women inside the house of worship. It is also noticeable that St John draws several analogies between the mosque and the Catholic church, to provide points of reference for the Western reader. It seems that the travellers were incapable of recognising the beauty of Islamic architecture without comparing it to the standard European criteria: 'the mosque of the Sultan Hasan is near the citadel: it is remarkable for the boldness of its construction, is very high, and has a fine nave, which calls to the imagination the style of the European churches'.[9] This continual comparison with Western churches seems to be a common feature in most travellers' descriptions of mosques. When considering the Muhammad Ali mosque, the travellers followed once more the general consensus that Christian/Western architecture is aesthetically more acceptable than and hence superior to any other: 'Mehemet Ali has lately commenced the building of a new mosque, of which we were shewn the foundation and superstructure. It will be finer . . . than any existing in Cairo.'[10] It was believed that in the construction of that mosque, Muhammad Ali was aiming to imitate the European churches. Similarly, the redeeming factor of the Mu'ayyad Mosque is its imitation of Christian decoration and art:

> The mosque of Moeyed has made its reputation on purely architectural grounds . . . As the representation of the human form . . . was forbidden to the Moslem architects, they were compelled to eke out the baldness of the earliest mosques by an ornament which was not vain and sensuous, but commemorative of the Deity and the leading doctrines of Islamism. The object, in the first instance, was just as in Christian art, to make it the vehicle of religious sentiment.[11]

Travellers did not have the capacity to appreciate and describe Egyptian architecture without reference to European artistic conventions. It took them some time to grasp alien artistic concepts and start to develop a taste for them. They constantly commented on the mosques' bare and simple interiors, which to them were incompatible with their decorative and magnificent exteriors:

> The walls are generally quite plain, being simply whitewashed; but in some mosques the lower part of the wall of the place of prayer is lined with coloured marbles, and the other part ornamented with various devices executed in stucco, but mostly with texts of the Kur-an, . . . and never with the representation of anything that has life.[12]

In their assessment of what is architecturally beautiful about the Islamic monuments travellers are constantly decoding the unfamiliar elements and comparing them to what is familiar in their own culture. Hence, 'every pilgrim', as Edward Said states, 'sees things his own way'.[13] This is exemplified in the following passages describing mosques in Cairo:

> I have little to say of the mosques; they considerably disappointed my expectation . . . the whole aspect of the building reminds one of a gutted cathedral . . . nothing can be more naked and cheerless than the interior of a Moslem mosque.[14]

Compare this to Sophia Poole's commentary: 'Of the public buildings of Cairo, the most interesting certainly are the mosques . . . They are extremely picturesque, and exquisite taste is displayed in the variety and elegance of the mad'nehs or minarets.'[15] It is significant that to the travellers the mosques were once again the epitome of the various motifs of the Orient – whether it is considered a place of pilgrimage, a spectacle or *tableau vivant* or a place that needs to be discovered and observed scientifically or realistically. In the first two cases the mosques then rendered themselves as suitable artefacts for romanticising and reinterpreting the East and Islam, and were rich material for the traveller who was re-informing the Western reader. Even the actual trip to Egypt was undertaken by travellers to fulfil a latent desire to experience the Orient and also to decipher, understand and unravel its inward reality, wondering about the difference between the world from which they had come and the world in which they found themselves. The Near East as a whole and Egypt in particular continued to be the object of British political interest because of its strategic importance as a route to India. Muhammad Ali's activities were thereafter followed with interest – and with a certain degree of approval, for, in English eyes, he had

> manifested the design, not merely to found a dynasty . . . but at the same time to regenerate and conduct into the track of European civilisation a people demoralised and degraded by a thousand years of political servitude.[16]

Egypt was beginning to attract attention as an area in which a new political force was gathering momentum. As Muhammad Ali gained in power, travellers visited the country chiefly to report on the new order. In addition, they felt safe in Egypt. As one of them wrote:

> Travellers, so far as their personal safety is concerned, have reason to speak in the highest terms of the security afforded by the measures of Mohammed Ali, for their protection in every part of Egypt. I do not know of any European country where one may travel with greater safety than in Egypt.[17]

Egypt was certainly gaining in popularity as a result of the overland route and the warlike as well as the peaceful activities of Muhammad Ali. Visiting the Pasha was an important part of a certain type of tourist itinerary, and an interview with him became one of the necessary embellishments of any Egyptian travel book – to leave out mention of his works or commentary on the people under his rule was considered a grave injustice to the reader. Consequently, I will be examining two interviews by two very different travellers. The first is with John Petherick, a British engineer who was asked by Egypt's viceroy to find coal. Muhammad Ali believed in the value of specialists and the virtue of the expert. He searched them out, learned from them and made use of that knowledge. This is from Petherick's report:

> On the following day I was presented to his Highness Mehemet Ali Pasha . . . He was sitting on a raised divan, in a beautiful kiosk, in his justly celebrated gardens. Having been honoured with a chair a short distance opposite to him, he saluted me by gently raising his right hand, scrutinising me severely with his searching dark eyes . . . Addressing me he said, 'Welcome to Egypt.' I bowed. 'I have sent for you to travel in my country to search for minerals, but particularly for coal, of which I stand much in need.'[18]

The second interview is with Augustus St John, a traveller who wanted to write about Muhammad Ali's governmental policies. He wrote:

> I rode to the palace, . . . and, on arriving at the entrance, found a number of janisaries and other attendants, in their costly and gorgeous uniforms, lounging about the grand flight of steps which leads to the divan. Having ascended these stairs, we crossed several spacious halls whose lofty ceilings were painted in a chaste and elegant style, and, making our way through crowds of courtiers of all nations, arrived at the audience-chamber, where we found the Pasha and his minister, Boghos Ioussouff, standing at the extremity of the apartment ready to receive us, saluted us in the Turkish manner, repeating the *salam*, or, 'peace and welcome,' and placing his right hand upon his heart. When we had returned his Highness's salutation, our names were pronounced; upon which he took his seat on his lofty crimson divan, and desired me to sit down by his side. On this occasion, he placed himself, as usual, in a corner of the room; where, his whole person being involved in shadow, it was extremely difficult to detect the expression of his countenance, or the uneasy rapid motion of his eye.[19]

It is noticeable how in both passages the Orientalised setting is highlighted, with emphasis on the divan, the crimson colours, the elegance and the overall glamorous and magical atmosphere of the *Arabian Nights*. In accordance with the preconceived setting of the East is the reference to the shadows and the blurred and obscured countenance of the Pasha – all echoing the standard associations of the Orient as being mysterious, dark and threatening. As a contrast to this depiction of Muhammad Ali is the factual description of his outstanding personality as reported by Ali Bey, the Spanish secret agent who assuming the character of a prince of the Abbasids, was received in Cairo by Muhammad Ali:

> He received me with every sort of politeness. This prince, who is very brave, is still young; he is thin, and is marked with the small pox; he has quick lively eyes, and a certain air of defiance.[20]

Ali Bey says little about Muhammad Ali (no doubt he said more in his reports), except that he had plenty of common sense but lacked finesse. Muhammad Ali certainly realised that Ali Bey was no Abbasid, but allowed the spy to continue, since it suited his purpose of playing the Great Powers off against each other. Badia, too, noted his 'deep distrustful eyes'. Muhammad Ali was a short, stocky man with distinctive short forearms. He had blond hair, deep-set hazel-grey eyes, a small mouth and beautiful hands. People immediately noticed his eyes, which were constantly animated. A.A. Paton, who met him when he was long past his prime, remarked, 'if ever a man had an eye that denoted genius, Mohamed Ali was that person. Never dead or quiescent, it was fascinating like that of a gazelle; or, in the hour of storm, fierce as an eagle's.'[21] All those who met Muhammad Ali, whether natives or foreigners, commented on his great charm and, above all, on his exquisite politeness, the hallmark of a true Ottoman gentleman. Muhammad Ali seemed, to his viewers, to surpass the normal courtesy of the Ottoman society, in which Court manners and rules of etiquette were the characteristic of people in authority.[22]

Muhammad Ali is simultaneously described in terms of the sensuous brilliance and the dream quality of the *Arabian Nights* as a modern European political leader. Occasionally he is depicted as a prince who desires, above all, inexhaustible riches and limitless indulgence in the pleasures of the senses – persistent *Arabian Nights* themes – and also as a shrewd, Machiavellian Western ruler. Furthermore, Muhammad Ali is a capable and successful politician only because of his Westernised qualities. The fact that Muhammad Ali was an Albanian, a member of a linguistic and ethnic minority group within the Ottoman family, is significant. The Albanians spoke a different language from Turkish, yet they were Muslims, and were not members of the despised Arab fellahin.[23] Muhammad Ali was illiterate, something highly unusual for a member of the Ottoman elite. He had in his favour cunning, native intelligence, a quick grasp of facts and the ability to think in broader terms than the immediate issue at hand.[24] His French education and ignorance of the Arabic language were seen as highly commendable assets:

> Mohammed Ali was perfectly indifferent as to old Arabic literature. He wished to create a new epoch in Egypt, both as a soldier and revolutionist, and it was the modern science of Europe that was more likely to suit his purpose than any amount of the curious theology and literature of the earlier Arabic period.[25]

Muhammad Ali is not considered a true Muslim leader but a clever Albanian, and hence European, soldier:

> Like Henry VIII, he converted the fat revenues of peaceful drones into the tough sinews of ambitious war; like Peter the Great, he made an army of steady soldiers out of slavish serfs, and a commanding navy out of a nest of pirates.[26]

And also:

> Mehemet Ali seems the only Mussulman whose mind is of that superior cast to qualify him to estimate at its real value the civilization of his epoch, while he has done nothing to alienate or disgust the prejudices of its race.[27]

Muhammad Ali could easily be compared with other adventurers who had reached the top of the ladder during the eighteenth and nineteenth centuries. What distinguished him from the others was the political and economic vision that he had for the country.[28] Above all, Muhammad Ali is seen as the father of modern Egypt as a result of his continual efforts to reform the administration and develop agriculture, irrigation, public works and industry. In general, his insistence upon the introduction of European technology in all activities and functions of the State resulted in his becoming quite popular in Europe:

> In Europe, the name of Mehmet Ali is familiar to every mind as one of the great powers that share the rule of this great world: we think of him, however, as seated on the throne of the Pharaohs and the Ptolemies; and seldom recur to the eventful and romantic career which shot him upward from the rank of a peasant to that of a prince.[29]

However, this birth of a 'modern' ruler was attended by a great deal of bloodshed and cruelty. Muhammad Ali's rivals were the Mamluk Beys, the allies of the British during their 1807 campaign; but instead of confronting them, the new Pasha showed great tact and courtesy. He even made a point of inviting them to attend the celebrations of his son, Toussun, before he led an army against the Wahhabis. Muhammad Ali proved on that day, 1 March 1811, that Eastern hospitality really was as dangerous as many travellers had claimed.[30] He trapped his Mamluk guests in the citadel at Cairo and murdered them all – 470, according to some accounts. This carnage is powerfully described in the following passage:

> The Beys came, mounted on their finest horses, in magnificent uniforms, forming the most superb cavalry in the world. After a very flattering reception from the Pasha, they were requested to parade in the court of the citadel. They entered the fortification unsuspectingly – the portcullis fell behind the last of the proud procession: a moment's glance revealed to them their doom: they dashed forwards – in vain! – before, behind, around them, nothing was visible but blank, pitiless walls and barred windows; the only opening was towards the bright blue sky; even that was soon darkened by their funeral pile of smoke, as volley after volley flashed from a thousand muskets behind the ramparts upon their defenceless and devoted band.[31]

The contrast between the decorative clothes of the Mamluks and the fate that befell them appears to justify the perception of the Orient as a place in which gore and gems went hand in hand. Muhammad Ali is portrayed as an Oriental despot who sits enthroned on his luxurious divan detachedly watching his subjects being stabbed to death. The massacre has been committed in secret, with little or no emotion and without judgment, as befits a capriciously cruel Orient. The whole scene becomes an exotic spectacle, voyeuristically observed by the onlooker who is both unsympathetic and brutal:

> The Pasha had placed himself on the summit of a terrace. Seated on a carpet, smoking a magnificent *narguile* (Persian pipe), from whence he could see every motion without being seen; . . . He regarded the scene below with a fixed and terrible look, without speaking a word; the signal was given to fire, and the massacre of the Mamlukes commenced.[32]

By way of contrast to this description of bloodthirsty barbarism, the Pasha is then compared to the great military and political leaders of the West, and also to a fairy-tale prince, reminiscent of the legendary kings of the *Arabian Nights*. By using these two models, one European and one Oriental, Eliot Warburton strikes the right note to appeal to the Western reader, who is only too familiar with both of them. He goes on to say:

> Like Mahomet, when he awoke from the dream of youth to the reality of manhood, he found himself in the depths of poverty; like him, too, he married a wealthy widow, who was the foundress of his fortunes. Unlike the Prophet, however, he had none of the prestige of ancient blood to buoy him up, and was indebted to himself, and not to his ancestry, for his rise.[33]

Warburton speaks of Muhammad Ali and the Prophet in the same breath, inviting comparison and completely ignoring the difference in stature between the two. He has brought down the sublime, in the figure of the Prophet, to the ordinary human level of a Napoleon and a Muhammad Ali, and in doing so has disregarded Islam's respect for the Prophet. Warburton regards Muhammad Ali as a 'super-hero', a larger-than-life figure who is simultaneously the successful politician and military man, an invincible legendary prince who is endowed with pure and virtuous qualities:

> Napoleon and Mehemet Ali came into the world in the same year of grace, 1769 . . . Each was an adventurer on a foreign soil; each attained political, through military power; each trampled fearlessly upon every prejudice that interfered with his progress; and each converted the crisis that appeared to threaten him with ruin into the means of acquiring sovereignty.[34]

Having drawn parallels between Muhammad Ali's positive qualities and those of Napoleon, Warburton quickly reminds his readers that the Pasha is not, after all, an Arab but a Turk who had the common sense of seeing 'the necessity of adopting European military tactics, and resolved to create an efficient army'.[35] Finally, Muhammad Ali's achievements are summed up as follows:

> Mehemet Ali had great aspirations, and of these he realised more than meaner minds could have believed possible, considering the

circumstances of his state, and the country he rules over . . . he endeavoured to make of the despised Arabs a martial people; of their exhausted and impoverished province, a fertile and manufacturing nation.[36]

Finally, it is important to note that the Pasha was not conversant with, sympathetic to, or concerned with such modern European concepts as the emancipation of the people, popular sovereignty and democratic representation. To him people were subjects who obeyed a forceful ruler, who, in turn, ruled alone and absolutely without their participation. The travellers did not attribute such modern sentiments to Muhammad Ali. He was simply a Muslim ruler whose conceptions about society and relations among men were essentially religious, with a strong instinct for domination and command. He understood that modernity had indispensable advantages when it came to attaining power and establishing a strong dynasty. If achieving these objectives required certain reform measures and the fulfilment of other conditions, he never hesitated to take action. Nevertheless, the consequences of the Pasha's pursuit of power and dominion provided the essential foundations of the development of modern Egypt – both as a state and a society.

It was the multifaceted nature of Egypt, with its Oriental, Muslim, Eastern and Arab traits, that lured and puzzled the travellers. Despite the fact that their imagination was sustained by a long tradition of Western scholarship and Western texts written about the East, along the lines of the *Arabian Nights*, the travellers were able to record their own subjective descriptions and observations that broke away from the stereotypical images held by the Western public.

In this paper I have tried to analyse the various strategies that the travellers adopted to unravel the East. At times they attempted to fictionalise it drawing from their *Arabian Nights* impressions. At other times they tried to come to terms with it as a reality, and not an extension of a fictitious and legendary world. Their accounts varied from mythologising and romanticising about the East to factual and realistic depictions of it. As a result the travellers' discourse was sometimes overworked and overburdened with metaphor, figurative language, reverie and fantasy; at other times it was controlled, accurate and free from all inherited representations. In both cases they succeeded in creating a literature of travel that is of historical, social and literary value.

Notes

1 Leila Ahmed, *Edward William Lane: A Study of his Life and Work and the British Ideas of the Middle East in the Nineteenth Century* (London and New York, Longman, 1978), p. 59.
2 Eliot Warburton, *The Crescent and the Cross: Romance and Realities of Eastern Travel* (London, 1841), p .79.
3 Rashad Rushdy, *The Lure of Egypt for English Writers and Travellers during the Nineteenth Century* (Cairo, Anglo-Egyptian Bookshop, 1954), p. 30.
4 Rana Kabbani, *Europe's Myths of Orient: Devise and Rule* (London, Macmillan, 1986), p. 38.
5 Warburton, *op. cit.*, p. 53.
6 {Georgiana} Dawson Damer, *Diary of a Tour in Greece, Turkey, Egypt and the Holy Land* (2 vols., London, H. Colburn, 1841), p. 152.
7 E.W. Lane, *Manners and Customs of the Modern Egyptians* (2 vols., London, Library of Entertaining Knowledge, 1836; repr. London, Charles Knight, 1846), p. 424.
8 James Augustus St John, *Egypt and Mohammed Ali: Or, Travels in the Valley of the Nile* (2 vols., London, Longman, 1834), vol. 2, p. 375.
9 St John, *op. cit.*, p. 17.
10 Damer, *op. cit.*, p. 150.
11 St John, *op. cit.*, p. 334.
12 Lane, *op. cit.*, p. 86.
13 Edward W. Said, *Orientalism: Western Concepts of the Orient* (London, 1978; repr. Harmondsworth, Penguin, 1991), p. 168.
14 Warburton, *op. cit.*, pp. 174–5.
15 Sophia Poole, *The Englishwoman in Egypt: Letters from Cairo Written during a Residence there in 1842, 3, & 4, with E.W. Lane, Esq.* (3 vols., London, Charles Knight, 1844; London, C. Cox, 1851), p. 153.
16 St John, *op. cit.*, p. 50.
17 R.R. Madden, *Egypt and Mohamed Ali* (London, Routledge & Kegan Paul, 1841), pp. 25–6.
18 John Petherick, *Egypt, the Sudan and Central Africa* (London, William Blackwood & Sons, 1861), p. 2.
19 St John, *op. cit.*, p. 50.
20 Ali Bey, *Travels of Ali Bey in Morocco, Tripoli, Cyprus, Egypt, Arabia, Syria, and Turkey. between the Years 1803 and 1807* (2 vols., London, Longman, 1816), p. 13.
21 A.A. Paton, *A History of the Egyptian Revolution from the Period of the Mamelukes to the Death of Mohammed Ali* (2 vols., London, 1863), vol. 2, p. 165.
22 Afaf Lutfi al-Sayyid Marsot, *Egypt in the Reign of Muhammad Ali* (Cambridge University Press, 1984), p. 29.
23 *Ibid.*, p. 38.
24 *Ibid.*, p. 58.
25 St John, *op. cit.*, p. 248.
26 Warburton, *op. cit.*, p. 197.
27 Damer, *op. cit.*, p. 267.

28 Marsot, *op. cit.*, p. 58.
29 Warburton, *op. cit.*, pp. 184–5.
30 Anthony Sattin, *Lifting the Veil: British Society in Egypt 1768–1956* (London, J.M. Dent, 1988), p. 29.
31 Warburton, *op. cit.*, p. 36.
32 Poole, *op. cit.*, p. 217.
33 Warburton, *op. cit.*, p. 185.
34 *Ibid.*
35 *Ibid.*, p. 189.
36 *Ibid.*, p. 194.

Select Bibliography

al-Abbasi, Ali Bey (Domingo Badia-y-Leblich), *Voyages d'Ali Bey al-Abassi en Afrique et en Asie pendant les années 1803–1807* (Paris, Didot, 1814).

—*Travels of Ali Bey: in Morocco, Tripoli, Cyprus, Egypt, Arabia, Syria, and Turkey, between the Years 1803 and 1807* (2 vols., London, Longman, Hurst, Rees, Orme and Brown, 1816; repr. Westmead, Farnborough, Gregg International, 1970).

Abdel-Hakim, Sahar S., 'British Women Writers in Egypt in the Middle Decades of the Nineteenth Century: Sophia Poole, Harriet Martineau and Lucie Duff Gordon', unpublished doctoral thesis, University of Cairo, 1996.

Ahmed, Leila, *Edward W. Lane: A Study of His Life and Work and of British Ideas of the Middle East in the Nineteenth-Century* (London & New York, Longman, 1978).

Akdag, Mustafa, *The Origin of the Great Jelali Disorders* [in Turkish] (Ankara, 1963).

Akinian, Nerses, *Travel Account, Annals and Colophons of Simeon the Scribe of Poland* [in Armenian] (Vienna, 1936).

Aldridge, James, *Cairo* (London, Macmillan, 1969).

Alpini, Prosper, *Historia Ægypti naturalis* (2 vols., Leiden, Lugduni Batavorum apud Gerardum Potvliet, 1735).

Anderson, M.S., *The Eastern Question 1774–1923: A Study in International Relations* (London, Macmillan, 1974).

Anonymous, 'Review of *Incidents of Travel in Egypt, Arabia Petræ, and the Holy Land*', *The North American Review*, 45 (July 1837), 247–50.

—'Review of *Incidents of Travel in Egypt, Arabia Petræ, and the Holy Land*', *The North American Review*, 48 (January 1839), 181–206.

—'The Nile', *Harper's New Monthly Magazine*, 69:410 (July 1884), 165–80.

Antoninus of Piacenza, 'Itinerarium', *Corpus Christianorum*, ed. P. Geyer and O. Cuntz Series Latina 175 (Turhout, Belgium, 1965), 127–74.

Arberry, A.J., *British Orientalists* (London, William Collins, 1943).
Arif Pasha, Mahmud Salih, *Les Anciens Costumes de l'Empire Ottomane depuis l'origine de la monarchie jusqu'à la réforme du Sultan Mahmoud* [*Majmu'at tesavir 'uthmani*] (Paris, Lermercier, 1863–).
Armander, Primrose and Askhain Skipworth, *The Son of a Duck is a Floater* (London, Stacey International, 1985).
al-Armani, Abu Salih, *The Churches and Monasteries of Egypt and Some Neighbouring Countries Attributed to Abu Salih, the Armenian*, trans. from the original Arabic by B.T.A. Evetts, with added notes by Alfred J. Butler (Oxford, Clarendon Press, 1895).
Arnold, Dieter, *Die Tempel Ägyptens – Götterwohnungen, Kultstätten, Baudenkmäler* (Zurich, 1992).
Atiya, Aziz S., *The Copts and Christian Civilization* (Salt Lake City, University of Utah Press, 1979).
Auldjo, John, *Journal of a Visit to Constantinople and Some of the Greek Islands in the Spring and Summer of 1833* (London, Longman, 1835).
Avcioğlu, Nebahat, 'Peripatetics of Style: Travel Literature and the Political Appropriations of Turkish Architecture, 1737–1862', unpublished doctoral thesis, University of Cambridge, 1997.
Baedeker, Karl, *Palestine and Syria* (Leipzig, Baedeker, 1898).
Balzac, Honoré de, *La Lys dans la vallée* (Paris, 1836).
Beaufort, Emily de [afterwards E.A. Smythe, Viscountess Strangford], *Egyptian Sepulchres and Syrian Shrines* (London, Macmillan, 1861).
Beauvan, Henri de, *Relation iovrnaliere dv voyage dv Levant* (Nancy, Iacob Garnic, 1615, 1619).
Behzad, Faramarz, *Adam Olearius' 'Persianischer Rosenthal,' Untersuchungen zur Übersetzung von Saadis 'Golestan' im 17 Jahrhundert* (Göttingen, Vandenhoeck & Ruprecht, 1970).
Bell, Gertrude, *Safar Nameh: Or, Persian Pictures, a Book of Travel* (London, R. Bentley, 1894).
—*Poems from the Divan of Hafiz* (London, W. Heinemann, 1897).
—*Syria: The Desert and the Sown* (London, W. Heinemann, 1907).
—*The Letters of Gertrude Bell*, ed. Lady Florence Bell (London, Ernest Benn, 1927).
—*The Earlier Letters of Gertrude Bell*, ed. Elsa Richmond (London, Ernest Benn, 1937).

Bélon, Pierre, *Les Observations de plusieurs singularitez et choses memorables, trouuées en Grèce, Asie, Iudée, Égypte, Arabie, et autre pays estranges*, redigees en trois Liures, par Pierre Bélon du Mans (Paris, Guillaume Corrozet, 1553).

Belzoni, G., *Narrative of the Operations and Recent Discoveries within the Pyramids, Temples, Tombs, and Excavations in Egypt and Nubia; etc.* (London, John Murray, 1820; 3rd edn, 1822).

Ben Arieh, Yehoshua, *Painting the Holy Land in the Nineteenth Century* (Jerusalem, Tel Aviv & New York, 1996).

Bendiner, Kenneth Paul, 'The Portrayal of the Middle East in British Painting 1835–1860', unpublished doctoral thesis, Columbia University, 1979.

Bevis, Richard (ed.), *Bibliotheca Cisorientalia: An Annotated Checklist of Early English Travel Books on the Near and Middle East* (Boston, J.K. Hall, 1973).

Bierbrier, M.L. (ed.), *Who Was Who in Egyptology*, 3rd revised edn (London, Egypt Exploration Society, 1995).

Binning, Robert B.M., *A Journal of Two Years' Travel in Persia, Ceylon, etc.* (London, W.H. Allen, 1857).

Black, Jeremy, *The British Abroad: The Grand Tour in the Eighteenth Century* (London, Croom Helm, 1985).

Blanch, Lesley, *Pierre Loti: The Legendary Romantic* (New York, Harcourt Brace Jovanich, 1983).

Blashfield, Edwin Holland and E.W., 'Afloat on the Nile', *Scribner's Magazine*, 10 (December 1891), 663–81.

—'Day with the Donkey-boys', *Scribner's Magazine*, 11 (January 1892), 32–50.

Blount, Sir Henry, *A Voyage into the Levant: A Briefe Relation of a Journey, Lately Performed by Master H.B. Gentleman from England by Way of Venice, into Dalmatia, Sclavonia, Bosnah, Hungary, Macedonia, Thessaly, Thrace, Rhodes and Egypt unto Gran [sic] Cairo: With Particular Observations Concerning the Moderne Conditions of the Turkes and Other People under that Empire* (1634; London, printed by I.L. [John Legatt] for Andrew Crooke, 1636). Reprinted in *Collection of Voyages and Travels . . .* (London, printed by assignment from Messierus Churchill, for Thomas Osborne in Gray's Inn, 1752).

Blunt, Anne, *A Pilgrimage to Nejd* (2 vols., London, John Murray, 1881).

Booth, Bradford A. (ed.), *The Letters of Anthony Trollope* (London, Oxford University Press, 1952).

Bourrienne, Louis Antoine Fauvelet de, *Mémoires de Napoléon Bonaparte* (Paris, 1829).

Bowmann, Glenn, 'Contemporary Christian Pilgrim to the Holy Land', *The Christian Heritage in the Holy Land*, ed. Anthony O'Mahony (London, Scorpion Cavendish, 1995).

Bowring, Sir John, *Report on the State of Finances in Egypt* (London, 1840).

Bramsen, John, *Travels in Egypt, Syria, Palestine, Egypt and Greece, in the Years 1814 and 1815* (London, H. Colburn, 1815).

—*Letters of a Prussian Traveller, Descriptive of a Tour through Sweden, Prussia, Austria, Hungary, Istria, the Ionian Islands, Egypt, Syria, Rhodes, the Morea, Greece, Calabria, Italy, the Tyrol, the Banks of the Rhine, Hanover, Holstein, Denmark, Westphalia and Holland* (2 vols., London, H. Colburn. 1818).

Brauer, Erich, *Ethnologie der Jemenitischen Juden* (Heidelberg, 1934).

Brimmer, Martin and Minna (Timmins) Chapman, *Egypt: Three Essays on the History, Religion and Art of Ancient Egypt* (Cambridge, Mass., Houghton, Mifflin, 1892).

Broadhurst, R. (trans.), *The Travels of Ibn Jubayr* (London, Jonathan Cape, 1952).

Brockelmann, Carl, *History of Islamic Peoples*, trans. Joel Carmichael and Moshe Perlmann (New York, Capricorn Books, 1960).

Bronkhurst, Judith, '"An Interesting Series of Adventures to Look Back Upon": William Holman Hunt's Visit to the Dead Sea in November 1854', *Pre-Raphaelite Papers*, ed. Leslie Parris (London, Tate Gallery/Allen Lane, 1984).

—'Holman Hunt's Picture Frames, Sculpture and Applied Art', *Re-Framing the Pre-Raphaelites: Historical and Theoretical Essays*, ed. Harding and Ellen (Aldershot & Brookfield, Vermont, Scolar Press, 1996).

Browning, Iain, *Palmyra* (Park Ridge, NJ, Noyes Press, 1979).

Buckingham, James Silk, *Travels in Palestine, etc.*, 2nd edn. (2 vols., London, Longman, 1821).

—*Travels among the Arab Tribes* (London, Longman, 1825).

—*Travels in Mesopotamia* (London, H. Colburn, 1827).

—*Travels in Assyria, Media, Persia etc.* (London, H. Colburn & R. Bentley, 1830).

—*Travels in Egypt, Nubia, Syria and the Holy Land* (London, John Murray, 1844).

—*Autobiography of James Silk Buckingham* (2 vols., London, Longman, Brown, Green and Longmans, 1855).

Burckhardt, John Lewis [= Ibraham ibn Abdullah], *Arabic Proverbs; Or, the Manners and Customs of the Modern Egyptians Illustrated from their Proverbial Sayings Current at Cairo, Translated and Explained*, ed. Sir William Ousely (1817; London, H. Colburn, 1830; repr. with an introduction by C.E. Bosworth, London, Curzon Press, 1984).

—*Travels in Nubia: By the Late John Lewis Burckhardt* (London, John Murray, 1819).

—*Travels in Syria and the Holy Land* (London, John Murray, 1822; repr. London, Darf, 1992).

Burton, Sir Richard Francis, *Personal Narrative of a Pilgrimage to Al-Madinah & Mecca*, Memorial Edition (3 vols., London, Longman, Brown, Green and Longmans, 1855–1856; 2 vols., Tylston and Edwards, 1893; repr. New York, Dover Publications, 1964).

Busbecq, Ogier Ghisele de, *The Turkish Letters of Ogier Ghisele de Busbecq* (Oxford University Press, 1927).

Butler, Alfred Joshua, *The Arab Conquest of Egypt* (Oxford, Clarendon Press, 1902).

Butler, Howard Crosby, *Sardis, The Excavations Part I 1910–1914* (Leiden, E.J. Brill, 1922).

Byron, George G.N. [Baron Byron], *Childe Harold's Pilgrimage* (London, John Murray, 1814).

—*Life of Lord Byron, with his Letters and Journals*, ed. Thomas Moore (1844; London, John Murray, 1851).

Cable, Lucy Leffingwell, 'On the Desert with Maude Adams', *The Ladies' Home Journal* (May 1907), 7–8, 72.

Cailliaud, Frédéric, *Voyages à l'oasis de Thèbes et dans les déserts 1815–18* (Paris, Imprimerie Royale, 1821).

Calvert, Frederick [Lord Baltimore], *A Tour to the East in the Years 1763 and 1764, with Remarks on the City of Constantinople and the Turks* (London, W. Richardson & S. Clark, 1767).

Campbell, Mary, *The Witness and the Other World: Exotic European Travel Writing, 400–1600* (Ithaca, Cornell University Press. 1988).

Capper, James, *Observations on the Passage to India, through Egypt, and across the Great Desert with Occasional Remark on the Adjacent*

Countries and also Sketches of the Different Routes (London, printed for W. Faden, Geographer to the King, 1783).

Carne, John, *Letters from the East: Written during a Recent Tour through Turkey, Egypt, Arabia, the Holy Land, Syria and Greece* (2 vols., London, H. Colburn, 1826; repr. 1830).

Casa, Jean Michel, 'Art From a Distance: Van Mour and Guardi', *Cornucopia*, 5 (1993–1994).

Çelebi, E., *Evliya Çelebi in Bitlis*, ed. R. Dankoff (Leiden, New York, Copenhagen, Cologne, 1990).

Chaillé-Long, Charles, *My Life in Four Continents* (London, Hutchinson, 1912).

Chardin, Chevalier, *Voyage en Perse et autres lieux de l'Orient* (London, Moses Pitt, 1686; repr. Amsterdam, 1735).

Chateaubriand, François-René, Vicomte de, *Itinéraire de Paris à Jérusalem* (Paris, Garnier-Flammarion, 1968; 3rd edn, Le Normant, 1812).

Chaudhuri, Nupur and Margaret Strobel (eds.), *Western Women and Imperialism, Complicity and Resistance* (Bloomington and Indianapolis, Indiana University Press, 1992).

Chiego, William J. (ed.), *Sir David Wilkie of Scotland 1785–1841* (Raleigh, NC, North Carolina Museum of Art, 1987).

Chirol, Valentine, *The Occident and the Orient* (Chicago, University of Chicago Press, 1924).

Chwolson, D., *Die Ssabier und der Ssabismus* (St Petersburg, 1856; repr. Amsterdam, 1965).

Clemens, Samuel Langhorne, *The Innocents Abroad* (Hartford, Conn., American Publishing Company, 1869).

Conder, Josiah, *The Modern Traveller* (30 vols., 1827; London, James Duncan, 1825–31), vol. 5.

Conner, Patrick (ed.), 'The Inspiration of Egypt: Its Influence on British Artists, Travellers and Designers', *1700–1900 Exhibition Catalogue* (Brighton, Brighton Borough Council, 1983).

Cook, J.M., *The Troad: An Archaeological and Topographical Study* (Oxford, Clarendon Press, 1973).

Cooley, James Ewing, *The American in Egypt; with Rambles through Arabia Petraea and the Holy Land, during the Years 1839 and 1840* (New York, D. Appleton, 1842).

Coullart, Paul and Jacques Vicari, *Le Sanctuaire de Baalshamin à Palmyre: Topographie et architecture* (Neuchâtel, Institut Suisse de Rome, 1969).

Cox, Percy Z., 'Some Excursions in Oman', *Geographical Journal* (1925).

Craven, Countess of, *A Journey through the Crimea to Constantinople: Letters* (London, H. Colburn, 1814).

Crinson, Mark, *Empire Building: Orientalism and Victorian Architecture* (London, Routledge, 1996).

Cunningham, Allan, *The Life of Sir David Wilkie and His Journals, Tours and Critical Remarks on Works of Art and a Selection from His Correspondence* (2 vols., London, John Murray, 1843).

Curtis, George William, *Nile Notes of a Howadji* (New York, Harper & Brothers, 1851).

Cyril of Jerusalem, 'Catecheses XIII:22', *The Works of Saint Cyril of Jerusalem*, ed. Leo McCauley (Washington, D.C., The Catholic University of America Press, 1968).

Daglish, R. (ed.), *The Cossacks: A Story of the Caucasus* [*Kazaki: Kavkazskasa povesm'*, written 1812–1863], trans. from Russian (Moscow, Foreign Languages Publishing House, n. d.).

Dalrymple, W., *In Xanadu: A Quest* (London, Flamingo/HarperCollins, 1989).

—*City of Djinns: A Year in Delhi* (London, HarperCollins, 1993).

Dalton, Richard, *Antiquities and Views in Greece and Egypt in 1751–2* (London, M. Cooper, 1791–1792).

Damer, Hon. M.G[eorgina] Emma (Seymour) Dawson, *Diary of a Tour in Greece, Turkey, Egypt and the Holy Land* (2 vols., London, H. Colburn, 1841).

Damiani, Anita, *Enlightened Observers: British Travellers to the Near East, 1715–1850* (Beirut, American University of Beirut, 1979).

David, Rosalie, *The Macclesfield Collection of Egyptian Antiquities* (Warminster, Aris & Phillips, 1980).

Davidson, A., *Muse of Wandering of Nikolay Gumilev* [in Russian] (Moscow, Nauka, 1992).

Davidson, Lilias Campbell, *Hints to Lady Travellers at Home and Abroad* (1887; repr. London, Iliffe, 1889).

Davies, W.D., *The Gospel and the Land: Early Christianity and Jewish Territorial Doctrine* (Berkeley, University of California Press, 1974).

Davis, Richard Harding, *The Rulers of the Mediterranean* (New York, Harper & Brothers, 1893).

—'Cairo as a Show-place', *Harper's Weekly*, 37 (8 July 1893), 642–3.

Deeken, A. and M. Boesel, *An den suessen Wassern Asiens* (Frankfurt, 1996).

Degenhard, Ursula, *Exotische Welten, Europäische Phantasien: Entdeckungs- und Forschungsreisen im Spiegel alter Bücher* (Stuttgart, Württembergische Landesbibliothek, 1987).

Demont, [Mrs], *Voyages and Travels of Her Majesty, Caroline Queen of Great Britain* (London, Jones, 1821).

Dye, William McEntyre, *Moslem Egypt and Christian Abyssinia* (New York, Atkin & Prout Printers, 1880).

Ebers, Georg Moritz, *Egypt: Descriptive, Historical and Picturesque*, trans. Samuel Birch with notes by Clare Bell (2 vols., London, Cassell, 1878; repr. 1887).

Edwards, Amelia, *A Thousand Miles up the Nile* (London, Longmans, 1877; repr. Century Publishing, 1982; also Leipzig, Bernhard Tauchnitz, 1878; also repr. London, Parkway, 1993).

—*Pharoahs, Fellahs and Explorers* (New York & London, James R. Osgood & McIlvaine, 1891).

Egeria, *Egeria's Travels*, trans. and ed. John Wilkinson (London, SPCK, 1971).

—'Itinerarium', *Corpus Christianorum*, ed. A. Franceschini and R. Weber, Series Latina 175 (Turnhout, Belgium, 1965).

Egerton, Henrietta Grey, 'Camp Life and Pig-Sticking in Morocco', *The Nineteenth Century*, 182 (April 1892), 623–30.

Elsner, Eleanor, *The Magic of Morocco* (London, Herbert Jenkins, 1928).

Elsner, John, 'Pausanius: A Greek Pilgrim in the Roman World', *Past and Present*, 135 (1992), 3–29.

E.M. [Emile Prisse d'Avennes, fils], *Notice biographique sur Emile Prisse d'Avennes voyageur français, archéologue, égyptologue et publiciste* (Paris, 1896).

Emerson, Ralph Waldo, *The Letters of Ralph Waldo Emerson*, ed. Ralph L. Rusk (6 vols., New York and London, Columbia University Press, 1929).

—*The Journals and Miscellaneous Notebooks of Ralph Waldo Emerson*, ed. William H. Gilman (Cambridge, Mass., Harvard University Press, 1973).

English, George Bethune, *A Narrative of the Expedition to Dongola and Senaar, under the Command of His Excellency Ismael Pasha, Undertaken by Order of His Highness Mehemmed Ali Pasha, Viceroy of Egypt by an American in the Service of the Viceroy* (London, John Murray, 1822).

Eraqi-Kloreman, Bat-Zion, 'Jewish and Muslim Messianism in Yemen', *IJMES*, 22 (1990), 201–28.

Erdbrink, C. Bosscha, *At the Threshold of Felicity: Ottoman-Dutch Relations During the Embassy of Cornelis Calkoen at the Sublime Porte 1726–1744* (Ankara, Türkīrih Kurumu Basimevi, 1975).

Esposito, John L., *Women in Muslim Family Law* (Syracuse University Press, 1982).

Fagan, B. *The Rape of the Nile: Tomb Robbers, Tourists and Archaeologists in Egypt* (New York, Mcdonald & Jane's, 1977).

Farman, Elbert Eli, *Along the Nile with General Grant* (New York, The Grafton Press, 1904).

Favart, Charles Simon, *Les Trois Sultanes* (Paris, 1761; repr. 1826).

Fay, Eliza, *Original Letters from India (1779–1815): Containing a Narrative of a Journey through Egypt, and the Author's Imprisonment at Calicut by Hydar Ally, to which is Added an Abstract of Three Subsequent Voyages to India* (Calcutta, 1817), ed. E.M. Forster (New York, Harcourt, Brace, 1925; repr. London, Hogarth Press, 1986).

Fetridge, William Pembroke, *Harper's Hand-book for Travellers in Europe and the East* (New York, Harper & Brothers, 1871).

Fife, Sir John (ed.), *Manual of the Turkish Bath* (London, Lond, 1865).

Flaubert, G., *Notes de voyages; voyage en Égypte, 1849–1850* (2 vols., Rouen, 1930).

—*Souvenirs, notes et pensées intimes* (Paris, Butchet-Chastel, 1965).

—*Flaubert in Egypt: A Sensibility on Tour*, ed. and trans. Francis Steegmuller (London, Bodley Head and New York, Little, Brown, 1972).

—*Correspondance*, 1re série (2 vols., Paris, 1910), ed. Jean Bruneau (Paris, Gallimard, Bibliothèque de la Pléiade, 1973).

—*Lettres à George Sand. Correspondance* (Paris, G. Charpentier, 1889; new edn, 1981).

Fodor, A., 'The Origins of the Arabic Legends of the Pyramids', *Acta Orientalia Academiae Scientiarum Hungaricae* 23:3 (1970), 335–63.

Forbin, Louis Nicolas Philippe Auguste, comte de, *Travels in Egypt, Being a Continuation of Travels in the Holy Land, in 1817–18* (London, printed for Sir R. Phillips and Co., 1819).

—*Voyage dans le Levant en 1817 et 1818* (Paris, Imprimerie Royale, 1819),

Forster, Charles Thornton and F.H.B. Daniell (trans.), *The Life and Letters of Ogier Ghiselin de Bushecq* (London, C. Kegan Paul, 1881) in *The Orientalists: Delacroix to Matisse. European Painters in North Africa and the Near East* (London, Royal Academy Exhibition Catalogue, 1984).

Forster, Edward Morgan, 'Eliza in Egypt' in *Pharos and Pharillon* (London, Michael Haag, 1983), 59–72.

Frank, Katherine, *Lucie Duff Gordon: A Passage to Egypt* (London, Hamish Hamilton, 1994).

Frankland, Captain Charles Colville, *Travels to and from Constantinople in the Years 1827 and 1828* (2 vols., London, H. Colburn, 1829).

Fresne-Canaye, Philippe du, *Voyage du Levant* (Paris, 1573; repr. 1897).

Frith, F., *Cairo, Sinai, Jerusalem, and the Pyramids of Egypt: A Series of Sixty Photographic Views by Francis Frith with Descriptions by Mrs. Poole and Reginald Stuart Poole*, Issued in 20 pts., 60 albumen prints, approx 8¾" x 6½" 225 x 165mm (London, J.S. Virtue, 1860; repr. 1861).

Gabriel, Alfons, *Die Erforschung Persiens: Die Entwicklung der abendländischen Kenntnis der Geographie Persiens* (Vienna, A. Holzhausen, 1952).

Galt, John, *Letters From the Levant: Containing Views of the State of Society, Manners, Opinions and Commerce in Greece and Several of the Principal Islands of the Archipelago* (London, Galt, 1813).

Geary, G., *Through Asiatic Turkey* (2 vols., London, 1878).

Gendron, Charisse, 'Lucie Duff Gordon's *Letters from Egypt*', *Ariel*, 17 (1986), 4–61.

Ghistele, Joos van, *Le Voyage en Égypte de Joos van Ghistele, 1482–1483*, trans. from the Flemish, introduced and annotated by Renée Bauwens-Préaux (Cairo, IFAO, 1976).

al-Ghoneim, A.Y., *Geography of Egypt from the Book al-Mamalik wa al-masalik* (Kuwait, 1980).

Gibson, Charles Dana, *Sketches in Egypt* (New York, Doubleday & McClure, 1899).

Gibson, Shimon and Joan Taylor, *Beneath the Church of the Holy Sepulchre Jerusalem: The Archaeology and Early History of Traditional Golgotha* (London, Palestine Exploration Fund, 1994).

Gidney, W.T., *The History of the London Society for Promoting Christianity among the Jews from 1809 to 1908* (London, LSPCJ, 1908).

Gilpin, Lillian C., 'To the Pyramids with a Baby Carriage', *Harper's Weekly*, 52 (12 September 1908), 30.

—'City of Noise and Flies', *Harper's Weekly*, 52 (31 October 1908), 17.

Ginzburg, E., *On Lyricism* [in Russian] (Moscow & Leningrad, Sovetskii pisatel, 1964).

Gliddon, George Robins, *Appendix to The American in Egypt* (Philadelphia, Merrihew & Thompson, 1842).

Göhring, L., 'Die Beziehungen des Malers Karl Haag zu seiner Vaterstadt Erlangen', *Erlanger Heimatblätter*, 46 (1930), 185–8.

Gordon, Lucie Duff, *Letters from Egypt 1863–1865* (London, Macmillan, 1865; repr. 1983; repr. Virago, 1986).

—*Last Letters from Egypt to which are Added Letters from the Cape*, ed. Janet Ross (London, Macmillan, 1875).

Greaves, J., *An Account of the Latitude of Constantinople and Rhodes; Written by the Learned Mr. John Greaves, Sometime Professor of Astronomy in the University of Oxford, and Directed to the Most Reverend James Ussher, Archbishop of Ardmagh* in *A Collection of Curious Travels & Voyages*, ed. John Ray (London, 1693).

Grelot, Guillaume-Joseph, *Relation nouvelle d'un voyage de Constantinople* (1680; repr. Paris, 1681).

Grohmann, Adolf, *Studien zur historischen Geographie und Verwaltung des frühmittelalterlichen Ägypten* (Vienna, In Kommission bei R.M. Rohrer, 1959).

Grove, Lady Agnes, *Seventy-One Days Camping in Morocco* (London, Longmans, Green, 1902).

Guiterman, Helen, *David Roberts R.A. 1796–1864* (London, Helen Guiterman, 1978).

Gumilev, N., *Collected works* [in Russian] (4 vols., Moscow, Terra, 1991).

Gurney, J.D., 'Pietro Della Valle: The Limits of Perception', *BSOAS*, 49 (1986), 103–16.

G[ushakian], Th[orgom] E[piskopos], *Ancient and Modern Armenian Churches in Egypt* [in Armenian] (Cairo, 1927).

H., G. S. and R. De P. Tytus, 'On the Nile', *Harper's New Monthly Magazine*, 109 (October 1904), 693–701.

Haarmann, Ulrich (ed.), *Das Pyramidenbuch des Abu Ga'far al-Idrisi* (Beirut-Stuttgart, 1991).

Habachi, Labib, 'The Monument of Biyahmu', *ASAE*, 40 (Cairo, 1940), 721–32.

Habesci, E., *The Present State of the Ottoman Empire* (London, 1984).

Hahn-Hahn, Ida Marie Louise Sophie Friederike Augusta, *Orientalische Briefe* (Berlin, Dunker, 1842).

Halls, John James (ed.), *Life and Correspondence of Henry Salt . . . Consul General in Egypt* (2 vols., London, R. Bentley, 1834).

Halévy, Joseph, 'Voyage au Nedjran', *Bulletin de la Société de Géographie de Paris*, 5 (1873), 5–31.

Halsband, Robert, *The Life of Lady Mary Wortley Montagu* (Oxford, Clarendon Press, 1956)

—(ed.), *The Complete Letters of Lady Mary Wortley Montagu* (3 vols., Oxford, Clarendon Press, 1965–1967).

Hamst, [Olphar Hamst], *Sketches of Turkey in 1831 and 1832* (New York, 1833).

Harman, Henry Martyn, *A Journey to Egypt and the Holy Land, in 1869–1870* (Philadelphia, J.B. Lippincott, 1873).

Hassan, Fekri, 'Town and Village in Ancient Egypt: Ecology, Society and Urbanization', *The Archaeology of Africa*, ed. I. Shaw *et al.* (London, Routledge, 1993), 551–69.

—'The Dynamics of a Riverine Civilization: A Geo-archaeological Perspective on the Nile Valley, Egypt', *World Archaeology*, 29:1 (1997), 51–74.

Hatem, Mervat, 'Through Each Other's Eyes' in N. Chaudhuri and M. Strobel (eds.), *Western Women and Imperialism* (Indiana, Indiana University Press, 1992).

Hentsch, Thierry, *Imagining the Middle East* (Montreal, Black Rose Books, 1992).

Herbert, Th., *Travels in Persia 1627–1629*, abr. and ed. Sir William Foster, with an Introduction and Notes (London, G. Routledge, 1928).

Hobhouse, John Cam, *A Journey through Albania and other Provinces of Turkey in Europe and Asia to Constantinople during the Years 1809 and 1810* (London, J. Cawthorn, 1813).

Hodgson, Marshall, *The Venture of Islam: Conscience and History in a World Civilization* (Chicago, University of Chicago Press, 1974).

Holland, Frederick W., 'Eastern Cities: Cairo the Victorious', *Lippincott's Magazine of Popular Literature and Science*, 7 (February 1871), 197–202.

Holland Sir Henry, *Travels in the Ionian Isles, Albania, Thessaly, Macedonia etc. during the years 1812 and 1813* (2 vols., 1815; repr. London, 1819).

Homayoun, Gholamali, *Iran in europäischen Bildzeugnissen vom Ausgang des Mittelalters bis ins achtzehnte Jahrhundert*, unpublished dissertation (Cologne, 1967).

Hopkins, Hugh E., *Sublime Vagabond: The Life of Joseph Wolff – Missionary Extraordinary* (Worthing, Churchman, 1984).

Howard-Vyse, L., *A Winter in Tangier and Home through Spain* (London, Strangeways, 1882).

Hughes, Rev. T.S., *Travels in Greece and Albania*, 2nd edn (2 vols., London, 1830).

Hunt, William Holman, 'The Pre-Raphaelite Brotherhood: A Fight for Art', *Contemporary Review*, 49 (June 1886), 828.

—*Pre-Raphaelitism and the Pre-Raphaelite Brotherhood* (London, Macmillan, 1905).

Hunter, William, *Travels through France, Turkey and Hungary to Vienna in 1792*, 3rd edn (2 vols., London, 1803).

Hutton, C.A., 'The Travels of "Palmyra" Wood in 1750–51', *Journal of Hellenic Studies*, 47:1 (1927), 102–29.

Ibn al-Akfani, *A Survey of the Muhammedan Sciences*, ed. A. Sprenger (Calcutta, 1849).

Ibn Battuta, *The Travels of Ibn Battuta, A.D. 1325–1354*, trans. H.A.R. Gibb with revisions and notes from the Arabic text, ed. C. Defrémery and B. R. Sanguinetti (Cambridge University Press for the Hakluyt Society, 1958).

Ibn Taymia, *Public Duties in Islam: The Institution of Hisba* (Leicester, Islamic Foundation, 1985).

Inalçik, Halil, 'The Heyday and Decline of the Ottoman Empire' in P.M. Holt, Ann K.S. Lambton and Bernard Lewis (eds.), *The Cambridge History of Islam*, vol. I (Cambridge, Cambridge University Press, 1970), 347–50.

Institut du Monde Arabe, *Jordanie, sur les pas des archéologues*, catalogue of the exhibition, 13 June–5 October 1997 (Paris, Institut du Monde Arabe, 1997).

Irby, Hon. C.L. and J. Mangles, *Travels in Egypt and Nubia, Syria, and Asia Minor, during the Years 1817 and 1818* (London, privately printed, 1823; repr. T. White Printers, 1823).

—*Travels in Egypt, Nubia, Syria, and the Holy Land* (London, John Murray, 1844).

Irwin, Eyles, *A Series of Adventures in the Course of a Voyage up the Red Sea, on the Coasts of Arabia and Egypt and of a Route through the Desarts of Thebais, hitherto Unknown to the European Traveller, in the Year M.DCC.LXXVII in Letters to a Lady* (Dublin, printed for W. Sleater, 1780; London, J. Dodsley, 1787). The two-volume London edition of 1787 contains in addition *A Supplement of a Voyage from Venice to Latichea, and of a Route through the Deserts of Arabia, by Aleppo, Bagdad, and the Tigris to Busrah, in 1780 and 1781* (2 vols., London, J. Dodsley, 1787).

—*Reise auf dem Rothen Meer auf der Arabische und Ægyptische Küste und durch d. Thebaischen Wüste* (Leipzig, Weidmann, 1781).

—*Voyage à la Mer Rouge sur les côtes de l'Arabie, en Égypte et dans les deserts de la Thébaïde; suivi d'un voyage Bassorah, etc. en 1780 et 1781*, trans. from English by J.P. Parraud (2 vols., Paris, 1792).

Isaacs, Albert Augustus, *Biography of the Rev. Henry Aron Stern: For More Than Forty Years a Missionary among the Jews – Containing his Account of his Labours and Travel in Mesopotamia, Persia, Arabia, Turkey, Abyssinia and England* (London, J. Nisbet, 1886).

al-Jabartī, Abd al-Rahmān, *Napoleon in Egypt: al-Jabarti's Chronicle of the French Occupation, 1798* (New York, Markus Wiener, 1993).

J[olliffe], T.R., *Letters from Palestine, Descriptive of a Tour through Galilee and Judaea, with Some Account of the Dead Sea, and of the Present State of Jerusalem*, 2nd edn, to which are added, *Letters from Egypt* (London, James Black, 1820).

Jomier, J., *Le Mahmal et la caravane égyptienne des pèlerins de La Mecque, XIIIe–XXe siècles* (Cairo, 1953).

Jones, George, *Excursions to Cairo, Jerusalem, Damascus, and Balbec from the United States Ship Delaware, during her Recent Cruise* (New York, Van Nostrand & Dwight, 1836).

Jones, Sir William, 'A Prefatory Discourse to an Essay on the History of the Turks', *The Works of Sir William Jones* (13 vols., London, 1807).

Juler, Caroline, *Les Orientalistes de l'école italienne* (Paris, ACR Edition, 1994).

Kabbani, Rana, *Europe's Myths of Orient: Devise and Rule* (London, Macmillan, 1986).

—*Imperial Fictions: Europe's Myths of Orient* (London, Pandora, 1994).

Kamal, Ahmad, *Tarwih al-nafs fi madinat al-Shams* (*Heliopolis*) (Cairo, 1896).

Kapoïan-Kouymjian, Angèle, *L'Égypte vue par des Arméniens, XIe–XVIIe siècles* (Paris, Fondation Singer-Polignac, 1988).

Kardashian, Ardashes H., *Material for the History of the Armenians in Egypt* [in Armenian] (Cairo, 1943).

Keane, John F., *Six Months in the Hejaz: An Account of the Mohammedan Pilgrimage to Meccah and Medinah* (London, Ward and Downey, 1887).

Kendall, James E., 'A Tour in Egypt', *The American Catholic Quarterly Review*, 31 (October 1906), 671–9.

Khalifa, Hajji, *Kashf al-zunun 'an asami al-Kutub wa'l-funun. Lexicon bibliographicum et encyclopaedicum a Mustafa ben Abdallah Katib Jelebi dicto et nomine Haji Khalifa celebrato compositum. Ad codicem Vindobonensium, Parisiensium et Berolinensis fidem primum edidit latine vertit et commentaria indicibusque instruxit Gustavus Fluegel* (7 vols., Leipzig, Leiden, 1835–1858).

al-Kindi, *Fada'il Misr*, a new edition by Ali Muhammad Umar (repr. Cairo, 1997).

Kinglake, A.W., 'The Rights of Women', *The Quarterly Review* (December 1844).

Kinglake, A.W., *Eōthen, or Traces of Travel Brought Home from the East* (London, John Olivier, 1844; repr. Marlboro, Vt., The Marlboro Press, 1992).

Knecht, Justin, *Belmont und Konstanze* (1787).

Knightley, Phillip and Colin Simpson, *The Secret Lives of Lawrence of Arabia* (London, Nelson, 1969).

Kobak, Annette, *Isabelle: The Life of Isabelle Eberhardt* (New York, Alfred A. Knopf, 1988).

Kosciow, Zbigniew, *Symeon Lehacy (Szymon z Polski). Zapiski Podrozne* (Warsaw, 1991).

Kurz, M. and P. Linant de Bellefonds, 'Linant de Bellefonds: Travels in Egypt, Sudan and Arabia Petraea, 1818–1828' in P. and J. Starkey (eds.), *Travellers in Egypt* (London, I.B. Tauris, 1998).

Laborde, Léon Emmanuel Simon Joseph, Marquis de, *Journey through Arabia Petraea, in Mount Sinai, and the Excavated City of Petra, the Edom of the Prophecies* (London, John Murray, 1836).

—*Pétra retrouvée. Voyage de l'Arabie Pétrée, 1828. Léon de Laborde et Linant de Bellefonds*, preface and notes by Chr. Augé and P. Linant de Bellefonds (Paris, Girard, 1830; repr. Paris, Pygmalion, 1994).

Lamartine, Alphonse de, *Voyage en Orient: souvenirs, impressions, pensées et paysages pendant un voyage en Orient (1832–1833) ou Notes d'un voyageur* (4 vols., Paris, C. Gosselin, 1835; repr. Paris, Firmin Didot, 1849).

Landow, George P., 'William Holman Hunt's "Oriental Mania" and his Uffizi Self-Portrait', *Art Bulletin*, 64 (December 1982), 648.

—'William Holman Hunt's Letters to Thomas Seddon', *Bulletin of The John Rylands University Library of Manchester*, 66 (1983–4), 152.

Lane, Edward William, *An Account of the Manners and Customs of the Modern Egyptians, Written in Egypt during the Years 1833–1835* (2 vols., London, 1836; repr. London, Charles Knight, 1846; repr. The Hague and London, East–West Publications, 1981; also repr. Cairo, Livres de France, 1978; repr. in 2 vols., London, 1849; 5th rev. edn, ed. E. Stanley Poole, London, John Murray, 1860; also repr. New York, Dover 1973).

—trans., *The Thousand and One Nights* (3 vols., London, Charles Knight, 1839–41).

Lansing, Gulian, 'A Visit to the Convent of Sittna (Our Lady), Damiane', *Harper's New Monthly Magazine*, 28:168 (May 1864), 757–74.

Lechevalier, J.-B., *Voyage de la Troade fait dans les années 1785 et 1786* (Paris, 1799).

Le Hay, Jacques, *Recueil de cent estampes representant différentes nations du Levant, tirées sur les tableaux peints d'après nature en 1707 et 1708 par les ordres de M. de Ferriol, ambassadeur du roi à la Porre. Et gravées en 1712 et 1713 par les soins de M. Le Hay*, with new editions in 1714 and 1715 (Paris, St le Hay; Sr Duchange, 1714; Jacques Collomat, 1715).

Leon, Edward De, 'A Bridal Reception in the Hareem of the Queen of Egypt', *Lippincott's Magazine of Popular Literature and Science*, 16 (September 1875), 379–83.

Lermontov, Mikhail Yur'evich, *Geroi Nashego Vremeni* (*A Hero of our Time*), 1841, trans. from the Russian by Vladimir Nabokov in collaboration with Dimitri Nabokov (New York, Doubleday, 1958).

Lewis, Bernard, *The Muslim Discovery of Europe* (New York, Norton, 1982).

—*Islam in History* (Chicago, Open Court, 1993).

Lewis, J.M., *John Frederick Lewis, R.A., 1805–1876* (Leigh-on-Sea, Lewis, 1978).

Lewis, Reina, *Gendering Orientalism: Race, Femininity and Representation* (London, Routledge, 1996).

Light, Capt Henry, *Travels in Egypt, Nubia, Holy Land, Mount Libanan and Cyprus in the Year 1814* (London, printed Weybridge, Rodwell & Martin, 1818).

Linde, Paul and Justin Wintie, *A Dictionary of Arabic and Islamic Proverbs* (London, Routledge & Kegan Paul, 1984).

Lithgow, William, *A Most Delectable and True Discourse of an Admired and Painful Peregrination from Scotland to the Most Famous Kingdomes in Europe, Asia and Affricke* (London, printed by Nicholas Okes, and are to be sold by Thomas Archer, 1614; 2nd impression 1616; repr. New York and Amsterdam, Da Capo Press and Theatrum Orbis Terrarum, 1971); 2nd edn, *The Total Discourse of the Rare Adventures and Painful Peregrinations of Long Nineteene Years Travayle From Scotland to the most famous Kingdoms in Europe, Asia and Africa*, 1632; repr. Glasgow, James MacLehose & Sons, Publisher to the University, 1906; new repr. ed. Gilbert Phelps, London, 1974.

Llewellyn, B., 'Petra and the Middle East', *The Connoisseur* (June 1980), 123.

—'The Islamic Inspiration. John Frederick Lewis: Painter of Islamic Egypt', *The Society of Antiquaries of London*, ed. S. Macready and F.H. Thompson, Occasional Paper (New Series), 7 (1985).

—(comp.), *The Orient Observed: Images of the Middle East from the Searight Collection* (London, Victoria & Albert Museum, 1989).

—'Luigi Mayer, Draughtsman to His Majesty's Ambassador at the Ottoman Porte', *Watercolours*, 5:4 (Winter 1990), 9–13.

—'Carl Haag', *The Dictionary of Art* (London, Macmillan, 1996).
—'J.F. Lewis and Frank Dillon: Two Interpretations of Islamic Domestic Interiors in Cairo', *Travellers in Egypt*, ed. P. and J. Starkey (London, I.B. Tauris, 1998).
Lloyd, Christopher, *English Corsairs on the Barbary Coast* (London, Collins, 1981).
Lockhart, Laurence, 'European Contacts with Persia', *The Cambridge History of Iran*, ed. Peter Jackson (Cambridge University Press, 1986).
Longford, Elizabeth, *A Pilgrimage of Passion: The Life of Wilfrid Scawen Blunt* (London, Weidenfeld and Nicolson, 1979).
Lorimer, J.G., *Gazetteer of the Persian Gulf, Omān, and Central Arabia* (2 vols., Calcutta, Government of India, 1908–1915; repr. Farnborough, Gregg International, 1970).
Loring, William Wing, *A Confederate Soldier in Egypt* (New York, Dodd, Mead, 1884).
Lovell, Mary S., *A Scandalous Life: The Biography of Jane Digby el Mezrab* (London, Fourth Estate, 1995).
Lowe, Lisa, *Critical Terrains: French and British Orientalisms* (Ithaca, NY, Cornell University Press, 1992).
Lutyens, Mary (ed.), 'Letters from Sir John Everett Millais, Bart, P.R.A. (1829–1896) and William Holman Hunt, O.M. (1827–1910) in the Henry E. Huntington Library, San Marino, California', *Walpole Society*, 44 (1972–1974).
MacFarlane, Charles, *Constantinople in 1828* (2 vols., London, Saunders & Otley, 1829).
Macgill, Thomas, *Travels in Turkey Italy and Russia during the years 1803, 1804, 1805 and 1806* (2 vols., London, John Murray, 1808).
MacKenzie, John M., *Orientalism: History, Theory and the Arts* (Manchester & New York, Manchester University Press & St Martin's Press, 1995).
Mackintosh-Smith, Tim, *Yemen: Travels in Dictionary Land* (London, John Murray, 1997).
Madden, Richard Robert, *Egypt and Mohammed Ali, Illustrative of the Condition of his Slaves and Subjects* (London, 1841).
—*Travels in Turkey, Egypt, Nubia, and Palestine, in 1824, 1825, 1826 & 1827* (2 vols., London, H. Colburn, 1829).
Madox, John, *Excursions in the Holy Land, Egypt, Nubia, Syria, &c. Including a Visit to the Unfrequented District of the Hauran* (2 vols., London, R. Bentley, 1834).

Select Bibliography

Manley, Deborah, *The Nile: A Traveller's Anthology* (London, Cassell, 1991).

Manoncourt, C.N. Sonnini de, *Travels in Upper and Lower Egypt*, trans. Henry Hunter (London, J. Debrett, 1800; repr. Westmead Gregg International Publishers, 1972).

—*Voyage en Grèce et en Turquie fait par ordre de Louis XVI* (2 vols., Paris, 1801).

Mans, P. Raphael Du, *Estat de la Perse en 1660, par Le P. Raphael Du Mans, Supérieur de la Mission des Capucins d'Ispahan*, ed. Ch. Schefer (Paris, 1890).

Mansel, Philip, *Constantinople: City of the World's Desire, 1453–1924* (Harmondsworth, Penguin, 1997).

al-Maqrizi, Ahmad ibn 'Ali Taqi al-Din Abu al-'Abbas, *Khitat*, I (Beirut, Dar al-Kutub al-'Ilmiyya, 1998).

Marana, Giovanni Paolo, *The Turkish Spy* (8 vols., 1687–1694; London, printed by J. Leake for Henry Rhodes, 1691).

—*L'Espion des grands seigneurs, dans les cours des princes chrétiens, ou Mémoirs pour servir à l'histoire de ce siècle depuis 1637 jusqu'à 1682* (6 vols., Amsterdam & Paris, 1684).

—*L'Espion du grand Seigneur, et ses relations secrètes envoyées au divan de Constantinople et découvertes à Paris* (2 vols., Amsterdam & Paris, 1684–1686).

—*L'Espion dans les cours des princes chrétiens, ou lettres et mémoires d'un envoyé secret de la Porte dans les cours de l'Europe* (54 vols., Cologne and Paris, 1696).

Markus, Robert, *The End of Ancient Christianity* (Cambridge University Press, 1990).

—'How on Earth Could Places Become Holy? Origins of the Christian Idea of Holy Places', *Journal of Early Christian Studies*, 2:3 (1994), 257–71.

Marsot, Afaf Lutfi al-Sayyid, *Egypt in the Reign of Muhammad Ali* (Cambridge University Press, 1984).

Martin, Abbé, *Voyage à Constantinople fait à l'occasion de l'ambassade de M le Comte de Choiseul-Gouffier à la Porte Ottomane* (1819).

Martineau, Harriet, *Eastern Life: Present and Past* (Philadelphia & London, Lee & Blanchard, 1848).

Masson, Flora, 'Holman Hunt and the Story of a Butterfly', *Cornhill Magazine*, n.s., 39:173 (November 1910), 644.

Masson, Paul R., *Histoire du commerce français dans le Levant au XVIIIe siècle* (1896; Paris, 1911; repr. 1967).
Matar, Nabil I., *Islam in Britain, 1558-1685* (Cambridge University Press, 1998).
Matran, R., *Istanbul dans la seconde moitié du XVIIe siècle. Essai d'histoire institutionelle, économique et sociale*, Bibliothèque Archéologique et Historique de l'Institut Français d'Archéologie d'Istanbul, 12 (Paris, l'Institut Français d'Archéologie d'Istanbul, 1962).
Mayer, Luigi, *Views in Turkey in Europe and Asia Comprising Romelia, Bulgaria, Wallachia, Syria and Palestine* (London, 1801–1806).
—*Views in Egypt from the Original Drawings in the Possession of Sir Robert Ainslie, taken during his Embassy to Constantinople* (London, Bowyer, 1801–1804).
—*Views in Palestine* (London, 1801–1804).
—*Views in the Ottoman Empire, Chiefly in Caramania* (London, 1803).
—*Views in the Ottoman Dominions* (London, 1810).
—*A Series of Twenty-Four Views Illustrative of the Holy Scriptures Selected from Sir Robert Ainslie's Celebrated Collection of Drawings* (London, 1833).
Mazuel, J., *L'Oeuvre géographique de Linant de Bellefonds: étude de géographie historique* (Cairo, Société Royale Géographie d'Égypte, 1937).
McClellan, George B., 'The War in Egypt', *Century Illustrated Monthly Magazine*, 24 (1882), 784–88.
Meath, Countess of, 'The First Woman's Hospital in Morocco', *The Nineteenth Century*, 43 (June 1898), 1002–7.
—'A Land of Woe', *The Nineteenth Century*, 49 (June 1901), 1050–5.
Melman, Billie, *Women's Orients: English Women and the Middle East, 1718–1918. Sexuality, Religion, and Work* (Ann Arbor, University of Michigan, 1992; London, Macmillan, 1992).
Melville, Lewis, pseud. [i.e. Lewis Saul Benjamin], *Lady Mary Wortley Montagu, Her Life and Letters 1689–1762* (Boston and New York, Houghton Mifflin and London, Hutchinson, 1925).
Merezhkovsky, D.S., *It Was and Will Be. Diaries 1910–1925* [in Russian], (Petrograd, 1915).
Meynell, Alice, 'William Holman Hunt, Part III, The Artist's Home and Studio', *Art Annual* (1893), 28.
Middleton, Dorothy, *Victorian Lady Travellers* (New York, Dutton, 1965).

Miles, S.L., 'On the Route between Sohar and el-Bereymi in Oman', *Journal of the Asiatic Society of Bengal*, 46 (1877).
—'Journal of an Excursion in Oman', *Geographical Journal*, 7 (1896).
—'Across the Green Mountains of Oman', *Geographical Journal*, 18 (1901).
—*The Countries and Tribes of the Persian Gulf* (London, Harrison, 1919; 2nd edn (London, Frank Cass, 1966).
Mills, Sara, *Discourses of Difference: An Analysis of Women's Travel Writing and Colonialism* (London, Routledge, 1991).
Mitchell, Timothy, *Colonising Egypt* (Cambridge University Press, 1988).
Monro, Rev. Vere, *A Summer Ramble in Syria, with a Tartar Trip from Aleppo to Stamboul* (2 vols., London, R. Bentley, 1835).
Montagu, John, *A Voyage Performed by the Late Earl of Sandwich Round the Mediterranean in the Years 1713 and 1739* (London, 1799).
Montagu, Lady Mary Wortley, *Complete Letters*, ed. Robert Halsband (Oxford, Clarendon Press, 1965).
—*The Turkish Embassy Letters*, ed. Malcolm Jack (London, Virago, 1994).
Montulé, Edouard de, *Travels in Egypt during 1818 and 1819* (London, printed for R. Phillips, 1821).
Morgan, David, *Medieval Persia 1040–1797* (London, Longman, 1988).
Morritt, J.B.S., *A Grand Tour: Letters and Journeys 1794–1796* (London, Century, 1985).
Murray, Elizabeth, *Sixteen Years of an Artist's Life in Morocco, Spain, and the Canary Islands* (London, Hurst and Blackett, 1859).
Musckau, Hermann Ludwig Heinrich Puckler, Prince, *Egypt and Mehemet Ali* (3 vols., London, T.C. Newby, 1845).
Nasr, Seyyed Hossein, *Ideals and Realities of Islam* (Cairo, American University in Cairo Press, 1989).
Nemoy, Leon, ed. and trans., 'The Treatise on the Egyptian Pyramids (*Tuhfat al-kiram fi khabar al-ahram*) by Jalal al-Din al-Suyuti', *ISIS*, 30 (1939), 17–37.
Netton, I.R., *Golden Roads: Migration, Pilgrimage and Travel in Medieval and Modern Islam* (Richmond, Curzon Press, 1993).
—(ed.), *Seek Knowledge: Thought and Travel in the House of Islam* (Richmond, Curzon Press, 1996).
Niebuhr, Carsten, *Travels through Arabia and Other Countries in the East*, trans. and ed. Robert Heron (Edinburgh, R. Morison, 1792).

Nightingale, Florence, *Letters from Egypt*, ed. Antony Sattin (London, A. & G.A. Spottiswoode, 1854; repr. London, Barrie & Jenkins, 1987).

Nochlin, Linda, 'The Imaginary Orient', *The Politics of Vision* (New York, Harper and Row, 1989), 35–59.

Norden, Frederic Louïs, *Voyage d'Égypte et de Nubie* (2 vols., Copenhagen, Imprimerie de la Maison Royale, 1755).

Oddie, E.M., *Portrait of Ianthe: Being a Study of Jane Digby, Lady Ellenborough* (London, Jonathan Cape, 1935).

Oelwein, Cornelia, 'Carl Haag (1820–1915). Ein Erlanger Künstler – "Well-Known" in England', *Bayernspiegel*, 4 (Munich, 1995).

—*Lady Jane Ellenborough. Eine Frau beeindruckt ihr Jahrhundert* (Munich, 1996).

Olearius, Adam, *The Travels of Olearius in Seventeenth-century Russia*, trans. and ed. Samuel Baron (Stanford, Stanford University Press, 1967).

—*Vermehrte Newe Beschreibung der Muscowitischen und Persischen Reyse* (1656), ed. Dieter Lohmeier, Deutsche Neudrucke 21 (Tübingen, Max Niemeyer, 1971).

—[*Vermehrte Newe Beschreibung der Muscowitischen und Persischen Reyse*] *Moskowitische und persische Reise: die holsteinische Gesandtschaft beim Schah, 1633–1639*, ed. Detlef Haberland (Stuttgart, Thienemann, 1986).

Olivier, G.A., *Voyage dans l'empire Othoman, l'Égypte et la Perse* (Paris, H. Agosse, (1801–7).

Ollier, Edmund, *Cassell's Illustrated History of the Russo-Turkish War* (2 vols., London, Paris, New York, 1885–1886).

Osterhammel, Jürgen, 'Reisen an die Grenzen der Alten Welt: Asien im Reisebericht des 17. und 18. Jahrhunderts', *Der Reisebericht*, ed. Peter Brenner (Frankfurt am Main, Suhrkamp, 1989), 224–60.

Packard, J.F., *Grant's Tour Around the World* (Cincinnati, Forshee & McMakin, 1880).

Palmer, Loomis T., *General U.S. Grant's Tour around the World* (Chicago, W.M. Farrar, 1880).

Pardoe, Julia S.H., *The City of the Sultan and Domestic Manners of the Turks in 1836* (2 vols., London, H. Colburn, 1837).

Paton, A.A., *A History of the Egyptian Revolution from the Period of the Mamelukes to the Death of Mohammed Ali*, 2nd edn, enlarged (2 vols., 1863; repr. London, Truebner, 1870).

SELECT BIBLIOGRAPHY

Perrier, Amelia, *A Winter in Morocco* (London, Harvey S. King, 1873).

Peters, F.E., *Jerusalem: The Holy City in the Eyes of Chroniclers, Visitors, Pilgrims and Prophets from the Days of Abraham to the Beginnings of Modern Times* (Princeton, Princeton University Press, 1985).

Petherick, John, *Egypt the Soudan and Central Africa* (London & Edinburgh, William Blackwood, 1861).

Philippe, Beatrice (ed.), *Voir Jérusalem: pèlerins, conquérants, voyageurs* (Paris, 1997).

Phipps-Jackson, M., 'Cairo in London: Carl Haag's Studio', *Art Journal* (1883).

Pick, Christopher (ed.), *Embassy to Constantinople: The Travels of Lady Mary Wortley Montagu* (London, Century, 1988).

Pigafetta, Marc Antonio, *Itinerario da Vienna a Constantinopoli di Marc'Antonio Pigafetta gentil'huomo Vicentino* (London, Giovanni Wolfio, 1585).

Piloti, Emmanuel, *L'Égypte au commencement du XVe siècle d'après le Traité d'Emmanuel Piloti de Crète (Incipit, 1420)*, ed. P.- H. Dopp (Cairo, 1950).

Pilz, Gerg, ed., *Paul Gavarni* (Berlin, Eulenspiegel Verlag, 1971).

Pleydell, Kathleen Mansel, *Sketches of Life in Morocco* (London, Digby, Long, 1907).

Pococke, Richard, Bishop of Meath, *A Description of the East and Some Other Countries* (2 vols., London, J. & R. Knapton, 1743–1745).

Poole, Sophia, *The Englishwoman in Egypt: Letters from Cairo, Written during a Residence there in 1842, 3, & 4, with E.W. Lane, Esq., Author of 'The Modern Egyptians'* (2 vols., London, Charles Knight, 1844).

—*The Englishwoman in Egypt: Letters from Cairo Written during a Residence there in 1842, 3, & 4, with E.W. Lane, Esq.* (3 vols., 1844; repr. London, C. Cox, 1851).

—*The Englishwoman in Egypt: Letters from Cairo, Written during a Residence there in 1845–46, with E.W. Lane . . . etc.*, 2nd Series (London, Charles Knight, 1846).

Poole, Stanley Lane (ed.), *The Thousand and One Nights, Commonly Called in England, The Arabian Nights' Entertainments, a New Translation from the Arabic, with Copious Notes by Edward William Lane* (London, Charles Knight, 1859).

—*Life of Edward William Lane* (London, Williams & Norgate, 1877).

—*Cairo: Sketches of its History, Monuments and Social Life* (1898; repr. New York, Arno Press, 1973).

Postel, Guillaume, *Des Histoires orientales et principalement des Turkes ou Turchiques* (Paris, H. de Marnef & G. Cauellat, 1575).

Potocki, Jan, Le Comte de, *Voyage en Turquie et en Egypte, fait en l'année 1784* (Varsovie, 1788).

Potter, W. (proprietor of the Turkish Bath, Manchester), *The Roman or Turkish Bath: Its Hygienic and Curative Properties* (Manchester and London, 1859).

Pratt, Mary Louise, 'Fieldwork in Common Places', *Writing Culture: The Poetics and Politics of Ethnography*, ed. James Clifford and George Marcus (Berkeley, University of Berkeley Press, 1986).

—*Imperial Eyes: Travel Writing and Transculturation* (London, Routledge, 1992).

Prime, William Cowper, 'Passages of Eastern Travel', *Harper's New Monthly Magazine*, 12:68 (1856), 224–34, 371–80, 482–90.

—'Passages of Eastern Travel', *Harper's New Monthly Magazine*, 13 (1856), 191–201, 323–35, 473–84, 609–18, 773–82; also 14 (1856), 32–44.

—'From Thebes to the Pyramids', *Harper's New Monthly Magazine*, 14:82 (March 1857), 463–77.

—*Boat Life in Egypt and Nubia* (New York, Harper, 1857).

Prisse d'Avennes, Emile, *Atlas de l'histoire de l'art Égyptien d'après les monuments depuis le temps les plus reculés, jusqu'à la domination romaine* (Paris, A. Bertrand, 1868–1878).

Quataert, Donald, 'Clothing Laws, State and Society in the Ottoman Empire, 1720–1829', *IJMES*, 29 (August 1997).

al-Qudsi, *Al-Fada'il al-bahira fi mahasin Misr wa-al-Qahira* (formerly attributed to Ibn Zahira), ed. M. al-Saqqa and K. al-Muhandis (Cairo, National Library Press, 1969).

Raguse, Marechal, Duc de, *Voyage en Hongrie, en Turquie . . . et en Egypte* (4 vols., Brussels, Société Typographique Belge, 1837).

Rapelje, George, *A Narrative of Excursions, Voyages, and Travels, Performed at Different Periods in America, Europe, Asia, and Africa* (New York, printed for the author, 1834).

Ray, John (ed.), *A Collection of Curious Travels and Voyages* (2 vols., London, S. Smith & B. Walford, 1693).

Rees, Joan, *Writings on the Nile* (London, Rubicon, 1995).

Repplier, Agnes, 'Christmas Shopping in Assuân', *Atlantic Monthly*, 75 (May 1895), 681–95.
Ribeiro, Aileen, 'Turquerie: Turkish Dress and English Fashion in the Eighteenth Century', *Connoisseur* (May 1979), 17–23.
Rice, Edward, *Captain Sir Richard Francis Burton: The Secret Agent Who Made the Pilgrimage to Mecca, Discovered the* Kama Sutra *and Brought* The Arabian Nights *to the West* (New York, Harper, 1990).
Richard, F., 'Raphaël du Mans missionaire en Perse au XVIIe siècle', *Moyen Orient & Océan Indien XVIe–XIXe siècle*, 9 (2 vols., 1995).
Richardson, Robert R., *Travel along the Mediterranean, and Parts Adjacent: In Company with the Earl of Belmore, during the Years 1816, 1817, and 1818, Extending as Far as the Second Cataract of the Nile, Jerusalem, Damascus, Balbec, etc.* (2 vols., London, printed for T. Cadell, 1822).
Richmond, J.C.B., *Egypt 1798–1952: Her Advance towards a Modern Identity* (London, Methuen, 1977).
Riedesel, Johann Hermann von, Baron, *Voyage en Sicile, dans la Grande Grèce et au Levant* [in German, 1771] (Paris, 1802).
Righi, Eleanor Rigo de, *Holiday in Morocco* (London, G.T. Foulis, 1935).
Roberts, Chalmers, 'Where East and West Meet', *Harper's New Monthly Magazine*, 100:596 (January 1900), 245–56.
Roberts, David, *The Holy Land, Syria, Idumea, Arabia, Egypt & Nubia* (2 vols., London, F.G. Moon, 1842–1849).
Robinson, Edward H.T., *Lawrence: The Story of His Life* (London, Oxford University Press, 1933).
—*Lawrence the Rebel* (London, Lincolns-Praeger, 1946).
Robinson, Gertrude, *David Urquhart* (Oxford, Basil Blackwell, 1920).
Robinson, Jane, *Wayward Women: A Guide to Women Travellers* (Oxford & New York, Oxford University Press, 1990).
Roche, Max, *Education, assistance et culture françaises dans l'empire Ottoman* (Istanbul, 1989).
Rodenbeck, Max, *Cairo: The City Victorious* (London, Picador, 1998).
Rodkey, Frederick Stanley, 'The Turko-Egyptian Question in the Relations of England, France and Russia, 1823–41', *University of Illinois Studies in the Social Sciences*, 11:3–4 (September–December 1923).
Rottiers, Colonel E.A., *Itinéraire de Tiflis à Constantinople* (Brussels, 1829).

Rozière and Rouyer, 'Mémoire sur l'art de faire éclore les poulets en Égypte par le moyen des fours', *Description de l'Égypte* (2nd edn, Paris, Panckoucke, 1822).

Rushdy, Rashad, *The Lure of Egypt for English Writers and Travellers during the Nineteenth Century* (Cairo, Anglo-Egyptian Bookshop, 1954).

Russell, Alexander, *The Natural History of Aleppo and Parts Adjacent* (1756; repr. London, G. & J. Robinson, 1794).

Said, Edward W., *Orientalism: Western Concepts of the Orient* (London, Routledge & Kegan Paul, 1978; New York, Pantheon, 1978, repr. New York, Vintage Books, 1979; and London, Penguin Books, 1991 & 1995).

—*Culture and Imperialism* (London, Chatto and Windus, 1993; New York, Alfred A. Knopf, 1993; repr. London, Vintage, 1994).

Sampson, E.D., *Nikolay Gumilev* (Boston, Twayne, 1979).

Sanderson, John, *Travels of John Sanderson in the Levant, 1584–1602*, ed. Sir William Forster (London, printed for the Hakluyt Society, 1931).

Sattin, Anthony, *Lifting the Veil: British Society in Egypt 1768–1956* (London, J.M. Dent & Sons, 1988).

Sauneron, Serge, 'Le Temple d'Akhmim décrit par Ibn Jobeir', *BIFAO*, 51 (Cairo, 1952), 123–35.

Sauveboeuf, L. Ferrières, Comte de, *Mémoires historiques, politiques et géographiques des voyages du comte de Ferrières-Sauveboeuf faits en Turquie, en Perse et en Arabie, depuis 1782 jusqu'en 1789* (2 vols., Paris, 1790).

Savory, Isabel, *In the Tail of the Peacock* (London, Hutchinson, 1903).

Savory, Roger, *Iran under the Safavids* (Cambridge University Press, 1980).

Sayyid, Ayman Fuad, *Le Manuscrit autographe d'al-Mawaʻiz wa-al-iʻtibar fi dhikr al-khitat wa-al-athar de Taqi al-Din Ahmed b. Ali b. Abd al-Qadir al-Maqrizi* (London, al-Furqan Islamic Heritage Foundation, 1995).

Schmidt, Margaret Fox, *Passion's Child: The Extraordinary Life of Jane Digby* (London, Hamilton, 1977).

Schuster-Walser, Sibylla, *Das Safawidische Persien im Spiegel Europäischer Reiseberichte (1502–1722): Untersuchungen zur Wirtschafts- und Handelspolitik* (Baden-Baden, Bruno Grimm, 1970).

Searight, Sarah, *The British in the Middle East* (London, Weidenfeld and Nicolson, 1969; New York, Atheneum, 1970; repr. 1979).

—*Steaming East: The Forging of Steamship and Rail Links between Europe and Asia* (London, The Bodley Head, 1991).
Seddon, [John Pollard], *Memoir and Letters of the Late Thomas Seddon, Artist by his Brother* (London, James Nisbet, 1858).
Sezgin, Ursula, *Light on the Voluminous Bodies to Reveal the Secrets of the Pyramids by Abu Ja'far al-Idrisi* (Frankfurt am Main, Institute For the History of Arabic-Islamic Science, 1988).
Shaw, Stanford, *History of the Ottoman Empire and Modern Turkey: Empire of the Gazis: The Rise and Decline of the Ottoman Empire, 1280–1808* (Cambridge University Press, 1978).
al-Shenawy, Abdel-Aziz M., *Qanat al-Suways* (Cairo, Maahad al-Buhuth wa al-Dirasat al-Arabiyya, 1971).
Shepheard's Hotel, *Cairo and Egypt: A Practical Handbook for Visitors to the Land of the Pharaohs* (Cairo, Shepheard's Hotel, c. 1897–1917).
Shirazi, Mosleh al-Din Sa' di-ye, *The Gulistan or Rose Garden of Sa'di*, trans. Edward Rehatsek (London, George Allen & Unwin, 1964).
Simeon of Poland, *Travel Account, Annals and Colophons of Simeon the Scribe of Poland* [in Armenian] (Vienna, 1936), with a German résumé, 485–93.
Skeet, Ian, *Muscat and Oman* (London, Faber and Faber, 1974).
Skilliter, S.A., *William Harborne and the Trade with Turkey, 1578–1582* (Oxford University Press, for British Academy, 1977).
Slade, Adolphus, *Turkey, Greece and Malta* (2 vols., London, 1837).
Slatter, Enid M., 'The Princess, the Sultan and the Pasha', *Art and Artists* (November 1987), 1417.
Smith, Byron Porter, *Islam in English Literature* (Beirut, The American Press, 1939).
Smith, Thomas, *Remarks upon the Manners, Religion and Government of the Turks* (London, Moses Pitt, 1678).
—*Historical Observations Relating to Constantinople by the Reverend and Learned Tho. Smith, D.D. Fellow of Magd. Coll. Oxon, and of the Royal Society* in *A Collection of Curious Travels & Voyages*, ed. John Ray (London, 1693).
Spitzer, Leo, 'The Epic Style of the Pilgrim Aetheria', *Comparative Literature*, 1:3 (1949), 225–58.
Spivak, G.C., *In Other Worlds: Essays in Cultural Politics* (London, Routledge, 1988).
—*The Post-Colonial Critic* (London, Routledge, 1990).

—'Can the Subaltern Speak?', *Colonial Discourse and Post-Colonial Theory*, ed. P. Williams and L. Chrisman (New York & London, Wheatsheaf & Harvester, 1993).

St John, James Augustus, *Egypt and Mohammed Ali: Or, Travels in the Valley of the Nile* (2 vols., London, Rees, Orme, Brown, Green & Longman, 1834).

Staffa, Susan Jane, *Conquest and Fusion: The Social Evolution of Cairo AD 642–1850* (Leiden, E.J. Brill, 1977).

Stanford, W.B. and E.J. Finopoulo, *The Travels of Lord Charlemont in Greece and Turkey in 1749* (London, Trigraph for A.G. Leventis Foundation, 1985).

Stephens, John Lloyd, *Incidents of Travel in Egypt, Arabia Petræ and the Holy Land* (New York, Harper, 1837).

Stern, Henry A., *Dawnings of Light in the East* (London, C.H. Purday, 1854).

—*Journal of a Missionary Journey into Arabia Felix: Undertaken in 1856* (London, 1858).

Stevens, Mary-Anne (ed.), *The Orientalists: Delacroix to Matisse, European Painters in North Africa and the Near East*, Exhibition Catalogue (London, Royal Academy of Arts, and Washington, National Gallery of Art, 1984).

Stevenson, Catherine B., *Victorian Women Travel Writers in Africa* (Boston, Twayne, 1982).

Stewart, Aubrey (ed.), *Itinerary from Bordeaux to Jerusalem: 'The Bordeaux Pilgrim' [AD 333]* (London, Palestine Exploration Fund, 1896.)

Stewart, Desmond, *T.E. Lawrence* (London, Paladin, 1979).

Stewart, Frederick William Robert [Lord Castlereagh, 4th Marquess of Londonderry], *A Journey to Damascus, through Egypt, Nubia, Arabia Petraea, Palestine and Syria* (2 vols., London, Henry Colburn, 1847).

Stoneman, Richard (ed.), *Across the Hellespont: A Literary Guide to Turkey* (London, Hutchinson, 1987).

Strack, Thomas, *Exotische Erfahrung und Intersubjektivität. Reiseberichte im 17. und 18. Jahrhundert. Genregeschichtliche Untersuchung zu Adam Olearius – Hans Egede – Georg Forster* (Paderborn, Igel Verlag, 1994).

Stucky, R.A. and N.N. Lewis, 'Johan Ludwig Burckhardt und Williams John Bankes', *Petra*, ed. Th. Weber and R. Wenning (Mainz, 1997), 5–12.

Sweetman, John, *The Oriental Obsession* (Cambridge University Press, 1988).
Symonds, John Addington, Review of *A Thousand Miles up the Nile*, *The Academy* (7 July 1877), 65–8.
Tabachnick, Stephen E. and Christopher Matherson, *Images of Lawrence* (London, Jonathan Cape, 1988).
Taylor, Bayard, *A Journey to Central Africa: Or, Life and Landscapes From Egypt to the Negro Kingdoms of the White Nile* (New York, G.P. Putnam, 1854).
Teixeira, Pedro [Muhammad ibn Khavand Shah, called Mir Khavand], *Relaciones de Pedro Teixeira d'el Origen Descendencia y Succession de los Reyes de Persia y de Harmuz y de un Viage hecho por el mismo Autor dende la India Oriental hasta Italia por tierra*, En Amberes En can de Hieronymo Verdussen (2 vols., Amberes, Hieronugmo, 1610).
—*The Travels of Pedro Teixeira*, ed. W.F. Sinclair and D. Ferguson (London, Hakluyt Society, 1902).
Temple Bt., Major Sir Grenville, *Travels in Greece and Turkey* (2 vols., London, 1836).
Thackeray, W.M., *Lovel the Widower and Notes of a Journey from Cornhill to Grand Cairo* (London, Collins' Clear-Type Press, 1846).
—*Notes of a Journey from Cornhill to Grand Cairo* (London, Chapman & Hall, 1846; repr. London, Macmillan, 1903; illus. repr. Heathfield, Cockbird Press, 1991).
Thesiger, W., *Arabian Sands* (London, Longmans, 1959).
Thévenot, Jean de, *Relation d'un voyage fait au Levant* (3 vols., Paris & Rouen, chez Thomas Jolly, 1665–1684).
Thomas, Bertram, 'The Musandam Peninsula and its Inhabitants: The Shihuh', *Journal of the Royal Central Asian Society*, 15 (1928).
—'Among Some Unknown Tribes of South Arabia', *JRAS* (1929).
—'Musandam and its People', *Journal of the Royal Central Asian Society* (1929).
Thompson, Jason, *Sir Gardner Wilkinson and His Circle* (Austin, University of Texas Press, 1992).
—'"OF THE OSMANLEES, OR TURKS": An Unpublished Chapter From Edward William Lane's Manners and Customs of the Modern Egyptians', *Turkish Studies Association Bulletin*, 19 (Autumn 1995), 19–39.

—'Edward William Lane's "Description of Egypt"', *IJMES*, 28 (November 1996).
—'Edward William Lane in Egypt', *JARCE*, 34 (1997), 243–61.
Thornton, Lynne, *Women as Portrayed in Orientalist Painting* (Paris, 1988).
—*La Femme dans la peinture orientaliste* (Paris, ACR Éditions Internationales, 1993).
Tidrick, Kathryn, *Heart-beguiling Araby: The English Romance with Arabia*, revised edn (London, I,B. Tauris, 1989).
Tillett, Selwyn, *Egypt Itself: The Career of Robert Hay, Esquire of Linplum and Nunraw, 1799–1863* (London, SD Books, 1984).
Tregaskis, Hugh, *Beyond the Grand Tour: The Levant Lunatics* (London, Ascent Books, 1979).
Trollope, Anthony, *Doctor Thorne. A Novel* (1858; New York, Harper and brothers).
—*The Bertrams* (1859; repr. London, The Folio Society, 1993).
—'An Unprotected Female at the Pyramids' (1860), *Tourists and Colonials* (London, The Folio Society, n.d.).
—'George Walker at Suez' (1861), *Tourists and Colonials* (London, The Folio Society, n.d.).
—*An Autobiography* (1883; repr. Oxford, Oxford University Press, 1928).
Tucker, Judith, 'Muftis and Matrimony: Islamic Law and Gender in Ottoman Syria and Palestine,' *Islamic Law and Society*, 1:3 (1994).
Turner, William, *Journal of a Tour in the Levant* (3 vols., London, John Murray, 1820).
Tuson, Penelope, *Records of the British Residency and Agencies in the Persian Gulf* (London, India Office Library and Records, 1979).
Twain, Mark pseud. (i.e. S.L. Clemens) *The Innocents Abroad* (Leipzig, Bernhard Tauchnitz, 1879; repr. London, 1914).
Urquhart, D., *The Spirit of the East: Illustrated in a Journal of Travels through Roumelia during an Eventful Period* (2 vols., London, 1838).
—*The Pillars of Hercules: Or, A Narrative of Travels in Spain and Morocco in 1848* (2 vols., London, 1850).
Valle, Petri della, *Petri della Valle: Eines vornehmen Roemischen Patritii Reiß-Beschreibung in unterschiedliche Theile der Welt* (3 pts., Genff, J.H. Widerhold, 1674).

Vann, R.L., *The Unexcavated Buildings of Sardis*, BAR International Series 538 (Hildesheim and New York, George Olms Verlag, 1976; Oxford, BAR, 1989).

Varthema, Ludovico de, *Itinerario . . . nello Egitto, nella Sorria, nella Arabia deserta e felice, nella Persia, nella India e nella Ethiopia* (Venice, 1525).

Vittone, Bernardo Antonio, *Corso d'architettura civile sopra li cinque ordini di Giacomo Barozzio da Vignola, disegnato da Giambatista Borra . . .* (Turin, 1737).

Volney, Constantin François Chassboeuf, Comte de, *Voyage en Syrie et en Égypte pendant les années 1783, 1784 et 1785*, 2nd edn, revue et corrigée (2 vols., Paris, Volland et Desenne, 1787).

Walker Art Gallery, *Collective Exhibition of the Art of W. Holman Hunt, O.M., D.C.L.* (Liverpool, Walker Art Gallery, 1907).

Walker, Peter, *Holy City, Holy Places? Christian Attitudes to Jerusalem and the Holy Land in the Fourth Century*, Oxford Early Christian Studies (Oxford, Clarendon Press, 1990).

Wallach, Janet, *Desert Queen: The Extraordinary Life of Gertrude Bell: Adventurer, Adviser to Kings, Ally of Lawrence of Arabia* (London, Weidenfeld & Nicolson, 1996).

Walsh, Rev. Robert A., *Residence at Constantinople, during . . . the Commencement, Progress, and Termination of the Greek and Turkish Revolutions* (2 vols., London, F. Westley & A.H. Davis, 1836).

Warburton, Eliot, *The Crescent and the Cross: Or, Romance and Realities of Eastern Travel* (2 vols., London, Henry Colburn, 1845; repr. London, Maclaren, 1908).

Ward, Philip, *Travels in Oman: On the Track of Early Explorers* (Cambridge, Oleander, c.1987).

Warner, Charles Dudley, 'At the Gates of the East', *Atlantic Monthly*, 36.

—'Cataracts of the Nile', *Atlantic Monthly*, 31.

—*My Winter on the Nile: Among the Mummies and Moslems in Egypt 1874–75* (Hartford, Conn., American Publishing Co., 1876).

Warner, Nicholas (ed.), *An Egyptian Panorama: Reports from the Nineteenth-Century British Press* (Cairo, Zeitouna, 1994).

Waterfield, Robin E., *Christians in Persia: Assyrians, Armenians, Roman Catholics and Protestants* (London, Allen & Unwin, 1973).

Wattins, Thomas, *Tour through Swisserland . . . to Constantinople* (2 vols., London, 1792).

Webster, James, *Travels through the Crimea, Turkey, and Egypt; Performed during the Years 1825–28, Including Particulars of the Last Illness and Death of the Emperor Alexander, and of the Russian Conspiracy in 1825* (London, H. Colburn, 1830).

Wedmore, F., 'Carl Haag R.W.S.', *The Magazine of Art* (December 1889), 52–61.

Weekes, Richard V., *Muslim Peoples: A World Ethnographic Survey* (Westport, Greenwood Press, 1978).

Weiss, Gerhard, 'In Search of Silk: Adam Olearius' Mission to Russia and Persia', *James Ford Bell Lectures*, 20 (Minneapolis, University of Minnesota, 1983).

Wellsted, Lt James Raymond, *Travels in Arabia* (2 vols., London, John Murray, 1838).

Wesseling, P., *Vetera Romanorum Itinera* (Amsterdam, 1735).

Whaley, Buck, *Buck Whaley's Memoirs, Including his Journey to Jerusalem* (London, Alexander Moring, 1906).

Wharncliffe, Lord (ed.), *Embassy to Constantinople: The Letters and Works of Lady Mary Wortley Montagu* (2 vols., London, Swan Sonnenschein & Co., New York, Macmillan & Co., 1893).

Wharton, Annabel, *Refiguring the Post-Classical City: Dura Europos, Jerash, Jerusalem and Ravenna* (Cambridge University Press, 1995).

Wharton, Edith, *In Morocco* (New York, Charles Scribner's Sons, 1920).

Wilbour, Charles Edwin, *Travels in Egypt (December 1880 to May 1891)*, ed. Jean Capart (Brooklyn, NY, Brooklyn Museum, 1936).

Wilken, Robert, *The Land Called Holy: Palestine in Christian History and Thought* (New Haven, Yale University Press, 1992).

Wilkie, Sir David, *Sir David Wilkie's Sketches in Turkey, Syria and Egypt 1840–41. Drawn on Stone by Joseph Nash* (London, Graves & Warmsley, 1843).

Wilkinson, John, *Jerusalem Pilgrims before the Crusades* (Warminster, Aris and Phillips, 1977).

Williamson, Capt. T., *The East India Vade-Mecum: Or, Complete Guide to Gentlemen Intended for the Civil, Military or Naval Service of the East India Company* (2 vols., London, 1810).

Wilson, C.W., 'Introduction', *Itinerary from Bordeaux to Jerusalem* (London, Palestine Exploration Fund, 1896).

Wilson, E., *The Eastern or Turkish Bath: Its History, Revival in Britain, and Application to the Purposes of Health* (London, 1861).

Wilson, Edward L., 'Sinai and the Wilderness', *Century Illustrated Monthly Magazine*, 36 (July 1888), 324–40.
—'From Sinai to Shechem', *Century Illustrated Monthly Magazine*, 37, 193–208.
Wilson, Jeremy, *T.E. Lawrence: The Authorised Biography* (London, Minerva, 1990).
Wilson, William Rae, *Travels in Egypt and the Holy Land* (London, printed for Longman, Hurst, Reese, Orme and Browne, 1823).
Winslow, William Copley, 'The Queen of Egyptology', *The American Antiquarian*, 14 (November 1892).
Wolff, Joseph, *Missionary Journal of the Rev. Joseph Wolff* (London, 1827–1829).
—*Researches and Missionary Labours among the Jews, Mohammedans and other Sects* (London, J. Nisbet, 1835; Philadelphia, 1837).
—*Journal of the Rev. Joseph Wolff in a Series of Letters to Sir Thomas Baring Bart.: Account of his Missionary Labours from the Years 1827 to 1831; and from the Years 1835 to 1838* (London, printed Leeds, 1839).
Wood, Alfred C., 'The British Embassy in Constantinople', *English Historical Review*, 40 (1925).
—*A History of the Levant Company* (Oxford University Press, 1935; repr. London, Frank Cass, 1964).
Wood, Robert, *The Ruins of Palmyra, Otherwise Tedmor, in the Desart* (London, 1753; repr. Westmead, Farnborough, Gregg, 1971).
—*The Ruins of Balbec, Otherwise Heliopolis in Coelosyria* (London, 1757; repr. Westmead, Farnborough, Gregg, 1971).
Woolson, Constance Fenimore, 'Cairo in 1890', *Harper's New Monthly Magazine*, 83 (October 1891), 651–74 (part II in November 1891 issue, 828–55).
Wright, William, *An Account of Palmyra and Zenobia* (London, Thomas Nelson, 1895).
Wustenfeld, F., *Die Geographie und Verwaltung von Ägypten nach dem Arabischen des Abul Abbas Ahmed ben Ali el-Calcaschandi* (Göttingen, 1879).
Ya'ari, Avraham, *Jacob Saphir: Sefer Masa Teiman* [in Hebrew] (Tel Aviv, 1941), abr. from Saphir's account, *Even Saphir* (2 vols., Lyck, 1866; Mainz, 1874).

Yegül, Fikret K., *The Bath-Gymnasium Complex at Sardis*, Archaeological Exploration of Sardis Report 3 (Cambridge, Mass. and London, Harvard University Press, 1986).
Yohannan, John, *The Poet Sa'di: A Persian Humanist* (Lanham, MD, University Press of America, 1987).
Zand, K.H. *et al.*, *The Eastern Key*, Arabic text published with translation and some notes (London, Allen & Unwin, 1965). Arabic text ed. Paul Ghalioungui (Cairo, General Book Organisation, 1985).
Zoller, Olga, *Der Architekt und der Ingenieur Giovanni Battista Borra (1713–1770)* (Bamberg, Wissenschaftlicher Verlag Bamberg, 1996).
Zulalyan, M.K., *The Jelali Movement and the Condition of the Armenians in the Ottoman Empire* [in Armenian] (Erevan, 1966).

Index

A
Aaron's tomb   193, 198
al-Abbasi, Ali Bey   87–8, 261, 269
Abgar, King   10
Abraham   27
Abu Simbel   180, 187, 242
accessibility of the Orient   50, 269
Adams, Maude   246–7
Adrianople, palace of   158
Africa Association, the   78, 184, 195, 206
Ahmad, Imam Sayyid Sultan bin   132–3
Ahmed, Leila   66, 75–6
Ainslie, Robert   44, 53
Akinian, Father Nerses   112
Alaouin guides   196, 198, 205
Albania   56
Aleppo   42, 44, 48
Alexandria   56, 67, 75, 80, 176
   consular life in   170, 222
   description   112, 226–7, 245
   people   231–2
Along the Nile with General Grant (Farman)   245
Alte Geographie Arabiens (Sprenger)   135
Amasya, courtiers at   68
Americans in Egypt   239, 249
   list of   250–7
Amicis, Edmondo De   225
Anastasius' (Hope)   54–5
Anastasis   12–13
Anatolia   47, 54–5, 77, 232
ancient monuments, drawing of   199, 200–6
Antiquities of Athens, The (Stuart)   49
antiquities, removal   49, 53–5, 190, 201, 248
   ethics of   187
Aqaba   197–8, 205
Araba   198
Arabian Nights, influence of the   47, 264, 268
Arabs   69, 231

architecture, oriental influences   45–6, 49–51, 55, 150–1, 265–9
Armenian diaspora   111, 113, 115
Artemis, temple of   147–8
artists
   influenced by the orient   72–3
   working in the orient   44–5, 48, 68–9, 70–1
Asher, Michael   140
Asia Minor   111, 146
Aswan   186
Athens   49–50, 54–5, 57, 59
Atik, Khalil   86
al-Azhar mosque   265

B
Baal   19–20
Baalbek   50–1, 143, 145, 176
Bacon, Francis   103
Baedecker   86
baksheesh   186
Banian merchants   135–6
Bankes, William John   57, 176–7, 190, 194, 220
baptism   22, 30–3
Barry, Charles   55
Barzini, Luigi   225
bath of Cornelius   20–2
Bayezit II   68
Beechey, Henry   183, 185–8, 190
Beechey, Sir William   55, 73, 185, 187–8, 190
Beirut   44, 81
Belgioioso, Princess Cristina   225, 232
Bellefonds, Linant de   81, 85, 188, 193–207
Bellini, Gentile   68–9
Belmore, Earl   179–80
Belzoni, Giovanni   183, 185–6, 190, 219, 235
Belzoni, Sarah   240
Bethel   14
biblical influences   8–15, 18–25, 28–9, 102

[311]

Bin Tepe cemetery 147
Blackstone, Sir William 162
Blount, Sir Henry 70, 79, 102–5
Blunt, Wilfred Scawen 85–7
Boat Life in Egypt and Nubia (Prime) 242
Bombay merchants 175–6
Bonaparte, Napoleon 59, 74–5
Bonomelli 230, 234
Bordeaux Pilgrim, itinerary 16–17
  see also *Itinerarium Burdigalense*
Borra, Giovanni Battista 50–1, 143–51
  decorative schemes 150–1
  history 144–5
Bouverie, John 144, 150
Braudel, Fernand 76
Brimmer, Martin 246
British in the Middle East, The (Searight) 75
Brook, Juliana Eleanor 182
Brüggemann, Otto 119
Buckingham, James Silk 58, 80, 169–77, 220
Buraimi 133, 135, 138
Burkhardt, Johan Ludwig 58, 75, 80, 173–5, 184, 186, 195–6, 201, 222–3
Burton, James 87–8, 211–18
Busbecq, Ogier Ghiselin de 68
Buselli, Franco 228–9, 234
Bushnell, David 241
Butler, Howard Crosby 147
Byron, Lord George 55–6, 59, 73

C
Cable, Leffingwell 247
Caffi, Ippolito 82–3
Cailliaud, Frédéric 181
Cairo 81–2, 174,
  descriptions 171, 266–9
  European lifestyle 171–2
  living conditions 230
Cairo in 1890 (Woolson) 248
Calkoen, Cornelius 71
Campbell, Mary 12
Capper, James 67
Caroline of Brunswick 57–8
Cartwright, John 105

Casanova 47
Cassas, Louis-François 52
Castle Coole 179–80, 190
Cesana, Augusto 229–30, 234
Chaillé-Long, Charles 244
Champollion, Jean François 78, 235
Chandler, Richard 51
Charlemont, Lord 46, 48, 50
Charrington, Lt Harold 86
Chateaubriand, Viscomte de 55
Le Chevalier 52
Choiseul-Gouffier, Comte de 51–3
Chosen People 32–3
Christian
  early beliefs 7, 30–3
  shift in priorities 11
Christian holy sites 25–6
  and water 10, 20–3, 24–7, 30–1, 33
  martyrs and 7–8
  sanctification of 7, 8–11, 13, 23
  see also Jesus of Nazareth
circumcision 137
cities, criteria for recording ancient 146
Clapperton, Hugh 78–9
Classical and Topographical Tour Through Greece, A (Dodwell) 58
classics, influence of 47, 102, 105, 145
Cockerell, C. R. 50, 55–6
coffee trade 135
Cohen, Colonel 240
Colocci, Adriano 230
Constantine 8, 26–7
Constantinople 44–6, 47, 52, 54, 70, 87
Constantinople Ancient and Modern (Dallaway) 54
Cook, J. M. 146
Cooley, James Ewing 241
Copts 113, 234
Corinthian tomb 203–4
Coryate, Thomas 105–6
Cossacks 74, 84
Cox, Sir Percy 138–40
Craven, Lady 53
Crescent and the Cross, The (Warburton) 261

INDEX

Cromer, Lord   86, 234
curiosity travel   3, 43, 103, 169
Curtin, James   181
Curtis, George William   242
Cyril of Jerusalem   9–10

D

Dalkeith, Lord   85
Dallaway, James   54
Dalrymple, William   77
Dalton, Richard   46
Damascus   48, 81
Davis, Richard Harding   244
Dawkins, James   50, 143–4, 150
De Sacramentos (St Ambrose)   32
Dead Sea   27
Deftardar Bey, the   186, 232
Deir monastery   205
Deraa episode   90–1
Description of England (Harrison)   70
Description of the East, A (Liotard)   48
Dhofari tribes   136–7
Digby, Jane   85–6
Diocletian   11
Disputa di Santa Catarina (Pinturicchio)   69
Disraeli, Benjamin   59
Divan Club   49
Doctor Thorne (Trollope)   59
Dodwell, Edward   58
Donne, John   103
dress *see* European dress, oriental dress
Drovetti, Colonel Bernardo   181, 186–7, 188–9, 235
Dudu, Burtons mistress   214–16
Dye, William   244

E

East India Company   131, 133–4, 176, 219
Eberhardt, Isabelle   88
Edessa   10
Edfu   188
Effendi, Osman   82, 212
Effendi, Yirmisekiz Çelebi zâde Mehmet   71
Egeria   8–10, 12–14
Egypt   75, 111–16, 179–90, 225–35

Egypt: Three Essays on the History, Religion and Art of Ancient Egypt (Brimmer, Chapman)   246
Egyptian
  politics   233–5, 270
  religion   114, 232
  society   113–14, 230–3
Egyptian Society, the   49
Elgin, Lord   56
Elijah   18–23, 29–30
Elisha   29
  spring of   21
Elizabeth I, Queen   69–70
empiricism   102–6
English travellers   75, 189
Eōthen (Kinglake)   81
Esna   173, 188
espionage   66, 90–1
European dress   57, 83–4, 171–2
  see also Oriental dress
Eusebius of Caesarea   9, 12–13, 26
Exodus   87
Extended, New Description of the Journey to Moscow and Persia, The (Olearius)   119–20
Ezekiel, Khoja   132

F

Farman, Elbert   245
fashion   68–70
Fay, Eliza   67, 80
fellahin, the   113–14, 198, 231
Ferriol, Charles de   70
fez, decree to wear   83–4
Fiennes, Ranulph   140
film, eastern influences on   87
Finati, Giovanni   181, 194
Fitzclarence, Captain   184
Fitz-gerald, Desmond   151
Flaubert   83
Fleming, Paul   119
Forbin, Comte de   58, 75, 189, 219
Forni   229, 234
Fortress of Aqaba (Léon de Laborde)   198
Freer, Charles Lang   247
Fuller, John   59
Fynes, Morrison   70, 103, 105

[313]

G
Galland, Antoine 47
Gara tribe 136–7
garden of Eden, whereabouts 105
Garden Tomb 205
Garofalaki, Adriana *see* Dudu
Geary, Gratton 134
German embassy to Persia 125–8
Ghislanzoni 234
Gibb, Graham 57
Gill, Captain William 86
Gilpin, Lilian C. 248
Gliddon, George Robbins 240–1
Gospel and the Land, The (Davies) 23
Gottorp, Persian embassy to 128
Grand Tour
    Italian, end of 50, 59
    Ottoman Empire 41–59
    see also travel, travellers
Grant, Ullyses S. 244–6
Greece 49–50, 58
Greeks 50, 53
Greenblatt, Stephen 102
Greenough 212–15
Gregory of Nyssa 9–10
Gresham, Frank 59
guides to travel 15, 86, 219–23, 248–9
    see also travel books
Guilford, Lord 53, 56
gypsies 135

H
Haines, Captain 136
Hamerton, Captain Atkins 132
Hamilton, Gavin 50
Hanbury-Tenison, Robin 78
Hanfmann, George M. A. 147
Haqq-werdi 128
harem 158–60, 173, 212, 232–3
Harman, Henry Martyn 243
Harrison, William 70
Hassun, Bakhur 86
hatcheries, artificial 115
Hebron 27
Helene Glavani and the English Merchant, Mr Levett (Liotard) 45
Henry VIII, King 69
Herbert, Thomas 103, 106

Herodotus 247
Hezekiah 25
Hilair, Jean-Baptiste 52
Hindus in Oman 135–6
History of English Law, A (Holdsworth) 162
Hobhouse, J. C. 47, 55–6, 59
Holdsworth, W. S. 162
Holstein Embassy, Shāh Safī's banquet for the 127
Holt, Reverend 187
Holy Land 8–33, 48, 226
Homer's geography 145
Hope, Thomas 54, 73
Howell, James 103, 106
Hughes, Reverend 190
Humphreys, Charles 212–15
Hunt, E. D. 12
Huxley, George 145–6

I
Incidents of Travel in Egypt, Arabia Petraea and the Holy Land (Stephens) 207, 248
Instructions for Forreine Travell (Howell) 103
interior design, Eastern influences 150–1
Iran *see* Persia
Irby, Charles Leonard 76, 181, 194, 196
Isaiah 25
Isis, statue of 202
Israelites 28–9
Istanbul *see* Constantinople
Italian travellers to Egypt 225–35
Itinerarium Burdigalense as a guide 14–16, 24
    biblical references 18–25, 26–30
    critique 11–12, 30–3

J
Jabal al-Khubthah, tombs of 201
Jacob's well 22
Janissaries 59, 83
Jellany, Araby 175
Jerash 57, 195
Jericho 21, 220

INDEX

Jerusalem 14, 27, 176
Jesus of Nazareth 22–3, 25–8
Jewish holy sites, destruction of 25–6
Jolliffe, Reverend 221–5

K

Kabbani, Rana 66
Kalabsha 187
Karnak 188
Kāshān 123
Kauffer 52
Kerak 193
Khan al-Khalili bazaar 114
Khazneh, The 193, 201–2
Khojas, The 136
Kinglake, Alexander 81–2
kiosks, Turkish 45, 47, 55
Kobak, Annette 88–9
Kumazara tribes 137

L

Laborde, Léon de 81, 193–207
Ladies Home Journal, The (Leffingwell) 247
Lamartine, Alphonse de 59
Lane, E. W. 65–6, 76–8, 82, 84
Lane-Pool, Stanley 84–5
Lawatiyah, the 136
Lawrence, T. E. 87, 89–90
Le Chevalier 52
Leake, William Martin 58
Ledyard, John 240
Lee, Peter 170, 220
Legh, Thomas 181, 190
Lepsius 83
Lettre sur l'Égypte (Savary) 53
Levant, scales of 44
Levant trade 41
L'Hôte, Nestor 78
Light, Captain 171
Liotard, Jean Étienne 44–5, 48, 71–2
Lithgow, William 70, 106
local people
  attitudes to travellers 48, 75–6, 79, 86, 201
  travellers perceptions of 50, 81, 159, 104, 114, 157–60, 233
Loring, William Wing 244

Lydian royal burial mounds 149

M

Macgill, Thomas 54
Madden, Dr 75–6
Mahmud II, Sultan 59, 83
Makrani Balouch 136
Mamluk Bey 233
  massacre of 271
Mangles, James 52, 76, 181, 184, 190, 194
mapping and maps 120, 133, 146
Markus, Robert 7
markets 114–15
Marmont, Marshal 59
marriage 161–4
marriage à cabine 46
Matar, Nabil 67
Matariyya 115
Matrah, map of 133
Medinet Habou 188
Mehmet II 68
Miles, Colonel Samuel 134–6
milking 137
miraculous spring, the 10
Missett, Colonel 170, 172, 220
Montagu, Edward Wortley 71
Montagu, John 44–5
Montagu, Lady Mary Wortley 71, 157–65
Morrissey, Mr 190
Morritt, J. B. S. 54
Morrison, Fynes 70, 103, 105
mosques 264–6
Mu'ayyad mosque 265–6
Muhammad Ali 59, 67, 80–2, 84–5, 174–5, 227, 234, 267, 269–75
  description 174–5, 234
Murat IV, Sultan 67
Murray, John 177–8
Murshid, Imam Nasir bin 131
Muscat 131–3, 135, 139–40
Muslims, perception of 232
My Winter on the Nile (Warner) 244

N

Nabada, the 138
Nabatean art, perceptions of 207

Nabatean tombs   199
Nablus   81
Natural History of Allepo and Parts Adjacent (Russell)   48
Nazareth   10–11
Neale, Thomas   103
Niebuhr, Karsten   73, 159
Nile Notes of a Howadji (Curtis)   241
Nile, river   229–30, 245–6, 248, 262–3
Nizami style of Egyptian dress   83–4
    see also Oriental dress
Nizzoli, Amalia   225–7, 234–5

O
Occidentalists   66, 68
Oettingen-Wallerstein, Wolfgang   43
Old House by the River, The   242
Olearius, Adam   119–29
Olivier, G. A.   160
Oman   131–41
Omanis   136
On Zephania (St Jerome)   25
Orient, perceptions of   121, 266
Oriental dress   67, 82–4, 177, 220
    influence on army uniforms   74, 84
    items of   67, 73, 77, 79, 83
    travellers and   65–91, 186, 198, 220, 262
    see also European clothing
Orientalism (Said)   121
Ortelius, Abraham   106
Osman II, Sultan   112
Ospray, the   181–2
Ottoman Empire   41–59
    accessibility of   41, 47
    trade   42
    reasons for visiting   43

P
Palestine   13, 77, 82
Palmer, E. H.   86
Palmyra   42, 50–1, 143, 145
Parousia   30–2
Pars, William   51
Pasha, Ali   56
Pasha of Egypt see Muhammad Ali
Paton, A. A   269
Pechorin   73

Pengelley, Lt W. M.   133, 135–6
Persepolis   106
Persia   79, 119–29, 160
Persians   121–2, 124–5, 128
Persianisches Rosenthal (Saʻdī)   128
Petherick, John   261, 267–8
Petra   57, 193–207
Philae   187, 245
Philipi   22
Piacenza Pilgrim   10–11
pilgrimage   7–33, 225
pleasure travel   3, 46–7, 101–8
Pococke, Rt Rev Richard   48–9, 71
Poland, Armenian emigration to   111
Poole, Sophia   261, 266
Potocki, Jean   53
Prime, Cowper William   244–5
promised land, the   32
prostitution   46–7
pyramids   52, 180, 183–4, 189, 228, 262–3

Q
Qaitbay, Sultan   69
Qara tribe   136–7
Qasr al-bint   199–200

R
Rainsford, Colonel Henry   131
Ramage, C. T.   80
Relation, The (Sherley)   107
religious fanaticism   48–9
religious influences   7–33, 102
Repplier, Agnes   248
Ricci, Alessandro   181, 195
Richardson, Dr Robert   179–80, 182–6, 188
Riedsel, Baron de   53
Rifaud, Jean-Jacques   188
Roberts, David   67, 82, 207
Ruins of Baalbec (Wood)   50, 143, 145
Ruins of Palmyra (Wood)   50, 143, 146
Russell, Alexander   48

S
Safī, Shāh   119
Said, Edward   55, 65, 121, 266
Saida   44

Index

Salonica   54
Salt, Consul General Henry   78, 176, 181–6, 189, 220
Sandys, George   102, 106–7
Sardis   147, 149
Savary, Claude Etienne   53
scholarship travel   47–8, 51
Schoubra garden   263–4
scientific discovery   120
Searight, Sarah   79, 82
seasickness, causes of   120
Seetzen, U. J.   57
Sechar   20–1
Semail   134
Serao, Matilde   225, 230
Serena, Carla   225
Seti, tomb of   185
Seven Pillars of Wisdom (Lawrence)   90
sex trade   46
   see also slavery
sexual behaviour   46–7, 125–6
Sheffield, Charles   212–13
Shepheard's hotel   247
Sherley, Sir Anthony   107
Sherley, Sir Robert   79
Shihuh people   137
Shuhites   137
silk trade   119
Siloam   25
Silsil, Hadjr   187
Simeon of Poland   3, 111–16
Sinai   8–9, 196
Sīq, gorge of   198–9, 202
Siwah   86
slave markets   115–16, 213–14, 216
slavery   209–16
   justification of   212
   Western attitudes to   211
Slavery Act, Abolition of (1833)   6, 209
Smirke, Robert   55
Smithsonian Institution   239, 246–7
Smyrna   44, 146, 170, 194
Society of Dilettanti   49, 51
Solomons temple   24
Sonnini C. S.   53, 159
Spon, F.   47
spring of Elisha   21
St Ambrose   32, 59

St Jerome   25
St John, Augustus   265, 268
St Mark Preaching in Alexandria (Bellini)   69
St Peter   21–2
Stanhope, Lady Hester   56–7, 180–1, 184–5
Stephens, John Lloyd   207, 241, 248
Stiffe, Captain Arthur   133, 135
Stoppani, Antonio   235
Stowe   151
Stuart, James   49–50
Suez canal   174–5, 231–2
Süleyman the Magnificent   68
Sultan Hasan mosque   265
Sultan, Sayyid Saʿid bin   132
sumptuary laws   67
   see also Oriental dress
Sur la Nil avec Champollion (L'Hôte)   78
surveying   58, 120, 133, 144, 145–6, 174
Sychar, well at   22–3
Synar spring of   20–1
Syria   52–3, 57, 75, 77, 81

T
Taberna, Major   172
Tanuf   138–9
Tarsus   22
Taylor, Bayard   242
Temenos Gate   199
Temple mount   24–5
Thebes   188
Thesiger, Sir Wilfred   140
Thomas, Bertram   136–8, 140
Thomas Cook and Son   243
Thompson, Jason   76–7
Thomson, William   175
Thousand and One Nights, influence of see *Arabian Nights*
Thurburn, Robert   172
Timberlake, Henry   106
Tolstoy, Leo   73–4
tombs   7, 23, 185, 193, 198–202, 203
tourism and tourists   225, 243–5
trade   41–2, 119, 135, 212, 269–70
   and British imperialism   174–5
Travel Account (Simeon)   111–16

[317]

travel books   59, 206–7, 223, 227, 241
    see also guide books
travel, reasons for   2–5
travel writers   42, 75, 241, 246
Travels Along the Mediteranean, (Richardson) (review)   182
Travels in Palestine (Buckingham)   177
Travels in Turkey, Egypt, Nubia and Palestine (Madden)   75
Travels Through France, Turkey and Hungary to Vienna in 1792 (Hunter)   43
travellers   186–7
    advice to   221–3, 242
    lifestyle   198, 214–15, 227
    safety   80, 186, 194, 198–9, 201, 204
    see also Grand Tour
Tripoli   44
Trollope, Anthony   59
Trumbell, Mr and Mrs Hammond   242
Turcomania   3, 71–3, 83
Turkish rooms   45–6
Turks   53, 69
Twain, Mark   244

U
Ubar, lost city of   140–1

V
Valley of the Kings   185
Vanmour, Jean Baptiste   70–1
veil, meaning of   158–9
Venetian Embassy to Damascus   69
Vergennes, Charles Gravier   52
Virmarcati, César   234
Volga   119
Volney, Comte de   52–3, 159–60
Voyage de Arabie Pétrée (Laborde)   206
Voyage en Syrie et en Égypte (Volney)   52–3
Voyage pittoresque de la Grèce (Choiseul-Gouffier)   51–2

W
Wadi Farasa   203
Wadi Musa   196, 198
Wahhabis   133, 174
Walpole, Horace   51
Warburton, John   261, 272
Warner, Charles Dudley   244

water and Christianity   10, 20–7, 30–1, 33
water purification   114
Watkins, Thomas   44, 50
weaving industry   134
Webster, James   78
Wellington, Duke of   42
Wellsted, Lt James   133, 135
West Africa   78–9
Whaley, Buck   47
Whitelock, Lt   133
Wilbour, Charles Edwin   245
Wilken, Robert   11–12, 15–16
Wilkie, David   82
Willey, Reveley   53
Willison, George   72
women in the Ottoman Empire   46–7, 157–65, 171, 209–16, 232–3, 265
Wood, Robert   50, 143, 145–50
Woolson, Constance Fenimore   248
world sanctification   13
Worsley, Richard   53
Wylde, Phillip   131

X
xenophobia   79–81

Y
Young, John Russell   245

Z
Zanzibar   132–3